Using Computers in Hospitality

Using Computers in Hospitality

Third edition

Peter O'Connor

THOMSON

Australia • Canada • Mexico • Singapore • Spain • United Kingdom • United States

THOMSON

Using Computers in Hospitality, 3rd edition

Copyright © 2004, Thomson Learning

The Thomson logo is a registered trademark used herein under licence.

For more information, contact Thomson Learning, High Holborn House; 50-51 Bedford Row, London WC1R 4LR or visit us on the World Wide Web at: http://www.thomsonlearning.co.uk

British Library Cataloguing-in-Publication Data
A catalogue record for this book is available from the British Library

ISBN 1-84480-045-8

First edition published 1996 by Cassell
Second edition published 2000 by Continuum
Reprinted 2000, 2002 by Continuum
Third edition published 2004 by Thomson Learning

Typeset by Kenneth Burnley, Wirral, Cheshire

Printed in Croatia by Zrinski d. d.

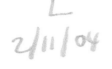

Contents

Preface

The use of computerization in the hospitality industry has changed greatly over the past twenty years. The launch of low-cost personal computers in the early 1980s started an explosion in the use of technology that is still continuing today. Technology still in development, such as truly integrated hotel systems and Internet-based reservations systems, will have a profound effect on how hospitality organizations transact their business and perhaps even on the structure of the industry itself. For hospitality businesses, it is no longer a question of whether to computerize, but which system will give the most benefits and should be installed first!

The role of computers in hospitality management and operations has become increasingly complex. Many different types of hardware and software are used, and it can be difficult even to begin to understand the array of technical terms that can be encountered. Computing isn't just about PCs any more: it's also about connectivity, networking and communications. Integrating this connectivity poses one of the greatest challenges for the future. The pace of change is also very swift, and thus it can be very difficult to keep up-to-date on what's happening in the area. That being said, knowledge of both the capabilities of computer systems and the benefits that can be gained by using them is essential for every hospitality manager.

While searching for a textbook to help in teaching my own students, I found that those available were unsuitable for a variety of reasons. General computing texts tended to concentrate too much on technical concepts and issues and, as a result, were not really suitable for use by hospitality students. Many existing hospitality-specific texts had become outdated because of the rapid pace at which computerization has developed over the last few years. Others approached the subject entirely from the perspective of the American hotel industry, which has very different size and ownership characteristics to that of most European countries, and thus did not address many of the issues in sufficient detail. To overcome these limitations, I set out to write a basic textbook that could be used to introduce students both to computers in general, and to how they are used in the hospitality industry. My aim has been to develop both the computer literacy and the practical skills of the reader. Having read the book and completed the case studies and exercises at the end of each chapter, readers should have a sound working knowledge and understanding of technology, especially as it relates to the hospitality industry. They should also appreciate that computers are only tools that must be managed carefully to bring maximum benefit to the organization.

Outline of chapters

Chapter 1 provides an overview of how and why computers are used in the hospitality sector. Its main purpose is to serve as an introduction to the book overall, and each topic mentioned is discussed in greater detail in later chapters.

Chapter 2 introduces computers by briefly outlining their development from the first mainframe computers of the 1960s to the personal computers, laptops and PDAs of today. A wide variety of technological terminology and concepts are explained, and the hardware and peripherals encountered in the hospitality sector are explored in detail.

Chapter 3 discusses the concept of computer software. Different approaches to operating systems are examined, and both general purpose and hospitality-specific software applications are introduced. The most commonly used general purpose software applications, namely word processors, spreadsheet packages, database packages, email clients and web browsers are also discussed in detail.

Chapter 4 concentrates on the issue of communications and integration. Various methods of allowing computers to transfer data between one another are discussed and the subject of interfacing/integrating systems is examined.

Chapter 5 focuses on the Internet and its growing use as a communications and marketing tool. Internet services such as the World Wide Web are examined in detail and their advantages and limitations critically assessed. Developing technologies such as Application Service Provider (ASP) are also examined and their potential for use in the hospitality sector explored.

Chapter 6 outlines the process of developing a web site from conception to publication and promotion. The process provides a useful framework for exploring many of the management topics surrounding the use of a web site as an effective ecommerce tool.

Chapter 7 explores the increasingly important area of electronic distribution of the hospitality product. Global distribution systems, central reservations systems and destination management systems are among the concepts examined and their use by hotel companies discussed.

Chapter 8 continues the theme of distribution by exploring the effect of the World Wide Web on the hotel electronic distribution arena. Strategies for distributing the hotel product online are explored, and trends for the future in this rapidly changing field are outlined.

Chapter 9 examines the use of computer systems in hotels. The features found in a typical property management system (PMS) are explored in detail, and the ancillary systems that interface with the PMS are also discussed.

Chapter 10 focuses on the use of computers in catering and food and beverage management. Recipe-costing systems, stock control systems, electronic point-of-sales systems and conference and banqueting systems are among those explored in detail, while several other specialized catering systems are also examined and assessed.

Chapter 11 focuses on the computer systems that work behind the scenes in a hospitality business. Various applications that assist in personnel, accounting, marketing and operations are described and their benefits for hospitality management and operations highlighted.

Chapter 12 explores the process that should be used when selecting and implementing a new computer system within an organization. By outlining a comprehensive checklist of steps that should be followed, it helps managers focus on the core issues and helps ensure that new systems will ultimately meet their objectives.

PETER O'CONNOR
January 2004

Acknowledgements

I would like to express my appreciation to the following people and organizations for their help and contributions to this book:

Everyone at Institut de Management Hotelier International, ESSEC Business School, France, especially Jeanine, Nicola, Florence, Genvieve, Joelle and Muriel for their continued support;

Andy Frew at Queen Margaret University College, Edinburgh for his continued support and encouragement;

Dimitrios Buhalis at University of Surrey for just being Dimitrios;

Everyone at Thomson for being so flexible and ceaselessly solving problems;

Sue Welch of Welshtech, Dan Hiza of Newmarket Software, Mark Talbert of Mark Talbert and Associates and Andrew Mitchell of Meeting Matrix for providing some of the illustrations;

All Microsoft® screenshots are printed with the permission of Microsoft Corporation. All Microsoft® products mentioned are Microsoft® trademarks.

And finally all the 'lads' for the help that only they know they gave!

Abbreviations

ADSL	Asynchronous digital subscriber line
ALU	Arithmetic logical unit
AMD	Advanced micro devices
ASP	Application system provider
ATM	Automated teller machine
B2B	Business to business
B2C	Business to customer
BCC	Blind carbon copy
bps	Bits per second
CC	Carbon copy
CD	Compact disk
CD-R	Compact disk recordable
CD-ROM	Compact disk read only memory
CIS	Catering information system
CLASS	Customer loyalty anticipation and satisfaction system
CLI	Command line interface
COM	Communications port
CP/M	Control program for microprocessors
CPC	Cost per click
CPM	Cost per 1000 impressions
CPU	Central processing unit
CRO	Central reservation office
CRS	Central reservation system
CRT	Cathode ray tube
CTR	Click through rate
DD	Double density
DMS	Destination management system
DNS	Domain name server
DPI	Dots per inch
DS	Double sided
DSL	Digital subscriber line
DTP	Desk top publishing
DVD	Digital video disk, digital versatile disk or nothing at all
DVOD	Digital video on demand
ECR	Electronic cash register
EDI	Electronic date interchange
EFT	Electronic funds transfer
EPOS	Electronic point-of-sales

FAST	Future automated screening for travellers
FTP	File transfer protocol
G/Gb	Gigabyte
GDS	Global distribution systems
GUI	Graphic user interface
HITIS	Hospitality industry technology interface standards
HTML	Hypertext mark up language
I/O	Input/output
IBM	International Business Machines
IP	Internet protocol
IRC	Internet relay chat
ISDN	Integrated services digital network
ISP	Internet service provider
IT	Information technology
K/Kb	Kilobyte
Kbps	Kilobytes per second
LAN	Local area network
LCD	Liquid crystal display
M/Mb	Megabyte
MHz	Megahertz
MS-DOS	Microsoft® disk operating system
NIC	Network interface card
OS	Operating system
OTA	Open travel alliance
PABX	Private automated branch exchange
PC	Personal computer
PDA	Personal digital assistant
PGP	Pretty good privacy
PLU	Price lookup
PMS	Property management system
POS	Point-of-sales
PPC	Pay per click
QBE	Query by example
RAM	Random access memory
RFP	Request for proposal
ROM	Read only memory
RTO	Regional tourism organization
SDSL	Symmetrical digital subscriber line
SQL	Structured query language
SVGA	Super video graphics array
T/Tb	Tetrabyte
TCO	Total cost of ownership
TCP/IP	Transmission control protocol/Internet protocol
TIC	Tourism Information Centre
UPS	Uninterruptible power supply

URL	Universal resource locator
USB	Universal serial bus
UTP	Unshielded twisted pair
VAT	Value Added Tax
VDU	Video display unit
VGA	Video graphics array
VPN	Virtual private network
WAN	Wide area network
WYSIWYG	What you see is what you get
WiFi	Wireless fidelity
WWW	World Wide Web

1 An introduction to computers in the hospitality industry

A computer system is made up of several components, including *hardware*, *software* and the *user*, which work together to perform various tasks (Figure 1.1). Each of these is independent, but is only productive when used with the other components. For example, hardware, the part of the computer that you can physically see and touch, will sit and do nothing unless given instructions by the user through the software.

Hardware includes both the actual computer itself, and the various peripherals (short for 'peripheral devices') which allow data to be input, output and stored (Table 1.1). There are many different types of computer, ranging from large *mainframes*, which are expensive and can support many simultaneous users, to *personal computers*, which are relatively cheap and are designed for use by a single person, to *personal digital assistants* (PDAs), which are small enough to be carried in a shirt pocket but provide limited functionality. Conceptually, all computers are based on the same principles. Each is composed of a central processing unit (which does the actual work), a system bus (which is an electronic pathway along which data travels) and memory (which is used to store data). On a physical level, these components are incorporated into tiny chips made of silicon, which are mounted on cards inside the system's unit – the case that most people refer to as the computer.

Software, on the other hand, is basically a series of instructions which tells the hardware what to do and how to do it! Software operates at several different levels. The bottom layer is known as an *operating system*. In simple terms, this controls the use of the hardware and supervises the running of other programs. Two different types of operating system are common. A *command line interface* is

Figure 1.1

A computer system

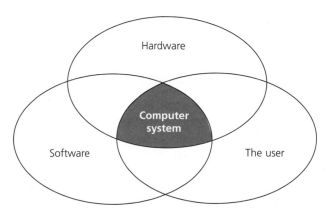

Table 1.1	Input	Output	Storage
Computer peripherals	Keyboard	Visual display units	Magnetic disk
	Mouse	LCD panel	CD-ROM
	Bar code reader	Printers	DVDs
	Magnetic-strip reader	Speakers	Magnetic tape
	Touch screen		Removable drives
	Punched card reader		
	Digital scanner		
	Pen entry		
	Voice entry		
	Direct entry		
	Biometrics		

text-based and is used by typing specific commands with a particular format and syntax. A *graphic user interface*, on the other hand, uses a more intuitive, picture-based format to perform the same tasks, and thus requires less technical knowledge from its users.

Applications software sits on top of the operating system; these are the programs with which the user works directly and uses as tools to perform various tasks. Some applications software is general purpose in nature. For example, packages such as spreadsheets, word processors and databases are relatively flexible and can be applied to a variety of tasks. While, as can be seen from Table 1.2, each is particularly useful for a particular purpose, the boundaries between different types of package are rapidly being broken down as new versions, incorporating increasingly diverse features, are launched.

Other applications software is both industry-specific and function-specific. Applications of this type are highly specialized, and can only be used for a very specific set of tasks. Some examples from the hospitality industry are outlined in Table 1.3.

Table 1.2	Application type	Main functions
General-purpose applications	Word-processing package	Allows text to be typed, stored, have its appearance manipulated and be printed
	Spreadsheet	Allows numerical models to be set up and modified interactively
	Database	Allows data to be stored and processed using powerful sorting and selective retrieval facilities
	Email package	Allows messages and data to be sent electronically from one computer to another
	Web browsers	Allow web pages to be displayed on screen while surfing the World Wide Web
	Utilities package	Adds extra features to a computer system – for example, to enhance ease of use or security

Table 1.3	Application	Main functions
Hospitality-specific applications	Reservations system	Processes enquiries for room availability; tracks the number of rooms booked for each future date; accepts and stores reservations for both individuals and groups; tracks travel agents' commission due; provides a variety of operational and management reports
	Property management system	Stores a list of the guests registered in the hotel: identifies which rooms are occupied; helps maintain guest folios by tracking charges and payments; provides a great variety of operational and managerial reports to both the front office and most other departments in the hotel
	Recipe-costing system	Generates an accurate and up-to-date cost for individual dishes and complete menus; automatically recalculates the cost of all recipes when an ingredient price changes; generates a stores requisition list detailing both the ingredients and quantities needed to produce a specific number of portions of any menu
	Stock-control system	Manages and controls stock by identifying the variance between the amount of each ingredient used and the amount which should have been used based on the number of portions sold; generates a variety of managerial and operational reports including usage rates and automatic reorder lists
	Conference and banqueting	Assists in the management of the banqueting department by accepting and storing reservations for events, tracking audio-visual and other equipment needs, coordinating the provision of services from the food and beverage department, and simplifying the process of billing clients for services provided

Sometimes specialized pieces of hardware are combined with software to automate a particular function. Although we tend not to think of these systems as computer based because they do not resemble the big beige boxes that we have come to associate with computers, they form an essential part of the information technology infrastructure of the hospitality organization. Some of the most common examples of such systems are outlined in Table 1.4.

Each of the systems outlined in the tables above and below can be, and often is, used independently. However, efficiency and productivity are greatly increased if the systems are integrated, allowing data to flow freely between the interlinked systems and thus improve guest service, security and control. Unfortunately, many computer systems in use in hospitality operations are not well integrated. Poor planning and the lack of an accepted technology standard for hospitality computer systems have resulted in the majority of systems operating in isolation. This 'islands of automation' problem has resulted in many of the benefits that the use of a computer system can bring being lost in the hospitality sector.

	System	Main functions
Table 1.4		
Hybrid computer systems in the hospitality industry	Call accounting system	Automatically posts charges for telephone calls to the guest's bill, and provides a variety of other services such as voicemail and wake-up calls
	Electronic point-of-sale system (EPOS)	Assists in food and beverage service by electronically transmitting orders to remote printers in production areas such as kitchens or dispense bars; increases control by automatically posting charges on the guest's bill and by providing a variety of management information and analyses
	Minibar system	Provides beverage facilities in bedrooms and automatically posts charges for items consumed to the guest's bill
	Electronic door-lock system	Improves security by generating a unique electronic key for each new guest
	Energy management system	Helps reduce energy costs by automatically shutting off services to unoccupied areas, and by controlling temperatures more precisely than is possible using manual or mechanical methods
	Entertainment systems	Provide cable television, interactive games, movies on demand and Internet access on the television in the guest room

Why use a computer system?

Before discussing the benefits that the use of a computer system can bring to an operation, let us examine some of the characteristics that make them useful:

- Speed: computers work at electronic speeds and can process thousands of transactions per second. As a result, large and complex tasks can be completed very quickly.
- Accuracy: computers always do exactly what they are told to do. As a result, they do not make mistakes and all calculations are performed correctly.
- Discipline: computers can perform the same tasks over and over again, and never get tired, bored or distracted.
- Capacity: computers can process large amounts of data easily. As a result, they can perform more in-depth analysis and consider more variables than would be possible manually.

As a result of these four characteristics, the use of a computer system brings many benefits when compared with manual procedures. First, there is a reduction in the amount of clerical work that must be carried out. Many boring, repetitive tasks can be automated, which makes employees' jobs more varied and fulfilling, thus helping to increase job satisfaction. The accuracy of the computer helps to reduce mistakes, which leads to increased guest satisfaction and better control over operations. Computers also increase productivity, because the same amount of work can be completed with less effort. This can be translated into cost savings by reducing staff numbers, or can help to further increase guest satisfaction as staff have to concentrate less on routine clerical work and thus have more time for personal interaction with the guest. Computer systems also allow larger amounts of data to be processed, in a wider variety of ways, than would be possible manually, which results in more timely, accurate and relevant management of information.

What makes a computer system work successfully?

Despite their promise and potential, it must be realized that these benefits are not automatic. Computers are not a panacea for every management or operational problem. They are simply *tools* that can be used to automate manual procedures to increase efficiency and control. If the underlying policies and procedures are faulty, then the use of a computer system will only make the problem worse.

> The effectiveness of a . . . system is directly related to the quality of the management using it: it cannot compensate for management shortcomings and will only accentuate them. In a well managed hotel, a system is perceived as a tool for better performance, while in poorly managed properties, a system often serves as a convenient excuse for all operational problems.
>
> (Marko and Moore, 1980)

To help ensure that technology-based systems work successfully, it's useful to think of technology in three forms – programs, processes and people. Programs (in this analogy, confusing both the hardware and the software) are the things that we normally think of when we think of technology-based systems – the computers themselves, the applications that are used to automate particular functions and so on. However, focusing on these elements in isolation will not bring many of the benefits of automation. Equal if not more emphasis must be placed on the processes – how the computerized systems interact with your organization – and the people, ensuring that the users have the will, ability and training to successfully use their systems. These last two points are often neglected, resulting in systems that look fine on paper but result in suboptimum performance. The only way to ensure that each of these three elements gets the attention that it deserves is to actively manage the use of information technology within the organization.

Information technology management

As discussed above, computerization promised many benefits to hospitality organizations, including improved service quality, enhanced profitability and efficiency, better integration of departments, speedier communications and reduced costs. As a result, hospitality organizations have adopted a wide variety of

Case Study *Guest history at Ritz Carlton*

Ritz Carlton is acknowledged as one of the leading hotel companies in the world in terms of customer service. It has won countless awards, including being chosen by *Global Finance* readers in 1997 as the best hotel chain in North America. The strategy that lies behind this success is simply to offer the best customer service possible by anticipating guests' needs. This is reflected in the company's mission – 'to provide the finest personal service' and 'fulfil even the unexpressed wishes and needs of its guests'. Their outstanding level of customer service is achieved by having a common set of goals and procedures throughout the world – known as the Gold Standards – in which all members of staff are trained and follow passionately. In fact staff are the key to Ritz Carlton's success. Each member is carefully selected and matched to their particular position, and then extensively trained both in the technical components of their position and also in the company's customer service philosophy. Each is empowered 'to move heaven and earth' to ensure that the customer is satisfied and that any complaints are quickly and efficiently resolved.

Technology is used extensively to support the efforts of employees. Using a computerized system known as CLASS (Customer Loyalty Anticipation and Satisfaction System), Ritz Carlton is able to turn guest preference data into actionable information, which employees can subsequently use to provide a more personalized level of service. The goals of the system are lofty – to give 100 per cent reliability and consistency in recognizing repeat guests, fulfil guest preferences and anticipate their needs and to help personalize each guest experience. Each employee carries a guest preference pad, on which they can write guest preferences. These are consolidated and entered into CLASS on a daily basis, and consequently available to employees at any of the 33 Ritz Carlton immediately. 'The idea is that if a guest wants the Pittsburg Press in his room where ever he goes, or wants rocks in his pillow, the next time he stays with us, he won't have to express that desire' says Bruce Speckhals, Vice President of Information Systems. CLASS is integrated with MARSHA, the Marriott Central Reservation System on which the Ritz Carlton properties are now distributed, and bookings are linked to guest profiles during the reservation process. At each property, the guest recognition manager prints a guest recognition report on a daily basis and circulates it to each department. Thus, arriving guests are immediately recognized as repeat customers, their needs anticipated and selective elements of their stay customized in line with their preferences in order to provide more personalized service.

The system also helps Ritz Carlton to create loyalty programmes that recognize the value of repeat guests. Returning customers are classified into one of three groups. *Repeat customers* have less than twelve stays within a year, *key repeat customers* have more than twelve stays in one or two properties within a year and *loyal customers* have more than twelve stays in at least three properties within a year. CLASS allows the company to determine the travel patterns and revenue contributions of each guest, and make projections as to their lifetime value. Thus one of the keys to the success of the overall system is linking the reservation to the guest profile, a process that is managed by the guest recognition manager at each property. And, despite the wealth of data available for direct marketing purposes, Ritz Carlton has only comparatively recently begun to exploit this opportunity. However, as the trust and confidence of its customers are so important, guest data is never sold or passed on to outside companies, and direct marketing is coordinated on a global scale to record who has received what and when, and to ensure that the amount of mail that an individual receives is carefully managed.

Is the system successful? According to independent research, over 90 per cent of their customers say that they would come back. The question now for Ritz Carlton is how to maintain this competitive advantage. With the continuing reduction in the costs of technologically based systems, an opportunity exists for its competitors to use similar systems and similar levels of recognition for their customers.

technology-based systems at a phenomenal rate, with most now using multiple systems to automate different functions. Unfortunately, the use of information technology within the sector is to a large extent unplanned and unmanaged.

This has not always been the case. As will be discussed (see Chapter 2), mini-computers were used to automate hotel operations in the late 1960s and early 1970s. Although these systems were expensive to operate and slow to respond to users' needs, they had one major advantage: responsibility for their operation and management was clearly defined. All aspects of computing were the responsibility of one person – the information systems manager – and, as a result, computer use and growth was planned and coordinated. However, this has changed. Personal computer-based systems are now the norm, having augmenting and in most cases replaced mini-computer-based systems. While personal computers have a lot of advantages when compared to mainframe-based systems, their flexibility also gives rise to problems with regard to management of the information technology (IT) resource. As they are relatively cheap, they can be purchased by individuals or departments and used to automate individual functions. Similarly, software can be purchased literally off the shelf, with little or no thought being given to its suitability for the task, or how it will interact with other systems. Such flexibility gives rise to a variety of problems and may mean that the resulting systems are incompatible with each other. Different hardware platforms, operating systems, software and data standards mean that information cannot be shared across systems. As a result, many of the main benefits of computerization are lost. However, such incompatibility is really just a symptom of a much deeper problem. In reality, it is caused by a lack of management of IT within the organization. As personal computers have been installed, the role of the information systems manager has declined in importance, or, in many cases, disappeared altogether. As a result, responsibility for the use of technology within the organization has become ill defined. However, because of its importance and undeniable benefits, investment and adoption of IT-based systems has continued unabated. Systems have grown haphazardly, without any planning and control, ultimately resulting in the confusion which can be seen today.

Information systems planning

Decisions regarding technology must be based on a clear idea of the company's fundamental purpose. By grounding technological change in your corporate strategy, implementation of new strategies will center around common goals.

(Haywood, 1990)

To be effective, the role information technology plays in the management and operation of the hospitality organization must be planned and must integrate with the overall long-term plans of the business.

Introducing a new technology-based system means managing changed relationships; any decisions with regard to new technology must be based on a clear understanding of the organization's fundamental purpose. Therefore a strategic viewpoint must be taken when thinking about technology. This can only be done by first defining and documenting the goals of the business as a whole. Specific objectives must be set and quantified, so that everyone has a clear understanding of where the organization is going and what it is setting out to achieve. In many cases, the effective use of IT can contribute significantly to these objectives. A classic example is the airline sector, where computerized distribution systems were used to promote the host airline's flights over those of competitors. Eventually these systems became such a strategically competitive weapon that governments were forced to regulate their use. Similarly Pizza Hut, through effective use of both hand-held EPOS systems and an innovative cooking method, were able to achieve their objective of dominating the lunchtime pizza market by ensuring quick and efficient service.

Once the overall strategic plans of the organization have been considered, an IT plan must be drawn up. This should clearly outline the role that technology will play in achieving the objectives of the business. It should also assess the business's current and future technology needs, and outline how these are going to be satisfied. Last, it should assign responsibility for the development and control of computerization within the organization. Employees at all levels of the organization should be involved in the technology planning process. Top-level management involvement is especially important as it allows departmental interests to be overridden for the good of the business as a whole. Also, if managers at the highest level in the company are seen to use technology, an ethos flows through the whole organization that technology is important. Involving employees at lower levels of the organization is also essential. If users are consulted

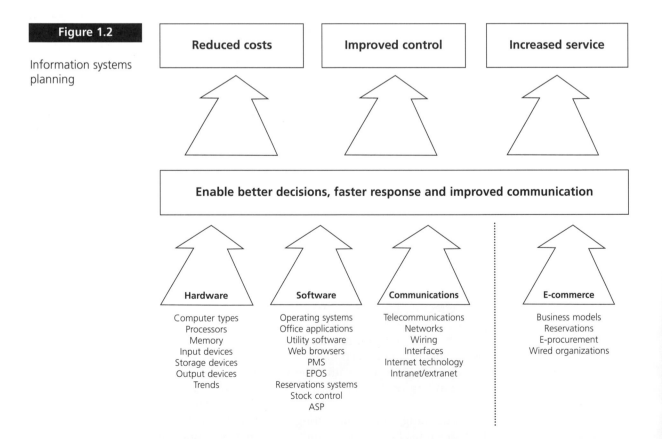

Figure 1.2

Information systems planning

about where and how technology could be used to make operations more efficient, they are more likely to accept a system when it is eventually installed.

Once the objectives of using technology have been established, they must be translated into more practical policies to ensure that the overall aim is achieved. Key aspects of this process include the provision of an appropriate budget and the setting of appropriate standards. Even the simplest plan is doomed to failure unless given sufficient financial resources to implement it successfully. Unfortunately, many hoteliers are slow to invest adequate amounts on technology on a regular basis. This may be because the functions automated by hospitality systems are generally ones where previous capital expenditure lasted for a very long time. For example, many billing machines or room racks purchased twenty or thirty years ago are still in use today. Despite the expectations of many hoteliers, computerized systems will not be efficient for anywhere near as long. Common hospitality accounting practice is to write off capital expenditure over a five-year period. However, five years is a very long time when considering anything to do with technology. For example, in 1997 the typical business computer was generally a 486-based machine. Today, such equipment is regarded as obsolete, but many are still being used in hotels all over the world to automate business-critical functions! New products, new technologies and new features are constantly evolving, and systems need to be continually updated to take advantage of the benefits that such developments can offer. Both hardware and software standards must be defined for the business as a whole. These standards may be deliberately vague (for example, that all computers must be PC compatible) or very specific, such as those shown in Figure 1.3. In either case, what is important is that adequate thought is given to the issue, decisions are made, standards are set and then implemented. When this happens, systems that conform to these standards should then be more easily able to exchange data, thus reducing the 'islands of automation' problem discussed earlier. In addition, software standards (in terms of operating systems and standard applications to be used throughout the organization) help to reduce the costs of purchasing, training and maintenance, as will be discussed in Chapter 12.

Figure 1.3

A hardware
standards
specification

Heather Hotel

Specification of Minimum Computer Hardware

Last Updated 1 December 2003

Minimum standards for the purchase of computer hardware are specified below. These guidelines are necessary to ensure compatibility between the computer systems within the company. The purchase of any equipment that does not conform to these standards must be agreed in advance with the computer services manager.

Processor standard:	IBM compatible
Minimum processor:	Pentium® 4 (or equivalent)
Speed:	1.2 Ghz or better
Memory:	512 Mbs or greater, expandable to 1024 Mbs
Hard disk:	40 Gbs or greater
Operating system:	Windows® 2000 Pro
Screen type:	18 inch SVGA or better
Ports:	1 serial, 1 parallel, 3 USB 2.0
Disk drives:	3$\frac{1}{2}$ inch diskette drive, CD-ROM drive
Network card:	Internal Ethernet 10/100-base-T

In addition, all computers should have the operating system pre-installed, and be pre-loaded with Microsoft® Office XP Professional Edition. For any questions or clarifications, please contact the computer help desk on extension 3456.

Discussion questions

1. Think about a specific IT-based system currently being used in a hospitality organization with which you are familiar. Consider the investment that the company has made in each of the 3 'P's – programs, processes and people. What effect has the level of investment in each case had on the success (or otherwise) of the system? How are these effects manifested? Would a different investment strategy have resulted in a different result?

2. A hotel company is considering introducing a standardized property management system (PMS) throughout the entire chain. What types of benefits could be expected from such a step?

3. In the manufacturing sector, one of the key arguments used to justify investments in technology is a reduction in labour cost. Do the same arguments hold true for the hospitality sector? What other (additional or alternative) arguments could you make to convince management that such investments are necessary?

4. Read the 'Guest history at Ritz Carlton' case shown earlier in this chapter. Identify the technologies that the company is using to recognize its guests. Why does the system work so well? What lessons can we learn from this example in terms of how we should go about using technology in our own organizations?

5. The growth in the use of personal computers has given rise to a variety of problems with regard to incompatibility of data. Standardization is cited as a possible solution. Within a hotel chain, what barriers might there be to adopting such an approach?

2 Computer hardware

Buying a computer can be an intimidating experience. The technology seems complicated and ominous, and the terminology is anything but welcoming. Terms like byte, CPU, RAM, ROM and hertz all whiz over the novice's head. While you do not have to be a computer expert to buy or use a computer, a little bit of understanding can help you a lot. Just as knowing a little bit about how a car works can improve your driving, having a basic understanding of how a computer works can help you to use it more effectively. In addition, a basic knowledge of computer terminology is also useful. You have a better idea of what to expect from different types of systems and can therefore choose the most appropriate one with confidence.

As an introduction, this chapter outlines the development of computer technology from the mainframe computers of the 1950s and 1960s to the personal computers (PCs) and hand-held computers of today. The internal structure of a computer and its peripheral devices are examined and many common technical terms are explained. Particular attention is paid to two components, the central processing unit (CPU) and the computer's memory, because of their importance in the overall performance of a system.

A brief history of computers

The concept of a computer is generally attributed to Charles Babbage, who devised his analytical and difference engines in the 1830s. Conceptually these bore an uncanny resemblance to the modern computer, with the ability to input and store data, to perform mathematical operations, and to output results. Babbage's devices were never produced, because the technology of the period was not sufficiently advanced to manufacture the parts required. However he was clearly ahead of his time and most modern computers follow his basic design.

The first electronic computer, known as ENIAC (Electronic Numerical Integrator And Computer) was built around 1940 in the University of Pennsylvania, but, as a result of secrecy during the Second World War, it was not introduced to the public until 1946. ENIAC was essentially created as a giant calculating machine. During the war, a vast pool of people was needed to calculate the firing tables used by artillery units. It took one person working flat out for over a week to calculate a single trajectory, using only an adding machine and a lot of perseverance. ENIAC, on the other hand, could calculate over 5000 additions or 14 ten-digit multiplications in a second, and could thus work out a trajectory in less time than it took the shell to travel to its target. Having said that, ENIAC was big! It weighed over 30 tons, drew 174 kilowatts of electricity and had 18,000 vacuum tubes, 6000 switches and miles of wiring. The use of vacuum tubes in computers of this era meant that they generated vast amounts of heat, and, as a result, could only be used for a few minutes at a time before they overheated and shorted out. However, in these short bursts of activity, they were capable of processing thousands of calculations per second and could carry out a tremendous amount of work. They thus demonstrated their worth and the age of computing was born.

With mainframes such as ENIAC and its successors, *batch processing* was used to maximize the work that could be carried out in the periods when the machine was actually in operation. Jobs from different people were collected, placed in sequence and coded onto punched cards by a special data-processing department. These cards were then fed into the computer and processed in a 'batch', thus keeping the amount of time that the computer was in actual use to a minimum. The major problems associated with batch processing were the time lag between submitting work for processing and receiving the results, and the difficulty in detecting and correcting errors. This time delay was caused by the fact that anything to be processed had to be submitted to the specialist department, punched onto cards, batched and run through the computer. The results then had to be translated back into text and sent back to their owners. As a result, the work cycle could take anything from a few hours to several days. The gap between submission and receiving results was greatly extended if any error occurred. Generally the owner of the work did not become aware of the error until the results of the batch were obtained, perhaps hours or days later. The error then had to be corrected and the work resubmitted to be processed again – a time-consuming and frustrating process.

The development of transistors and then integrated circuits in the early 1960s allowed computers which were smaller, consumed less power and generated less heat to be built. An integrated circuit is basically thousands of electronic components etched onto a tiny sliver of silicon – known as a *silicon chip*. These chips can be mass produced, a fact which allowed IBM to launch the first commercial computer (the IBM 360 mainframe) in 1964. Subsequently computers began to fall in price. Mini-computers, which were far more powerful than the original mainframes but smaller in size and much cheaper, began to appear on the market. Although still expensive to purchase and to operate, computing power was now within the reach of large organizations.

As computers became more sophisticated, a new type of processing emerged. Instead of sending their work to the data-processing department to be batch processed, people began to work directly on the computer themselves, using a keyboard and a screen. *Online processing*, as this became known, is interactive in that the computer processes commands as they are entered and gives results straight away. Errors are immediately apparent and can therefore be corrected, and work continued, without any delay. However, having a single person using a powerful computer interactively is not very efficient. Even when the time spent thinking is ignored, the facilities of the computer are not being used the majority of the time. Computers are capable of processing many thousands of transactions per second, but the fastest human typist can only reach a speed of maybe a hundred words per minute. As a result, the computer would lie idle most of the time while it is waiting for the typist. Literally millions of processes could be completed between the keystrokes! To make better use of computing power, a process called *time-sharing* was developed. Using this strategy, the power of the computer is divided among several users, each using a *terminal*, which is basically a keyboard and screen. Each user is allocated a period of computer time called a time slice, during which the computer processes his or her work. This is then saved temporarily and the computer moves on to each of the other users' time slices. When each user has received his or her slice, the computer returns to the beginning of the queue, loads the first user's work and starts the cycle again. This process occurs at tremendous speeds, so it appears that each user has exclusive use of the computer. However, time-sharing can be problematic. Complex (and therefore expensive) software is required to control the allocation and management of the time slices. Furthermore, as there is only a finite amount of computing power available, a time-sharing system tends to become slower as the number of users increases. Eventually, if the number of users becomes too large, the computer 'trashes' – each user's time slice becomes so small that there is no time available to do anything apart from load and then immediately save the work before moving on to the next user's time slice. Although limiting the number of simultaneous users can control this problem, this unreliability in terms of speed (along with a massive reduction in hardware costs) helped to fuel the growth of the personal computer.

The development by Intel of the first microprocessor (computer on a single chip) at the beginning of the 1970s began a path that ultimately led to massive cuts in the cost of computing power. The first personal computers (PCs) designed

Figure 2.1

A personal computer and a mainframe

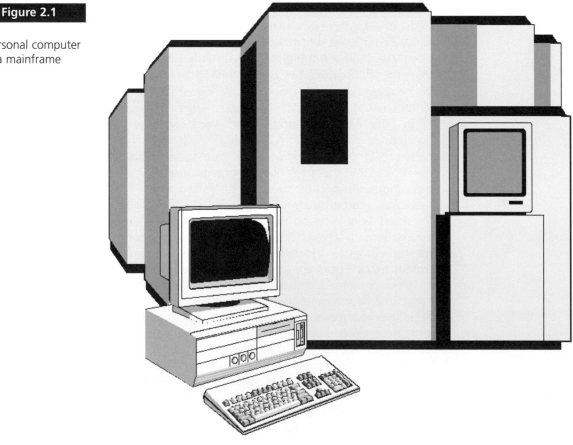

specifically to be used by a single person, appeared in the 1970s. Each had its own central processing unit and operated independently. As a result, the number of people using computers had no effect on the speed of operation of each user's machine. However, independence also had disadvantages. Information could not be shared easily among users, as is the case with a mainframe system. Data entered on one machine was only available to the user of that machine. Each personal computer also had to have its own peripherals, such as printers and disk drives, while multiple users connected to a mainframe could share these expensive devices. To overcome these drawbacks, methods of allowing personal computers to communicate with each other were developed. While each machine remains *stand-alone* and thus retains a reliable speed of operation, the use of a *network* allows computers to share both information and peripherals. This and other methods of allowing computers to communicate with each other are discussed in Chapter 4.

The IBM PC, which was the first personal computer to become a standard throughout the business world, was launched in 1981. After this, the 'personal computer revolution' occurred, and computers have continued to fall drastically in price and rise rapidly in power. It has been estimated that computers double in speed, processing power and storage capacity every eighteen months, while also halving in price. As a result, the dividing line between different categories of computer has become blurred. For example, even the most basic PC of today is more powerful than many of the mainframes of the 1980s, while at the same time costing less than £1400 instead of hundreds of thousands of pounds. Apart from a rapidly closing speed difference, the main method used to distinguish between different types of computers today is by the number of simultaneous users or more technically terminals – the machine in question supports. A personal computer is normally used concurrently by just a single user, and a mini by between five and 80 users, while a mainframe is generally regarded as any computer with over 80 terminals.

The trend towards smaller and more powerful computers continues today with the introduction of extremely portable devices. Portable computers (sometimes called laptops or notebooks) combine the monitor, systems unit and keyboard into one casing, usually smaller than a briefcase, and are designed for people on the move who want to take their work with them. While they are small and relatively lightweight, laptops are generally more expensive than desktops, while at the same time being less powerful and having less flexibility. Despite this, portable computers continue to become smaller, lighter and cheaper. Miniaturization has allowed the development of hand-held computers, sometimes known as personal digital assistants (PDAs). In general, these tend to lack conventional keyboards, instead relying on character recognition technology for input, and tend to have a much narrower range of functions, usually relating to maintaining the user's schedule and contact management, although a variety of specialist applications have also been developed. Some companies (for example Carlson) have developed their own proprietary hand-held computers. Known as MACH-1 (Mobile Access to Carlson Hospitality Version 1), this interfaces with their property-based systems and allows managers to be more mobile and less desk-bound. A more recent development has been the tablet PC. Designed like a notebook, the screens of these devices can be rotated and laid flat across the keyboard, giving a highly mobile computer that can be used in places where a laptop would not be appropriate. Most tablet PCs use pen-based entry in a manner similar to the PDAs discussed above, and are designed to be lightweight and highly portable. In general they use wireless networking (see Chapter 4) and, unlike PDAs, have the full capabilities of a normal PC and thus can be used to run normal business applications. So, for example, they could be used throughout the hotel to run the PMS, eliminating the need for a front desk!

There are some occasions where a full computer is just not necessary. For example, computers at the front desk of a hotel do not need to be state of the art, full-featured computers. While staff in this area obviously need computers to access the PMS (see Chapter 9), their needs, both in terms of processing power and also in terms of peripherals, are fairly basic. Why should PCs in this situation be equipped with modems, CD-ROM drives, expansion ports and other expensive add-on materials? Similar situations in other industries have driven the development of what have become known as '*network computers*' or '*thin clients*' – stripped-down computers that can be used where the limited nature of the tasks to be performed do not merit the use of a full-featured, full-powered PC. Thin clients are essentially cut down workstations – each with their own processors but with their level of 'thinness' determined by what else is included. At their most extreme level, they may just include a keyboard, screen, processor and memory, but omit both hard and floppy drives as well as any other peripherals. While applications run on the processor of the individual thin client, all data storage is done on the network.

Note that the thin-client concept differs from the mainframe and dumb terminals approach discussed earlier. Each thin client has its own processor and works independently, and thus it could be said that the concept combines the advantages of the centralized mainframe approach in terms of security, data sharing and manageability, while eliminating its limitations. The big advantage of thin clients is that their simplicity makes such machines easy to manage and reduces their total cost of ownership. Companies can lock down the functions

Figure 2.2

Hand-held
computing device

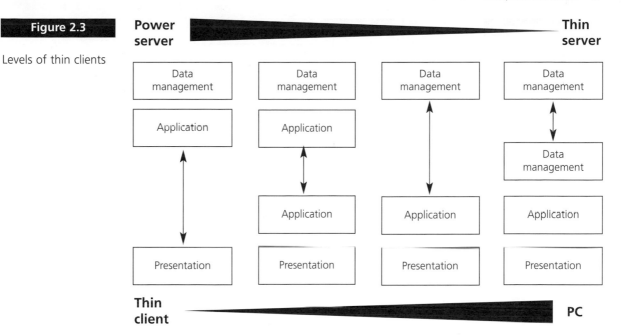

Figure 2.3

Levels of thin clients

and features of the machine much more effectively than they can do with today's PCs. Only the applications that the company wants the user to run – delivered from the server – are available, and the user cannot change the settings or otherwise reconfigure the machine. As a result, the costs of setting up and supporting such systems are much lower. Other variations on the thin-client idea may include disk drives or other peripherals, but the overall concept is to eliminate features that are not needed to reduce management overhead and costs. Thin clients are not for everyone – they can only be used in situations where the range of functions needed is limited – but the economic arguments for using them are compelling. Companies that have switched from PC networks to network computers typically cite savings in the region of 30 per cent in operating costs.

The structure of a computer

While technology has changed, the underlying concepts behind how a computer works have not. Information is input and processed in some way, and the results either stored for further processing or reported to the user. All computers, whether mainframes or PCs, follow the basic design outlined by Babbage.

Within a computer system, all information and instructions are stored and processed in *binary* form. The use of the binary number system derives from the electronic nature of computers. Any storage location can be either positively or negatively charged, and its state is represented in writing as 1 or 0 respectively. Each of these charges is known as a *binary digit*, or *bit* for short. Groups of bits (usually eight) are combined in unique patterns to form characters. For example, the letter A is represented by the combination 01000001. Each group of eight bits is known as a *byte*, which is the basic unit of measurement for memory and

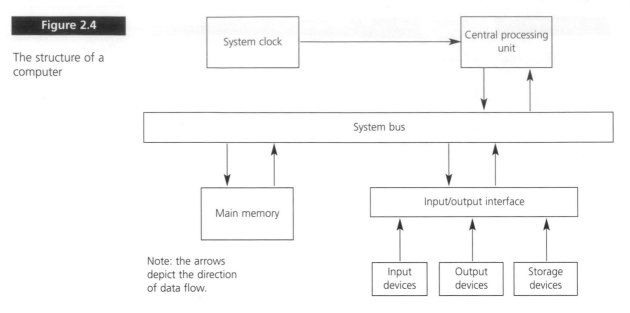

The structure of a computer

Note: the arrows depict the direction of data flow.

storage capacity (Table 2.1). For example, the capacity of a 3.5 inch floppy disk ranges is normally 1.44 megabytes (which means that it can store one million four hundred and forty thousand characters), while the storage space on a hard fixed disk is typically measured in gigabytes. Computer memory is also measured in bytes, with typical configurations ranging from 128 Mb upwards.

Information is entered into the computer system through an *input device*. This converts outside signals into binary data, which can then be processed and stored by the computer. The keyboard is probably the most common input device, although, as will be discussed later in this chapter, others such as the mouse, magnetic-strip readers and touch sensitive screens have become more common. All the actual work of the computer is carried out by the *central processing unit*, which could be described as the 'brain' of the computer. This is itself composed of two components: the arithmetic logical unit, which performs all of the calculations, and the control unit, which controls the sequence in which the work is performed. All operations are synchronized using the pulses of the *system clock*, which is often described as the heartbeat of the computer. The speed of the clock is measured in megahertz (MHz), that is, in millions of cycles per second. High clock speeds mean that the computer can execute commands at greater speed, and thus can achieve the same results faster. All data, as well as the program being executed, is stored in *main memory*, and travels along the *system bus* to the

Table 2.1

Bits and bytes

Term	Symbol	Explanation
Bit		One-eighth of a character
Byte		1 character
Kilobyte	Kb or K	1024 characters
Megabyte	Mb or M	1024 K or approximately 1 million characters
Gigabyte	Gb or G	1024 Mb or approximately 1 billion characters
Tetrabyte	Tb or T	1024 Gb or approximately 1 thousand billion characters

processor when requested by the control unit. The results then travel back along the bus to be stored in main memory until needed again. *Output devices* take the binary signals of the computer and convert them into a form suitable for interpretation by the user. The most common output devices are *visual display units* (VDUs), which display the results on a computer screen, and *printers*, which print the results on paper.

All data entered into or output from the computer travels through the *Input/Output interface* (*I/O interface*). This forms a buffer between the electronic speeds of the computer and the much slower speeds of the outside world. For example, when a computer sends data to a printer, it encounters the mechanical speed of the printer head as it goes back and forth across the page. If the computer was to wait for each character to be printed before sending the next, it would spend most of its time doing nothing. Instead, a portion of the data to be printed is stored in the I/O interface and sent to the printer at the correct rate, freeing the CPU to perform other tasks. Similarly, key-presses are stored in the keyboard buffer, which is checked and processed periodically (perhaps several times a second) by the computer, which is then free to perform other tasks while the user is typing.

The central processing unit

The central processing unit (CPU) is a small chip (usually smaller than your thumbnail) encased in black plastic and located on the motherboard of your computer. As we saw earlier, the CPU is basically the 'brain' of the computer. Consequently, the type of CPU present in a computer has a great effect on its functionality and performance. Many software packages require a certain type of CPU to operate. For example, Windows® XP Professional (one of the current industry standard operating systems) requires the computer to have a minimum of a Pentium®-type processor operating at 300 Mhz to be able to run. Anything less and the operating system will simply not be able to work. Therefore choosing an appropriate CPU is important when purchasing a computer.

The CPU is composed of three parts: the arithmetic and logic unit, the control unit and working memory.

- The arithmetic and logic unit (ALU) performs the mathematical and logical operations into which all functions of the computer are ultimately broken down.

- The control unit coordinates the operation of the entire computer. It determines what calculations are to be performed by the ALU and what data is necessary to complete these calculations, fetches this data from main memory or an input device and places it in working memory, and finally returns the result to main memory.

- A small amount of temporary storage space, known as working memory or memory registers, is also contained within the CPU.

Although the term 'personal computer' is generic, and simply means a computer designed to be used by a single person, the majority of computers used in

Table 2.2	Introduced	Brand name	Processor size	Bus size	Typical clock speed
Characteristics of the Intel 80X86 family of processors	1978	8086	16-bit	16-bit	4 MHz
	1979	8088	16-bit	8-bit	4 MHz
	1982	80286	16-bit	16-bit	12 MHz
	1985	80386	32-bit	32-bit	33 MHz
	1989	80486	32-bit	32-bit	66 MHz
	1993	Pentium®	32-bit	32-bit	200 MHz
	1997	Pentium® II	32-bit	32-bit	400 MHz
	1998	Pentium® III	32-bit	32-bit	500 MHz
	2000	Pentium® 4	32-bit	32-bit	2 GHz
	2003	Pentium® M (Centrino)	32-bit	32-bit	1.4 GHz

business are IBM compatible and have processors based on the 80X86 series of chips from Intel. This series started with the 8086, which was the processor incorporated into the original IBM PC, and worked through successive generations to the 80586 (known as the Pentium®) and its successors. As can be seen from Table 2.2, each chip has grown in capacity both in terms of speed and of the amount of data that can be processed at one time. The 8086 was a 16-bit chip, which means that the processor can work on two characters (2 × 8 bits = 16 bits) at a time. In contrast, more modern chips are 32-bit, which means that they can process data four characters at a time. In theory, this means that all other things being equal, newer chips should be able to complete the same work in half of the time taken by an 8086. In practice, however, other factors – namely bus size and clock speed – also have a considerable effect.

As mentioned above, the system bus is an electronic pathway along which data travels between main memory, the CPU and the input/output interface. The most important characteristic of the system bus is its width, which is measured in bits. The wider the bus, the faster data can be transported, resulting in faster performance. With an 8-bit bus, data can only be transferred one character at a time, while with 16-bit and 32-bit buses, data can travel two and four characters at a time respectively. A useful analogy is that of cars travelling along a single lane road compared to those on a dual carriageway or a four-lane motorway. Even if the speed of the individual cars on the different roads is the same, those on the motorway arrive faster because they can travel four abreast. The 8086 chip had an 8-bit bus, and therefore data could only travel along it one character at a time. As a result the processor, which was 16-bit, had to wait for data to arrive and therefore could not operate at its maximum potential speed. More recent chips have a fairer balance between bus width and processor speed. For example, the Pentium® has both a 32-bit bus and a 32-bit processor, and thus the processor is not kept waiting. The clock speed in more modern chips is also far higher than that of an 8086, and the combination of the higher clock speed and the 32-bit processor capacity can makes them several hundred times faster in operation. However, it is not the design of the chip or its clock speed that determine overall performance but the sum of all the chip's parts working together. For this reason, it is difficult to compare the performance of CPUs from different manufacturers simply by looking at their specifications. For example, the AMD chip shown in Table 2.3 below theoretically has a clock speed of 2.2 GHz, but in reality delivers performance similar to that of a 2.8 GHz Pentium® 4. The only true way to tell is to run performance tests where each processor is asked to perform a certain set of tasks and to compare the results.

The prior point raises the issue of non-Intel processors. Despite the dominance of Intel (nearly 80 per cent of the world market in 2002), there are a variety of other processors available from alternative manufacturers. These fall into two categories – those that attempt to clone the capabilities and facilities of the Intel chips (such as those from Advanced Micro Devices [AMD] and Cyrix), and those that are specifically designed to be very different (such as the PowerPC processors that power the Apple Macintosh). In the former case, the competing companies have been able to consistently produce clones that more or less exactly imitate the corresponding Intel chip (and in some cases surpass them in terms of performance) but at a price approximately 25 per cent lower. As the cost of the processor to a large extent determines the selling price of a PC, users can buy a computer based on such chips much cheaper than the equivalent Intel processor.

Processors continue to get faster, in terms of clock speeds, bus sizes and processor capacity. The first commercially successful 64-bit processors were introduced by AMD at the end of 2002 and Intel is racing to catch up. However, the question remains – does a user really need the latest and greatest high-performance processor? The short answer is a qualified no. For those who primarily do word processing, spreadsheet, Internet browsing and email, or even those who run general business applications, 'slower' processors – those one or two generations behind the cutting edge of processor technology – work perfectly. More powerful processors will give limited performance enhancements in these situations, and at a very high price. Only those that need to work with video or other graphically intensive digital content really benefit from the newest technology.

Table 2.3	Chip	Manufacturer	Intel clone	Typical speed
Comparison of alternative chip manufacturers	Celeron	INTEL	Yes	2.22 GHz
	Pentium® 4	INTEL	Yes	3 GHz
	Athlon XP	AMD	Yes	2.2 GHz
	PowerPC G4	Motorola	No	1.2 GHz

Computer memory

Memory is where all programs and data are stored while they are active in the computer. Memory comes in chips – small gray and black rectangles containing tiny electronic circuitry encased in plastic and attached to the motherboard of the computer. There are basically two types of memory: read only memory, more commonly known as ROM, and random access memory, known as RAM.

- Read only memory (ROM), as the name suggests, is permanent and its contents cannot be changed. As a result, it cannot be used for normal, day-to-day storage. Instead it contains programs which are essential for the operation of the computer and which are permanently 'burned' into ROM at the manufacturing stage. For example, a program called the *bootstrap* is included in ROM on most PCs. This runs automatically when the computer is turned on (this process is called *booting the computer*, hence the name 'bootstrap'). It performs a diagnostic check and, provided everything is working correctly, attempts to load another program called the operating system (see Chapter 3) from disk.

- Random access memory (RAM), on the other hand, can be changed and is used by the computer to store any programs or data required by the user. Although it can be overwritten as many times as is needed, RAM is only a temporary storage facility, as its contents are erased whenever power is removed. To keep the data permanently, it must be transferred to a secondary storage device such as a floppy disk. The amount of RAM present on a computer has a major effect on its performance. In order for a computer to use a program or a piece of data, it must be in memory. Over the years programs have grown greatly in size and, as a result, the minimum amount of memory required has grown in tandem. Until quite recently, many computers were sold with as little as 640 K of RAM. Now all industry standard PCs are shipped with at least 128 Mb of memory. However, most users purchase much more to help improve performance. For example, while Microsoft® Windows® XP Professional operating system will theoretically run with just 64 Mbs of memory, at least 256 but preferably 512 megabytes of memory are needed to run applications at an acceptable speed! Increasing the amount of memory available is the best and easiest way to increase the performance of a computer.

The external appearance of a personal computer

When talking about the structure of a computer, an average user is more likely to be referring to a large, cream-coloured box with slots on the front and various sockets on the back than to things such as processors, buses or memory. Figure 2.5 shows a typical personal computer. Apart from peripherals such as the keyboard and monitor, the most noticeable features on the front are the *disk drives*. The computer shown has two different types of drives: a 3.5 inch drive for floppy disks and another drive for loading information from CDs and/or DVDs.

The back of the machine is a little more confusing (see Figure 2.6). There is generally a selection of connections, called *ports*, to allow peripherals such as screens, keyboards, mice and other devices to be connected. The largest and most noticeable item on the rear panel is the fan opening, which is used to keep the internal components cool while the computer is in use. Both the serial and the parallel ports are used for data transfer, either between two computers or to send data to a device such as a printer. The serial ports, often known as COM1 and COM2 (short for communications), allow the transmission of data one bit at a time. The parallel port, on the other hand, sends eight bits, or one byte, simultaneously over eight separate lines in a single cable. As a result, transmission through the parallel port is faster and is often used to connect the computer to a printer. Another type of port, known as a universal serial bus (USB) is also present

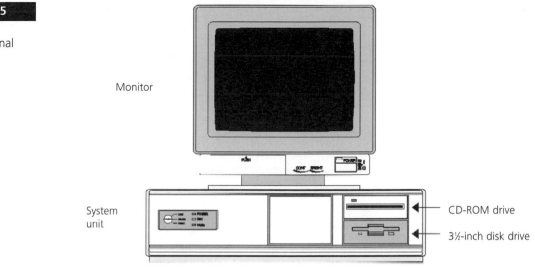

Figure 2.5

A typical personal computer

Monitor

System unit

CD-ROM drive

3½-inch disk drive

on many modern computers. This has been promoted as a replacement for the serial and parallel ports, and offers far higher data transfer rates. It also allows up to 127 devices to be daisy-chained together for connection to the computer, thus helping to overcome the 'port famine' most users experience as they try to add peripherals to their computer. USB connections can also carry power, allowing each device to be connected through a single cable and eliminating the pile of transformers that normally help warm the user's feet! Firewire ports (also called iLink ports) are similar to USB ports in that they allow peripherals to be connected at high speeds and can be daisy-chained together, and are generally used to connect audio-visual devices such as digital camcorders to the computer. *Expansion slots* allow additional features to be added to the computer system to enhance its functions. Common examples include things such as additional hard disk drives, network cards, modems, sound cards and specialized graphics cards. Such cards fit inside the computer case, with any external connections showing through the expansion slot space. Laptop computers normally have a special type of expansion slot, known as a PCMCIA slot, which allows credit card-sized expansion cards to be inserted to add extra features.

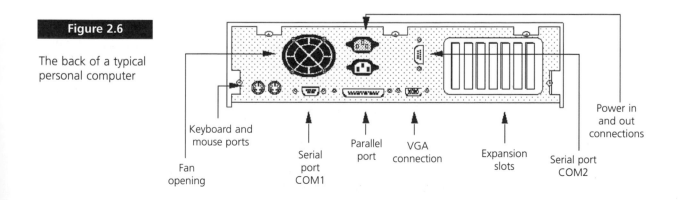

Figure 2.6

The back of a typical personal computer

Keyboard and mouse ports

Fan opening

Serial port COM1

Parallel port

VGA connection

Expansion slots

Serial port COM2

Power in and out connections

Peripheral devices

The phrase 'peripheral devices' is used to describe any piece of equipment connected to the computer. They can broadly be divided into three sections: input devices, output devices and secondary storage devices.

Input devices

Information is entered into a computer system using an input device – the most common of which are keyboards of various types. However, these are not ideal for all purposes and other input devices are increasingly becoming common. The input devices most often used in the hospitality industry are described below.

The keyboard

The keyboard may take many forms, from the normal typewriter-style keyboard shown in Figure 2.7, to the membrane keyboards used in point-of-sales (POS) systems in fast-food outlets (Figure 2.8), to the key pads used in a bank's automatic cash teller machines and even the normal telephone handset. Each has a common feature: it allows the user to input information quickly and easily by pressing buttons. In the case of a typewriter-style keyboard, each key-press enters a single letter, while on other keyboards, such as those used on a POS system, each key can be pre-programmed, so that pressing a single button may enter an order for a complete meal.

The computer keyboard was derived from the QWERTY keyboard (so called because of the first six letters on the top left row of alphabetical keys) used on a typewriter. However, a PC keyboard also has several extra keys, as can be seen from Figure 2.7.

At the extreme top left of the keyboard can be found the *Escape* key, which is usually marked with the letters 'Esc'. This is normally used to cancel (or escape from) an operation or go back a step in a process. At the bottom left-hand side of

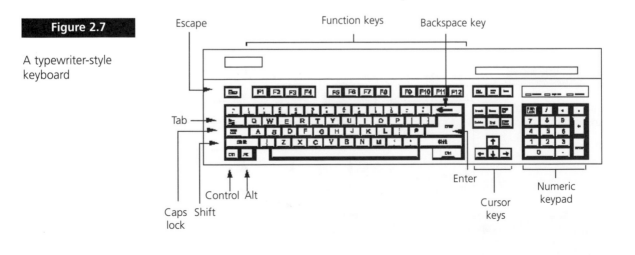

Figure 2.7

A typewriter-style keyboard

the keyboard can be found three other important keys: the *Shift* key (which is sometimes marked with a hollow arrow pointing upwards), the *Control* key (which is usually marked 'Ctrl') and the *Alt* key. The Shift key is used to access the upper-case letters and symbols, such as the £$%^&* which are located over the numbers. The Alt and Control keys are used in conjunction with other keys to give access to various commands. For example, holding down the Alt key and pressing the first letter of the desired menu accesses drop-down menus in Microsoft® Windows®. Above the Shift key is the *Caps Lock* key, which, as the name suggests, locks the capital letters in place. When it is depressed, every letter typed will come out in upper case, until the key is pressed again to release it and return the data entry to lower case. Usually you can tell if Caps Lock is on or off from a small light either on the key itself or over the numeric keypad. The *Tab* key works in a similar way to the Tab key on a typewriter and moves the cursor to the next tab mark (usually set by default at every half-inch). The Tab key is also used by many software programs to select options from menus displayed on the screen.

On the opposite side of the alphanumeric keyboard, another set of Ctrl and Shift keys can be found. Above these is the most important key on the keyboard: the *Enter* key, sometimes known as *carriage return* or simply *return*. To get the computer to process something the user presses the Enter key. This tells the computer that data entry is finished and to get on with processing the information entered. Above the Enter key is the *Backspace* key, which, as the name suggests, moves the cursor back one space. If there is something in that space, it is erased. This is different from the *Delete* key, which erases the character to the right of (or forward from) the cursor. Along the top of the keyboard (or sometimes down the left-hand side) can be found the *Function keys*, which are labelled from F1 to F12. These are special-purpose keys that are used by software programs to carry out different functions – hence the name 'function keys'. They allow commonly used tasks to be performed at the touch of a single button, and the exact purpose of each key varies from program to program. There are, however, some common conventions. For example, pressing the F1 key generally gives the user access to a software package's help screens. Four arrows, known as the *cursor keys*, can be found towards the bottom right-hand side of the keyboard. These are used to move a 'highlighted area' called the cursor around the screen to show the computer where to start typing or to choose options from a menu.

Immediately above the cursor keys can be found a group of six keys labelled *Home, End, PgUp, PgDn, Ins*, and *Del*. The first four of these move the cursor to the beginning, end, previous page or next page of a document respectively. The Del or delete key is similar to the Backspace key but deletes forwards (instead of backwards), and the insert key is used to insert something which has previously been deleted. On the extreme right can be found the numeric keypad, which allows numbers to be entered more efficiently than by using the 'normal' number keys. In addition, the cursor keys and the group of six keys discussed above are duplicated on this numeric key pad.

A membrane keyboard from an EPOS used in a bar

Pint Guinness	1/2 Pint Guinness	Bottle Guinness	Long Neck Beer	Irish Whiskey	White Wine	Special Cocktail 1			Slippery Nipple
Pint Lager	1/2 Pint Lager	Bottle Lager	American Long Neck	Scotch Whiskey	Dark Rum	Special Cocktail 2	Manhattan	Dry Martini	
Pint Beer	1/2 Pint Beer	Bottle Beer	Holsten Pils	American Whiskey	Brandy	Special Cocktail 3	Old Fashioned		
Pint Cider	1/2 Pint Cider	Bottle Cider	Bottle Export Lager	Tequila	Liqueurs	Snacks	Cigarettes	Cigars	Bar Food
Bottle House Red	1/2 Bottle House Red	Glass House Red		Vodka	Campari	TAKE AWAY	Manager	Refund	Charge
Bottle House White	1/2 Bottle House White	Glass House White	No Alcohol Beer	Gin	Martini	CLEAR	PLU	VOID	QTY
Bottle Champagne	1/2 Bottle Champagne	Glass Champagne	Lucozade	Port	Sherry	SERVER NO	7	8	9
Teas Coffee	Babycham	Snowball	Mineral Water	Malibu	Pernod	NO SALE	4	5	6
Irish Coffee	Hot Toddy	Sprite	Orange	Fruit Juice	Baileys	SUB TOTAL	1	2	3
Iced Tea	Coke	Lemonade	Mixers	Splash Mixers	TOTAL		0		.

The mouse

The use of a mouse as an input device has become common because of the growth of graphic user interfaces such as Microsoft® Windows® which necessitate the use of a pointing device. A mouse is a small plastic device that fits comfortably in the palm of the hand (Figure 2.9). On the underside can traditionally be found a small rubber ball which sticks out of the casing. As this ball is moved around a desk or other flat surface, the movement is mirrored by an arrow – called a *pointer* – on the screen. A mouse generally has two or three buttons on its top surface for the user to click, and the combination of 'pointing and clicking' can be used to choose options from menus, select areas of text, draw shapes on the screen or whatever. While using a mouse is a very efficient method of choosing

A mouse

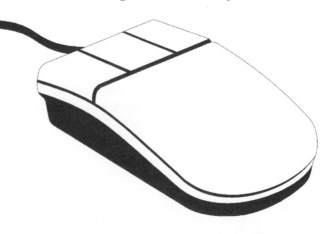

from predefined options or working with graphics and can allow the user to perform complex tasks without ever having to touch a keyboard, it is not generally suitable for entering textual or numeric data and, for that reason, it is rarely used alone, but as a supplement to another input device such as a keyboard.

Some modern mice dispense with the rubber ball and instead use infrared light to tell when they are being moved around the desk. This has the advantage that it can be used on a wider variety of surfaces than is possible with a traditional 'ball' mouse. Several other devices could be described as mouse-related. For example, trackerballs, games paddles and joysticks are all input devices with which many people are familiar from computer games. Each of these is based on the same principle: sending an electronic signal to the computer to tell it in what direction to move the cursor, which in this case could be a Pac-Man or a spaceship or whatever. Trackerballs, which are basically a mouse turned upside-down, are sometimes used with portable computers where the lack of a flat surface could make using a mouse difficult. Others use a 'Track pad' – a touch sensitive area on which the user can move their finger to control the pointer. Other manufacturers use a 'nubbin', 'eraser head' or 'pointing stick' – all different names for effectively the same thing – a tiny rubber joystick-like device positioned in the middle of the laptop's keyboard. Both approaches take a little practice to be able to control the pointer effectively, and both have their own set of supporters arguing that their approach is best.

The bar-code reader

Most readers will be familiar with this technology from the bar codes found on consumer items, which are used by supermarket checkouts to calculate the cost of a person's shopping. Bar codes are a series of dark lines separated by white spaces. Variations in the thickness of the bars and the width of the spaces represent various pieces of encoded data. A bar-code reader (Figure 2.10) inputs the information by sweeping a small beam of light across the bar code. The dark lines reflect less light than the spaces and this difference is identified by the reader and translated into electrical signals, which are processed by the computer.

Figure 2.10

A bar-code reader

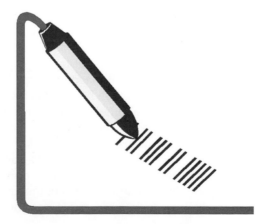

Figure 2.11

An airline luggage tag

The use of bar codes is becoming more common in the hospitality industry. For example, they can be attached to equipment such as tables, chairs and audio-visual equipment in the conference and banqueting department, or even televisions and other equipment in guest bedrooms. Security or maintenance staff can then use a hand-held computer with a bar-code reader to keep track of the location of each asset. Airlines also use bar codes in their luggage-tracking systems. A bar code is used to record the passenger's flight information on the tag attached to each piece of checked luggage (Figure 2.11). This can be read by sensors located on the baggage belts and the luggage automatically diverted to the correct trolley for transfer to the correct plane.

Punched-card entry

Figure 2.12

A punched-card-style key for an electronic locking system

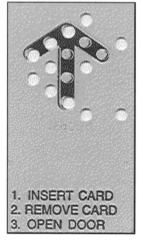

Although one of the first computer input methods, punched cards are now almost obsolete as an input device. As was discussed earlier, data was originally punched onto cards and fed into the computer through a punched-card reader to make the maximum use of computer time. As computers became cheaper and were used interactively, the need to pre-punch data was eliminated. However, punched cards are still used to a limited extent in the hotel industry. Some computerized door-locking systems use a plastic punched card instead of a metal key (Figure 2.12). Each door lock contains a reader that reads the information encoded on the card and compares it to the combination stored in the computer. Where these match, it unlocks the door.

Magnetic-strip reader

Magnetic-strip technology is ubiquitous today, and is used in everything from credit and ATM cards to pre-paid cards for photocopying, automatic vending or car parking. Data is encoded on a strip of magnetic tape attached to the card and can be read by a computer by 'swiping' this strip through a special card reader. An important feature of magnetic strips is that they are re-recordable – for example, a card purchased with fifty credits for a photocopier has its remaining balance re-recorded several times as the card is used. When it is 'empty' it can be recharged using an encoder. Magnetic strips store a lot more data than bar codes. A typical bar code holds just twelve characters, while a magnetic strip can store up to 300.

The use of magnetic-strip cards has naturally becoming common in the hospitality sector. Some electronic door-locking systems (see Chapter 9) use magnetic-strip cards instead of metal keys (Figure 2.13). In the industrial catering sector, magnetic-strip cards can help simplify cash control. Employees can

Figure 2.13

A card with a magnetic strip

1.
Introduire et retirer la carte-clé
Insert and remove the keycard
Schlüsselkarte einstecken und herausziehen
Kaart insteken en uittrekken

2.
Tourner la poignée au vert
Turn handle while green light is flashing
Wenn grün, Türgriff drehen
Bij groen licht, knop omdraaien

E

pre-pay by placing cash into a machine at a central location, which encodes the value of their payment onto a card with a magnetic strip. This can then be used to pay for meals, snacks and beverages from canteens or vending machines. All cash transactions are centralized and cash floats are not required at each service location.

Touch recognition systems

Touch recognition allows users to enter data into a computer by touching predefined areas, usually on a computer screen. The 'screen' is composed of a layer of electrically conductive material covered with a layer of glass. This transparent layer is then placed over a conventional VDU. Special software displays coloured areas to form 'buttons' on the screen. When the user touches one of these, the pattern of the electric current is disturbed and the computer can calculate which button has been pressed. In addition to displaying buttons, the underlying VDU can also be used to display prompts or messages to guide the user through a process. This makes touch screens a hybrid device as they can be used to both input and output information at the same time. This saves space and is ergonomically more sound than having a separate keyboard and monitor,

Figure 2.14

A touch screen from an EPOS system

Filet Mignon

1	Prawn salad	4.50	1
2	Caesar salad	3.00	1
3	Sirloin steak	14.50	1
	Med rare		
	Baked potato		
4	Filet mignon	12.50	1
5			
6			
7			
8			
9			

Enter meat temperature

TBL 2/1   CHK 284

11 May 2003 12.13pm   GST 2   Server 201

Subtotal   34.50
Service charge   0.00
Amount tendered   0.00

Total   34.50

Void/Return/Lbs		Cancel ?

Enter	Clear

Blue	Med rare	Med well
Rare	Medium	Well

7	8	9
4	5	6
1	2	3
0	Done	

which makes them useful in cramped conditions. The outer layer of glass also makes them durable, which makes them a popular choice for use in electronic point-of-sale (EPOS) systems (see Chapter 10). Because they are more capable of resisting the rough-and-tumble environment, they can be located in food and drink service areas, where they take up less space than separate keyboards and screens. In addition, because their buttons are interactively created by the software which drives them, they can display an unlimited number of menu items, thus overcoming the physical limitation of the traditional membrane keyboards, which have a fixed number of keys (Figure 2.14).

Pen entry

Using a technology similar to the touch screen, pen-based entry is becoming more common, particularly on the developing range of hand held and tablet computers. With pen-based entry, the user writes using a special pen, called a *stylus*, directly onto a screen, which is covered with two layers of electrically conductive transparent material. When the stylus touches a portion of the screen, the currents meet and software is able to calculate the position of the pen and reflect this on the liquid crystal display (LCD) screen below, thus giving the impression that the pen is actually writing on the screen. Special software can be used to interpret this writing and convert it into printed text.

The success of pen entry depends on this handwriting recognition software. There are a great number of variations in handwriting styles and we ourselves can have problems reading our own writing. To overcome this, some software uses word recognition, which compares its interpretation of the squiggles to words in a database and selects what it considers to be the closest match. An alternative to trying to understand the user's writing is to store the entry in the form of a picture, a process known as *inking*. The credit-card companies in particular are experimenting with the inking process in an attempt to cut down on credit-card fraud. An image of the customer's signature is captured on a special pad. The key features of the signature can then be identified by special software, and a comparison made with data stored either on the magnetic strip on the credit card or in a central database.

Digitization devices

There are now a wide variety of inexpensive devices available that allow the easy digitization of text and images. Examples of such devices include *scanners* and *digital cameras*, and although such devices may seem unrelated, both convert material into digital form so that it can be stored and manipulated on a computer. Scanners, which may take different forms such as flatbed or hand-held, can be used to digitize either images or text. Digital cameras can be used to capture still or video images onto the computer system. In both cases, the digital material can be manipulated easily using a variety of software programs once it has been saved on the computer. With devices of this type the key issue is resolution, which determines the quality of the digitized image. While most consumer-orientated devices do not provide a high enough image quality for marketing purposes, their output is good enough to be used in internal publications and on the Web.

Other input devices

New forms of input device are constantly evolving. Possibly the three most important ones from the point of view of the hospitality industry are voice entry, linking equipment directly into the computer and biometrics.

- Voice entry has the potential to be a very effective data-entry method. The average person talks at about two hundred words per minute but can only type at less than forty words per minute. If speech could be effectively captured and converted into a form that the computer could understand, the rate at which data could be entered would be greatly increased. There have been some limited successes in developing speech-recognition systems. However, differences in dialect and pronunciation and problems with background noise have made the development of commercial applications difficult. Those systems currently available have limited vocabularies (somewhere between 30,000 and 250,000 words, although only a proportion of these may be active at any one time) and tend to be 'speaker dependent'. As a result, they must be trained by each user to recognize his or her pronunciation of each word. Nonetheless, voice recognition products such as Dragon Dictate and IBM's Via Voice are gaining increasing acceptance by the marketplace. Both allow the user to speak into a headset microphone, and attempt to convert this speech into typed text. Errors can also be corrected using spoken commands, and indeed the program learns and adapts itself from these corrections. Given the recent speed at which this technology is progressing, most observers agree that it will become standard on home and office computers in the near future.

- Direct connection is a form of input that is becoming more important in directly linking pieces of equipment to the computer to provide it with data. Many readers will be familiar with the sensor in some microwave ovens that measures the internal temperature of the item cooking and switches off the power when it reaches a certain level. Technology of this type is widely being used in the fast-food sector. For example, research has shown how to cook perfect French fries consistently, and this process has been incorporated into automated systems. Controlled by a microprocessor, the oil in a deep-fat fryer is heated to a precise temperature. The fries are then dropped in automatically and the oil is reheated to the optimum temperature to cook the food. After a predefined cooking period, the fries are automatically lifted from the oil and shaken.

- Biometrics involves converting unique human characteristics into numeric data, and using this data as input into a system. There are many different types of biometric readers such as fingerprint scanners, retinal or iris eye scanners, facial recognition systems and scanners that recognize hand geometry. Although such technology is futuristic, it is in fact becoming more common wherever higher levels of security than can normally be achieved are needed. For example, many airports now use iris recognition systems instead of magnetic card swipes to control staff access to the tarmac. To get through the door, an employee's ID card must match a live scan of his iris, preventing stolen ID cards or compromised keypad codes from posing a threat to the terminal's security. Similarly the US immigration service's FAST (Future Automated Screening for Travelers) system has for a number of years made use of hand geometry to identify travellers. On arrival at selected airports in the US, instead of meeting face-to-face with an immigration official, travellers participating in the program can insert their hand into a special ATM-style kiosk, whereupon it is scanned and compared to data stored on a pre-recorded smart card, allowing them to prove their identity and clear immigration quickly.

Now that the technology has proved its usefulness and reduced in price, it is likely to become more common. Fingerprint recognition is currently the most popular approach, as it is the least expensive and the easiest to implement. For example, some laptops now use fingerprint scanners to control the boot process. Without the right finger, the system simply will not boot and any attempts to bypass the system result in all of its data being deleted. Fingerprint recognition can also be used as a replacement for magnetic cards in controlling access to guest rooms. By scanning the guest's finger at check-in, a biometric reader can be used on the door lock to grant access to the bedroom. Similarly, some hospitality system vendors have incorporated similar technology into back-of-house time attendance systems to help prevent buddy punching and other time fraud.

Output devices

Output devices are used to communicate results to the user. The commonest forms of output devices include visual display units (which display the output electronically on a computer screen), printers (which create a permanent copy of the results on paper) and voice (which gives the output in audible form).

Visual display units

The most common output device is the computer screen, also known as a visual display unit (VDU) or a monitor. Most conventional monitors are based on cathode ray tube (CRT) technology, similar to that used on a television. The quality of a monitor is usually measured in five ways; by its viewable area, its resolution, its dot pitch, its refresh rate and by the number of colours that it is capable of displaying.

The number of colours is important, as colours make the monitor more pleasant to use. Obviously size is also important as the larger the monitor, the greater the viewing area. The size quoted by manufacturers is actually the size of the front of the tube measured diagonally, and the real viewable area is slightly smaller. Thus a 15 in. screen may actually only provide about 13 in. of viewable space. While 15 in. screens have been relatively standard on most low-priced PCs, 17 in. and 19 in. are becoming more common. Larger viewable areas increase both productivity and comfort. For example, a 17 in. monitor has about 35 per cent more screen area than a 15 in. one, thus allowing the user to see more of the application at once, with less scrolling around. *Resolution* refers to the sharpness of the image on screen, and is expressed as the number of pixels – the dots that make up the monitor's image. The more pixels on the screen, the higher the resolution. Monitors with low resolutions can fit less information on the screen at any one time, and their characters tend to be slightly blurred, which can result in eyestrain with continued use. Dot pitch refers to the distance – measured in millimetres – between each of the pixels. The smaller the dot pitch, the closer the pixels and the sharper the image. Dot pitches of 0.28 and 0.31 are typical for a 15 in. and 17 in. screen respectively. One other factor is also important. Better monitors are *non-interlaced*. The image on a computer screen is not constant – it has to be redrawn several times each second. The computer redraws the image by highlighting pixels across the screen, going from top to bottom. The *refresh rate* refers to the number of times per second that each pixel on the screen is redrawn. Manufacturers quote the refresh rate in hertz (Hz), with higher figures being better. Monitors with low refresh rates tend to flicker, and even if this is only barely perceivable it can lead to eyestrain and headaches. However sometimes manufactures take shortcuts and refresh only every other line on every pass, which is called interlacing. Just like having a low refresh rate, this can cause your monitor to flicker, so for best quality you should get a non-interlaced monitor that refreshes every line at every pass.

Monitors really don't have minds of their own – they simply do what the computer tells them to do. In general the monitor gets these signals from a special piece of hardware called a *graphics card*. The main characteristics of the major graphic card standards are summarized in Table 2.4. The three earliest standards (monochrome, CGA and EGA) have in general been surpassed by newer technology. Most of today's systems are packaged with at least a VGA but probably an SVGA video card, showing at least 256 colours at high resolution.

Although they are relatively cheap, the biggest challenges with CRT-based monitors are that they are big and heavy, and that they consume a lot of power and generate a lot of heat. They also have a large 'footprint' in that they take up a lot of space – a problem in areas such as the front desk where space is often at a premium. For these reasons, an alternative, known as LCD monitors, is becoming more popular. Liquid crystal displays (LCDs) have become popular in portable computers, where the combination of low size and weight with low power consumption (which places less of a strain on the portable's batteries) makes them suitable. Until recently, their relative high cost prevented them from being used on standard desktop systems. However, as a result of falling prices and increased consumer demand, LCD-based monitors are now available for use on desktop systems. While prices are still double or triple that of a similar sized CRT screen,

Table 2.4	Type	Resolution	Colours
Graphic card standards	Monochrome	80 × 25 characters	1
	CGA (colour graphics array)	320 × 200 pixels	4
	EGA (enhanced graphics array)	640 × 350 pixels	16
	VGA (video graphics array)	640 × 480 pixels	256
	XGA (extended graphics array)	800 × 600 pixels	Millions of colours
	SVGA (super video graphics array)	1024 × 768 pixels	Millions of colours
	SXGA	1280 × 1024 pixels	Millions of colours
	UXGA	1600 × 1200 pixels	Millions of colours

Figure 2.15

An LCD panel saves a
lot of desk space

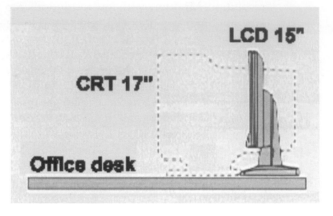

they will continue to fall as yields increase and production capacity meets demand. Today they are becoming more and more common in distinct niches, such as where space is at a premium. For example, many EPOS systems now use LCD panels in place of conventional monitors. Similarly space is usually at a premium in the front office, and the use of LCD screens can help ease congestion as a result of their much smaller footprint. In addition to being smaller and thus taking up less space, they have lower electromagnetic emissions and are also easier on the eyes as there is no flicker. Their viewable area is the same as the quoted figure, so a 15 in. LCD panel has a similar usable area to a 17 in. CRT.

Related to LCDs are what are known as *smart displays*. Incorporating a touch sensitive display and wireless networking, these flat panel devices allow the user to remotely access their existing PC's resources without actually being physically present at the system's unit. Acting in effect as a supplemental but highly portable monitor, these devices usually incorporate touch sensitive screens that allow the user to control the computer using either a stylus or even their fingertips. In general smart displays are light and highly portable, as they do not have hard disks or expansion ports, and normally include an on-screen virtual keyboard rather than a physical one. However, it's important to differentiate between such devices and the table PCs discussed earlier. While the latter are fully functional computers, smart displays are just remote wireless monitors – all the processing and storage still needs to be done on its wirelessly attached PC. While initially targeted at the home market, offering facilities such as surfing the Web from bed or checking email from the comfort of your armchair, such devices have the potential to be used in the hospitality sector. Imagine registering guests in the lobby of a hotel rather than making them queue up at the reception desk. All of the normal features of a PMS could be available, with the added advantage of electronic capture of the guest signature directly on the smart display itself.

Printers

Printers are the second most common form of computer output device and are used to transfer data onto paper. Printers can be classified by how they form their impression on paper.

Impact printers work like a typewriter and use a mechanical mechanism to push small, blunt-ended wires or 'pins' against an inked ribbon to form an image on a sheet of paper.

- Dot matrix printers (Figure 2.16), form characters on the page using a matrix of dots in the same way as pixels form characters on a computer screen. Because dot matrix printers employ dots to form characters, tint gaps occur in letters produced in this way. One way to close the gaps and improve print quality is to add more dots in the same amount of space, either by using more pins (24 pins instead of 9) or by making two passes of the print head over each character.

- In contrast to dot matrix printers, daisywheel printers use solid type to print characters, and as a result have a much higher quality output. The pre-formed characters are mounted on stems radiating from the centre of a wheel. To print a character, the wheel is rotated to the correct position and a hammer pushes the character against the inked ribbon. By changing the daisywheel, different fonts (typestyles) can be used to print documents. While daisywheel printers give higher quality textual output than dot matrix printers, they suffer from a major disadvantage in that they cannot print graphics. Dot matrix printers print diagrams and graphs by using combinations of dots to form the shapes required: daisywheel printers are limited to their pre-formed characters and therefore cannot create the pattern of dots needed to print graphics.

Non-impact printers form characters on the page not by mechanical means but electronically. This means, in theory at least, that any font or shape can be printed. The output need not have a typewritten appearance but can look as if it has been professionally printed. Non-impact printers are also quicker and quieter than impact printers, as there are fewer moving parts and a hammer does not have to push through a ribbon.

Figure 2.16

A dot matrix printer

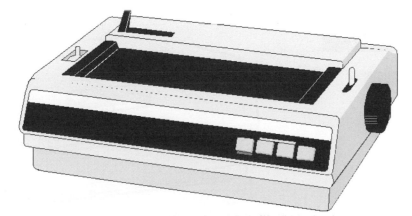

The three main types of non-impact printers are:

1. Ink-jet printers, which form images on paper using a carefully controlled, fine spray of quick-drying ink. Characters are not printed completely in one move but are built up gradually as the print head goes back and forth across the page. These printers are capable of giving high-quality output, but suffer from a slight drawback in that the ink takes a few seconds to dry, during which it may be smudged. Ink-jets are also unsuitable for printing full page artwork or illustrations, as the large amount of ink tends to make ordinary office paper soggy and a banding or stripping effect often occurs as it passes back and forth across the page.

2. Laser printers (Figure 2.17) work on the same principle as photocopiers and generally produce the highest quality output. Laser printers differ from other printers in that, rather than printing one character or line at a time, the entire page is printed in one step. Carbon toner is attracted electronically onto the surface of a rotating drum using a laser. The image formed on the drum is then transferred onto paper and fixed by gently applying heat to the page. Because the toner runs together when it is heated, it makes the character's edges smoother. Instead of a collection of dots as with dot matrix and ink-jet output, laser printing produces a solid black mass with smooth edges that is very pleasing to the eye.

3. Thermal printers form an image by moving a heated stylus over specially treated paper. Thermal printers are quiet, require no ribbons or ink and produce a relatively high quality output. The special heat-sensitive paper used is sometimes expensive, and often has a waxy feel that makes it unsuitable for many uses. However thermal printers have become common in some specialized situations, for example in the printers of cash registers and EPOS systems (see Chapter 10).

Irrespective of their type, measurement of the quality of all printers is usually based on two factors – speed and resolution. Speed is measured in terms of the number of pages per minute the printer can output under normal operating conditions (note that many manufacturers differentiate between text and graphics, and between printing in colour and in black and white, when quoting this figure). Resolution is measured in dots per inch (DPI). As most printers print documents

Figure 2.17

A laser printer

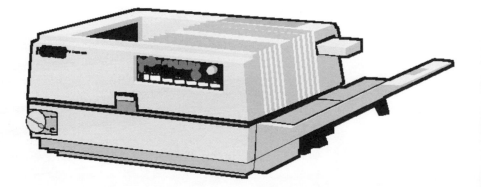

one dot at a time, the finer the dots the more detail the printer can show in a document. Higher resolutions mean that text is crisper and less jagged, and pictures have more subtle shades and tones as well as finer lines. Most printers now offer output in the 720 to 1440 DPI range at a reasonable cost.

Cost of operation is also important. Obviously all printers need paper – for dot matrix, ink-jet and laser this is relatively equal. However, as we mentioned earlier, thermal printers need special heat-sensitive paper that may be more difficult to obtain and which costs marginally more than normal paper. For dot matrix printers, the main consumable is the printer ribbon, which is comparatively cheap, working out at less than half a penny per page. With ink-jet printers the ink cartridge(s) must be replaced periodically. Cheaper ink-jet models use a single three-colour cartridge, mixing the ink in equal proportions to produce black. Since colour cartridges are more expensive, purchasing a printer such as this can be a false economy in the long run. Cost savings can be made by buying a model that has separate cartridges for black and for colour inks, or even better one that has separate cartridges for each colour – that way only the red cartridge has to be replaced when the printer is out of red ink. In the past, some users tried to economize by buying refill cartridges from other manufacturers or by refilling empty cartridges with ink. Since the printer manufacturers make lots of money from replacement cartridges – in many cases more than they make from selling the printer in the first place, the latter have come up with all sorts of reasons why this is not a good idea. More recently they have started building technology into the printers that monitor the quality and ink level of the cartridge, thus preventing 'non-approved' refills from being used. Checking the price of cartridge refills is essential when estimating the running cost of an ink-jet printer. A useful rule of thumb is that a monochrome printout will cost about one penny a page. Colour printouts will obviously cost more. For laser printers, the main consumable is the laser cartridge, which incorporates both toner and drum. Generally these are expensive, and a useful guideline is about 3 pence per page. This is more expensive than either dot matrix or ink-jet, but that's the price you pay for higher quality.

Sound

The use of sound as a means of outputting data has become increasingly common in recent years, particularly since sophisticated sound cards have become a standard feature in most new PCs sold. Sound output may take the form of music or effects, but computer-generated voices can also be used in certain situations. For example, services are now available that will 'read' your email to you, thus saving you from the necessity of having to look at your computer screen! Similarly, certain telephone companies use a digitized voice to announce numbers on their directory inquiry service, while newer personal computers use voice to draw attention to errors discovered during their start-up diagnostics. Some of these voice-output systems make use of 'phonemics', pre-recorded sounds strung together in an attempt to imitate natural speech. However, it can be difficult to get speech to sound natural using this method. An alternative involves pre-recording complete words and phrases, but this is only possible where a relatively limited vocabulary is required, as in the directory assistance service mentioned above.

Data storage devices

As we have already seen, data held in the memory of a computer is only 'stored' temporarily. If power is removed, RAM is blanked and any data held there is lost. To keep any data held in memory permanently, it must be saved to an external storage device. Common storage mediums include disks, CD-ROMs, DVDs, magnetic tape and other forms of removable media.

Magnetic disks

Disks use magnetic surface technology to store data. A magnetic record/playback head moves in a single plane across the disk's surface. This movement, combined with the rotation of the disk, allows data to be written to or retrieved from anywhere on the magnetic surface of the disk. Disks come in two main types: fixed (usually called hard disks) and removable (usually called floppy disks or diskettes).

Floppy disks were available in a variety of sizes, but the 3.5-inch diskette is the most common type used today. On a diskette, the magnetic media itself is sandwiched inside a tough plastic cover, which is lined with a thin furry material to help prevent scratches on the disk surface. Despite their portability, floppy disks suffer from a capacity problem. A typical high-density disk (DS HD) only stores approximately 1.44 Mbs of data (or about the equivalent of 700 pages of text) which, given the growth in the size of files, is simply not enough. As a result, a variety of other forms of removable storage have developed, all of which attempt to address this capacity issue. For example, the Iomega Zip disk acts as a floppy replacement, giving up to 500 Mbs of storage capacity respectively on each disk. CD-Recordable and CD-Rewritable formats (see p. 39) are an alternative solution

Figure 2.18

A cut-away of a hard disk

offering nearly 800 Mbs of storage, and many computers are now being shipped with just this storage solution.

A hard disk is actually of a set of disks made in a dust-free environment and heat-sealed to protect against foreign matter (Figure 2.18). The disk set is permanently mounted inside the system unit of the computer. In this sealed unit, the disks are spun at high speed and multiple read/write heads move over the disks' surfaces. As a result, the time taken to begin reading a file into memory (known as the *access time*) is much shorter than with floppy disks. Hard disks also have considerably higher storage capacities, typically ranging from 800 Mbs to 200 gigabytes. However, they are not transportable, as they are mounted within a machine's system unit and thus can only be accessed from that particular machine.

Clearly the question of how big a hard disk to buy in a computer is an important one. The usual rule of thumb is that the operating system and standard software applications (word processor, spreadsheets, Web browser, email client and so on) on a new PC should occupy no more than 25 per cent of the hard disk's capacity, leaving the user with 75 per cent for non-critical applications and data files. Given that the full installation of Microsoft® Windows® XP Professional eats up about 1.5 Gbs, and the latest version of the Microsoft® Office suite demands another 250 Mbs, hard disks with a capacity of 20 Gbs or more have become standard in most new PCs. When shopping for a hard disk, the phrase 'bigger is better' is particularly relevant. Get a disk with as much capacity as you can afford, because just like with cupboard space at home, on a hard disk you never seem to have enough room. Dig deep and buy the highest capacity drive you can afford!

Figure 2.19

Disk care

Handle gently!	**Avoid temperature extremes!**	**Beware of magnetic fields**
Don't bend them, put things on top of them, or otherwise mistreat them	Anything that is comfortable for you is acceptable	Magnetic fields generated by electric motors, TVs or mobile phones can wipe disks

CD-ROM

Compact disk read only memory (CD-ROM) uses optical technology for data storage. A small laser detects microscopic etchings on the surface of the CD as it spins in the drive, and translates these into binary data. A CD can store far more data than conventional magnetic disks (about 800 Mbs or roughly the same amount as 500 standard floppy disks), and is normally used these days both for distributing software and databases of information that do not need to be updated often, such as encyclopedias and online bibliographies. Most modern software applications are too large to fit on a single or even several floppy disks.

Even a word-processing package may include several disks for the program, and several more for spelling checkers, thesaurus and graphics modules. Instead of having the cost and logistical problems of supplying the package on multiple floppy disks, a single CD can be used. Normal CDs are read only, and thus cannot be used to save data. However newer CD-R (CD-Recordable) and CD-RW (CD-Rewritable) standards are also available that allow users to burn their own CDs from their personal computers. CD-ROM drives come in different speeds, defined by how quickly data is transferred from the disk onto your computer. 8X drives (meaning eight times the speed of the original specification of 150 K per second) are now standard and obviously you should purchase as fast a drive as possible when selecting a new system.

Another related development is DVD, which, depending on who you talk to, stands for Digital Versatile Disk, Digital Video Disk or nothing at all. DVDs look like CDs but have far larger storage capacities. Current DVD standards give a storage capacity of between 4.7 Gbs and 17 Gbs – enough for over two hours of high quality video at their lowest configuration. Just like CDs, DVDs can be both readable and writable, and thus are an attractive (if currently expensive) solution to mass removable data storage. However, this technology is still developing, and no one standard has yet emerged in the marketplace. Each of the competing systems is incompatible with the others, and thus smart users will tend to avoid DVD-R technology until standards settle down.

Magnetic tape

Magnetic tape, similar to the tape found in audiocassettes, can also be used as a data-storage medium. Although to a large extent obsolete, tape does still retain one major application – making back-ups, where its relatively unlimited storage capacity makes it very useful. Tapes were initially used because of their relatively low cost, but they suffer from a major drawback: on tape, data must be stored and accessed sequentially. This means that to find a particular piece of data, the tape must be wound and rewound until the starting point of the desired file is found, just like trying to find the start of a song on an audiocassette. This makes magnetic tape too slow and cumbersome for normal, day-to-day storage. Disks and CDs, on the other hand, are random access: the computer can read from and write to any part of the disk and, as a result, does not have to play through irrelevant data to find the file needed. Magnetic tape is useful for storing large amounts of data that will not be accessed regularly; for example, making a back-up copy of a hard disk. In such cases, its cheapness and its vast storage capacity far outweigh the limitations of sequential access.

Media	Capacity	Year first available	Price	Cost per Mb	Pros	Cons
Floppy diskette	720K	1985	€2.60	€16.25	Easy availability, can be used in most PCs	Small storage capacity, fragile
Tape drive	2 Gbs	1965	€5.00	€11.40	Low media cost; large capacity	Relatively slow; serial storage
Removable drive (e.g. zip disk)	100 Mbs	1995	€16.65	€0.17	Inexpensive, portable	Slow, limited in capacity
Additional hard drive	40 Gbs	1990	€80.00	€0.032	High speed; high capacity	Limited to one computer, not portable
CD-R	650 Mbs	1996	€1.79	€0.003	Low cost; disks can be read by most CD-ROM drives	Limited capacity
DVD-R	9.4 Gbs	2002	€7.89	€0.0008	Low cost; high capacity	Standards not stable as yet

Table 2.5 Graphic card standards

Source: Adapted from 'It's a removable storage feast', *PC World*, March 2003, p. 91.

Practical questions

1. Purchasing a personal computer

Shown below is an advertisement for some computer hardware that your hotel is considering purchasing.

The computer has the following features:

- Intel Pentium® 4 running at 800 MHz
- 100% IBM compatible
- 20 Gbs hard disk
- In-built 3.5 inch floppy disk drive
- 64 Mbs RAM, upgradeable to 512 Mbs
- 15 inch SVGA monitor
- 2 serial ports
- 1 parallel port
- 2 USB 2.0 ports
- Pre-loaded Microsoft® Windows® 2000 or Windows® XP professional operating systems

(a) Explain the significance of each of the features.
(b) You are thinking about using these computers at the front desk of your hotel. Can you foresee any problems?

2. Testing the power of personal computers

In your college or hotel, there are probably some different types of computer, of varying ages and processor types and with different amounts of memory. Try the following 'benchmark' exercise:

- Establish what type of processor and how much memory is in each machine. (Sometimes this information is displayed on the screen while the computer is booting, or you can use a diagnostic program to see the features of the machine.)
- Run the same software package, such as a word processor or a spreadsheet, on each machine. Use a stopwatch to time the delay between pressing the Enter key and the package being ready for use on the screen. Is this delay different on each machine?
- What factors are having an influence on the amount of time it takes the package to load?

Review questions

1. What four functions are common to both Babbage's 'analytical and difference' engines and modern computers?

2. Why were Babbage's devices never built?

3. What is meant by each of the following terms:
   (a) online processing;
   (b) time-sharing;
   (c) personal computer;
   (d) thin client;
   (e) Pentium®;
   (f) font;
   (g) hard disk;
   (h) DVD?

4. Explain what is meant by each of the following abbreviations:
   (a) bit;
   (b) K;
   (c) RAM;
   (d) CPU;
   (e) USB;
   (f) COM1;
   (g) VGA?

5. What are the two major problems associated with batch processing?

6. Are mainframe computers currently used in the hospitality industry? Why?

7. Briefly describe the function of each of the following:
   (a) the central processing unit;
   (b) the I/O interface;
   (c) the system bus.

8. Does the amount of memory in a computer have an effect on its performance?

9. Give three examples of uses for expansion slots.

10. Name five common input devices.

11. Describe how a bar-code reader works.

12. Suggest two applications for magnetic-strip readers in the hospitality industry.

13. Why, at present, is voice entry unsuitable for large-scale data entry?

14. Name three output devices.

15. What are the main differences between a dot matrix and a laser printer?

16. What are the advantages and disadvantages of ink-jet printers compared to laser printers?

17. What is the storage medium most commonly used today?

18. Why have floppy diskettes declined in popularity as a storage medium?

19. What are the two main advantages of hard disks over floppy disks?

Discussion questions

1. Compare the use of a mainframe computer with the use of a personal computer. What are the advantages and disadvantages of each type? Why have PCs become so popular?

2. Many of the personal computers used in the industry were purchased four or five years ago. Does this have an effect on their performance? What benefits could be gained by replacing them?

3. Moore's law states that computers double in speed, processing power and storage capacity every 18 months, while size and cost fall by half. To what extent do current trends in hardware support this theory?

4. Thin clients seem ideal for use in the front office of a hotel. Explain the advantages and disadvantages of such a strategy.

3 Computer software

Chapter 2 discussed computer hardware – the electronic and mechanical components that make up a computer. However, hardware on its own is of little use. A helpful analogy is that of an orchestra without sheet music; each part could theoretically work independently, but needs some coordination before it can make beautiful music. Computer software is the sheet music that guides the operation of the computer. Each piece of software (known as an application or a package) is composed of thousands of instructions written in a programming language. These tell the hardware, in minute detail, how to perform each task. This chapter gives a broad overview of computer software, describing both operating system and general applications software in detail, and giving a brief introduction to the more specific software used in the hospitality sector (these will be discussed in detail in subsequent chapters). Each application is discussed in very general terms, without reference to any particular brand name or specific package.

This approach has been taken for two reasons. First, within each category, a vast range of different packages are available. For example, some of the word-processing packages currently available include Microsoft® Word, WordPerfect®, WordStar® and many others. Each has different commands and menu structures. As a result, a 'press this key and then press that key' approach is of limited use, as the commands learned for one package do not work with the others. Second, packages are constantly being updated and new versions are released periodically. As a result, any discussion that focused on the use of a particular package would quickly become outdated. A more general approach, focusing on the concepts underlying each application, is more useful in developing understanding.

Types of software

What is described by the term 'software' may be broken down into three broad categories: *operating systems* (sometimes known as system software) *programming languages* and *applications software*. An operating system is a highly complex program that performs relatively basic functions, such as accepting input from the keyboard, displaying something on the screen and reading/writing data to disk, on behalf of the user or a software application. Since the tasks that it performs are so simple, much of its work occurs behind the scenes, and many casual users may not even be aware of its existence. Software applications, on the other hand, are the packages with which everyone is familiar. These are the tools with which work, such as writing a letter, calculating a budget or registering a guest, is carried out on a computer. Because of their visibility, most users are aware of which software applications they use regularly, and indeed many, such as Word and Excel, are household names. Both operating systems and applications are written in a programming language – a structure series of instructions that is interpreted by the computer and which tells the computer what to do.

Operating systems

The area of operating systems has given rise to much unnecessary 'techno-speak'. Terms such as 'MS-DOS', 'UNIX', 'Windows®', 'GUI' and so on are used casually by computer professionals but mean little to anyone else. This section gives a broad, non-technical introduction to what an operating system actually is, what it is used for and the types available.

Put simply, an operating system is a piece of software that allows a user to communicate easily and effectively with a computer (Figure 3.1). It is a layer of instructions that sits between the hardware – the actual physical chips and circuit boards inside a PC – and the applications software – the programs which are used directly by the person operating the computer. It manages the hardware and provides generalized services, such as opening a particular file, reading an entry from the keyboard, displaying a character on the screen or printing text on a printer, to the applications software. This makes the computer easier to use, as without an operating system the way in which each and every task should be performed would have to be specified in great detail for the computer. This can be illustrated using an oversimplified example. To copy a file from one disk to another in the absence of an operating system, the user would have to specify the exact physical location (using tracks and sectors) of the file on the original disk. The data from these locations would then have to be read into RAM. At this stage, the new location for the copy of the file would have to be identified, again by track and sector, and the data written onto the disk. However, many different things could go wrong, so some way of comparing the original with the new file would have to be found to make sure that the copy was completed successfully. Thus, it can be seen that even the ordinary, everyday task of copying a file from one location to another is really quite complex when closely examined. Operating systems simplify life for the user by taking care of such minute details automatically. In this example, they would track the locations of the files on each disk and automatically verify that copying has been successful, as well as ensuring that

Figure 3.1

The functions of an operating system

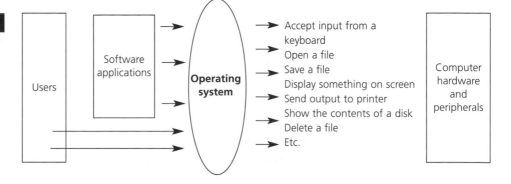

other files are not accidentally overwritten in the copying process. By taking care of such simple but important housekeeping tasks, operating systems make the use of the computer, from the user's point of view, far easier.

Operating systems also perform another role. Each brand and model of computer is different in terms of hardware architecture. However, since the operating system takes care of standard tasks and forms a buffer between the hardware and the applications, each computer running a particular operating system will 'appear' the same to both users and applications software. This has several implications. First, computer manufacturers can ensure that there is a ready-made 'store' of software applications available for use by users when a new machine is launched, by making sure that the new product makes use of an industry standard operating system. By doing this, they can be sure that a variety of programs are available for use on the machine straight away, without having to wait for software developers to bring out new versions specifically for the new machine. (In fact, one of the reasons why mainframe computers became less popular was that there was no widely accepted standard mainframe operating system. As a result, whenever a new model of mainframe was released, there was little or no software available to use on it. Everything had to be developed from scratch, thus adding to the expense of using such systems.) Second, because certain operating systems are very widely used (often referred to as *industry standard operating systems*), software companies that write applications that run under a particular operating system have a vast potential market for their programs. In the past, software programs were machine-specific – that is, they were written specifically to run on a particular computer. As a result, the potential market for any package was limited to the number of that particular computer sold. When the hardware was updated or replaced, the package had to be heavily modified or even totally rewritten so that it would run on the new hardware. This has changed, and software is now written to run under a particular operating system rather than on a particular type of hardware. As a result, it will operate on every computer that uses that operating system, irrespective of its make, model or specification, meaning that a package written to run under an industry standard operating system such as Microsoft® Windows® has a potential market of millions of machines. Last, developing a software package to run under a standard operating system is considerably easier than developing one to run on a specific machine. As we discussed above, most of the basic functions (such as accepting input from the keyboard or disk access) are taken care of by the operating system. A programmer can thus use these basic operations as building blocks to make program development easier, quicker and less error prone.

Command line interfaces and graphic user interfaces

As well as using an operating system 'through' applications software, computer users also use it directly to perform housekeeping chores, such as formatting disks, running programs, viewing directory contents or printing files. When accessing the operating system directly, two different approaches are common – using a text-based interface known as a 'command line interface', or using an icon-driven approach known as a 'graphic user interface'.

The first popular micro-computer operating system was called CP/M (Control

Program for Microprocessors), which was a relatively simple program that drove early computers based on Intel's 8080 processor. Users of other early PCs, such as the Apple II, needed to fit this processor into their machines to make them compatible with the growing range of software available for the CP/M operating system. Many of these hardware adaptations were supplied by a young teenager called Bill Gates and his company Microsoft®. In 1980, IBM turned to Microsoft® to develop an operating system for its next generation of computers, which it planned to launch the following year, and MS-DOS (Microsoft® disk operating system) was born. Both MS-DOS and CP/M are examples of the traditional approach to operating systems which was inherited from the world of mainframes. This uses a *command line interface*. Commands are typed in a particular format, interpreted by the computer when the Enter key is pressed and, if correct, executed. For example, an MS-DOS user who wished to delete a file called 'letter.doc' from disk drive A would type:

Del A:letter.Doc

and press the *Enter* key. If the command was typed correctly (with just one space, between the 'l' of 'Del' and the 'A'), the file would be deleted. However, any mistakes in the syntax, spelling or spacing of the command mean that the system would not understand, resulting in an error message, the command not being executed and, as a result, the file not being deleted. This complex syntax makes command line interfaces relatively technical, as they demand a considerable amount of knowledge on the part of their users.

For that reason, a different approach, which is more geared towards the casual user, was developed. Graphic user interfaces (GUIs) were originally conceived by Xerox®, but were popularized by Apple® with the Macintosh® range of computers and by Microsoft® with its Microsoft® Windows® series. GUIs are based on the use of pictures, known as *icons*, which are manipulated using a pointing device such as a mouse or a touch screen. Because the user interface is graphic, it is far more intuitive and the complex syntax demanded by command line interfaces is not needed. To take the same example, the file 'letter.doc' could be deleted by simply pointing at its icon using the mouse and dragging it onto another icon resembling a wastebasket. This approach is clearly more intuitive and easier to learn. As a result, the concept quickly became popular; particularly when Microsoft® launched Microsoft® Windows® in 1983, and has now to a large extent eliminated the command line approach with the exception of very specific legacy applications such as the airline reservation systems.

The spread of GUIs caused a further development that makes applications friendlier from the user's point of view. Different software applications running under a particular GUI typically have similar commands and menu structures. For example, all applications on the Macintosh® and on Microsoft® Windows® have their 'Open', 'Save' and 'Print' commands on the 'File' drop-down menu, which is always on the extreme left of the menu bar . This gives applications a familiar look and feel, which greatly reduces the time needed to learn how to use a package. Thus, once a user has learned how to use one program, they generally find it much easier to learn how to use another, as many of the features and facilities are more or less the same. This feature is particularly important in hospitality, where people often tend to be mobile across many jobs and department, and has major implications for training costs, as the use of GUI-based system both makes it easier to train employees initially and also reduces retraining costs in the long run. Companies that have switched from CLI to GUI have seen significant reductions – from 26 days down to 10 days per employee, largely because GUI driven operating systems are so intuitive. Users of older systems find it easier to work out what the new system can do, while new users are familiar with look and feel of the interface and are able to navigate and use the system with minimal instruction.

There is one major drawback, however, in using a GUI. The GUI program itself tends to be more complicated and thus larger in size than that of a simpler operating system. Computers, as has been discussed, are limited in terms of both their processing power and their memory. GUIs take up a larger proportion of these resources, and can therefore significantly reduce a machine's performance. A computer running a GUI has less free resources for applications and data than one using a more basic operating system. This makes it slower in operation, as more time must be spent 'swapping' data and applications into and out of the free memory area. This is a particular problem with older PCs, which have less powerful processors and smaller amounts of memory. A faster processor and larger amounts of memory are needed to run a GUI at an acceptable speed (see Table 3.1).

GUIs are obviously revolutionary when compared to command line interfaces such as MS-DOS and UNIX, and have significantly changed the way in which people work. People can now concentrate on what they need to do, rather than on learning the commands to do it. Also, because of the graphic nature of the interface, the actual type of computer or operating system has become less

Figure 3.2

A Microsoft®
Windows® XP screen

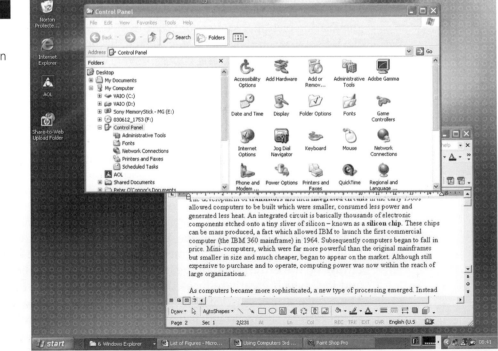

(setq.

Table 3.1

Minimum and recommended hardware specifications for different operating systems

Operation system	Minimum processor	memory	Recommended processor	memory
MS-DOS	8086	512 K	8086	640 K
Microsoft® Windows® 3.11	80286	2 Mb	80386	4 Mb
Microsoft® Windows® 95	80386 DX	4 Mb	80486	12 Mb
Microsoft® Windows® NT 4	80486	16 Mb	Pentium®	32 Mb
Microsoft® Windows® 98	80486 DX	16 Mb	Pentium®	32 Mb
Microsoft® Windows® 2000	Pentium® 133 MHz	64 Mb	Pentium® 166 MHz	128 Mb
Microsoft® Windows® XP Professional	Pentium® 233 MHz	128 Mb	Pentium® 300 MHz	256 Mb
Linux	Pentium® 120 MHz	32 Mb	Pentium® 120 MHz	64 Mb

important from the point of view of the average user. While some of the commands may differ from one computer or system to another, the basic concepts are the same, which allows users to worry less about technicalities.

Programming languages

All software, be it an operating system or a software application, is written in one or other of the programming languages. Examples of languages include Pascal, Cobol and BASIC, as well as the more modern C++ and Visual Basic.

Obviously, most software applications are written by professionals known as programmers (increasingly known as software engineers). This is because writing a computer program is a quite complex process as, at the end of the day, the processor at the heart of every computer is actually quite an ignorant device. It has to be told both what to do and how to do every single task, and these instructions have to be specified in minute detail. Even though it needs such detailed and precise instructions, it is only capable of understanding a very limited number of commands or instructions. Thus telling it what to do is a difficult task. All these instructions are translated into binary – the series of ones and zeros that is the language understood at the most basic level by the processor. However, as this is complex and unwieldy, it is rarely used directly by programmers to give instructions to the processor. Instead they turn to assembly language, which consolidates the machine code instructions into commands to accomplish particular tasks. Although reducing flexibility, this makes it (comparatively) easier to work with, but also means that the resulting program has to be either compiled or interpreted before being used by the computer. Today such low-level languages are only used in limited situations, such as in creating operating systems or device drivers, where speed and efficiency are critical. Instead, high level languages are used to develop most software applications. These use keywords which group together large numbers of assembler commands to automate commonly used functions. So for example the 'If' keyword in the Visual Basic language compares the values of two variables and does one of two predefined tasks depending on the result of the comparison – a complex and long result for such a little keyword!

Sources of software

When purchasing software, you have three basic choices – bespoke, packaged or customized. Bespoke (or customer written) software is most likely to meet the information needs of your organization, as it is (or rather should be) written specifically to automate them. However, as all the development costs must be borne by the purchaser, such a strategy tends to be expensive, and also requires time and skilled personnel to both design and create the system. There can also be significant problems communicating exactly what the system needs to be able to do – an issue made worse by the inability of managers and computer professionals to speak the same language. Furthermore, once written, the software needs to be extensively tested and debugged, again resulting in further delays. While having software especially written should result in a closer match between what is needed and the resulting package, the expense and time delay associated with this approach make it unrealistic in many cases. Packaged software, on the other hand, is usually available immediately and, because of its potential mass market, is likely to be much cheaper. Such software is usually already in use in other companies, and is likely to be well tested and thus more reliable. However, to use the analogy of an 'off the peg' suit, packaged software is unlikely to perfectly match all aspects of the organization's information needs. To benefit from

Table 3.2 Sources of applications summary

Choice	IS strategy	Suit analogy	Cost	Advantages	Disadvantages
Do nothing!	Status quo	Go naked!	Zero????	• No capital or transaction costs • Less hassle as no need to change anything	• System not working • Opportunity cost
Buy standard industry software	Package software	Off-the-shelf	€€	• Up and running quickly • Already working in other organizations • Relatively cheap • Conforms to standards (thus reducing training, interface costs)	• Availability of suitable systems • Not adapted to company needs
Develop their own software from scratch	Application development	Made to measure	€€€€€€	• System personalized to needs of the organization	• Time delay • Development process
Customize a software package	Customization	Seamstress-adjusted	€€€€€	• More closely match company needs • Up and running quicker	• Time delay • Costs increase exponentially with degree of customization • Danger of brittle code

the cheaper price, certain compromises have to be made, and each company has to think carefully before making the decision 'to build or to buy'. A third possible strategy is to customize an existing package by changing it to more closely match the needs of the organization. In practice, however, it is difficult to persuade software companies to make such modifications as having multiple versions of an application makes support nearly impossible. In addition, making such modifications is a very technical (and therefore time-consuming and expensive) process, which often introduced errors into the logic of the program code, making it brittle and likely to crash easily.

As we can see, each of the approaches has its advantages and limitations, making the choice of an appropriate strategy difficult. The main issues are summarized in Table 3.2. An examination of the process that should be followed to help ensure that the correct decision is made appears in Chapter 12 – Selecting and implementing a computer system.

Software copyright

In general, you do not actually 'buy' a software package. Instead you pay for a *non-exclusive licence* to use the package on (generally) a single computer. As a result, if you load the package onto more than one computer, you may be breaking the law! Software copyright legislation is complex. Most packages are governed by *software licence agreements*, such as the one shown in Figure 3.3, which details the conditions of use of the package. The terms of such licences can vary greatly, so it is important to read them carefully. For example, a package could be licensed for use by a single user, by a single concurrent user or on a single computer. In the first case, only a single person can legally use the package; in the second, a variety of people can use the package, but not at the same time; and in the third, the package can be used by anybody, but only on a specific computer.

Most licences include a disclaimer that states that the package is sold 'as is'. This means that the supplier does not claim that the software is fit for any particular purpose, and, as a result, is not responsible if the package does not do what it is supposed to do. On a related note, many licences also limit the liability of the supplier for damage caused by the use of the package. As a result, if data is lost or other programs are damaged because of a fault in the package, the software company cannot be held responsible. Both these clauses mean that responsibility for both choosing and using a package rests solely with the user, so the software company cannot be sued if anything goes wrong. And if the software is riddled with bugs and simply doesn't work – tough! While software companies would like people to believe that this is truly the situation, in practice consumer protection laws overrule these disclaimers. There have been a variety of cases where software companies have tried to hide behind such conditions when things go wrong, but the courts have decided to award substantial damages (including loss of revenue) to claimants. However, instead of doing what they should do – making their products work correctly – many software companies continue to insert such clauses into their conditions of use in the hope of discouraging action by uninformed (and dissatisfied) customers.

Soft Solutions Licence Agreement

This agreement constitutes a legal agreement between you, the end user, and Soft Solutions Ltd. You should read the following terms and conditions carefully before opening this package, Opening this package indicates your acceptance of these terms and conditions. If you do not agree to them, promptly return the unopened package and your money will be refunded.

Licence. Soft Solutions grants to you a non-exclusive licence to use the software on a single computer (i.e. with a single CPU). You may not network the software or otherwise use it on more than one computer at the same time.

Copy Restrictions. You make back-up copies of the software for that machine, always including copyright notices provided that (a) these copies are only for your own use, and (b) only one copy is in use at any time.

Transfer Restrictions. You may transfer the software with a copy of this agreement to another party only on a permanent basis and only if the other party accepts the terms and conditions of this agreement. Upon such transfer you must inform Soft Solutions in writing of the name and address of the other party and the serial number of the software package, transfer all accompanying written materials to the new owner, and either transfer or destroy all copies of the software in your possession. You may not lease, rent, reverse engineer, de-compile or disassemble the software.

Termination. Failure to comply with any of these terms will terminate this agreement and your right to use the software. You may also choose to terminate the agreement at any time. Upon any termination of this agreement, you must immediately destroy all copies of the software and accompanying written materials.

Limited Warranty. As its only warranty under this agreement. Soft Solutions warrants the media on which the software is provided to be free from defects under normal use for a period of 90 days from the date of delivery to you as evidenced by your purchase receipt.

This software is licensed 'as is' without warranty as to its performance. Except for the diskette warranty provided above, there is no warranties expressed or implied, including but not limited to implied warranties of merchantability or fitness for a particular purpose, and all such warranties are expressly disclaimed, in no event will Soft Solutions, or its suppliers, be liable for any direct, consequential or indirect damages (including damages for loss of business profits, information or use), even if Soft Solutions has been advised of the possibility of such damage.

Governing Law. This agreement is governed by the laws of the State of California.

Applications software

While an operating system performs generalized tasks, applications software is used to automate particular functions. Application software is composed of many diverse types of package, each of which has its own particular purpose. Such software can basically be divided into two major sub-categories: 'vertical-market' (or industry-specific) and 'horizontal-market' (or general-purpose) software.

- Vertical-market software is designed specifically to meet the needs of a particular market sector. As a result, it is highly specific and a package designed for use in one sector is of limited use in any other. For example, Figure 3.4 shows four broad industrial classifications and gives examples of tasks for which software applications are used in each. Banking software, used for controlling customer accounts, would be pointless in a retail outlet, a hotel or practically anywhere else. Similarly, a reservations system would only be of use in a hotel or similar type of business. Because of their limited market, vertical-market software packages tend to be relatively expensive but, as they are designed specifically to service the needs of that sector, they are more likely to provide all of the functions required by businesses operating in that specific sector.

- Horizontal-market software, on the other hand, is general-purpose in nature, and can be applied equally well across a broad range of industries and to a wide variety of situations. When compared to vertical-market software, applications in this category are more flexible and can be applied more broadly. For example, a word processor could be used for writing reports in a bank, drawing up orders for suppliers in a retail outlet, typing menus in a hotel, and writing letters to prospective clients in an insurance

Figure 3.4		Banking sector	Retail sector	Hotel sector	Insurance sector
Vertical- and horizontal-market software	**Typical vertical-market software tasks**	Controlling customer accounts Assessing suit-ability for loans	Stock control Automatic re-ordering Sales analysis	Reservations Guest billing Guest history	Calculation of premiums Tracking payments and claims
	Horizontal-market software	Speadsheets Word processors Databases Graphics packages Communications packages Utilities			

company. As they have a wider potential market, such packages tend to be comparatively cheap, but since they are designed to cater for as wide a market as possible, they may not contain all the functionality that you need and at the same time have hundreds (if not thousands) of superfluous features.

Horizontal-market software

This section introduces the most common types of general-purpose software, namely word-processing packages, spreadsheets, databases, email packages, Web browsers and utilities packages. Each is discussed in general terms below.

Word-processing packages

These are the most widely used computer application. At a simple level, they allow you to create, manipulate, format and ultimately print text-based documents. However, a word-processing package is much more than just an automated typewriter. By allowing documents to be saved, word-processing packages make life easy for the user. Any document saved can subsequently be reloaded, modified if necessary and printed again. As a result, pages or entire documents do not have to be retyped because of typing errors or other small changes.

Manipulating text

Word-processing packages typically include a variety of other features to make life easy for the user. For example, the word-wrap feature makes it simpler to enter text in the first place. Unlike manual typewriters, where the typist has to hit the carriage return key at the end of each line, a word-processing user does not have to worry about line length. The 'word-wrap' facility automatically determines when a line is full and moves any text which does not fit onto the beginning of the next line. Furthermore, changes can easily be made in a document by positioning the cursor at the required point and typing. What happens depends on whether the package is in *overtype* or *insert* mode. In overtype mode, existing text is replaced by the new text, while in insert mode, the existing text moves to the right and wraps downward to make room for whatever is typed. Most word-processing packages also allow the user to move portions of the text around the document. This is a powerful facility as it allows the writer to restructure what they have written by changing the order of words, sentences and paragraphs. In some cases, text can be moved by *highlighting* a block of text, *copying* this to a special area known as the *clipboard*, and then *pasting* it back into the document in the new position. Others use a facility called *drag and drop*. Text is highlighted and the physically dragged to the new location using the mouse (Figure 3.5). As this method is graphic in nature, it is very intuitive and, as a result, allows text to be reorganized very quickly.

To aid with editing, many word processors provide *search* facilities that can be used to locate specific words or phrases within the text. This is particularly useful when working with long documents, as a particular point can be found without

Figure 3.5

Using drag and drop to move text

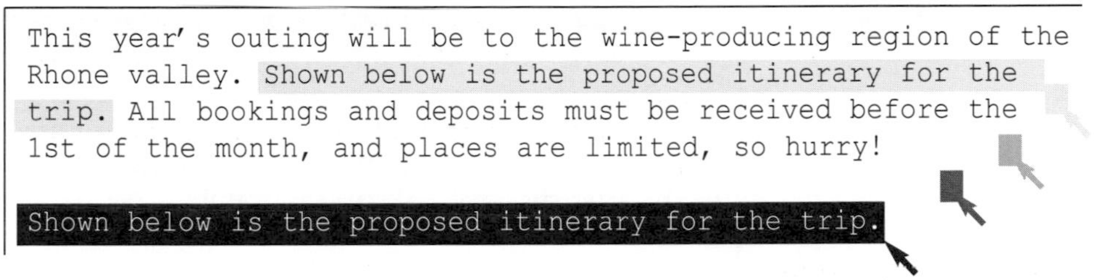
This year's outing will be to the wine-producing region of the
Rhone valley. Shown below is the proposed itinerary for the
trip. All bookings and deposits must be received before the
1st of the month, and places are limited, so hurry!
Shown below is the proposed itinerary for the trip.

having to scroll through pages and pages of text. These facilities are extremely accurate, but also require the user to be very precise. Differences in spelling or spacing often result in phrases not being found. For example, searching a document for the phrase 'I.B.M.' would not find either 'IBM' or 'I B M'. Searches can also be case-specific (whether 'IBM' matches 'ibm') and can be set to match either whole words only or partial words (whether 'computer' will match 'computerization', for example). The search facility is also used as part of another facility known as *search and replace*. This allows all instances of a particular word or phrase to be changed to another. Each matching word found is displayed on screen and the user asked to confirm that the replacement should take place, or, alternatively, all instances can be changed automatically (Figure 3.6). This facility is powerful and should be used with care. For example, replacing the word 'application' with the word 'package' in the text of this book would be dangerous, as the word 'application' is used in two entirely different contexts: computer applications, and the application of a theory. In the former case, 'package' might be acceptable, but in the latter it clearly would not make much sense.

Most word-processing packages provide powerful facilities to check the spelling of a document. *Spelling checkers* check each word by comparing it with those in an in-built dictionary. Words not found in the dictionary are selected and presented to the user for 'correction'. Most packages also now include interactive spell checking facilities that automatically check each word as it is typed and

Figure 3.6

Find and replace facilities from Microsoft® Word

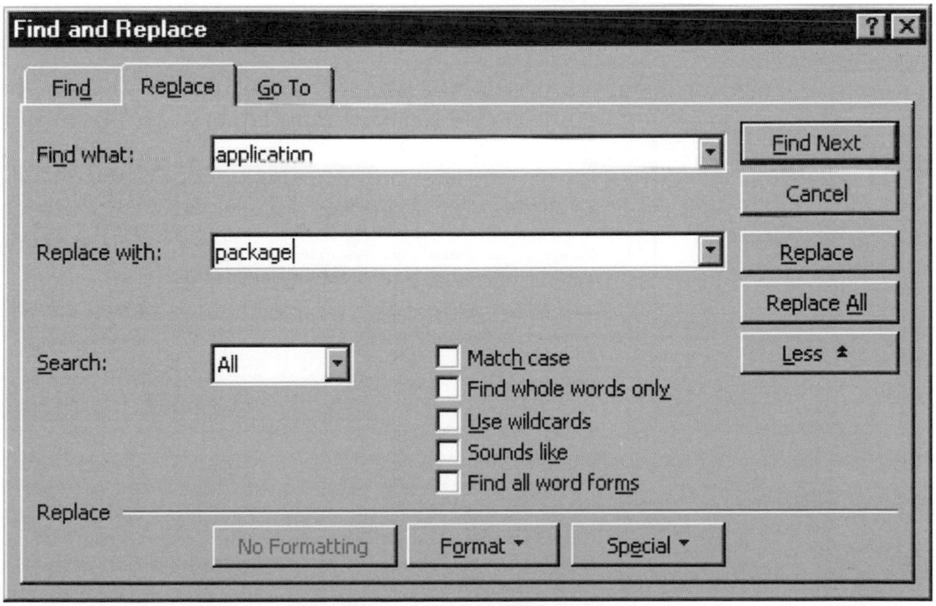
Find and Replace
Find
Replace
Go To
Find what:
application
Replace with:
package
Find Next
Cancel
Replace
Replace All
Less
Search:
All
Match case
Find whole words only
Use wildcards
Sounds like
Find all word forms
Replace
No Formatting
Format
Special

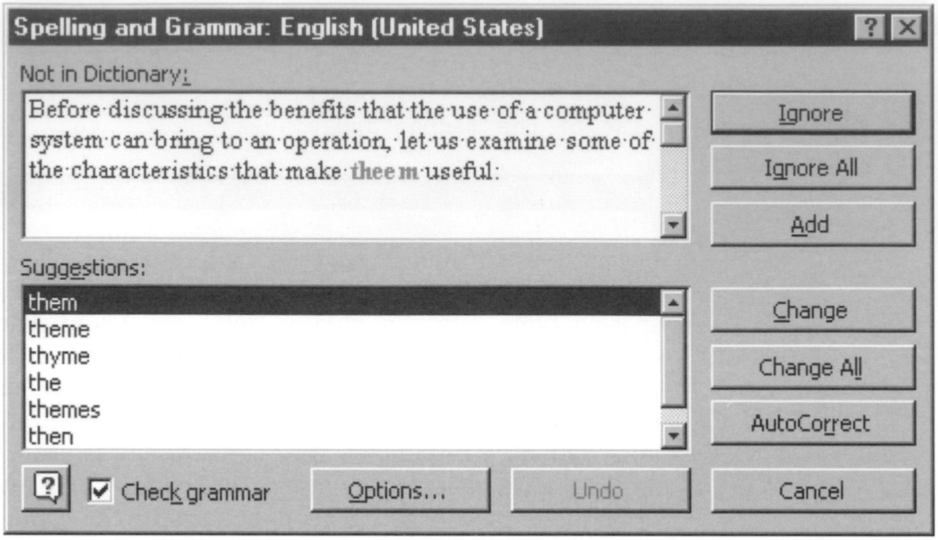

Figure 3.7

A spelling checker from Microsoft® Word

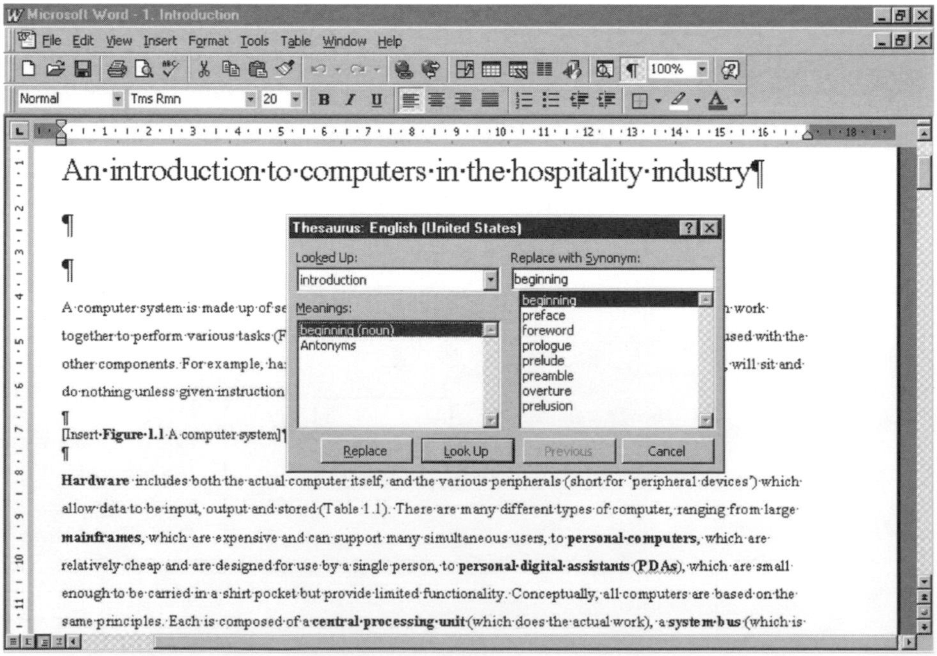

Figure 3.8

A thesaurus from Microsoft® Word

highlight unrecognized ones by underlining them in red. In both cases, the user can indicate that an unknown word is spelt correctly, or manually correct the spelling, or can ask the application to suggest the correct spelling. In the latter case, words like the word in question are displayed, and the correct one can be chosen from the list suggested (Figure 3.7).

Having the user manually confirm the correct spelling of unrecognized words is necessary as spelling checkers are far from perfect. For example, the in-built dictionary is finite, so technical words and proper nouns (such as the names of people or places) in a document are usually highlighted as being incorrect. To help overcome this, most packages allow *user dictionaries* to be created to store such words. However, a more serious limitation is the inability to check the context of a word in a sentence. If a word is included in the dictionary, it is regarded as correct, even if it is used out of context. For example, consider how the following words could be used incorrectly: 'their' and 'there', 'form' and 'from', or 'to', 'too' and 'two'. Spelling checkers will not identify such mistakes, as in each case the *spelling* of each word is correct. Broadly related to spelling checkers are *grammar checkers,* which examine documents and highlight common grammatical errors, such as split infinitives or overuse of the passive voice, and in many cases can also identify contextual errors such as those discussed above. Many also assess the readability of a document by calculating readability indexes. Another related facility is the *thesaurus,* which displays the synonyms (words with a similar meaning) of a selected word (Figure 3.8). This helps the writer to avoid repeating the same word unnecessarily, and can also be used as a mini-spelling checker to see whether a particular word is spelt correctly.

Formatting text

Formatting refers to the manner in which an item is displayed on the screen or in print. In a word-processing package, formatting can be applied either to the entire document, to individual paragraphs or to individual characters. Document-formatting changes the appearance of the entire document. Examples of this include:

- **Orientation** – this refers to the direction in which text is displayed on the page. There are two possible orientations: portrait and landscape (Figure 3.9). Portrait is normally used for typed documents, but landscape can also be useful – for example, to display a large table which would be cramped on a portrait page.

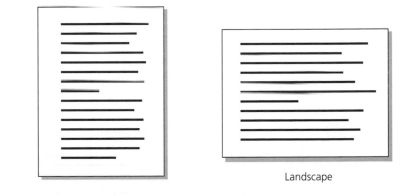

Portrait

Landscape

- **Margins** – these determine the boundaries within which text is displayed (Figure 3.10). If the margins are changed after text has been typed, word wrap automatically adjusts each line to make the text fit within the new margins.

Figure 3.10

Document margins

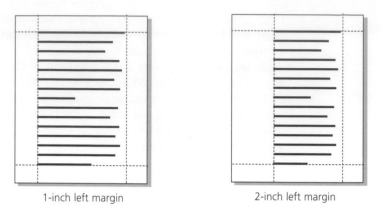

1-inch left margin   2-inch left margin

- **Columns** – most documents have just a single column of text. However, in some situations, such as when designing an advertising brochure or writing an article for publication, it can be useful to divide the page into two or more columns (Figure 3.11). Each column behaves like a mini-document, with words wrapping within the column boundaries in the same way as within document margins.

Figure 3.11

Text columns

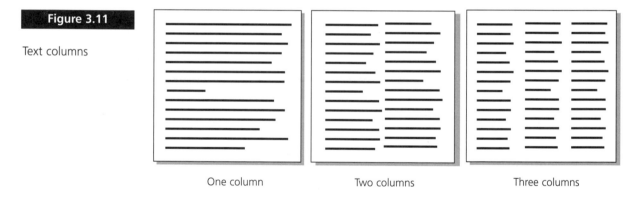

One column   Two columns   Three columns

- **Headers and footers** – these are special lines which can be inserted at the top and bottom of a page respectively (Figure 3.12) and are typically used to display information such as page numbers or chapter titles.

Figure 3.12

Headers and footers

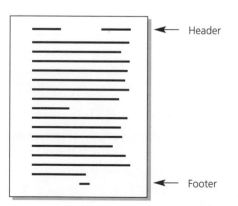

← Header

← Footer

Paragraph formatting features are applied to individual paragraphs. Examples include:

- **Alignment** – this refers to which edges of a paragraph are straight and which are ragged. For example, if a paragraph is left aligned, its text begins a fixed distance from the left-hand side of the page and its right margin is ragged. Similarly, if a paragraph is right aligned, each line of its text ends an equal distance from the right-hand side of the page and its left margin is ragged. Text may also be centred between the margins, or may be justified, which means that both margins are straight (like most paragraphs in this book). This is achieved by minutely adjusting the spacing between each word and is mainly used in published works such as books, articles and magazines (Figure 3.13).

Figure 3.13

Text alignment

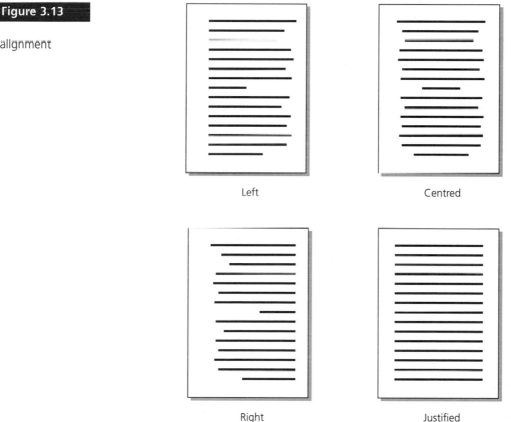

Left   Centred

Right   Justified

- **Spacing** – this refers to the vertical distance between each line of text. The larger the spacing, the fewer lines fit on each page and therefore the more pages the document occupies. For example, a typical A4 page contains sixty lines of single-spaced text, forty lines when one-and-a-half spaced, and thirty lines when double-spaced (Figure 3.14). Therefore a sixty-line document would fit on a single page if single-spaced, but would cover two pages if double-spaced.

Figure 3.14

Line spacing

Single spacing   1½ spacing   Double spacing

- **Indentation** – this refers to the starting point of the text on the first line of a paragraph (Figure 3.15). The style of this paragraph is known as a hanging indent, because the first line 'overhangs' the rest of the text – particularly useful for displaying bullet (or numbered) points.

Figure 3.15

Indentation

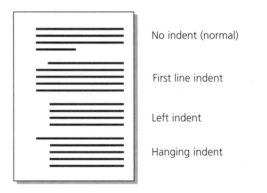

No indent (normal)

First line indent

Left indent

Hanging indent

The appearance of individual characters can also be changed. Character formatting includes features such as:

- Font – different type styles (such as `Courier`, Times or **Arial**) can be used.
- Size – different sizes of each font (such as 10 point, 12 point, 14 point or 18 point) can be used.
- Attributes – different font attributes (such as **bold**, *italic*, underlined, superscript or subscript) can also be set.

Formatting is usually applied in two stages. The area to be formatted is first of all selected using the mouse or the cursor keys. The formatting feature required is then applied to the selected area. Many packages use a *toolbar* (such as the one from Microsoft® Word shown in Figure 3.16) with *buttons* representing the most regularly used formats to help speed up this process.

Figure 3.16

A toolbar from Microsoft® Word

Another facility related to formatting is *styles*, which are user-defined combinations of character and paragraph formats. Using styles ensures that the appearance of text is consistent throughout a document or series of documents. For example, a style with the characteristics 'Bold, Centred, Font: Times, Size: 24pt' could be defined for the headings in a series of documents. This could then be applied to all the headings, thus ensuring that they are all consistent in appearance. Furthermore, changing the definition of the style would automatically change the appearance of all the headings in the document in a single step.

Printing text

While word-processing packages allow users to type characters on a computer screen, most people eventually want to print their work on paper, and it is at this stage that several additional benefits of using a word-processing package become apparent. For example, print preview facilities allow the user to see a graphical representation of their printed document on the computer screen before committing it to paper (Figure 3.17). This is useful as, although most packages are now WYSIWYG (pronounced 'whizzywig' – What You See Is What You Get), most computer screens are not big enough to display an entire A4 page in one go. Using print preview, any problems with a document's layout can be identified and corrected before it is actually printed. At the moment, most people still print on paper. However, as communications technology develops, it is likely that most letters, memos and reports will be sent electronically, thus giving rise to the famed 'paperless office'. Email clients, the software application that facilitates this process, are discussed in detail later in this chapter.

Figure 3.17

Print preview

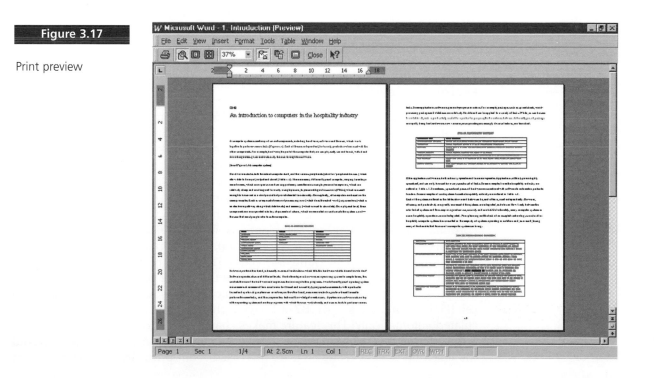

Most word-processing packages now routinely include powerful facilities to control layout and presentation, as well as to position graphics (such as charts, drawings or pictures) within documents. This was once the function of another classification of software, known as *desktop publishing* (DTP) packages (common examples include Microsoft® Publisher, Adobe® PageMaker® and Quark XPress™). However, the distinction between DTP and word-processing packages has to a large extent become blurred. As on many other occasions when using computers, it may be possible to do a particular task using either package, but one is usually more appropriate. The question as to which type of package should be used for a particular printing task often arises. To answer this question, you must remember that at a fundamental level, word processing is about manipulating words, while DTP is about working with layout. In general, DTP packages give users more precise control over the appearance of each page, but have limited text-editing and spell-checking facilities. Similarly, word processors have excellent facilities for entering, editing and manipulating text in a variety of ways but limited capabilities for positioning objects on a page. Each package should be used for the task at which it excels: text should be typed on a word-processing package and exported to a DTP if a complex layout is required.

Spreadsheets

After the word-processing package, the spreadsheet is probably the next most widely used application. Spreadsheets are designed primarily to manipulate numbers and their main advantage comes from a feature known as *automatic recalculation*. When calculating something manually, changing one number at the beginning of the problem would mean that each number dependent on it would have to be recalculated. If the same problem was set up on a properly constructed spreadsheet, and a number changed, all recalculations would be made and the new answer displayed automatically.

Performing calculations

Spreadsheets are composed of *columns* and *rows* (Figure 3.18). Each column is identified by a letter (A, B, C, and then AA, AB, . . .), and each row by a number (1, 2, 3 . . .). The intersection of a row and a column is known as a *cell*, which has a unique *cell reference*. This is composed of the letter from the column and the number from the row. For example, cell D5 is in column D and row 5.

An individual cell can contain one of three types of data: a number, a piece of text (known as a label) or a formula (which is used to perform calculations). Formulae are set up using combinations of cell references and calculation symbols, such as '+' (addition), '−' (subtraction), '*' (multiplication) and '/' (division). For example, to add up the numbers in cells B1, B2 and B3 and display the answer in another cell, say B5, the user would place the cursor on B5, type '=B1+B2+B3' and press the Enter key. The result of the calculation would then be displayed in cell B5. If the numbers in B1, B2 or B3 were changed, the answer would be recalculated automatically! This feature makes changes easy to make, and as a result, a spreadsheet is very useful for answering 'what if' questions, such as 'What would the effect on sales revenue be if we increased room prices by 5 per cent?' 'What

Figure 3.18

A spreadsheet

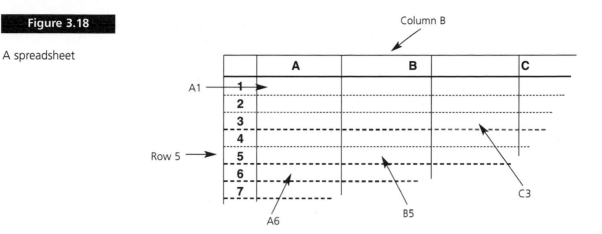

would the effect on the break-even point be if the sales mix changed in a particular way?', and so on. Once a scenario is set up on a spreadsheet, different analyses can be tried, and the spreadsheet will calculate the results instantly. This gives spreadsheets tremendous flexibility. Many different types of mathematical, statistical or accounting problems can be set up on a spreadsheet and then modified on a trial-and-error basis. If something is omitted, rows or columns can be inserted and the relevant formulae are altered automatically. Sections of the spreadsheet can be moved around at will and any references to these cells in formulae are adjusted automatically.

Figure 3.19

Entering formulae

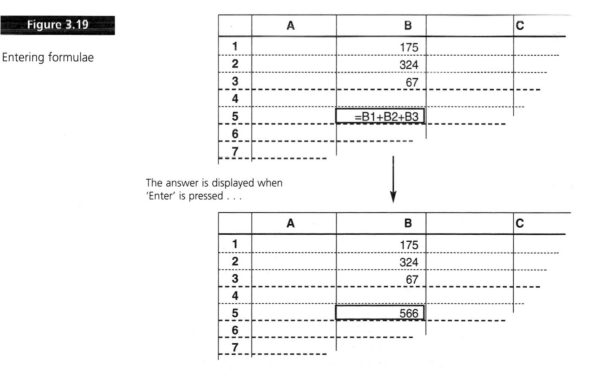

In addition to simple calculation symbols such as plus and minus, spreadsheets also use *functions* in formulae. Basically, a function automates a series of calculations, so that instead of having to enter several separate formulae to find the answer to a problem, the user only has to enter one (Figure 3.20). For example, to work out the correlation between two sets of numbers, the user could use separate formulae to work out each separate stage of the correlation calculation, or could do the entire series of calculations in one step by using the =Corr() function.

Figure 3.20

Some examples of formulae

=Average(A1:A10)	Calculates the average of a range of cells.
=Count(A1:A10)	Counts how many numbers are in a range of cells.
=If(A5>100,30,20)	Returns the value 30 if the value in A5 is greater than 100, otherwise it returns the value 20.
=Max(A1:A10)	Finds the highest number in a range of cells.
=Min(A1:A10)	Finds the lowest number in a range of cells.
=Sum(A1:A10)	Finds the total of a range of cells.

Another advantage of spreadsheets is that the contents of one cell can be copied into other cells. Using this feature with formulae makes it particularly useful. Take, for example, a spreadsheet which has been set up to work out a budget for twelve months, such as the one shown in Figure 3.21. Each column contains the figures for one month. If examined closely, it can be seen that the formulae needed to calculate the results for February, March and subsequent months are identical to those used to calculate January's figures, except that the letters representing the columns are different in each case. Apart from that, each

Figure 3.21

Copying formulae

The formula shown in B5 can be copied into C5, D5 and E5

	A	B		C	D
1			Profit	Analysis	
2		January	February	March	April
3	Sales	12000	13000	12000	12000
4	Purchases	4500	5000	4500	4500
5	Gross Profit	=B3–B4			
6					
7					

and the column letters in each formula adjust automatically.

	A	B		C	D
1			Profit	Analysis	
2		January	February	March	April
3	Sales	12000	13000	12000	12000
4	Purchases	4500	5000	4500	4500
5	Gross Profit	=B3–B4	=C3–C4	=D3–D4	=E3–E4
6					
7					

formula has the same structure – subtracting the figure in row 4 from the figure immediately above it. As a result, essentially the same formula has to be typed twelve times. However, using the 'copy' command, the formula structure in B5 can be used to produce the formulae from C5 to E5 and onwards. As the formula is copied, the column letters in each new formula are automatically adjusted to reflect their new locations. As a result, the formula relationships remain the same and each formula subtracts the figure in row 4 from the figure immediately above it in its respective column.

Most spreadsheets provide powerful graphing and charting facilities. Graphs can be created quickly by simply selecting the data to be charted, and telling the spreadsheet what type of graph to create. Legends, axis labels and titles can also be added to the chart easily (Figure 3.22). Windows®-based spreadsheets allow graphs to be placed directly on the spreadsheet worksheet, which allows both the graph and the data on which it is based to be displayed on the same screen or printed page (Figure 3.23). The automatic recalculation feature also works with graphs – if a value in the data is changed, the graph is automatically redrawn to reflect that change.

Figure 3.22

Components of a spreadsheet graph

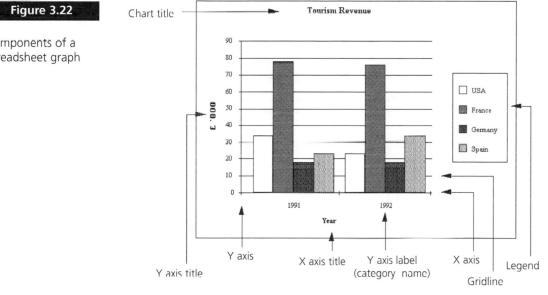

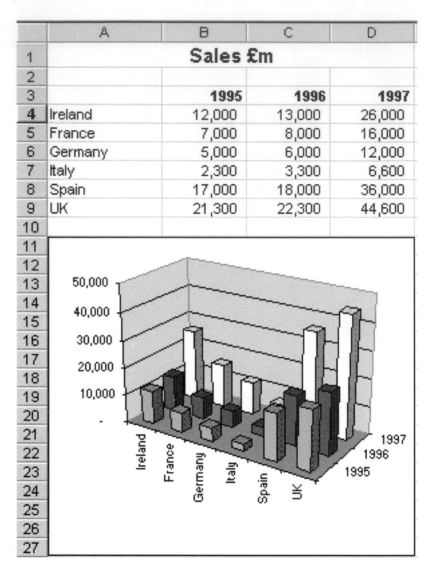

Figure 3.23

Data and graphs displayed on a spreadsheet worksheet

Formatting

As with a word-processing package, the appearance of the spreadsheet can be customized using powerful formatting commands. For example, numbers can be formatted in many different ways. A cell containing the value 1234.67 could be formatted as currency, as an integer or with one decimal place, as can be seen from Figure 3.24. However, formatting only changes the appearance, and not the value, of numbers. For example, if a cell containing the value '123.45' were formatted as an integer, '123' would be displayed on the screen. However, if this cell was multiplied by 100, the answer would be 12345, and not 12300. Such 'hidden values' can make the answers to calculations on a spreadsheet appear to be wrong when in fact they are correct.

Figure 3.24		

Spreadsheet number formats

Normal	1234.67
Integer	1235
Comma	1,234.67
Currency	£1,234.67
Scientific	1.23E+03

Normal	0.125
Two decimal places	0.13
Percentage	0.125
Fraction	1/8

Character formats such as bold, italic and underlining can be applied to both numbers and text, and the alignment of values within a cell can be changed. Column widths can be adjusted and extra rows or columns inserted to create 'white space', which makes a spreadsheet easier to read. Different typefaces and font sizes can be used to improve the appearance of a document, and areas can be shaded or enclosed in borders for emphasis. Spreadsheets can be printed as shown on the screen, or can be made more 'presentation-quality' by removing the borders (the ABCs and 123s) and the grid lines between cells.

Spreadsheet macros

Frequently used tasks can be automated using a facility known as a *macro*, which is basically a series of commands which can be executed by clicking on a button or pressing a particular key. Macros can be created in two ways: by recording keystrokes, or by using a special 'English-like' macro language. Using the former method, the spreadsheet records the user performing the task, and then converts the keystrokes and menu commands used into the macro language. For example, the macro shown in Figure 3.25, which prints a part of the spreadsheet, was recorded in this manner. Experienced users can also write macros directly (without recording) in Visual Basic, but to do so requires a thorough familiarity with the language, the package and some programming skills.

While macros are mostly used for automating simple tasks, they can, at their most complex level, be used to create user menus and help messages and to restrict access to areas of the spreadsheet, thus converting the spreadsheet into a kind of mini-application for use by other people. Such a spreadsheet is known as a *spreadsheet template*. A template is usually designed and created for a particular purpose, and contains all the necessary labels and formulae to complete that task.

Figure 3.25		

A simple spreadsheet macro which prints an area of the worksheet

Select the range A1 to D15

Macro command	Explanation
=SELECT("R1C1:R15C4")	Selects the area from row 1 column 1 (cell A1) to row 15 column 4 (cell D15)
=SET.PRINT.AREA()	Defines the selection as the print area
=PRINT(1,,,1,FALSE,FALSE,1,FALSE,1)	Selects the Print command
=RETURN()	Ends the Macro

Such a spreadsheet should be thought of as a blank form, waiting to be filled in by the user. Once the data is entered, the formulae automatically perform their calculations, and the answer to the problem is displayed. Macros may be built to perform tasks such as saving, printing, and quitting at the touch of a single button, so that the user of the 'application' does not need to be familiar with how to use a spreadsheet. As templates are usually created so that other people can use them, careful and logical design is essential. The developer should try to make the application as complete as possible for the eventual user. Instructions should be included, and each number on the spreadsheet should be clearly labelled. Print areas should be set, grid lines and borders removed, and formulae for all calculations included. However, the most important development task is to test the template comprehensively and completely. While dummy data can be used initially, the template should also be checked using real data, preferably some which has been processed previously by a manual system. Both sets of results should then be compared to ensure that the template is working properly. Remember Murphy's Law – 'Anything that can go wrong, will!' – and also remember that people rarely think to question results obtained from a computer.

Databases

Database packages are the third most popular type of horizontal-market software, and are primarily used to allow information to be stored, sorted and selectively retrieved in electronic format. The easiest way to explain the concept is to discuss an example of a non-computerized database with which everyone is familiar – the telephone book. A database is composed of *records*, each of which represents all the information in the database about one entity. In the telephone book example, a record is all the data about an individual person – his or her surname, first name, address and telephone number. Each record is composed of *fields*, which are the categories of information contained in the database (Figure 3.26). In a telephone book, there is the surname field, the first-name field and so on. Each field has a *data type* that determines what information can be stored in that field. While the actual types available vary from package to package, most databases have textual, numeric, currency, date, time, memo and graphic fields. These are self-explanatory. For example, textual fields can store text (numbers and letters), date fields can store dates and graphic fields can store various types of graphics, such as pictures, photos or illustrations.

Figure 3.26

Records and fields

	Surname	First name	Street	City
	Smith	Fred	12 Main St.	Cork
	Jones	Mary	Lakeshore Drive	Ennis
Record	Brown	Harry	12 Main St.	Cork
	Black	George	Lakeshore Drive	Ennis
	Green	Susan	Lakeshore Drive	Ennis
	White	Peter	Lakeshore Drive	Ennis

Field

There are several types of database. The most basic form are *flat-file* databases which store all their data in one table. To find a particular record, the user skips through all the records one by one, or goes straight to a particular one using an *index,* just as they would with a rotary card index. However, such a data structure is inefficient. For example, if a flat-file database was used to store company names and addresses, a separate record would have to exist for each contact name at each company. Where there are several contacts at one company, the address, telephone number, etc. needs to be repeated on two or more cards. If that company moves, the duplicate information has to be updated individually in each separate record. *Relational databases* overcome this data-duplication problem by allowing links to be created between tables. To use the same example, two tables are set up – one with the company name, address and telephone number, and another with the contact names. These tables are then linked using a *key field* – a field which uniquely identifies each record, such as, for example, a company reference number. If the company moves, the address only needs to be updated once – in the address table – which saves time, effort and needless repetition (Figure 3.27).

Figure 3.27

A flat-file versus a relational database

With a 'flat-file' database, a lot of data must be repeated in different records . . .

Surname	First Name	Company Name	Street	City	County	Telephone Number
Smith	Fred	XYZ Electronics	12 Main St.	Cork	Cork	(021) 34567
Jones	Mary	Regal Resorts	Lakeshore Drive	Ennis	Clare	(061) 98765
Brown	Harry	XYZ Electronics	12 Main St.	Cork	Cork	(021) 34567
Black	George	Regal Resorts	Lakeshore Drive	Ennis	Clare	(061) 98765
Green	Susan	Regal Resorts	Lakeshore Drive	Ennis	Clare	(061) 98765
White	Peter	Regal Resorts	Lakeshore Drive	Ennis	Clare	(061) 98765

. . . while with a relational database, an extra 'key' field is added and tables linked to avoid duplication.

Reference No.	Company Name	Street	City	County	Telephone Number
100	XYZ Electronics	12 Main St.	Cork	Cork	(021) 34567
101	Regal Resorts	Lakeshore Drive	Ennis	Clare	(061) 98765

Reference No.	Surname	First Name
100	Smith	Fred
101	Jones	Mary
100	Brown	Harry
101	Black	George
101	Green	Susan
101	White	Peter

Creating a database

Irrespective of the type being used, the first step in using a database is to create a structure to store the data. This is done by defining the field names, data types and, in some cases, the length of the fields to be included. This creates a blank table – a kind of skeleton that is then filled with data by the user (Figure 3.28). When creating fields, it is important to break data down into the smallest possible units and to create separate fields for each one. For example, a person's name could be stored in a single field, or it could be broken down into three separate fields: title, first name and surname. Using the latter approach gives the data more utility. For example, the database could be sorted by surname, or all the records which have 'Smith' in the surname field could be found. If the former approach was used, such data would be trapped within the larger field and would be inaccessible to the database.

It is also important to choose the correct data type for each field. This is not as simple as it appears. As mentioned above, database packages provide various different data types, each of which has its own characteristics. For example, textual fields can store both numbers and letters, while numeric fields can only store numbers, but can have their contents used in calculations. If a field such as 'Number of visits' were defined as being textual, then the 'number' (that is, the textual characters '1', '2', '3', etc.) could be stored, but could not be used in any calculations. Such a field would clearly be more useful as a numeric field. The difficulty in choosing the 'correct' field type can be further illustrated by discussing the storage of data such as telephone numbers. An inexperienced database creator might choose a numeric field type, but would then find it difficult to actually enter telephone numbers in the field. When examined more closely, one can see that telephone numbers contain things such as brackets and spaces, as in '(020) 7234 5677', and sometimes even text, as in 'ex 73'. None of these can be stored in a numeric field, which must, by definition, contain only numbers.

Figure 3.28

Creating a database structure

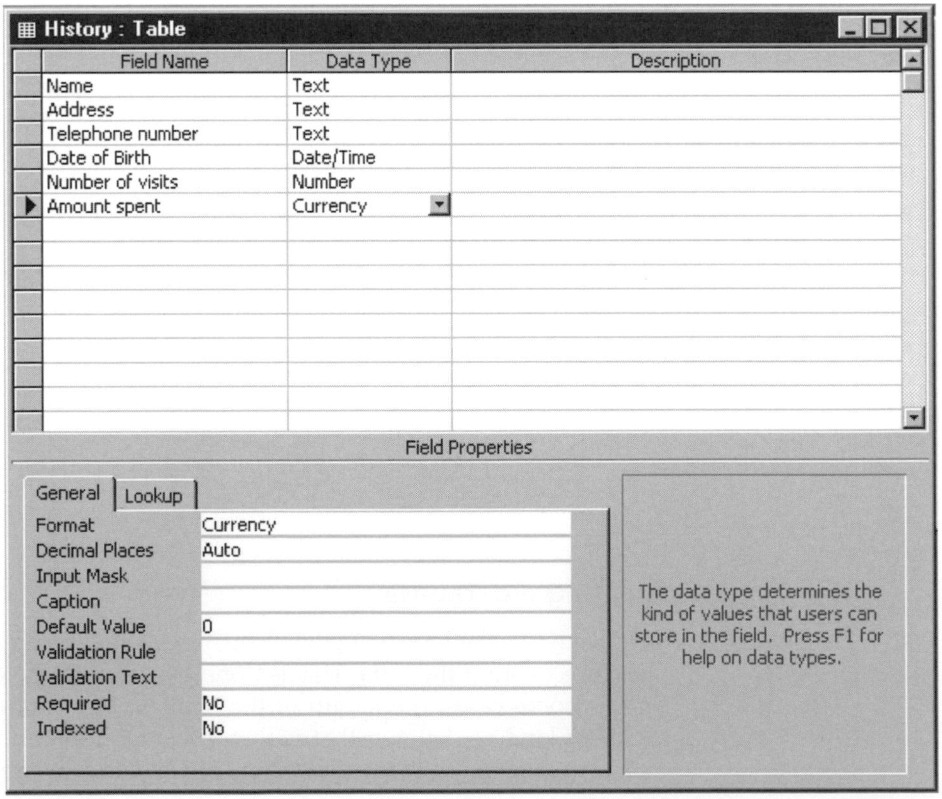

Furthermore, no one (I think!) performs calculations on telephone numbers, so a textual field type would be more appropriate.

Many databases allow validity checks to be defined to check data as it is entered. While most provide some automatic checks (to ensure, for example, that a date actually exists, or that currency figures only have the appropriate number of decimal places), users may wish to set up extra checks to make sure that the data being entered conforms to their own particular set of rules. The actual types of validity check allowed vary from package to package. Common examples include checks to ensure that data fall within certain minimum and maximum limits, that fields are not left blank, or that data is in a particular, user-defined format (such as the 'eight numbers followed by a letter' pattern of a US social security number).

Viewing data

The records in a database can be viewed and edited in two different ways. *Normal* or *table view* displays records on the screen in a row and column-like structure. Part of the data from several records is displayed at once, but as the screen is generally not wide enough to see all the data in any individual record, the user has to scroll over and back to see different fields. *Form view*, on the other hand, displays just one record on the screen at any time. All the information stored in the database about that entity can be seen, but all other records are hidden (Figure 3.29).

Figure 3.29

Table versus form view

In 'Table' view, parts of several records are visible on the screen at the same time . . .

Surname	First name	Company name	Street	C
Smith	Fred	XYZ Electronics	13 Main St	C
Jones	Mary	Regal Resorts	Lakeshore Drive	B
Brown	Henry	XYZ Electronics	13 Main St	C
Black	George	Regal Resorts	Lakeshore Drive	B
Green	Stuart	Regal Resorts	Lakeshore Drive	B
White	Peter	Regal Resorts	Lakeshore Drive	B

. . . while in 'Form' view, all of a single record's fields can be seen

COMPANY CONTACT DATABASE

Surname:	White	Company type:	Hotel
First name:	Peter	Credit rating:	AA
Company name:	Regal Resorts	Days credit:	30
Street:	Lakeshore Drive		
City:	Ennis		
Country:	Ireland		
Telephone No:	061 67343		
Fax No:	061 36730		

Most packages allow the user to create their own forms, which can be used for data entry and display. In this way, data can be laid out in a familiar or useful manner. Forms on paper and on the screen can be set up to have a similar structure, which can greatly speed up data entry and interpretation.

Sorting and selective retrieval

Apart from storing data, the main functions of a database are sorting and selective retrieval. *Sorting* refers to putting the database into order, based on the contents of one or more of its fields. For example, a telephone book could be sorted into alphabetical order by surname, or into ascending order by telephone

Figure 3.30	**List 1**	**List 2**
Secondary sorting	*Sorted by surname*	*Sorted by surname and then by first name*

	List 1		List 2	
	Smith	George	Smith	Alice
	Smith	Mary	Smith	Fred
	Smith	Alice	Smith	George
	Smith	Fred	Smith	Mary
	Smith	Sean	Smith	Sean
	Smyth	Ciaran	Smyth	Ciaran
	Smyth	Peter	Smyth	Mary
	Smyth	Mary	Smyth	Peter
	Toner	Ian	Toner	Alan
	Toner	Alan	Toner	Ian

number. If new records are entered, or existing records deleted, a database can be re-sorted in seconds to move the records into their appropriate positions. When a database is sorted using just one sort criterion, subgroups are created within the data. For example, if a telephone book were sorted alphabetically by surname, all the people with the same surname would be lumped together randomly, as is the case on the first list shown in Figure 3.30. A secondary sort (which can be thought of as a sort within a sort) would put these mini-groups into order. For example, if the same list were sorted first by surname and then alphabetically by first name, the subgroups would be placed in the order shown in the second list in Figure 3.30. In a similar way, tertiary and lower level sorts can be defined on other fields.

Selective retrieval means instructing the database to select all the records which match certain search criteria. This facility allows the user to ask questions about the data being stored in the database. These can be relatively simple (such as 'Find Alice Smith's record') or very complex (such as 'Find all the records of guests who have stayed in the hotel more than three times and spent more than £100 each time between the dates of 1 January and 31 March last year, and who paid their bill using a credit card'). Naturally it would be possible to find the answers to both of these questions by going through the database manually. However, particularly in the case of the second example, such a search would take a long time, during which the person searching could become bored or distracted and, as a result, miss records which should be selected. A computerized database, on the other hand, works at electronic speeds, is extremely accurate and does not get bored, so the correct answer is delivered in seconds.

There are two major standards used for selective retrieval. These are *query by example* (QBE) and *structured query language* (SQL). In both cases, the database is asked to create a subset of the information in the original table – a subset limited in terms of both the fields displayed and the records included.

- **Query by example** uses a graphical representation of the database(s) to set up the question. The illustration of a query shown in Figure 3.31 will find the surnames, first names and telephone numbers of everyone in the database whose surnames begins with 'D'. Fields are limited by placing a tick mark in those to be displayed in the answer, and records are limited by specifying

Figure 3.31

A query

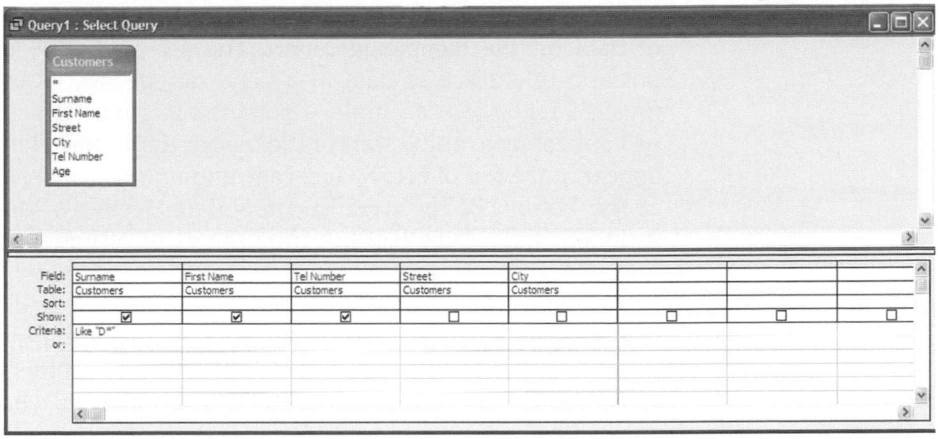

search criteria using an example of the sought data. So to ask the above question using QBE, the user would mark the surname, first name and telephone number fields with tick marks, and give the example 'D*' in the surname field.

- **Structured query language**, on the other hand, is text-based. The question is typed in an English-like language which uses special keywords with a particular format and syntax. For example, to find the answer to the question discussed above from a database called 'Contact' table, the user would type:

Select Surname First Name Telephone from Contacts where Surname = "D*"

Once a search has been performed, reports allow information to be output in a user-defined format. There are two basic types of reports: tabular and freeform, which broadly resemble the table and form views of a database. Tabular reports, as the name suggests, must have a table-like structure of rows and columns, while freeform reports have less structure and are therefore more flexible. User-defined reports are created using a report design screen (Figure 3.32).

Figure 3.32

A report design screen

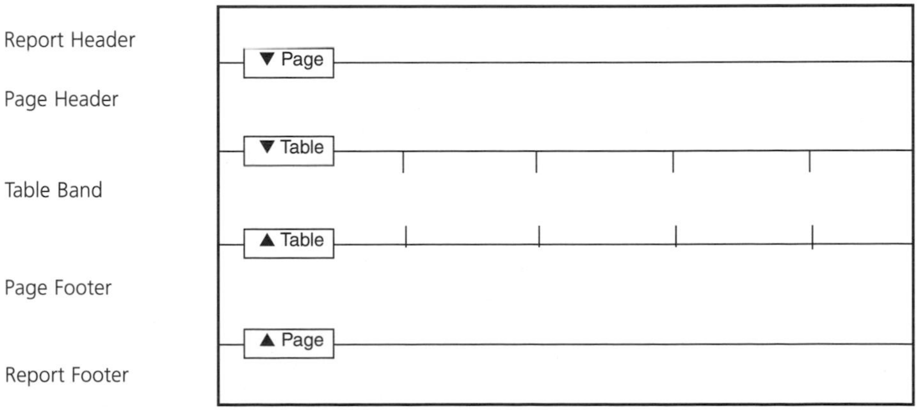

Report Header

Page Header

Table Band

Page Footer

Report Footer

▼ Page

▼ Table

▲ Table

▲ Page

The report designer allows a template to be created which dictates the position of data on the completed report. The screen is divided into bands, and the position of a piece of data in a band determines its eventual position on the finished report. For example, if something is positioned in the report header, it will appear once at the start of the report. If it is placed in the page header, it will appear at the top of every page. Page and report footers work in a similar manner at the bottom of the page and report respectively. Most of a report's data is included in the table band. A mini-template of how one printed record should look is created using field masks. Every record printed in the report then follows this pattern. Calculations, based on the value of fields in the record, can be included, as can summary fields which work out totals and averages (Figure 3.33). Reports and selective retrieval are often used together. For example, the user could ask the database to select the records of guests who stayed in the hotel last August. A freeform report, in the format of a letter offering a special promotion, could then be designed. By incorporating personal details from the database, each letter would appear to have been individually written and addressed to the client.

A package which provides all of the above facilities – namely table creation, data-entry forms, validity checks, sorting facilities, selective retrieval and a reports generator – is known as a *database management system* (Figure 3.34). If most hospitality-related software packages are examined closely (as they will be in the following chapters), it can be seen that many are clearly based on the concept of a database management system. For example, in a hotel reservation system, data-entry screens, validity checks, sorting, pre-recorded selective retrieval and reports can all be clearly distinguished. Data is entered into the reservation system using a customized data-entry form that has been laid out to appear like a paper booking form. As it is entered, the data is checked for validity – for instance, to see that the booking is not for a date which is past. Various customized reports form the output from the system. For example, an arrivals list is created by using selective retrieval to select the appropriate data based on the 'date of arrival' field, sorting the answer into alphabetical order by surname, and outputting the result as a tabular report which has been laid out in the required format.

Figure 3.33

A database report

Notice that everything in the 'page header' appears at the top of the page, everything in the 'table band' is repeated once for each record in the report, and the total (in the 'page footer') appears at the bottom of the page.

31.12.03			Page 1
	Monthly Sales Report		
Product	**Quantity**	**Unit cost**	**Total**
Becks beer	36	32.50	1320.00
Bulmers	100	36.00	3924.00
Carlsberg	45	37.90	3955.50
Guinness	17	30.00	1360.00
Harp	19	30.00	1377.00
Heineken	30	35.00	3015.00
Kronenberg	91	92.50	3417.50
Miller	302	41.00	12382.00
Ritz	47	33.50	1663.50
Stag	12	35.50	426.00
		Page total	40545.50

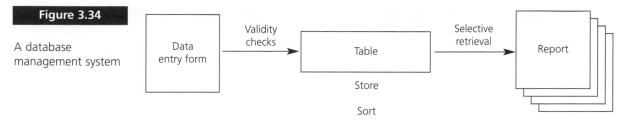

Figure 3.34

A database
management system

Email packages

The fourth most common type of application is an email client, which is used to send and receive electronic messages either internally over a company network, or externally over the Internet. Using email gives several advantages. First it is cheap, as hundreds of emails to destinations all over the world can be sent either for free or at most for the price of a local phone call. They are also more efficient: if the person to whom the email is being sent isn't present, the message is stored for them until they next use their computer system. Common examples of email clients include Eudora® from Qualcomm® and Outlook from Microsoft®. In both cases, shareware/freeware versions of the application are available that provide most of the basic features, which is adequate for most normal users. At the same time, upgrading to the full commercial version gives access to a more comprehensive range of functions, many of which are very useful when using email on a regular basis.

Sending an email

When sending a message, you generally start by entering the *email address* of the person you wish to contact. Email addresses generally have a particular format. For example, the author's email Internet email address is oconnor@essec.fr (a more detailed discussion of Internet addresses in included in Chapter 5 while examining the Internet). The address must be followed exactly, as any mistakes will result in the message *bouncing* – being returned to the sender as undeliverable. Each message should also have a subject line containing a short concise description of what the message is about. This courtesy to the recipient is becoming more and more important, particularly as the use of email grows and people are receiving increasing numbers of messages each day. Other fields that could be completed before starting to compose the email include the 'Cc' (carbon copy) field, which will send a copy of the message to anyone specified there, and the 'Bcc' (blind carbon copy) field, which does the same but without the main recipient being aware that a copy has also been sent.

The main body of the text can then be typed in the space below. Most email messages have traditionally been plain text, although multimedia features (in the form of colour, graphics sound and even voice) are becoming increasingly common. However, these should be used with caution, as you must be sure that the recipient is capable of receiving such enhancements before sending them. Text is the lowest common denominator, and should be used unless you are sure that the person can read the more advanced features at the other end. In other cases, you should use attachments to send files that are non-text along with your

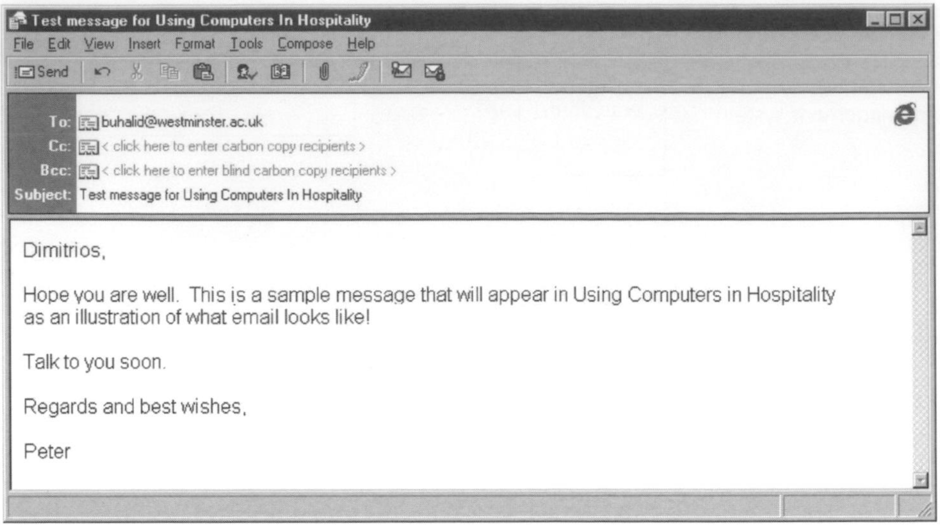

Figure 3.35

A typical email
message

Figure 3.35

A typical email message

message. Attachments are files in their native format (such as Microsoft® Word, Microsoft® Excel or an AVI video clip), which are encoded and travel along with your email message. This allows them to be sent without trying to include them in the text-only portion of the message, and they are dealt with automatically at the other end. Most email clients allow the user to set various options, such as that the message be stored and sent some time in the future, or that the sender be automatically notified when the message is delivered to or opened by the recipient. Most clients also allow the user to create one or more signature files. These are blocks of text that usually contain contact details such as addresses and telephone numbers etc. which are added automatically to the end of all messages sent.

Receiving email

Depending on whether you are permanently connected to a network, or you use a dial-up connection, you will receive email in different ways. In the former case, your email will periodically poll your mail server (usually about every 15 minutes) and download any messages waiting there for you. With a dial-up connection, on the other hand, you need to explicitly tell the client to connect to the Internet using your modem and contact your email server to download your messages.

Each message is preceded by various headers. Although cryptic at first, these tell you the sender of the message, its subject and the date it was sent. Sometimes you can also see the route that the message took between the sender's computer and the recipient's (Received by mail@aol.com at 23.55 on 23/12/98), which although normally of little use to the average user can be invaluable in diagnosing why a message is undeliverable. Many email clients automatically strip the headers from the messages, only allowing the user to see the 'From' and 'Subject' fields. Most email clients also now automatically decode attachments, returning them to their original file format and placing them in a special sub-directory on the recipient's PC. In such cases, their presence is usually indicated by an icon of a paper clip or a file within the email message.

Users can usually reply to a message by clicking on a single button. The email address and subject field are then completed automatically, and the text of the original message is included in the reply (with each line proceeded by an angle bracket '>' to help distinguish who has written what). The user can then add comments and answers to queries, making it easier for both parties to understand what the correspondence is all about. Emails can be forwarded or redirected to other people for attention, in which case the 'From' field changes to show that the message has passed through someone else's hands. Messages can also be stored in folders on the user's PC, which allows them to be sorted and archived in a logical way.

Most email clients provide a range of other facilities to make life easier for their users. Particularly useful is a nickname or address book facility. Even at the best of times, email addresses can be tricky to remember and difficult to type. Nickname facilities allow the user to specify shorter words that can be entered into the address field in place of the full email address. For example, instead of oconnor@essec.fr, the user could set up a nickname of 'Peter', which is all they would subsequently need to enter to send a message to the author. The email client would encounter 'Peter' in the recipient field and send the message to the full email address. Most systems also allow multiple addresses to be included in one nickname. So, for example, all the general managers in a hotel group could be included under a single nickname, making it easy to send a message to all of them in one quick easy step.

Another useful facility provided by many email clients is automatic filtering of incoming messages. Rules can be set up that tell the client what to do when it encounters particular conditions. For example, the client could be instructed to

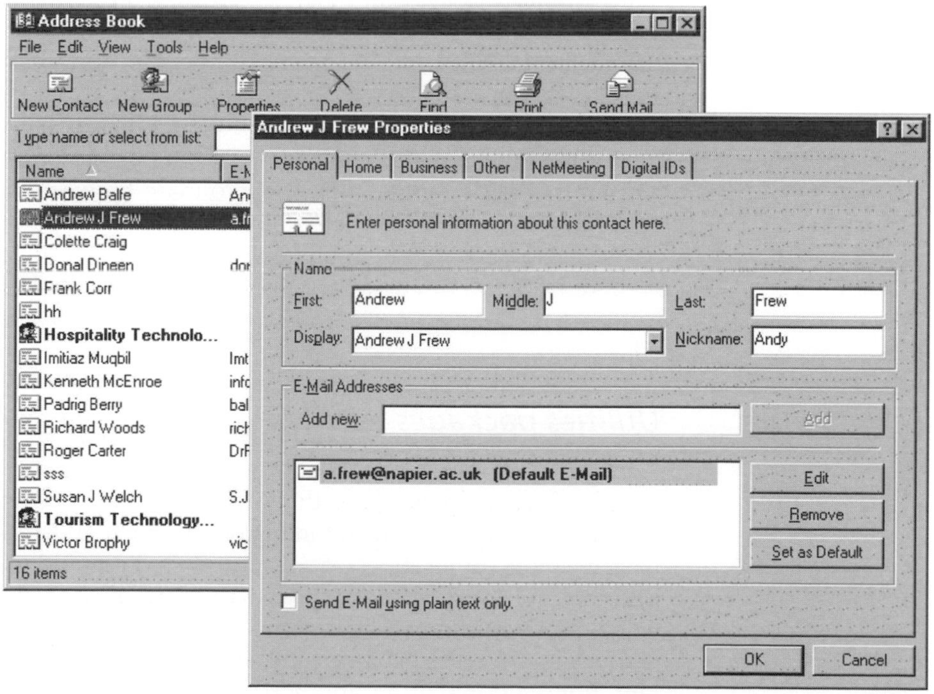

Figure 3.36

The address book from Microsoft® Outlook

send a message telling anyone who sent an external email to a particular address to tell the sender that their query is being dealt with by a particular employee, and then to forward the original message to that employee. In this case, internal emails would not get the reply, as the filtering facility would be able to tell the difference between them. Most email clients now also provide security features. Because email passes through a large number of computers on its route between sender and recipient, there is a (very small) possibility that other people could intercept and read it. Given increased concerns about security and confidentiality, many clients provide facilities to encrypt messages before they are sent, thus preventing any unauthorized eyes from reading them. Although several standards have arisen, Pretty Good Privacy (PGP) seems to be becoming accepted as the industry norm. Many email systems also allow you to see the time and date that an email was received or read by the recipient, thus preventing people from claiming that they never got your message.

Email has basically revolutionized the way in which work is carried out. The amount of paper in offices has been drastically reduced, as many messages, invoices, orders, reminders and even payments are now sent and stored electronically. Many hotel groups are using email for their normal communication. For example, many unit managers now use email to send their periodic reports and budgets to their group's head office. These can be read and approved by head office, and sent back to the hotel for implementation, all without ever being printed on paper.

Web browsers

Web browsers allow users to surf the World Wide Web – a vast multimedia database of information available over the Internet (see Chapter 5). The main function of a browser is to translate documents written in Hypertext Mark-up Language (HTML) into an image on the user's screen. The browser interprets special tags as instructions for layout and formatting, and places the data and other elements in their required position on the user's screen. Hyperlinks can also be included to allow the user to move from page to page and thus surf their way around the Web (Figure 3.37). The two main browsers available on the marketplace are Microsoft® Internet Explorer and Netscape's Navigator, and while the packages do have minor differences, these are not important to the average user. A more in-depth discussion of the function and capabilities of Web browsers is included in Chapter 5 – The Internet and the World Wide Web.

Utilities packages

Although the four types of software discussed above are probably the most commonly used applications, they are by no means the only ones available on the marketplace. Apart from the industry-specific software discussed below and in later chapters, other types of software include graphics packages, project-management software, accounting and financial management packages, desk-top video-conferencing packages, forms generators, statistical analysis packages, and many different types of games and simulations. The list is endless. What is important, however, is that an appropriate software tool is chosen for each task. An

A screen from
Microsoft® Internet
Explorer

analogy that has often been used is that it is possible to drive in a screw using a hammer, but it is a lot easier, quicker and more efficient to do so using a screw-driver!

Utilities packages are software programs that do general housekeeping tasks for a user. If computers were perfect, then you would not need utilities software. Unfortunately they are not and you do! While not even the best utilities can make your computer perfect, the right utilities can make many of its imperfections tolerable. Today's utilities cover an enormous range that starts with disaster recovery and disaster prevention applications that no one should be without. The range goes on to include valuable (and often indispensable) programs that help you compress files or otherwise manage files, optimize the performance of your computer, uninstall software – the list is endless.

Unless you are one of the fortunate few that has never lost files and whose computer never fails, back-up software is the first utility that you need, and you need it now! While Windows® includes basic back-up and restore facilities, in most cases a third-party utility is necessary to make up for the limitations of Microsoft®'s package and to make life more convenient for the user. A good utility of this type allows back-ups to be set up to run periodically and automatically, will allow back-ups to be made to a variety of different storage media (see Chapter 2) and will also make incremental back-ups (only copying the files that have changed) rather than backing up every file every time. While back-ups are your ultimate disaster recovery resource, disk maintenance and recovery utilities offer lifesaving benefits that are just as great. These monitor your disks for errors; un-erase deleted files and can help to recover disks that have crashed. Again, while basic facilities are provided in Windows®, most people can benefit from the added level of protection provided by Norton® and other utilities of this type. And of course, an essential utility is a virus scanner . . .

Viruses are devious. They do not discriminate and can be very destructive. They are currently stalking cyberspace, could strike at any time and could cost your company thousands of pounds and incredible inconvenience. Yet many people treat them as a joke, or believe that it could never happen to them. Welcome to the world of the computer virus!

Viruses come in many forms, from relatively harmless pests to intruders intent upon destruction. They are easily and unobtrusively transmitted, and the methods they use to avoid detection nearly match the sophistication of the tools designed to find and eradicate them. And today the threat of infection is greater than ever, as the widespread use of email and the Internet makes file swapping an everyday event.

Put simply, a virus is an illicit computer program that is designed to replicate itself on execution and create undesirable effects. In some cases, viruses cause relatively little damage, limiting themselves to symptoms such as displaying silly messages on the user's screen. Examples include *Stoned*, which flashes up the message *'Your PC is now stoned! Legalize Marijuana!'* and *Ping Pong*, which creates a tiny ball that bounces around the screen and deletes letters. There are, however, many that are destructive, corrupting files or emailing themselves to everyone in the user's address book. While some viruses only activate themselves on specific dates – like the famed Michelangelo, which triggers on 6 March, the famous painter's birthday, deleting data files – the majority are active all of the time, waiting for an opportunity to do mischief!

Traditionally viruses took the form of small chunks of code that attach themselves to the code of a program or system file. Such files were loaded into memory when the system was booted or when the infected program was run, and the virus began infecting other programs as well as, perhaps, delivering its payload by attacking the operating system, playing tricks with your screen or crashing the machine. Such viruses could cause sudden damage. Commonly referred to as Trojans, time bombs or logic bombs, they often waited for a certain date or event to trigger them. Usually the user had no idea that they had been infected until the virus released its deadly payload. However, protecting your computer against such viruses was comparatively easy, because as long as you didn't exchange program files with other users – a relatively rare occurrence – there was little chance of becoming infected.

A more modern form of virus, known as a 'macro virus', has the potential to be far more dangerous. While traditional viruses only infected software programs, macro viruses attach themselves to data files. When the user opens the infected document, the macro virus is activated and can perform any task allowed by the macro language, including deleting files, inserting random data, rebooting the system, preventing other files from saving or even reformatting the hard disk! Because users are far more likely to exchange data files than software programs –

Case Study *Are you in danger of infection? Take the test*

You run anti-virus software:

(a) Whenever the computer is on.
(b) Only when you install new files.
(c) Only when your network administrator makes you.
(d) At gun point!

The last time you updated your program's virus signature database was:

(a) Last month.
(b) Last year.
(c) Sometime this decade.
(d) When Bill Clinton was US President.

You sometimes let colleagues:

(a) View your computer from a distance.
(b) Copy data files off the computer using a floppy disk.
(c) Copy files onto the computer.
(d) Use your computer when you are out of the office.

You sometimes run programs you found on:

(a) A floppy disk you just scanned for viruses
(b) America Online®, or another commercial online service
(c) The Web.
(d) A floppy disk you found in the coffee room.

You recently viewed:

(a) A naughty picture from the Internet.
(b) An Excel file received as an email attachment.
(c) A Word document on a Microsoft® promotional CD-ROM.
(d) Someone booting your computer with a floppy in the A: drive.

Scoring
For every A answer, score 0 points.
For every B answer, score 1 point.
For every C answer, score 2 points.
For every D answer, score 3 points.

12–15 – Your computer is a danger to both yourself and others! Turn it off now and re-read this section.
8–11 – You're heading towards disaster!
4–7 – So you feel lucky, do you?
0–3 – Breathe easy, you obviously practise safe computing.

an absolute necessity in this age of email, e-business and collaborative working – macro viruses also tend to spread rapidly. Many have used the macro language capability of Microsoft® Outlook to automatically spread themselves. In such cases, the simple act of reading the infected email causes it to be emailed to all the contacts in the user's address book – a highly embarrassing situation.

To combat viruses effectively, you have to arm yourself with knowledge. Prevention is better than cure, and thus every computer should have a memory resident anti-virus program installed on it to prevent infection. These scan all existing and new documents and programs for viral signatures (specific pieces of code that can identify a virus). When a virus is found, the infected file can often be quarantined and cleaned before it does any damage, thus helping to prevent serious infection. However, anti-virus programs are limited in that they can only recognize viruses listed in their dictionaries. The latter need to be kept up-to-date by periodically downloading the latest versions from the supplier's website, but vigilance can also help. Determining if your computer is infected can be difficult, but at the first sign of odd behaviour – improper booting, strange sounds, a commonly used program refusing to run or documents refusing to save – you should scan your disks using the most recent version of an anti-virus program available. Don't delay – waiting until tomorrow could be disastrous!

Integrated packages

It is always better to figure out what you want your software to do before you buy it. But what if you are someone who has trouble telling one type of software from another – how can you cope with choosing the right application? One way to get over this hurdle is to purchase an integrated software package. Often given away 'free' as part of a bundle when you purchase a new PC, these generally contain a basic word processor, a spreadsheet, a simple database, an email client and possibly a drawing program. They provide basic features relatively cheaply and are called *integrated* packages because the different components usually work well together and allow information to be transferred easily between each package, so that, for example, a budget can be created using the spreadsheet, and then transferred for inclusion in the relevant portion of a word-processed report.

For users whose needs are simple, integrated packages can provide all the facilities that will ever be required. For example, the average home user or student, whose main uses would be the creation of simple reports, spreadsheets and basic databases, may find all the features he or she needs in an integrated package. However, in a normal business situation more powerful facilities are usually required, and it is often found that the features provided by most integrated packages are not adequate. Still, they are a good starting point, and allow less experienced users to identify the features they actually need so that they can subsequently buy the right combination of full featured packages to meet their processing needs.

Hotel and catering software applications

Vertical-market software for the hospitality industry can be divided into three broad categories: hotel, catering and back-office. Each is outlined briefly below, and they are examined in more detail in Chapters 8, 9 and 10 respectively.

An important concept when discussing hospitality-related software is the *integrated hotel system* – a set of computer applications that, together, assist in managing and controlling all aspects of hotel operations. Such a system helps management to satisfy the needs of the guest better, and should be capable of handling every transaction from the guest's initial telephone inquiry to their final billing.

Figure 3.38   An integrated hotel system

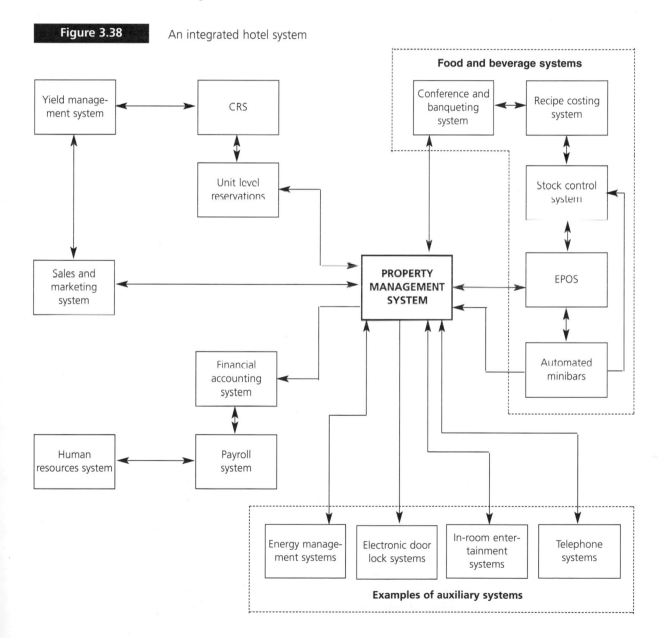

As can be seen from Figure 3.38, an integrated hotel system is composed of many different systems linked together. These include:

- **Reservation systems.** Many authors include the reservation function within the property management system. However, with the growing importance of central reservations systems (CRS) and other forms of electronic distribution, and the development of techniques such as 'yield management', reservation systems need to be discussed separately. A reservation system has two primary functions: to manage room availability and to accept bookings. Other functions can include the ability to track guest deposits and travel agent's commission, and the ability to provide important management and operational information.

- **Property management systems (PMS).** Sometimes referred to as 'front-office systems', these track which rooms are currently occupied or vacant in the hotel, and maintain the guests' folios by recording details of all sales and payment transactions. A PMS is now a necessity for most hotels as it would be difficult, if not impossible, to manage a hotel of 100 bedrooms or more without one.

A multitude of ancillary systems are used to support the hotel's PMS. For example, electronic door-locking systems generate a unique electronic key each time a new guest is registered, thus helping to increase security. Energy-management systems help to reduce heat and power costs by automatically turning off heating or air conditioning in rooms or sections of the hotel which are unoccupied. In-room entertainment systems provide extra services such as information screens, video-on-demand or computer games to guests, while at the same time generating additional revenue for the hotel. Telephone systems record data on each call made from the direct-dial telephone in the guest's room for billing purposes.

Several computer systems from the catering area also interface with the PMS. For example, electronic point-of-sale (EPOS) systems record the transactions that occur in the hotel's food and beverage outlets, while minibars are used to provide drinks and small food items in the guestroom. In the last three cases, integration between the systems allows charges to be posted automatically to the guest's account folio on the PMS. As soon as a transaction is completed its relevant charge appears on the folio, thus helping to increase control and ensure that the guest does not leave without paying for all services received.

- **Catering information systems (CIS)** manage and control all aspects of food and beverage production and sales. A CIS is composed of several separate systems linked together. Recipe-costing systems accurately cost food and beverage items and automatically update costs when ingredient prices change. Stock-control systems track inventory movements, record deliveries and issues and identify variances between actual and theoretical stock. EPOS systems transfer orders electronically from the service area to the kitchen, and ensure that guest bills are legible, accurately priced and up-to-date. Conference and banqueting systems manage and control the complex tasks of function reservations, organization and billing. Other examples of catering-related software packages focus on specialist areas such as club management, beverage control, nutritional analysis and menu engineering. Integration is very important for the efficient operation of these systems. For example, the recipe-costing system uses up-to-date prices from the stock-control system to calculate the cost of various recipes, which are then combined into menus. These are then sold to the customer through both the conference and banqueting system and the EPOS. They are also used, together with sales data from the EPOS, to detect variances in stock levels by the stock-control system.

- **Back-office systems**. Software is also widely used in what could be described as the 'normal' business areas of the hospitality industry. For example, accounting systems track debtors and creditors and generate final accounts and management reports periodically. Payroll systems automate the process of calculating wages and salaries, as well as maintaining period-to-date balances. Software is also used in the marketing area for data warehousing, database marketing and customer relationship management.

Case Study *The Royal Garden Hotel, London*

The Royal Garden Hotel, situated adjacent to Kensington Palace, is one of London's premier five-star properties, boasting 404 luxuriously appointed rooms. The hotel has recently undergone a multi-million dollar refurbishment programme, and no expense has been spared in providing general manager Graham Bamford and his team with the most up-to-date facilities and guest services. A key element of the redevelopment has been the installation of new information technology-based systems to help ensure full control and enhance guest service. Having a completely integrated system to help in both operations and management was regarded as essential. And for this, the company turned to Hotel Information Systems (HIS) and selected a totally integrated suite of packages, including;

- Front office
- Conference and banqueting
- Point of sale
- Stock control
- Accounting
- Sales and marketing
- Payroll and personnel

Interfaces have also been developed with the hotel's existing telephone call accounting system as well as with new electronic door locks and the hotel's pay-TV system, and they have been configured to satisfy the most demanding and discerning needs of the hotel and its guests. The entire system is based on Microsoft® Windows® NT Server and runs on Pentium®-based PCs.

Graham Bamford says

I am impressed by the flexibility and openness of the system. It definitely saves money as the staff training time is reduced and regular PCs can be used to run the system. Check-in is very simple. You click on a name and 'drag' the name to a room number and the guest is checked in. The same applies to check out and billing. The system enables us to offer guests top class service and we are very pleased with it.

Each of the above hospitality systems can be (and often is) used separately. However, the systems are much more effective if integrated and allowed to communicate with each other. For example, recipe costing is much more accurate if the recipe-costing system can access the latest purchase prices from the stock-control system. Similarly, security and control are greatly increased if ancillary systems such as electronic door locks and EPOS are linked directly into the PMS. It is connections at this level that have given rise to the concept of the integrated hotel system – a suite of software packages which are linked and assist in managing and controlling all aspects of a hospitality establishment's operations.

Practical questions

The following exercises have been designed to introduce you to the features of your word-processing, spreadsheet and database packages. Each exercise is based on real tasks that you could encounter while working in a hotel and catering operation. The menu commands necessary to complete each task are not given. These are obviously different in every package, and can be obtained from the package's manual or from your instructor. Tick off the exercises as you finish them.

Word processing

1. Text entry and editing concepts

You are working in the reservations department of a hotel. Type the letter shown in Figure 3.39, following it *exactly*. (Ignore any mistakes that you find, as these have been included deliberately.) Only press the Enter key when you wish to start a new paragraph (marked with a ¶ symbol in the diagram). At other times, the word-wrap feature will move to the beginning of a new line automatically for you.

(a) When you have finished typing, save the file as 'Hewson1'.
(b) Make sure that your word processor is in Insert mode. Place the cursor on the space after 'conference room' and add a comma and the words 'a patio' to the list of facilities. Notice how the existing text moves over and down to accommodate the new words.
(c) Change the departure date from the 17th to the 18th.
(d) Remove the incorrect word 'room' from the third paragraph.
(e) Place the cursor on the comma after 'beverage requirements'. Remove the comma, replacing it with a period ('.') and change the next sentence to 'These will be billed separately,'.
(f) Add the following paragraph before 'As discussed':

During the month of November, we are running a special traditional Irish promotion. A special menu, featuring the best of Irish food and drink, will be available in our restaurants, and an Irish ceilidh, with traditional music and dance, will be held each evening. Further details will be sent to you in the near future.

Letter for word-
processing
Question 1

```
The Hibernian Hotel,¶
Main Street,¶
Killarney,¶
Ireland.¶
¶
Mr Paul Hewson,¶
127 Grange Rd.,¶
Rathfarnham,
Dublin 24.¶
¶
12th August 1995.¶
¶
Dear Mr Hewson,¶
We are delighted to confirm your booking for our
Presidential Suite from the 11th to the 17th of November.¶
The Presidential Suite is composed of thrae en-suite
bedrooms, a lounge area, a conference room and a kitchen.
As agreed, a chef will be available 24 hors a day to met
your dining requirements.  You will also have exclusive use
of the large room garden adjacent to the suite.¶
As discussed, the rate for you stay is £500.00 per day.
inclusive of service and taxes.  However, this does not
include food and beverage requirements, which will be
billed separately.¶
We look forward to welcoming you and hope that you enjoy
your stay here in Killarney.¶
¶
Yours sincerely,¶
¶
Fred Smith,¶
Front Office Manager.¶
```

(g) Insert another paragraph mark after 'Yours sincerely,' to move the manager's name down a line.

(h) Spell check the document and correct any misspelled words. Notice that proper nouns, such as the names of people, and technical terms such as 'en-suite', are displayed as being incorrect. Also notice that 'you stay', from the second last paragraph, is overlooked, because 'you' (which should be 'your') is spelt correctly.

(i) Move to 'you' and add an 'r' to make it 'your'.

(j) Use the move facility to reverse the order of the sentences starting 'As agreed, . . .' and 'You will also . . .'.

(k) Use search and replace to change all instances of 'Killarney' to 'Galway'.

(l) Save the changes.

2. Formatting text

Load the letter that was typed in the previous question.

(a) Use the formatting commands of the word processor to centre the name and address of the hotel.

(b) Bold and italicize the hotel's name.

(c) Put a 4-inch indent on the date.

(d) Change the line spacing of each paragraph in the text of the letter (not the addresses) to one-and-a-half spacing.

(e) Put a 2-inch indentation on the manager's salutation.

(f) Underline the manager's name.

(g) Print the formatted letter.

(h) Save the changes.

You need to send a similar letter to John Smith of 17 Hill St., Birmingham, BR1 S3J. Mr Smith will arrive on 20 November and will stay for three nights.

(i) Edit the above letter, make appropriate changes and print Mr Smith's letter.

(j) Save the modified letter as 'Smith1'.

3. Formatting and font sizes

You need to type the menu shown in Figure 3.40. Begin by typing all the text and then apply the formatting commands detailed below.

(a) Centre all the text.

(b) Change the font to Times.

(c) In the case of each dish title, increase the font size to 14 point and make it bold.

(d) In the case of each description, decrease the font size to 10 point.

(e) Increase the font size used in the restaurant name to 18 point, and make it bold and italic.

(f) Make 'Dinner Menu' bold.

(g) Save and print the menu.

Spreadsheets

1. Revenue analysis

(a) Shown in Figure 3.41 are the departmental revenue figures for the Hibernian Hotel for a week.

(i) Calculate the total revenue for each day.

Figure 3.40

Menu for word-processing
Question 3

The Hibernian Hotel

Dinner Menu

Deep Fried Camembert

Breaded Triangles of Camembert, served with a Cumberland Sauce

Wild Irish Smoked Salmon

Thinly sliced, served with Capers and Irish Soda Bread

Dublin Bay Prawn Cocktail

Fresh Jumbo Prawns, served with Marie Rose Sauce and Irish Soda Bread

French Onion Soup

Beef Consommé, served with sliced Onions and topped with a Garlic and Cheese Crouton.

-ooo-

Chicken Cordon Bleu

Breaded supreme of Chicken, stuffed with Ham and Mozzarella cheese

Roast Wicklow Spring Lamb

Flavoured with Garlic and Thyme

Roast Crispy Duckling

Served with Orange and Honey Sauce

Prawns Provencale

Fresh Jumbo Prawns, served in a Tomato and White Wine Sauce accompanied by Saffron Rice

Fresh Corrib Salmon

Grilled or poached, served with a Prawn and Lobster Sauce

-ooo-

Profiteroles

Choux pastry served with fresh whipped cream and Chocolate Sauce

Strawberry Cheesecake

Baked American-style Cheesecake with fresh Strawberries

Baked Alaska

Made with fresh Black Cherries and home-made Vanilla Ice Cream and flamed with Brandy

-ooo-

Freshly Brewed Coffee

£20.00 per person, inclusive of service and taxes

(ii) Calculate the total weekly revenue for each department.
(iii) Calculate the overall revenue for the week.
(iv) Calculate the average daily revenue for each department.
(v) Save the spreadsheet.

Figure 3.41

Departmental revenue for Spreadsheets Question 1(a)

	A	B	C	D	E	F	G	H
1		Monday	Tuesday	Wednesday	Thursday	Friday	Saturday	Sunday
2	Accommodation	19,560	18,340	11,345	14,980	17,120	8,340	4,510
3	Food	4,856	4,585	2,836	3,745	4,280	2,085	1,128
4	Beverage	3,950	1,559	1,290	1,273	1,455	709	383
5	Sundries	807	624	516	509	274	284	153
6								
7	Total							
8								
9								

(b) Shown in Figure 3.42 is the number of guests who stayed in the hotel on each of the nights analysed above. Add the information to the previous spreadsheet and then:
(i) Calculate the average spend per guest on each day.
(ii) Calculate the average spend per guest for the week as a whole.
(iii) Calculate the average spending on each of accommodation, food, beverage and sundries.
(iv) Save the revised spreadsheet.

Figure 3.42

Number of guests for Spreadsheets Question 1(b)

	A	B	C	D	E	F	G	H
9		Monday	Tuesday	Wednesday	Thursday	Friday	Saturday	Sunday
10	No. of guests	279	262	180	214	213	99	58

2. Calculating redecoration costs

The dimensions of a number of conference rooms in the Hibernian Hotel are shown in Figure 3.43.

Figure 3.43

Dimensions for Spreadsheets Question 2

	A	B	C
1		Width (metres)	Length (metres)
2	Grand Ballroom	40	80
3	Tara Room	50	40
4	Kells Room	20	40
5	Achill Room	20	30
6			

(a) Calculate the floor space in each of the rooms.
(b) You wish to re-carpet each of the rooms. The carpet that you have chosen costs £37 per square metre. Underlay costs £4 per square metre. You have agreed to pay a fee of 5 per cent of the carpet and underlay cost for fitting. Calculate the cost of carpeting each room, and the overall cost of the carpet.
(c) Assuming that each guest needs a minimum of 3 square metres at a banquet, 2 square metres in a classroom and 1.5 square metres at a reception, calculate the capacity of each room using each of the above-mentioned seating styles.
(d) Save the spreadsheet.

3. A simple cash flow statement

Shown in Figure 3.44 is an estimate of the cash inflows and outflows of the Hibernian Hotel for the next quarter. Using the format shown, calculate the size of overdraft facility that will be necessary to meet the cash-flow needs of the hotel over this period. The cash balance at the beginning of the period is £500.

Figure 3.44

Estimate for Spreadsheets Question 3

		A	B	C	D
	1		January	February	March
	2	Sales			
	3	Accommodation sales	18,700	23,970	24,450
	4	Food & beverage sales	10,900	8,340	8,760
	5				
	6	Wages	14,800	16,155	16,605
	7	Variable costs	3,848	4,200	4,317
	8	Loan repayment		15,000	
	9	Rent due			1,000
	10	Power & light	300	450	370
	11	Payment due		9,000	
	12				
	13	Month end balance			
	14				

(a) In addition, calculate the totals for each category for the month. Use these to generate a simple trading account. Calculate the gross-profit and net-profit percentages.
(b) Save the spreadsheet.

4. Calculating stock values

A stock sheet from the Ivy Restaurant is shown in Figure 3.45. Use appropriate formulae to calculate the value of each stock item held and the page total.

Figure 3.45

Stock sheet for
Spreadsheets
Question 4

Stock Take Sheet – Dry Stores

Shelf number	Description	Size	Re-order level	Unit value	Quantity
567	Heinz Baked Beans	450g	30	0.27	45
568	Heinz Baked Beans	900g	30	0.51	17
569	Heinz Baked Beans	2000g	10	1.10	3
570	Batchelors' Peas	450g	30	0.28	32
571	Batchelors' Peas	900g	30	0.51	47
572	Knorr Stock Cubes – Beef	100g	70	1.35	79
573	Knorr Stock Cubes – Chicken	100g	70	1.35	56
574	Knorr Stock Cubes – Veg.	100g	70	1.21	70
575	El Pasco Taco Sauce	10oz jar	24	8.95	23
576	Plain flour	1kg	36	0.70	41
577	Self-raising flour	3kg	36	0.83	75
578	Whole grain flour	1kg	24	0.91	26
579	Sugar (white)	1kg	24	1.40	39
580	Sugar (brown)	1kg	12	1.45	17
581	Sugar (cubes)	1kg	12	2.35	26
582	Salt	500g	12	0.62	19

(a) The reorder level of each stock item is also shown on the sheet. Use an appropriate formula to highlight those products that need to be reordered.

(b) Save the spreadsheet.

Databases

1. Creating a personnel information system

The following database question is divided into several parts, each dealing with a separate topic related to databases. Each can be completed separately, but they must be completed in the order shown, as later parts use components created while completing the earlier parts.

(a) Creating a database

You wish to design a database that will store information about the hotel's employees. The field names and data types on which you have decided are shown in Table 3.3. Examine the table structure carefully. Why are 'telephone number' and 'social insurance number' both textual and not numeric?

(i)   Create a table to store this information.

(ii) Test the table by entering the records shown in Table 3.4.

(iii) Modify the structure of the database to include a new textual field for the employee's gender.

(iv) Edit the records of the two existing employees and add their genders.

(b) Validity checks

To prevent mistakes being entered, you wish to set up some rules for the data being entered into your system. These are detailed in Table 3.6.

Table 3.3	Field name	Data type
	Social insurance no.	Text
Field names and data types for Databases Question 1(a)	Surname	Text
	First name	Text
	Date of birth	Date
	Street	Text
	City	Text
	County	Text
	Country	Text
	Telephone no.	Text
	Annual salary	Currency
	Days' annual holiday	Number
	Department	Text

Note: some database packages only allow field names to contain eight characters and do not allow spaces. The field names shown here are longer and have spaces for clarity. If your database does not allow this, shorten the names but try to keep them understandable. For example, you could shorten 'First name' to FName'. Some packages also require a field length for some data types. If your package is like this, then make up appropriate lengths yourself.

(a) Set up appropriate validity checks to make sure that any new entries conform to these rules.

(b) Test your checks by entering the employees shown in Table 3.5. If your validity checks are working correctly, then the following should happen:
- The database should not accept the first record because it does not have a surname. Use 'Black' as the surname.
- The salary of £9,500 should be rejected as it is below the minimum. Change this to £10,000. (If you defined your validity check as being greater than £10,000, you are *wrong*. You were asked to make sure that the salary was *at least* £10,000.)
- The database should not accept 27 days' holidays. Change this to 25.

Figure 3.46	**The Hibernian Hotel**
	Personnel department
Paper form for Databases Question 1(c)	Confidential Employee Information

Social insurance number: 12121212A
Surname: White   First name: Michelle
Date of birth: 13/9/67

Address
Street   7 Church St
City   Paris
County
Country   France
Tel.   (1) 345 6789

Position
Department: Kitchen
Annual salary (£) 15,000
Annual holidays (days) 20

(c) Data-entry forms
Until now, you have been entering data in table view. Most databases allow data-entry forms to be created. You wish to create a form which resembles the paper form (shown in Figure 3.46) used by the personnel department.

Table 3.4   Records for Databases Question 1(a)

National Ins. no.	Surname	First name	Date of birth	Street	City	Country	Telephone no.	Annual salary (£)	Days' holiday	Department
12345687A	White	Fred	13.9.70	17 Main St.	Cliften	Galway	(091) 54321	12,000	20	Housekeeping
98765432B	Brown	Mary	31.6.71	7 Brewery Rd	Macroom	Cork	(021) 45678	17,000	18	Kitchen
98765499C	Brown	Frank	1.5.67	2 Francis St.	Dalkey	Dublin	(01) 8747886	14,000	20	Housekeeping
23234545D	Brady	Richard	14.6.65	Main St.	Cavan	Cavan	(091) 78987	22,000	20	Bar

Note: of course 31 June does not exist. The automatic validity checks on your database package should notice this and not allow this date to be entered. The date should be the 21st.

Table 3.5   Employees for Databases Question 1(b)

National Ins. no.	Surname	First name	Date of birth	Street	City	Country	Telephone no.	Annual salary (£)	Days' holiday	Department	Gender
11112222C	White	Tom	7.1.70	Blackrock	Dublin	Ireland	(01) 444444	9,500	20	Kitchen	Male
22223333R		Dolores	29.2.72	Macroom	Cork	Ireland	(021) 78456	15,000	27	Restaurant	Female
33334444R	Connell	Sean	1.1.70	Anslesea St.	Dublin	Ireland	(01) 8888888	14,000	10	Bar	Male

Field name	Check type
Table 3.6	

Field name	Check type
National Insurance no.	Cannot be left blank
Surname	Cannot be left blank
Annual salary	Must be at least £10,000
Days' annual holidays	Must be 25 days or less
Gender	Must be either 'Male' or 'Female'
Department	Must be one of the following: 'Kitchen', 'Reception', 'Restaurant', 'Housekeeping', or 'Accounts'

Validity checks for databases Question 1(b)

(i) Create a data-entry form for the database. Follow the layout of the paper form as closely as possible.
(ii) Change to form view. Examine the records already in the database. Notice how only one record can be seen at any time.
(iii) Enter the data from the paper form in Figure 3.46.
(iv) Which view is easier to use for entering date?

(d) Sorting data
If you have completed all of the above exercises, you should now have eight records in your sample database. These are used in the next two exercises to demonstrate sorting and selective retrieval.

Sort your database in each of the following ways:

(i) On the 'Annual salary' field – when sorted, you should be able to see who has the highest and the lowest salaries.
(ii) On the 'Date of birth' field.
(iii) On the 'Department' field – note how the records form into little groups representing each department.
(iv) Alphabetically (in ascending order from A to Z) on the surname field. When the sort is complete, examine the database. Look at the records for the people called 'White'. How are these records sorted within the group?
(v) First alphabetically by surname (as above) and second by first name. This should sort the 'Whites' into alphabetical order.

(e) Selective retrieval
Use the selective retrieval facilities of the database to carry out the following tasks:

- Find all the people whose surname is 'White'.
- Find all the males.
- Find all the people who work in the 'Restaurant'.
- Find all the people who work in the 'Restaurant' or in the 'Kitchen'.
- Find all the people whose surname begins with 'B'.
- Find all the people who live in Ireland.
- Find all the people called 'White' who live in Ireland.
- Find all the males called 'White'.
- Find all the people who earn less than £13,000 per year.

- Find all the people who have more than 25 days' annual holidays.
- Find all the people who are over 21 years old.
- Find all the people who have more than 20 days' holidays and who earn less than £18,000.

(f) Reports

Design the following reports for your database: A report listing the national insurance number, surname, first name and annual salary of all employees. This report should have the heading '**List of current employees**' at the top of each page.

(i) A letter confirming the employee's appointment.
(ii) A suggested report design and a sample of how each report might look in print are shown in Figure 3.47 (see p. 97). Do not peek!

2. Hotel reservations

Design an appropriate table to store the information taken when a room reservation is made. Remember to break information down into the smallest possible units when creating fields.

(a) Set appropriate validity checks and design an appropriate data-entry form.
(b) Last, design two reports: one in the format of an arrivals list, showing the guests to arrive on each day, and the other in the format of a letter to the guest confirming the reservation details.

Email

This exercise is designed to be used in class in a computer laboratory. By sending messages and files to each other, students can experience how email works.

Using the email package provided by your college, complete each of the following tasks.

(a) Find out the user name (and if relevant the email address) of the instructor, the person on your left and the person on your right.
(b) Send a message to the instructor. When prompted for the address, enter the instructor's user name. When prompted, enter a short description of what the message contains. When the screen clears, type your full message and send it.
(c) Send another message to the person on your left, and one to the person on your right.
(d) At this stage, you should have had at least one prompt to tell you that there is some new mail for you. Choose the menu option to read this mail.
(e) Reply to the person who sent you a message. His or her user name and address should be shown on the message he or she sent to you.
(f) Work in pairs. Exit the mail system, go into a word processor and type a paragraph of text. Save this as a file on your hard disk. Then start the mail program again, and attach this file to a message to your partner. After you have sent the message, go to your partner's computer and see whether the file got there.

Figure 3.47   Suggested report design and sample report output for databases Question 1(f)

Sample report design

Social Security No.	Surname	First name	Annual salary
AAAAAAAAAA	AAAAAAAAA	AAAAAAAAA	99999.99

▼ Page
List of current employees
▼ Fax to

▲ Fax to

▲ Page

Sample report output

List of current employees

Social Security No.	Surname	First name	Annual salary
12345678A	White	Fred	17,000.00
9876543B	Browne	Mary	17,500.00
11112222C	Black	Todd	12,000.00
222444567D	Jones	Jonah	15,000.00
775431879H	Smith	Jane	13,800.00

Sample report design

▼ Page

▼ Table

The Hibernian Hotel
Main Street
Killarney
Ireland

(First name)(Surname)
(Street)
(City)
(County)
(Country)

dd.mm.yy

Dear (First name)

We have great pleasure in offering you a position in our (Department) department. Welcome to the team! As agreed in the interview, your salary will be £(Annual salary) and you will have (Annual holidays) days holidays per year.

We look forward to having you work for us.

Sincerely

Fred Bloggs (General Manager)

▲ Table

▲ Page

Sample report output

The Hibernian Hotel
Main Street
Killarney
Ireland

Fred White
17 Main Street
Cliften
Galway
Ireland

12.03.2004

Dear Fred

We have great pleasure in offering you a position in our Housekeeping department. Welcome to the team! As agreed in the interview, your salary will be £15,000 and you will have 24 days holidays per year.

We look forward to having you work for us.

Sincerely

Fred Bloggs (General Manager)

Review questions

1. Explain the difference between hardware and software. ·
2. How are programs created?
3. What is the function of an operating system?
4. What are the implications for hardware manufacturers of having industry standard operating systems?
5. What are the implications for software writers?
6. What is the most commonly used operating system?
7. Describe what is meant by a command line interface.
8. Give two examples of operating systems which use a command line interface.
9. Describe what is meant by a graphic user interface (GUI).
10. Give two examples of operating systems which use a graphic user interface.
11. What are the main advantages and drawbacks in using a GUI?
12. What is meant by the term applications software?
13. What are the five most common types of general-purpose software?
14. Describe (in a single sentence for each application) the main functions of each type.
15. Which software package would you use to perform each of the following tasks:
    (a) Working out next year's budget;
    (b) Keeping a list of past customers;
    (c) Graphing last year's sales on a pie chart;
    (d) Working out the cost of a recipe;
    (e) Typing the restaurant menu?
    In each case, explain how the application's facilities would make the task easier than using manual methods.
16. What is the main function of a Web browser?
17. Explain what is meant by the term word wrap.
18. Explain what is meant by drag and drop.
19. Any word identified as being incorrect by a spell checker is spelt incorrectly. True/False. Why?
20. Give an example of when you might use the search and replace facility of a word-processing package.
21. Explain what is meant by the term formatting.
22. Give three examples of:
    (a) Document formatting;
    (b) Paragraph formatting;
    (c) Character formatting.
23. A document that is three pages long in double line spacing would be six pages long if single-spaced. True/False.

24. Explain the meaning of a formatting style.

25. Explain what is meant by the term WYSIWYG.

26. What is the major difference between a word-processing package and a desktop publishing package?

27. Explain why the automatic re-calculation facility on a spreadsheet is useful.

28. Name two other advantages in using a spreadsheet over using a calculator or manual methods.

29. Explain what is meant by a spreadsheet function.

30. Why would you use a macro?

31. What is the most important stage in developing a spreadsheet template for use by other people?

32. Explain the difference between a record and a field.

33. What is the main advantage in using a relational, as opposed to a flat-file, database?

34. What is meant by the term secondary sort?

35. What are the two major selective retrieval standards and what is the principle difference between them?

36. What is the function of the Bcc field on an email package?

37. Why would you send a document using an attachment rather than building it into the body of the email?

38. Describe what is meant by the term hotel-specific software.

39. Give four examples of tasks for which software is used in the hospitality industry.

40. What is meant by ancillary systems?

41. Name three hotel-related ancillary systems.

Discussion questions

1. Has the development of industry standard operating systems had any effect on the spread of computer use?

2. What is the difference between general-purpose software, such as spreadsheets and databases, and industry-specific software, such as property management systems?

3. Why, despite its limitations, is MS-DOS still widely used in the hospitality industry today?

4. Most hotel groups now use Microsoft® Windows®-based applications for both vertical and horizontal applications. Discuss the advantages and limitations of such a strategy:
   (a) From the point of view of an individual hotel company.
   (b) From the point of view of the industry as a whole.

4   Computer networks and communications

Computers are capable of storing and processing vast amounts of data. However, such data is of limited use if it is stored on a single computer because it is isolated and can only be used by a single person. Data becomes much more powerful if it can be shared by many people. To facilitate this, various methods of electronic communication have been developed which allow data to be transferred or shared electronically between computers. This chapter discusses different aspects of data communications and their implications for the hotel and catering industry. The various types of hardware and software used to transfer data electronically are described. Computer networks, the backbone of hospitality technology, receive special attention and the various types of network available, their component parts and their topologies are discussed in depth. The chapter concludes with a discussion of integration and its implications for the hospitality sector.

Communications theory

Conceptually communication is quite simple. A message is transmitted from a source, through a communications medium to a destination. The aim is to reproduce the source's message at the destination. However, sometimes this does not happen, as the message becomes distorted because of noise or interference as it passes through the communications medium. There are three different modes of communication:

1. **Simplex** communication allows data to flow in one direction only. The sender is always the sender and the receiver is always the receiver. An example of simplex communication is a television broadcast, where a signal is sent from the television station to people watching their television sets.

2. **Half-duplex** communication allows data to flow in both directions, but not at the same time. The sender and the receiver alternate, with each side waiting for the other to finish before responding. A good (although slow) example of a half-duplex mode is communicating by post. Each person waits for the other's letter before replying. Similarly, to communicate effectively on a walkie-talkie or two-way radio, half-duplex communications must be used, with one person waiting for the other person to finish speaking ('Over!') before starting to reply.

3. **Duplex** communication allows data to flow in both directions simultaneously. Both ends send and receive at the same time. People are not good at duplex communication, as can be seen when two people try to talk at the

same time. Computers, on the other hand, do not have this limitation and duplex communication can be used very successfully when dealing with electronic devices.

An important characteristic of any communications medium is its capacity to carry data, which is known as its *bandwidth*. This can best be explained using the analogy of a pipe – in this case the medium is the pipe itself, the data is the water flowing through it and the diameter of the pipe is the bandwidth. The greater the bandwidth, the faster a fixed amount of data (say a bucket of water) that can be transported from one place (the sender) to another (the recipient) in a given unit of time. One way to increase the speed of communications is to increase the diameter of the pipe by using a medium with a higher bandwidth. The rate at which data is transferred is known as the *baud rate*, which is measured in *bits per second* (bps). In general, an average of eight to ten bits are used to transmit each character, so a baud rate of 1200 bps means 120 characters per second.

Traditional methods of computer communication

The most basic level of computer communication is one where two devices are linked together to exchange data. These devices could be, for example, two computers, or a computer and a peripheral such as a printer. The simplest way to link the devices is to connect them directly to each other. As was explained in Chapter 2, most computers are equipped with serial, parallel, USB and infrared ports, which allow such connections to be made easily. However, direct connection is obviously limited by distance. While computers in the same room or perhaps the same building could be linked in this way, it would be difficult or impossible to use this method across a city or country. Clearly some other communications medium must be used.

The traditional method of linking computers over long distances has been to use telephone lines as the communications medium. However, telephone lines are designed to carry voice signals and are *analog* in nature. This is fundamentally different from computers, which are *digital* (Figure 4.2). As a result, the digital signal of the computer must be converted to analog before being transmitted along the telephone line, and it must then be reconverted back to digital at the other end so that it can be understood by the receiving computer.

These conversions are carried by a device called a *modem* (modulator–demodulator), which acts as an interface between the computer and the telephone line (Figure 4.3). There are many different types of modem, ranging from external (connected to the computer through the serial or USB port) through internal

Figure 4.1

A serial and a parallel port

Serial

Parallel

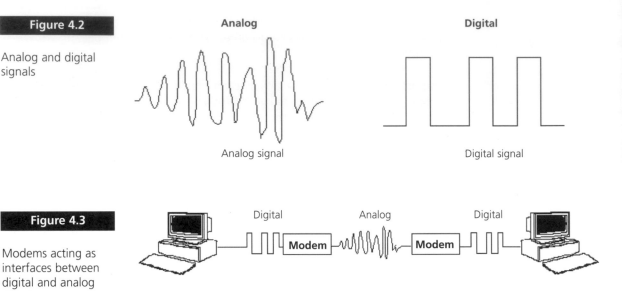

Figure 4.2

Analog and digital signals

Figure 4.3

Modems acting as interfaces between digital and analog signals

(fitted inside the computer in an expansion slot) and data-only through fax-data (able to send and receive facsimiles). However, the most important characteristic of a modem is its baud rate, as this determines the speed at which data is transferred. Modems typically have baud rates ranging from 28,800 bps (28.8 Kbps) to 56,000 bps (56 Kbps). Using a modem with a low baud rate means that it takes longer to transfer data, which results in more expensive telecommunications charges.

Two different types of telephone line can be used.

- Dial-up lines use normal public telephone lines to carry data. When two computers need to exchange information, the telephone number of the receiver is dialled, just like a normal telephone call. However, dial-up connections are problematic. Time must be spent waiting for an outside line dialling the telephone number, connecting and handshaking, which slows down the communications process, and background noise from other lines can result in errors.

- The other alternative is to use leased lines. These are dedicated, high-quality lines which permanently connect two points ('dedicated' means they perform only this task). Because the computers are always linked, time is not wasted dialling and connecting. In addition, the line is often specially 'treated' to reduce interference, which helps reduce transmission errors, and as a result, leased lines can transmit data at much higher speeds (typically in the region of 1 Mbps to 1.5 Mbps).

However, the most important difference between the two types of line is the way in which cost is calculated. The cost of a dial-up line is based on normal telephone charges and, as a result, depends on the amount of time spent connected and the distance involved. Users of leased lines, on the other hand, pay a fixed monthly fee, which is based on the distance between the two points and the bandwidth required. The option that works out cheaper depends on the amount of usage. Where small amounts of data have to be transferred infrequently, then dial-up lines are cheaper. However, if a connection is needed for several hours a day (for example, when a hotel's computer is linked to a central reservation system for online updating of availability), then a leased line is generally less expensive.

A relatively new development provides an alternative to using phone lines for connectivity. Broadband – basically media that promise speeds higher those that can typically be achieved over a conventional modem – are becoming more common. At present, broadband is focused on three different media – cable, digital subscriber line (DSL) and satellite.

- Cable broadband uses spare capacity on the wires normally used to deliver television signals to people's homes. Connection to the PC is made using a cable splitter, which routes TV signals to the set-top decoder box and data to the cable modem, which is in turn connected to the computer. Theoretical connection speeds of 2.5 Mbps are offered, although in practice actual speed is influenced by the number of users accessing the local loop simultaneously, and most people achieve a connection speed of about 512 Kbps.

- Digital subscriber line (DSL) uses high frequency transmission to enhance the carrying capacity of the existing telephone network to give higher band-width. As telephone lines go practically everywhere, this allows broadband to be used anywhere without having to dig up the roads to lay cable or fibre optic connections. However, while the telephone lines themselves can carry the enhanced signal, in many cases the existing local telephone exchanges cannot cope with the higher frequencies required and have to be replaced before DSL can be offered in an area. As with cable, the signal from the tele-phone line is split within the home or business, with voice being routed to the telephone and data to the DSL router. DSL offers a theoretical maximum speed of between 700 Kbps and 10 Mbps and, like cable, actual connection speeds are influenced by the number of users connected, in practice there is less fluctuation. DSL is normally sold to consumers as ADSL – the 'A' stands for asynchronous meaning that the downstream channel offers more band-width than the upstream link, based on the premise that most home users download more data than they upload. For business users with heavier uploading requirements, symmetrical DSL (SDSL) offers less disparity between upstream and downstream capacities.

- Where your telephone exchange will not cope with DSL and cable television companies do not service your area, satellite broadband may be your only solution. In theory is can be used anywhere – in terms of hardware all that is needed is a dish on the outside of the building and an transceiver/modem unit to hook up your computer. Satellite can now match DSL in terms of speed, with downstream capacity of 300 Kbps and upstream speeds of 150 Kbps typically being offered. However satellite broadband is much more expensive, making it primarily a solution for businesses rather than consumer use.

While broadband offers an interesting alternative to using leased lines, for com-mercial use it suffers from one major drawback – none of the three solutions presented above offer guaranteed service levels in terms of connection speed. In each case, the actual speed of the connection is influenced by factors such as the number of users, the quality of the medium and several other uncontrollable issues. Where reliability in terms of speed is a critical issue, businesses still prefer leased lines because despite the expense they promise consistency in terms of speed. Perhaps the old adage 'You get what you pay for' is relevant here!

Computer networks

The phrase computer network is used to describe any system of computers linked together to share resources. It is usually composed of a central computer, called a *server*, which provides a variety of services to multiple *client* computers (hence the term *client–server network*). Each client is independent and works separately, but can share files and resources on the server. This contrasts with using a mainframe linked to dumb terminals, where all the work (processing) is performed centrally. With a network, the processing is *distributed* to the client computers, and therefore the system does not slow down as the number of users increases. A client server approach therefore delivers the best of both worlds – the security, accessibility and manageability of a central data repository coupled with the reliability and flexibility of local processing.

Networks may, in theory at least, be divided into two categories. Computers located in the same physical area, such as a set of rooms or a building, are normally referred to as a *local area network* or LAN. A link covering a larger geographical area is known as a *wide area network* or WAN. However, the distinction is rather imprecise and the point where a LAN becomes a WAN is difficult to determine. For example, a network connecting computers in the front office of a hotel is clearly a LAN. Similarly, one connecting hotels in different cities is clearly a WAN (Figure 4.4). But is a network linking computers in a large resort hotel a LAN or a WAN? Perhaps a good rule of thumb might be that a network becomes a WAN where communications media are supplied by an outside agency, such as the telephone company. Many hotels now have several networks – a LAN within the property to facilitate the integration of the PMS and various other operational system (see the section on integration later in this chapter), a WAN to facilitate exchange of data with the corporate office, provide access to the Internet and sometimes some telephone services, and the guestroom network, connecting devices such as the television, minibar, energy management system and door locks, as well as providing Internet access to the guest from the hotel room (see Chapter 8).

Advantages of using a network

Installing a network is complex, time-consuming, expensive and often frustrating. However, several important benefits can be gained from using one. These include:

- **Shared data**. With stand-alone systems, data on a computer is isolated and can generally only be accessed by the user of the machine in question. A network allows data to be stored centrally and accessed by all the users. For example, in a hotel, room-availability data could be stored on the network. As a result, every user would be able to tell when rooms are available for

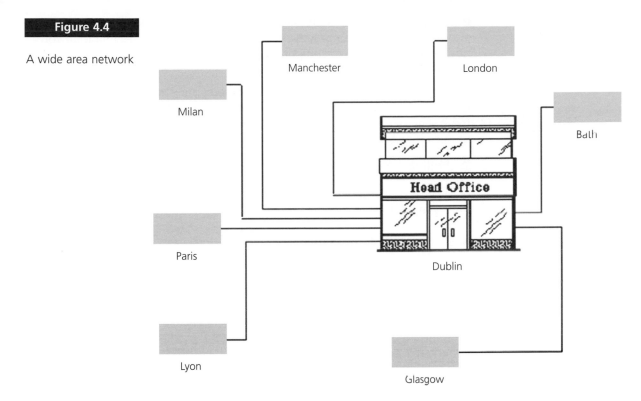

Figure 4.4

A wide area network

sale, which is clearly more efficient than limiting the information to a single computer. Data can also be transferred from one user to another over the network. As a result, documents such as budgets, reports, mailing lists, etc., can be sent from one person to another electronically.

- **Shared software**. As we saw in Chapter 3, purchasing a piece of software generally licenses the use of just a single copy of that particular package. Where a company has thirty computers, and wishes to use the package on each machine, then thirty licences must be bought. With prices of £400 to £550 for standard applications such as spreadsheets and databases, the total cost of equipping each machine in an organization with software can be substantial. Using a network allows a special type of licence to be purchased. Called (imaginatively!) a *network licence*, it allows multiple copies of an application to be used at a fraction of the cost of purchasing individual copies. Limited network licences restrict the number of copies that can be used to an agreed, fixed number, such as twenty users at any one time. If the agreed number of copies is already in use, then any additional users will not be able to load the package until one of the other twenty finishes. Unlimited network licences, on the other hand, allow as many copies as necessary to be used on the network in question.

- **Shared hardware resources**. Hardware can also be shared over a network. This allows further savings to be made, as each machine does not have to be equipped with peripherals such as printers, scanners, CD-ROM drives and modems. Instead peripherals such as these can be connected to the network and used by all the computers. Such an approach is less wasteful than connecting them to a single computer, where in general they would lie idle the majority of the time.

- **Communications**. Networks allow users to contact each other easily using electronic mail (email) and Instant Messaging facilities. Both allow messages to be sent and files to be transferred electronically, and can increase communications both within and outside the organization.

- **Reliability**. Compared to using a mainframe system, a network is more reliable from two points of view. First, its speed is unaffected by the number of users. Each computer is independent and processes all of its own work. This is in contrast with a mainframe-based approach, which uses time-sharing to distribute its processing power among several dumb terminals (see Chapter 2). As extra users connect to a mainframe, the entire system slows down as the finite processing power must be distributed between a greater number of terminals. Each computer on a network, however, has its own processing power and therefore its speed remains the same irrespective of the number of users. Second, a networked system is less dependent on the performance of a single computer. If a mainframe breaks down, then every user connected to it is out of action. However, if a single computer on a network breaks down, the others are unaffected. Even if the server fails, users can continue to work, using each computer's own local resources.

- **Security**. When data is stored centrally on the network, it can be backed up more easily than if it is spread over multiple computers. Software can be configured to make these back-ups automatically, thus helping to protect and safeguard valuable data.

- **Expandability**. While the initial costs of installing a mini-computer and a large network may be similar, it is easier and cheaper to expand a network. When more users are needed, extra computers can simply be plugged into the existing system with few if any technical limitations.

- **Control**. As many of the facilities of a network are based on the server, management and control of computer use are simplified. Software management and support are simpler, because everyone uses the same packages and the same versions, accessed from the server. Similarly, upgrading to new software is easier: change the version on the server, and everyone is immediately upgraded. Access to resources can also be controlled simply. The network manager, through the use of passwords and rights, can specify which programs, data and hardware are available to each user, and can even limit the times at which a user can access the system, which could be useful in preventing employees using the system outside of working hours.

Network components

Networks are composed of many complex and interrelated parts. This section explains the function of these parts and how they fit together.

File servers

The *file server* runs the network-operating system (discussed below) and makes its attached disk drives, printers, modems and other hardware devices available for use by the client computers. It is usually dedicated, which means that it performs only this task and is not also used as a client computer. When choosing a server, factors such as the size and speed of its hard disk, the speed of its processor and the quantity of RAM are very important. These determine the speed at which the server can respond to client requests, and thus the overall speed of operation of the network. For this reason, very large networks sometimes use a mainframe or a mini-computer as their server, but, in general, a powerful personal computer is sufficient.

Network-operating systems

The *network-operating system* is the software that controls the operation of the network. It is composed of a series of programs, some of which run on the file server and others on the client computers. The former controls the network and facilitates multiple simultaneous accesses to the server's disk drives and other hardware devices. In this respect, it resembles the multi-user operating systems of mainframe computers. The software in the client computer makes the facilities provided by the network appear to be local. Requests for services, such as loading data from disk or sending data to print, are intercepted and sent down the network to the server. Here they are re-routed to the appropriate hardware device, such as the server's hard disk or the network printer. Even if a network is only composed of a few dozen machines, it can benefit from some level of management. Most network operating systems provide facilities to monitor and control network traffic, track down troublesome links and automatically generate error alerts if things start to go wrong.

Workstations

When a computer is attached to a network, it is referred to as a *workstation*. Workstations can be personal computers, network computers, mainframes, minicomputers or a mixture of different types. However, in general, most networks encountered in the hospitality industry are composed entirely of personal computers. Floppy or hard disk drives are not needed on many workstations because users can store data on the server (see the discussion of network computers in Chapter 2). As a result, considerable savings in hardware costs are possible. However, disk drives may still be necessary in certain circumstances. For example, workstations located at the reception desk do not need floppy disk drives, as they would rarely, if ever, be used. On the other hand, users in offices use disk drives regularly to do things such as back-up data or install software. Similarly, hard disk drives may still be needed where an operating system such as Microsoft® Windows® is being used. Because of its large program size, Windows® spends a lot of time swapping data into and out of memory. Where this is done to a network drive, the data to be swapped must be sent down the network to the server, and the new data must be read into memory. As a result, 'traffic' on the network is greatly increased, which can slow down the speed of operation of the network as a whole. However, if the data is 'swapped' to a local hard disk, network speed is unaffected.

Network topology

Network topology refers to the physical construction of the network. This is composed of three parts: the type of cable used, the layout of this cable, and the network adapters or interface cards. These are discussed below.

Cable type

The cable is the physical medium used to connect one computer with another. Traditionally, either unshielded twisted pair cable (similar to telephone wiring) or coaxial cable (seen in cable television wiring) is used. However, alternative media, such as fibre optics and wireless, are becoming more common, as will be discussed later in this chapter.

- Unshielded twisted pair (UTP) cable is composed of a pair of insulated copper wires braided together and sheathed (Figure 4.5). It is relatively cheap, needs no special tools to install, and may already be present in the area to be networked in the form of spare telephone cabling. However, it is limited in the length over which it can be used (approximately 100 m) and is prone to picking up noise and interference from other electrical devices.

- Coaxial cable, on the other hand, is like a circular sandwich composed of a thick central copper conductor wrapped in foam and covered with a braided metal sleeve and plastic insulation (Figure 4.5). The latter acts as an electrical shield and reduces interference, which means that it can be used over greater distances (up to 500 m). However, it is more expensive, needs special connections and is less flexible, which makes it more difficult to install.

Functionally, there is little reason to prefer one cable type to the other.

Figure 4.5

Coaxial cable (left) and UTP (unshielded twisted pair) cable (right)

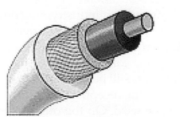

The distance limitations of either type can be partially overcome by installing an electronic device known as a repeater. This boosts the signal and allows the network to extend over a greater range. Similarly there are few differences in terms of carrying capacity – each can be used to carry Ethernet (10 mbps), Fast Ethernet (100 Mbps) or Gigabit Ethernet (1000 Mbps). Choice of cabling is usually based on convenience. For example, UTP is popular because of its flexibility, which makes it easy to fit through ceilings and walls during installation, although its lack of electrical shielding can be a problem in situations where interference could occur from other electrical devices. In many cases, a combination of cable types is used. Coaxial cable (or sometimes fibre-optic cable) is used to form a central 'backbone' in a building, to which a series of client computers are connected using UTP. Whatever cabling type is chosen, it must be flexible in terms of what it can be used for, and must be future proof, thus having the potential to

Case Study *Cabling at ITT Sheraton*

Mark F. Hedley, manager of special projects and development for hotel systems and communications for ITT Sheraton, describes how a standard cabling system was chosen for the group:

Choosing a cabling system for the entire group was a momentous task. Whatever solution was selected had to be able to support advanced communications, while at the same time having enough flexibility and reliability to adapt to changing demands as the nature of our business evolved. It had to be application and hardware transparent, and have the potential to be cost efficient over many years and yet still suitable for installation in more than 450 properties worldwide.

Finding a single solution was a monumental undertaking. Coaxial cable, shielded twisted pairs and/or twin axial cable are commonly used in proprietary cabling systems throughout the hotel sector. We selected a less common alternative – unshielded twisted pair (UTP) copper wire. However, even standardization brought problems. As any MIS manager knows, equipment manufacturers typically insist that a unique cabling system be installed before they will guarantee the performance of their products. Many vendors were also reluctant to accept the concept of a shared wiring plan because it would reduce their revenues by eliminating the need for their proprietary cabling plan. However, we were successful in showing them the benefits of a common wiring infrastructure. Many found that the easy access to cabling made installing and testing systems much simpler. We, of course, realized immediate savings as only one set of wires had to be installed to run all of our systems. Savings also accrued because we were able to serve any terminal at any information outlet with minimum cross-connect changes and no new cabling. Within minutes, obsolete or defective systems or terminals can be replaced while reusing the original wire. In addition, we save money on wiring new properties while the floors and walls are open as opposed to returning and rewiring each time a terminal, system or host has to be moved or replaced. And we gained flexibility.

(Adapted from: Hedley, M.F., 'How Sheraton cabled its properties', *Hotels*, May 1993, p. 82.)

cope with potential demands to carry voice, data, video or whatever other demands might be made of it in future.

Cable layout

The cable is usually structured in one of three main patterns, known as *bus*, *ring* and *star* (Figure 4.6):

1. A bus layout is linear in nature, with *terminators* at both ends. Data travels along the cable in both directions, with collisions prevented by special software. Hardware devices (technically known as nodes) may be connected at any point on the cable, which makes this pattern relatively flexible.

2. A ring layout links computers to each other in a closed loop, with signals being passed from one node to the other in a given direction. Each node regenerates the signal, which means that a ring layout can spread over a greater distance without using a repeater than either of the other patterns. However, if one node on the ring crashes (or someone simply disconnects the cable from the back of a single PC), the ring connection is broken and the entire network fails.

3. A star layout links all the client computers to a central node, which may either be the file server or a special piece of hardware called a *hub*. In either case, all messages are received by the central device and redirected to their proper destination. The principle advantage of a star pattern is reliability. As each client computer is isolated from the others, if the connection between it and the central node breaks, only that single computer is out of action. All other nodes are unaffected. However, star wiring uses much more network cable than the other patterns as each geographically dispersed node has to be connected to a single, central point.

Network interface cards

Each computer connected to the network, including the server, must have a *network interface card* (NIC) installed in one of its expansion slots (Figure 4.7). This fits inside the systems unit, connects to the network cable and converts the serial signals used by the network into the parallel data stream of the system bus. Most new computers can be purchased with a network card pre-installed, which means that it is immediately ready for use, and can be plugged straight into the network.

Other network hardware

A variety of specialized pieces of hardware facilitate the operation of a typical network. *Routers* and *switches* act as 'junction boxes' along the network, sending messages along to their desired destinations. *Gateways* and *bridges* facilitate connection to other networks, the former to ones that use a different networking standard or protocol and the latter to networks that use the same network operating system. The network may also be connected to the outside world using broadband (see earlier) or a leased line, and in both cases it should be protected

Figure 4.6

Alternative network
wiring layouts

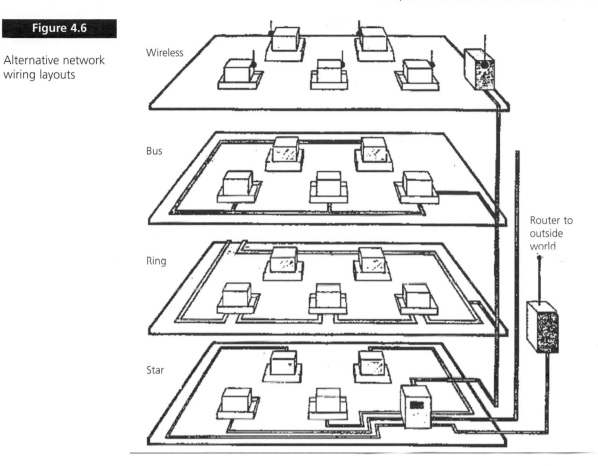

Wireless

Bus

Router to
outside
world

Ring

Star

Figure 4.7

A typical network
card

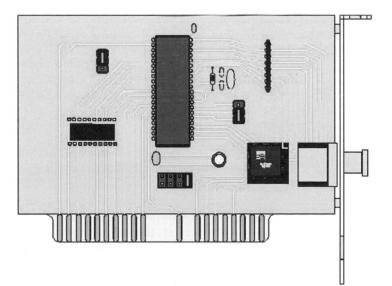

by a *firewall*. While specifying and installing hardware such as this has become considerably easier, in most cases a specialist is needed to ensure that it is being configured and used in an optimum way.

Using a network

Before using a network, special software, which establishes a connection with the server, must be run on the client computer. Once connected, a user logs on by entering a unique user name and password, and is then able to use the facilities of the network as if they were located on the local client. Each user has a personal user directory, which can store software or data just like a normal disk drive. User directories are private, in that their contents can only be seen and accessed by their owner. Other directories may be shared, which means that any user with sufficient rights can access their contents. This allows data and software to be shared over the network. Data can also be transferred from user to user by copying it onto a shared drive, and then copying it again down onto the destination computer.

Because a network is used by many people, security is an important issue. As already mentioned, each user has a unique user name and password. Time restrictions can also be used to limit when individual users can access the network's facilities. For example, office staff might only be allowed to log in between 9 a.m. and 5 p.m., to prevent use after hours, or the night auditor might only be permitted to log in between the hours of 10 p.m. and 8 a.m., to prevent the night run starting accidentally. Similarly, station restrictions can limit the locations from which each user is allowed to connect, helping to prevent unauthorized access and protect the company's data.

Developing communications media

As discussed above, networks have traditionally used either UTP or coaxial cable as their communications medium. However, several alternative media have been developed recently and are increasingly being used to overcome the limitations of cable. They can be divided into two groups, based on the way in which they carry the signal: cable-based systems and wireless systems. These are discussed below.

Cable-based systems

Fibre-optic cable uses pulses of laser-generated light travelling down a hair-thin strand of glass to carry data. Fibre optics offer dramatically more bandwidth at far higher speeds than conventional copper wires. The cable is also physically smaller, and can be used over far longer distances because light (unlike electric current) travels further without amplification. Fibre optic is also more secure, because it cannot be tapped without detection. However, while obviously superior to conventional cable, fibre-optic cable suffers from a major drawback: it is many times more expensive than traditional media and costs can be as much as ten times higher than that of UTP.

Digital lines carry a digital as opposed to the normal analog signal and therefore remove the necessity for a conventional modem. *Integrated services digital network* (ISDN) offers a worldwide, high-speed communications network based on special, wide-band digital lines. Users get the security of a leased line at a far lower cost because it operates as a dial-up service. As a result, users only pay for the amount of time that they are connected. ISDN typically operates at speeds of 64 Kbps, but is usually used in pairs to give the user a bandwidth of approximately 128 Kbps.

Wireless systems

Traditionally, networks have been constrained by the need to stretch cables between the points to be connected. Space under floors and above ceilings can be used for this cable, but this space is often already cluttered with telephone, electricity and other wires. Sometimes, holes have to be knocked in walls or trenches dug in floors to allow cabling to be laid. Once the system is set up, moving a computer, or adding more workstations, can be a nightmare. Wireless communication media offer a solution to this problem. Eliminating wires reduces clutter and allows computers to be repositioned at will. Wireless networks are particularly useful where computers need to be portable. For example, the hand-held electronic point-of-sale (EPOS) terminals used in many restaurants are based on wireless communications (Figure 4.8). These media use one of the following technologies:

- Infrared technology uses high frequency light to transmit data from point to point. However, this approach is limited in that it cannot penetrate solid objects such as walls. As a result, the transmitter and the receiver must be in direct sight of each other and is best suited in two situations – in large open spaces or at very close range. For example, infrared links are now used routinely to connect computers to both printers and PDAs to allow data to be transferred without actually physically connecting the devices. However,

Figure 4.8

An EPOS using wireless communications

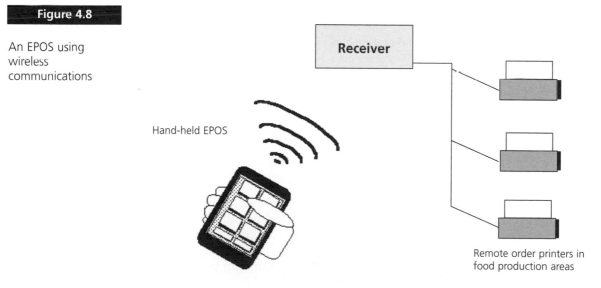

Hand-held EPOS

Receiver

Remote order printers in food production areas

the technology can also only be used over a relatively limited distance (20 and 30 feet). Infrared does have the advantage of being immune to electrical interference, which potentially makes it useful in locations such as kitchens where machinery could interfere with cabled or other wireless signals. And, unlike the other forms of wireless communications, it is not subject to government regulation, which makes it quick and easy to set up. Last, infrared links are highly secure, since their inability to penetrate solid objects means that the data being transmitted never leaves the room.

- Radio frequency technology uses small radio receivers and transmitters, called transceivers, instead of cables. It has a greater range than infrared, typically up to 500 feet, and does not require the computers to be in direct sight of each other. As a result, it can be used around corners or between different rooms. However, the use of radio presents its own problems. Government regulations allow only a narrow band of frequencies to be used. These are already cluttered with a variety of signals from television and radio stations, cellular phones and even car alarms and garage-door openers. As a result, signals can easily get jumbled, resulting in errors. Radio communication is also less secure in that anybody can listen in simply by tuning a receiver to that frequency. As a result, data encryption may be necessary to protect the security of the network. Two standards are currently becoming common in the marketplace. WiFi (802.11b) is used extensively in both commercial and home networking and allows laptops and other mobile computing devices to be connected to a network quickly and easily. WiFi 'hot spots' are becoming common in both hotels (where the property can charge customers for using its facilities), in coffee shops (Starbucks throughout the USA operates this service) and in areas where large numbers of business travellers congregate, such as airports and train stations. To log into one of these networks, all the user needs is a laptop or PDA equipped with a WiFi card and (depending on whether it's free or not) a username and password from the service provider.

Bluetooth is an alternative radio frequency technology, designed more specifically to allow mobile devices in proximity to each other to communicate and exchange data rather than for general network access. Bluetooth is relatively short range and is commonly found in devices such as PDAs and mobile phones. Already the hotel sector is starting to take advantage of this new standard. For example, the Holiday Inn in New York has become the first Bluetooth-enabled hotel. When you make a reservation, you quote your cell phone number, and when you arrive for your stay, your phone is detected by the hotel's system and you receive a message greeting you and telling you your room number. When you get to your room, your cell phone automatically talks with the door lock, identifies you and opens the door.

Taken together, WiFi and Bluetooth complement each other well. United Parcel Service, for example, is installing a worldwide network employing both technologies. Bluetooth will replace the cable between a waist-mounted terminal and a hand-held scanner, and the terminal will use WiFi to send the data – in this case, tracking information from packages – to the UPS central computer. However, as mentioned earlier, security can be a problem with wireless networks, especially with standards as common as WiFi. As the signals are not blocked by physical walls, data transported over the network flows outside your building and could potentially be intercepted by anyone with a suitably equipped laptop and some commonly available hacking software. However, simple actions such as limiting access rights and turning on 128-bit wired equivalent protection (WEP) on your wireless access point go a long way towards eliminating this problem, and if users are also authenticated (made to log in as though they were dialling in remotely), the danger is minimal.

Microwave technology can also be used as a communications medium. Communication can occur over longer distances, but, once again, there must be a clear line of sight between the two antennae. Microwave technology is very expensive and is highly government-regulated, with a special licence required for its use.

While offering flexibility, wireless communications also has its limitations. The average cost per node is considerably higher, averaging about £200 per node in comparison with about £40 for a fixed connection. In addition, transmission speeds are almost always slower than with fixed connections. For example, 2 Mbps is speedy for a wireless product, not good when compared with the 10 or 100 Mbps (and even 1000 Mbps of Gigabit Ethernet) provided by 'conventional' connections to the desktop. Even though this is more than fast enough for the average user, in many cases it is a good idea to ask if you really need a wireless network. Many buildings are already wired for conventional networking, just needing the appropriate equipment to be plugged in and configured. However, where speed and price matter less than flexibility and mobility, wireless networking can be an attractive option.

Peer-to-peer networks

Particularly for a small business, client–server based networks are relatively inefficient. A powerful computer must be dedicated to managing the network, expensive software must be purchased and a lot of time must be invested in installing and managing its use. An alternative, known as a *peer-to-peer network*, has become common. These networks do not need a dedicated file server, because every computer connected to the network acts both as a server and as a client simultaneously. A user at one machine can access data on all the others, and can use their peripherals, such as printers and modems, as if they were available on their own machine. In this way, the benefits of using a network are available, without the trouble and expense.

Another advantage of peer-to-peer networks is the ease with which they can be purchased and installed. Complete packages, with all the cables, cards and software needed to set up and operate the system, are available off-the-shelf. Sometimes your existing operating system is all you need to set up and run such a network. For example, various versions of Microsoft® Windows® effectively have an entire network-operating system built in. Users can share files and peripherals, and have email facilities. All that is needed to make the system work are some standard network cards (which can be purchased pre-installed in new machines) and appropriate cabling. The network can be up and running, sharing data and peripherals in minutes. The major limitation is that only a relatively small number of users can be networked using peer-to-peer technology. Like a mainframe system, the amount of time spent on administration increases proportionally with the number of users. As a result, the overall 'system' slows down and becomes inefficient when too many machines are attached. For that reason, peer-to-peer networks are most suitable on small networks with about ten users or less. Another (more minor) problem with peer-to-peer is that management of the network can become a real headache. Every computer has to be configured and maintained independently, and it's all too easy for these settings to be (accidentally or maliciously) changed. With a client server network and a dedicated server running a network operating systems such as Novell® Netware® or Microsoft® Windows® NT, everything is managed centrally and less problems of this nature are likely to occur. In addition, you get better security and a much higher level of performance.

Electronic data interchange and electronic funds transfer

The concept of email – allowing users to send electronic messages to each other – was discussed in Chapter 3. Two related but fundamentally different concepts are *electronic data interchange* (EDI) and *electronic funds transfer* (EFT). While email is designed to allow communication between people, using the computer as a communications device, EDI and EFT allow computers, not people, to communicate with each other, although its true usefulness can best be exploited when it is used for application to application communication. EDI automates business transactions by using a standard electronic message format to transfer data directly from a software application on one computer to another software application on a second computer. This sets it apart from other forms of communication such as voice, letter, fax or even email, all of which must be received by humans and acted upon. A computer receiving an EDI message is generally programmed to acknowledge receipt of the message, extract the relevant data and process it or pass it on to another application for processing. When used correctly, EDI has the potential to totally remove the need for human intervention in routine data transfer, saving time, allowing for faster responses and giving greater flexibility. EFT is similar to EDI, but is designed to allow banking transactions to be carried out electronically. The main difference is that three parties (the bank, the person paying and the person being paid) are involved in each EFT transaction. Apart from this, the principle is the same, with electronic messages being used to transfer money from one bank account to another.

There are many benefits to using these electronic business processes. Transactions are completed at great speed, with a typical turnaround of minutes as opposed to hours or days using other forms of communication. Costs are reduced and accuracy is increased, as data does not have to be retyped into a second system. Potential uses in the hospitality industry include reservations and ordering stock items. Reservations data could be transferred automatically from tour operators' computers to the PMS using EDI, and commission payment made automatically using EFT. Similarly, stock-control systems could order new supplies of stock items automatically when quantities go below a pre-set reorder level, and once again, payment could be made using EFT. The key to the successful use of both of these processes is *standards*. Without an agreed data format, applications do not know where to find data within a message. Use of EDI and EFT is being held back, not by a lack of standards, but by a proliferation of them. The retailing, banking and insurance sectors all have their own industry-standard data formats, none of which is compatible with any of the others. Large companies, which use EDI to transfer data internally, are not affected by this lack of a common standard because everyone within the company uses the same one. However, smaller companies, such as independent hotels and travel agents, whose main potential use of EDI would be to communicate outside their own company, are unlikely to accept EDI until an international standard is developed and adopted for use by all concerned.

Integration

The problems with standards discussed above in relation to EDI and EFT are also evident in other areas of computerization in the hotel and catering industry. As was discussed earlier, one of the prime uses of a network is to facilitate integration between systems. In a business that is characterized by a high volume of small transactions, integration between computer systems is very important. Often the same data is used for several different purposes, and integration removes the necessity for it to be re-handled again and again to enter it into multiple systems (Figure 4.9). In Chapter 9, the importance of the property management system (PMS) as an information hub is discussed. The computer systems used in most other departments either send data to or receive information from the PMS, leading to increased security and better service for the guest. For example, EPOS and telephone systems automatically post charges onto the guest bill, thus preventing guests leaving without paying. Similarly, guests' personal details can be transferred automatically from the reservation to the registration module at check-in, thus eliminating the need for the guest to give the same information twice. Typically integration helps to enhance guest service by expediting check-in and check-out, facilitating the generation of accurate guest bills, reporting room status in real time, automatically adjusting the temperature in the guest room to the desired level and making it possible to provide such conveniences as in-room check-out.

While the concept of integration between hospitality systems works well in theory, in practice it is often found that the systems being used in the sector (and often within individual properties) do not communicate very well. The phrase 'islands of automation' has often been used to describe how hotel systems currently integrate (or rather do not integrate) with each other. In addition to being highly complex, hospitality systems tend to work off software and hardware that are proprietary and customer designed. Few common standards exist to facilitate communications between systems. Until recently, reaping the benefits of new technologies meant developing custom interfaces between systems, at great expense and varying levels of success. According to Dick Moore, Professor Emeritus of the Cornell School of Hotel Administration, 'Interface troubles are costing the hospitality industry millions of dollars, wasting management and staff time, and holding back the industry's drive to use automation to improve service, cut costs and manage more effectively.' An example often quoted by Professor

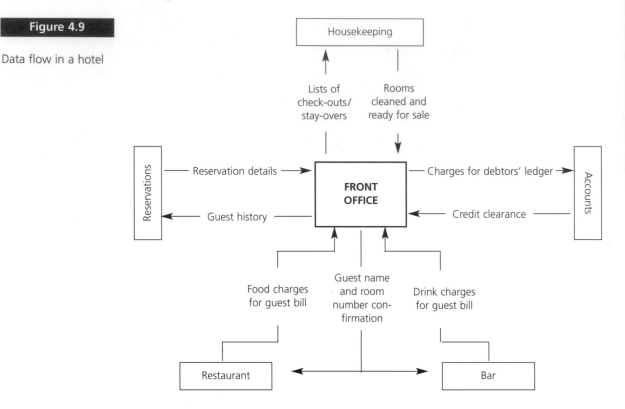

Figure 4.9

Data flow in a hotel

Moore clearly illustrates this point. When replacing the PMS in a 200-bedroom hotel, hardware and software costs could be expected to be around £50,000. However, if the PMS is connected to (say) ten auxiliary systems (such as telephones, electronic door locking, etc.), then twenty interfaces are necessary (since they usually work in pairs). Since these could cost an average of £2000 each, the cost of connecting the systems together could be as high as £40,000, almost as much as the cost of the system itself!

Suppliers of hospitality systems have been slow to try to solve this problem, preferring instead to blame each other for the fact that things do not communicate properly. By locking purchasers into a particular set of standards, they guarantee themselves future sales of upgrades, peripherals and software, as most customers would be unwilling to take the brave step of throwing out an existing system and starting again from scratch. However, there is some light at the end of the tunnel. Recent initiatives by vendors may help systems to integrate more easily. For example, the Hospitality Industry Technology Interface Standards (HITIS) project (now a part of the Open Travel Alliance or OTA), which was set up by a group of large, international, hospitality-system suppliers, is working to develop global interface standards to help reduce the need for interface customization. If this can be achieved, then the dream of a fully integrated hotel system may indeed come true, which should go a long way towards accelerating the adoption of technology by the hospitality sector.

Review questions

1. What is the major disadvantage of storing data on a stand-alone computer?
2. What are the three modes of communication?
3. What is the difference between bandwidth and baud rate?
4. What is the unit of measurement for baud rate?
5. What ports are provided at the back of most PCs to facilitate communication?
6. What is the major limiting factor encountered when linking computers directly to each other?
7. What is the function of a modem?
8. Why is it important to use a modem with a fast baud rate?
9. What are the advantages and disadvantages of using dial-up lines for communications?
10. What alternative type of line can be used?
11. What is the difference between a LAN and a WAN?
12. What is meant by a client–server network?
13. What are the advantages in using a network compared with a stand-alone system?
14. What is meant by a network licence?
15. What are the four components of a network?
16. What is the function of the network-operating system?
17. What is meant by a network's topology?
18. What are the two most common types of cable used in networking?
19. What are the three most common wiring patterns used in networks?
20. What is the function of a repeater?
21. What is the function of a network interface card?
22. Distinguish between client–server and peer-to-peer networking.
23. What are the advantages of using wireless rather than conventional networking?
24. Distinguish between Bluetooth and WiFi.

Discussion questions

1. Compare (in general terms) the use of a mainframe system with using a network, under the headings of set-up costs, expansion costs, reliability and control. Which option is probably more suitable for use in a small hotel operation?
2. A mainframe can be connected to a network, just like a normal personal computer. Suggest reasons why someone might want to do this.

3. What types of factor should be taken into account when choosing a computer to act as a file server for a network? Would the computer specified in the first practical question in Chapter 2 be suitable? Why?

4. Why is integration between computer systems important in the hotel and catering industry? Are the computer systems generally in use in the industry at present integrated? Why?

5. EDI and EFT have the potential to change many aspects of day-to-day operations in the hotel industry. Discuss examples of where these technologies could be used in the hotel business, explaining why these tasks are suitable for automation in this way, and what benefits could be expected from the use of EDI and EFT.

5 The Internet and the World Wide Web

In the last chapter, the concept and functionality of networks was explained. This theme is continued in this chapter, which addresses the Internet – a special type of network, linking computers and users all over the world using open communications protocols and standards. Although the Internet itself has existed since the 1960s, since the launch of the World Wide Web in the 1990s it has experienced phenomenal growth, and now acts as a powerful medium for electronic commerce, allowing buyers and sellers to communicate directly with each other to carry out commercial transactions. This chapter examines the origins and methods of operations of both the Internet and the World Wide Web, and introduces the concept of electronic commerce in general. The hotel industry's use of the Web as an information distribution and sales media is discussed in more detail in the next chapter.

The Internet

The Internet is the catch-all word used to describe a massive network of computer systems, linking users in practically every country in the world. Contrary to what many people believe, it is not, in fact, a single network, but an umbrella term for a series of participating networks that share common standards for addressing and exchanging information. Its origins lie in ARPANET, a network developed by the US military during the Cold War. This was purposely designed to be decentralized and also to have spare capacity and redundancy, so that in the event of part of the network being destroyed, electronic messages would still get to their destination. As a result, the structure (or rather lack of structure) of the Internet can best be described as being spaghetti-like, with millions of computers being connected in a haphazard and almost random fashion, knowing no precise shape or bounds and having no nucleus or central form of control. The lack of formal structure is emphasized by the fact that no one owns or controls the Internet, although a variety of organizations, such as the Internet Society (www.ISOC.org), set usage policy and provide support services on a voluntary basis.

A wide variety of statistics exist about the size of the Internet. However, growth is occurring at a phenomenal rate and estimates are out-of-date literally as soon as they are published. Thus, while selected statistics are presented here, they should only be used as illustrations to gain a broad overall picture of the size and scope of the Internet. Researchers try to estimate the size of the Internet in a variety of ways. Probably the most common method is to try to measure the number of 'hosts' or computers connected to the network. For example, Network Wizards periodically monitor this statistic, and as can be seen from Figure 5.1, growth has accelerated in recent years, with numbers doubling in the two-year period between 2000 and 2002. An alternative measurement is try to establish the number of people using the Internet. Again here results wary because of measurement difficulties. For example, a survey by Nielsen//NetRatings estimated that nearly 580 million people were online by late 2002. Another, from ITU, concluded that there were 655 million users worldwide. Other surveys estimate lower figures, but all agree that the overall trend is upwards. Instead of trying to estimate numbers, most studies now concentrate on establishing the demographics of the net. Most agree that over half of Internet users are US based, although Europe and Asia are rapidly catching up as more people get online. The average age of users is mid-thirties, and is gradually increasing. About two-thirds of users are male, although the proportion of female surfers is rapidly growing. Internet users also tend to be well educated (with two-fifths having college degrees), have a relatively high disposable income and a propensity to spend on leisure goods and services, making them an attractive market for travel products.

Internet operations

The Internet is the ultimate example of a peer-to-peer network, with every computer connected to it capable of acting as a client or a server (see Chapter 4). Communication is facilitated by a protocol known as Transmission Control Protocol/Internet Protocol (TCP/IP). This system of standards controls the way computers communicate, and the use of a common protocol means that different types of computers, using different operating systems and with other technical differences, are able to communicate without difficulty. TCP/IP acts as both an addressing system and a controlling mechanism to help messages reach their destination. Each computer connected to the Internet is assigned a cryptic but

Figure 5.1

Number of Internet hosts 1990–2002

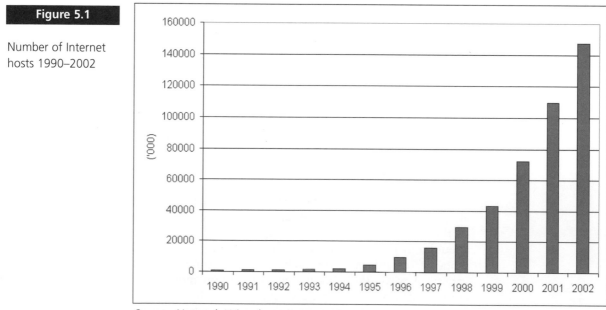

Source: Network Wizards www.nw.com

unique number known as an IP address. These consist of four sets of numbers separated by periods (e.g. 147.252.1.34). However, as we humans are not good at remembering numbers, each IP address is tied to a textual *domain name*, such as *Microsoft.com*. Such associations are maintained on dedicated computers known as domain name servers (DNS), which automatically translate between the two standards. A master list of associations worldwide is maintained by the InterNIC domain name registry in Reston, Virginia and this can be electronically queried by any DNS if it doesn't already know the IP address of the computer being requested. Anyone can register a domain name, by paying an appropriate fee to the coordinating body in their region. Names are assigned on a first come, first served basis, and thus the most logical name for a particular company might not necessarily be available as someone else could have registered it first! (A more thorough discussion of how to register your domain name is included in the next chapter.)

Most people's first experience of domain names is in Internet email addresses. Bill@microsoft.com is a typical example of an address. Most addresses represent pretty much what they sound like – in this case, a user called Bill in the domain name Microsoft.com. The last three letters of the domain name (.com) tell the user what type of organization they are sending a message to – in this case a commercial one. These three letter suffixes are known as first-level domains, and there are six commonly used examples, each representing a different type of organization, as can be seen from Table 5.1. As there are few vacant domain names left in the 'traditional' top-level domains, a variety of additional suffixes are currently in the process of being adopted. These include .biz, an extension/replacement for the .com suffix, .pro which will be limited to sites relating to professional activities and .name, which is aimed at individuals setting up personal sites.

Originally these first-level domain names were exclusively used within the USA, but their use has now expanded to other countries. Suffixes representing each country are also be used as first-level domain names. Although too numerous to list completely, some of the more common ones include .uk for the United Kingdom, .fr for France, .de for Germany and .ie for Ireland. Many of these country-specific domain names also have sub-domains for specific types of sites, for example .co.uk and .ac.uk for commercial and education sites respectively within the overall United Kingdom domain.

Electronic messages (be they emails, files or whatever) are not sent over the Internet as a single unit. Instead they are broken down into *packets* – smaller bundles of data that can be more easily moved around the network. Each of these

Table 5.1

First-level domain names

First level domain name	Meaning
.com	Commercial
.edu	Education
.gov	Government
.mil	Military
.net	Network
.org	Organization

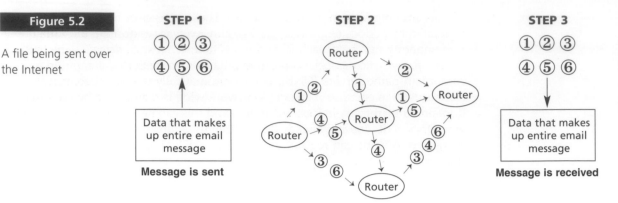

Figure 5.2

A file being sent over the Internet

is individually addressed and dispatched over the network, where it is forwarded from point to point until it reaches its destination, where the smaller units are reassembled to form the original document (see Figure 5.2). This process, known as packet switching, helps to increase reliability, because if a packet is corrupted or goes missing during transmission, only that particular packet, and not the entire file, needs to be resent. Such a feature is becoming more important as the richness of the files being transported increases. Multimedia files tend to be larger, making corruption more likely during transmission, and thus the use of packet switching helps to decrease the amount of traffic being sent over the Internet. And, because each message is split into multiple parts, each of which travels over a different route, the danger of information being intercepted by a third party is very small, despite public concerns about security.

Internet services

As has been discussed above, the term 'Internet' refers to the physical structure and protocols of the global network. This structure in itself is merely an enabling mechanism for a wide range of services – actual facilities that can be used by people connected to the Internet to accomplish particular tasks. These include:

- Email: As was discussed in Chapter 3, electronic mail can be used to send messages to users all over the world. Messages, for the most part, tend to be textual in nature, although multimedia extensions are becoming more common and attachments can be used to exchange files in their original file format. Despite the growing importance of the World Wide Web (see below), email remains the most commonly used Internet service.

- List servers: This service allows users with a common interest to share infor- mation. Users subscribe to the list, and can then post messages by sending email to the list server. Any message sent to the list is automatically redis- tributed to the other subscribers, allowing information to be disseminated and threaded discussions to occur. Lists may be moderated, in which case a nominated individual has responsibility for editing the postings to insure that they are relevant to the list subject.

- FTP: File Transfer Protocol (FTP) allows files to be placed on or retrieved from remote locations. Although, as mentioned above, files can be sent as part of an email attachment, these are generally limited in size (usually to a maximum of about 2 Mbs, although in many cases, individual local mail systems have a much smaller limit). FTP allows files of any size to be transferred, and also allows users to 'anonymously' connect to a site, locate a particular file and download it for themselves. Many software companies use this facility to give users access to software updates and drivers, thus allowing them to be proactive in fixing problems rather than tying up valuable technical support resources.

- Telnet: The Telnet service allows a user to log onto and use the facilities of a computer (usually a mainframe or minicomputer) from a remote location. The service, however, has a very basic textual interface, and is usually only used by technical users for very specific purposes.

- Newsgroups: Newsgroups can be compared to interactive noticeboards, on which users can post messages or files which can then be accessed by other people. Most newsgroups tend to be very topic specific (such as, for example, *rec.simpsons*, which is devoted entirely to news and discussions about the cartoon series).

The ones listed above are by no means the only Internet services. Others include communications services such as IRC (Internet Relay Chat) or Instant Messenger, both of which allow users to send messages to each other in real time and in effect hold a virtual conversation. Desktop video-conferencing is still developing and has yet to gain widespread acceptance, but its use is becoming more and more common. However the fastest growing Internet service is the World Wide Web (WWW or Web) which is discussed in detail in the next section.

The World Wide Web

Since its launch in the early 1990s, the Web has taken the Internet out of the hands of academics and technicians and made it accessible to the public at large. The Web is, essentially, a graphic overlay onto top of the other Internet services, providing a multimedia interface that enables users to access a vast pool of inter-linked documents. A software tool known as a 'browser' and a protocol known as Hypertext Mark-up Language (HTML) facilitates Web use. The browser (the most common examples of which include Microsoft® Internet Explorer and Netscape® Navigator®) acts as a client, requesting pages from Web servers and displaying them on the user's screen. Universal resource locators (URLs) are used to point to pages or files on the Internet. These have a particular format, as can be seen from Figure 5.3. The first part (before the two slashes) specifies the service to be used to access the file, which is usually http (Hypertext Transfer Protocol), although ftp, telnet and other protocols can also be used. The second portion is typically the address of the computer on which the data or service is located. Subsequent parts (after the slash) specify the path and the filename of the file to access. Thus, in effect, by typing a URL into a Web browser or clicking on a hyper-link, the user is sending a request to the computer specified to use a particular service or to open a specified file. The server should then reply with the requested information, which is subsequently then displayed in the user's Web browser.

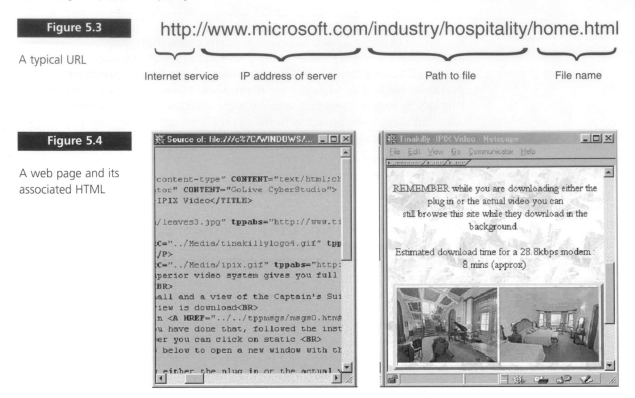

Figure 5.3

A typical URL

http://www.microsoft.com/industry/hospitality/home.html

Internet service   IP address of server   Path to file   File name

Figure 5.4

A web page and its
associated HTML

Web pages are written in HTML, which are essentially just plain text files. However they also contain special HTML 'tags' – formatting codes that tell the browser how the page should be laid out, what text should be highlighted and where graphics and other elements should be placed. For example, they may cause the browser to display a particular piece of text in a bold or different font size, change the background and foreground colours or display two columns of text instead of one. While originally tags dealt only with text formatting, the HTML vocabulary has been expanded to allow graphics, sound and even video to be incorporated into web pages.

HTML also allows words or other objects to be designated as *hyperlinks*. Such links are underlined or otherwise highlighted, and clicking on one takes the user to a predefined related page. This feature means that web pages do not have to be read sequentially. Hyperlinks allow users to plot their own course through the vast number of pages available on the Web – a process that has become known as 'Web surfing'. Clicking on a hyperlink loads another document or file, potentially stored on a server on the other side of the world. This nonlinear arrangement of information makes the Web unlike any other media, as it is the reader, not the publisher, who is in control of what is being accessed.

The use of browsers and HTML gives the Web certain characteristics. First, web pages are cross platform – they appear (relatively) the same irrespective of the type of computer being used to access them. This makes the Web particularly suitable for information distribution as practically everyone can access the pages as long as their computer is capable of running a Web browser. The dynamic nature of the Web, where information can constantly be updated without the

Figure 5.5   Selecting a hyperlink takes you to different page

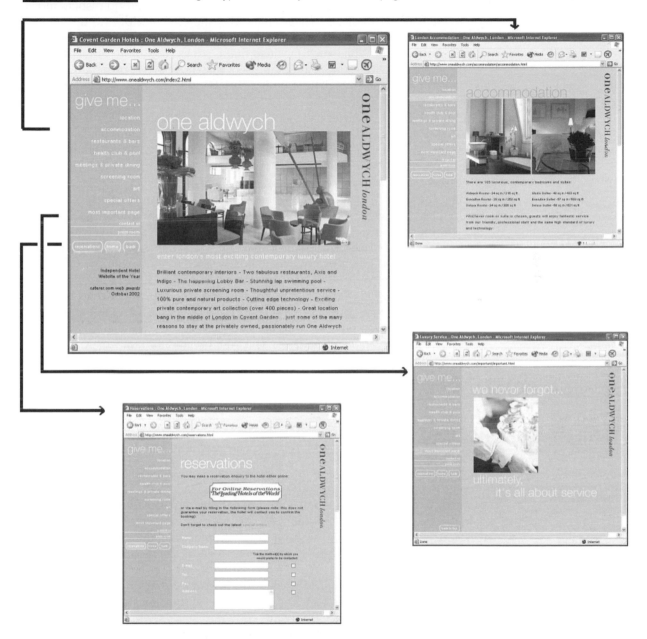

expense and delays associated with traditional paper-based publishing, means that data published on the Web need never be out of date. Last, the Web is graphical, and thus easy to navigate. It is this feature – the ability to display attractive mixtures of text and graphics in full colour – that has made the Web popular as an information medium with the general public.

However content on the Web is not limited to simply text and graphics. Multimedia information (such as sound and video) can now be routinely incorporated into web pages. While some such information can be viewed in a standard Web browser, in most cases additional software (known as a plug-in or extension) is required. Common examples of plug-ins include QuickTime® (to display movie files), RealPlayer® (to display streaming audio and video), IPIX® (to display 360 degree interactive pictures) and Macromedia® Flash® and Shockwave® (to display animation). While such facilities make pages look more attractive, they need to be used with caution, as some users may not have appropriate plug-ins to view them properly and thus would not be able to view any information displayed in this manner.

While HTML is used mainly for statistic displays, interactivity can also be added to web pages. For example, a feature known as a 'Form' can be used to allow users to enter information into a web page (Figure 5.6). What happens next depends on how the page is set up, but the data entered into the form can be processed either on the server or on the client. The server solution involves sending the data entered into the form over the Internet in the form of an electronic message, and processing this data using a facility known as common gateway interface (CGI). A typical example is the process that occurs when a user fills in a Web form to search a database residing on the Web server. The user enters their search criteria into the form, which is submitted to the server. The CGI script accepts the input, queries the database and returns the results to the user in the form of a web page. CGI thus allows pages to be generated on-the-fly, based on the current and up-to-date information stored in the database. However in some cases the data can be processed on the client itself. This usually uses programs written in special languages such as Sun Microsystems's Java® or Microsoft®'s ActiveX®. In both cases, small programs called 'applets' are downloaded along with the web page and tell the browser what to do with the data filled into the form.

Limitations of the Web

Despite being a vast source of information, the Web is not without its problems. Foremost among these is the difficulty in finding information. The Web offers a vast rich universe of information, with several billion pages of information available to be browsed at the last count. As was previously mentioned, it is to a large extent unstructured, with no single entry point or overall directory of content. In addition, each web site is free to develop its own hierarchy of information. As a result, finding a specific piece of information can be difficult for novice and experienced users alike. *Search engines* and *directory listings* help to reduce this difficulty. Search engines (such as Altavista www.altavista.com or Google www.google.com) run special software known as *spiders*, which, when informed of a site, go out onto the Web and come back with information about the location and content of the pages on that site. This is then stored on an online database that can be queried by users searching for information on any topic. The directory approach is different. Web developers submit details of their site to the directory owner, who then decides whether or not to include it on their directory list. Whether to use a search engine or a director to find information depends on the particular situation. For example, a user trying to find information about a particular hotel would probably have more success using a search engine. On the other hand, if a user wanted to find a hotel (i.e. any hotel) in a particular location, then

Figure 5.6	A Web form-based reservation enquiry

a directory listing would be more likely to give appropriate options. Yahoo (www.yahoo.com) is probably the ultimate example of a directory listing, with thousands of classifications broken down into regions and sub-categories.

Another major limitation of the Web is its speed, which has become so slow that some people have re-christened it the *World Wide Wait*! The cause of this drop in performance is twofold. As we will see, more and more people are getting online, leading to more demand for the same resources. Originally designed to cope with thousands of users, the infrastructure of the Internet is now straining under the burden of several million. Second, the information being transported over the network has become increasingly rich. Ten years ago, the majority of information being transferred over the network structure was textual in nature and thus small in terms of file size. Today, however, full colour graphics, sound and even video (with much larger file sizes – see Figure 5.7) are routinely being transported over the same resources, resulting in overcrowding and delays. Unfortunately in the hospitality sector, speed is one of the factors used to determine service quality. Consequently, slow response times (howsoever caused) can reflect badly on an organization's image. While surfers could view text only or low

Figure 5.7

A comparison of the file sizes of different media

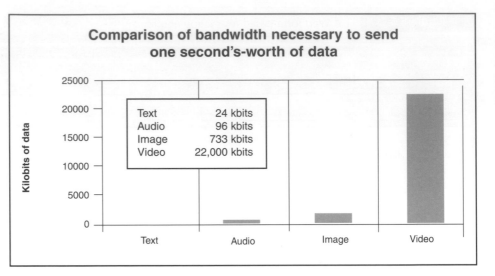

bandwidth versions of an organization's site, the Web loses much of its appeal without the inclusion of the complementary graphics, animation and other elements (assuming, that is, that they are relevant). Better bandwidth for users would help, but for now the challenge is to find an appropriate balance between simple and feature-enhanced pages to permit access to the site with an acceptable response time for the majority of users.

Security is also a concern. Correctly or incorrectly, many people perceive the Web to be insecure, and are thus reluctant to enter personal details such as credit card numbers into their Web browser – a perception that has until now limited the growth of ecommerce. Although, as we have seen, packets do flow through a variety of computer systems on route to their destination, the danger of interception, while theoretically possible, is very small. However, efforts by both the software companies – through their development of encryption technologies such as Secure Socket Layer (SSL), and the credit card companies – with the Secure Electronic Transactions (SET) standard, are helping to reassure the public. In any case, research has shown that concerns about security decline as users spend more time online; thus as users become more familiar with the Internet as an information and commerce tool, such concerns are likely to become less important.

A variety of other concerns also need to be addressed before the Web is completely accepted as a mainstream media. These include how to measure the credibility of information, because as it currently stands, anyone can place data or news on the Web, and distinguishing fact from fiction has become increasingly difficult. At the moment most information is in English which, although the main language of business, is limiting acceptance of the Web as a mainstream medium in many European and Asian countries. Intellectual property and copyright issues also need to be resolved, as most copyright legislation currently does not apply to material published on the Internet. Taxation of online sales is likely to be a major cause of turmoil in the near future. The problem of access is also an issue. If current trends continue, it is likely that we will soon have a society divided by not only economic or social factors but by access to information. Recent figures have shown that 97 per cent of Internet users live in high-income countries that account for just 15 per cent of the world's population. The moral and ethical issues of such a situation urgently need to be addressed.

Intranets and extranets

Two concepts related to the Internet that are currently receiving a lot of media attention are *intranets* and *extranets*. Both are based on Internet technologies, using the same browser technology, HTML and other protocols. They differ, however, in that in both cases only nominated people can access their facilities, in contrast with the Internet which is open to all. Where this closed user group is within a particular organization (irrespective of location), it is known as an intranet. Where usage is expanded to include those outside the organization, such as for example suppliers, customers or other business partners, the system is generally called an extranet. In both cases, the traffic on the private system runs on a secure virtual network known as a virtual private network (VPN) operating inside the Internet but invisible to public users on the same wires. The result is a virtual wide area network, crossing continents, for a fraction of the cost of a dedicated leased line. And it is quick to set up too – all you need are the right configurations and privileges for your users in the remote locations, and in a matter of minutes, they can be up and working as if they were based locally.

As a general rule, companies are using the Internet to make sales – either by improving communications with their existing customers or by attracting new ones. Intranet use is more focused on cost savings and efficiency, and it is the growing realization of just how big a difference that this can make to their bottom

Table 5.2		Internet	Intranet	Extranet
Key distinctions: Internet, intranet and extranet	User access	Publicly available to anyone with an Internet connection	Available to anyone on the company LAN, and carefully controlled users on the Internet	Available to internal users and selected third parties via direct or VPN links
	Server location	At ISP or in-house with a permanent internet connection	In-house on the company LAN	In-house but with external connections
	Information content	All manner of data, some useful, most irrelevant!	Specialized and proprietary	Extensions of proprietary data for ecommerce purposes
	Security	Non-existent	Medium to control access to sensitive data	High, with firewall protecting data from unauthorized users

line that is prompting many companies to start developing an intranet. Information is the lifeblood of any company, and it is important to make it available to those who need it in a timely manner. While many companies already have networks, in most cases these are based on specific (sometimes proprietary) standards, and the sharing of information is prohibited by the difficulty in making disparate networks talk to each other. Intranets, on the other hand, are based on TCP/IP, as discussed earlier, and can run on top of the existing networks, thus providing interoperability at a very low cost and allowing information to be distributed to those who need it.

In terms of content, most companies start with very simple applications such as a corporate phone book, which as a result is always accurate and up-to-date. As the benefits of using an intranet start to become apparent, the mountain of information known as the 'corporate knowledge base' gradually starts to move online. Reports, minutes of meetings, project schedules, marketing plans – every aspect of the organization's activities can be shared with few technical obstacles. One of the first things to go online is usually a company's internal employee communications. For example, Hilton Hotels Corporation has incorporated all its human resources manuals and forms onto its intranet, making them instantly available to employees around the world. And the advent of intelligent search engines makes the management of this information easier than ever before. With conventional networks, finding the file you need is usually a time-consuming and frustrating process, even when everyone in the organization conforms to standardized naming and filing conventions. With an intranet and a good search engine, it no longer matters to any great extent where the files reside, or what file-names they have been given, as the search engine will track down (and probably show you some other related ones that you didn't know existed). All the user has to do is type in the keywords and watch the matching documents come back to them in seconds! Intranets are not limited to simply information distribution. Internal functions can be automated using technologies such as Java® or ActiveX® to allow bureaucratic tasks such as filling in expenses claim forms or ordering sta-

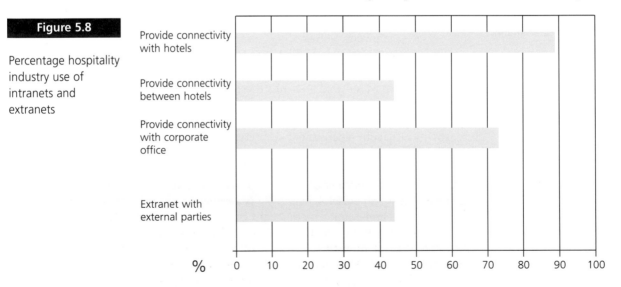

Figure 5.8

Percentage hospitality industry use of intranets and extranets

Source: Hospitality 2000, *The Technology*, NYU 2001

Figure 5.9

Information included
on hospitality
company intranets

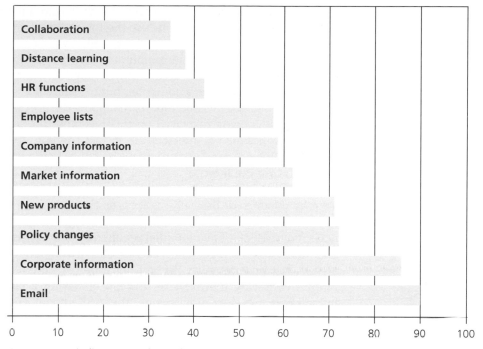

Source: Hospitality 2000, *The Technology*, NYU 2001

tionery to be carried out online, simultaneously eliminating the hassle of paper
forms and converting data into digital format straight away.

Having benefited from the sharing of data internally, many companies then
start to think about the benefits that could be gained by making information
available outside the boundaries of the company – to suppliers, customers or
partner companies. Once again the key benefits are in terms of lower costs,
greater coordination and leveraging the large amount of information that now
exists in digital form. However, security is a major concern with extranets. With an
intranet, company data is protected behind the firewall (or sometimes the
intranet server is not physically connected to the public Internet at all!). In
contrast, an extranet uses the Internet as its communications medium, and while
encryption and other technologies provide a layer of reassurance, worries about
sensitive company data falling into the wrong hands have limited the growth of
extranets to date.

Application service providers

A new type of technology, enabled by the Internet, has the potential to reduce one
of the longest standing deterrents to the use of technology in the hospitality
industry – cost. Investing in a computer system usually requires a significant
outlay of scarce capital on an asset that is often obsolete as soon as you buy it and
whose return on investment is difficult to demonstrate. Computer systems are
also troublesome to install, difficult to maintain and need to be updated
regularly. However, application service providers (ASP) – one of the hottest
technologies of the moment – has the potential to overcome these difficulties and

make it easier to both justify and implement computer systems in hospitality operations. ASP-based solutions use the Internet to deliver the functionality of a software package to a user, while at the same time storing the program itself and its database on a server at a remote location. The software application (be it a PMS, stock-control system, accounting package or whatever) appears to 'run' in a Web browser on the user's computer, but in reality it is simply the user interface – the data input screens and reports that allow the user to interact with the application – that is being displayed on this machine. The application itself, and the database with which it interacts, are in fact running on the central server, with input from the user and the program's reactions being instantly transported back and forth over the Internet.

The advantages of such an approach are many. First investment in hardware for users is minimized. Basically, as long as the machine runs a Web browser, the application will work! This means that older legacy PCs can be 'recycled' and even new purchases can have minimal requirements in terms of memory, peripherals and hard disk storage. Thin clients or network computers (see Chapter 2) are ideal for this approach. Second, software costs are reduced as most ASPs use innovative pricing mechanisms. Instead of having a large initial cost to either purchase or develop applications, the ASP model is characterized either by payment of a fixed monthly fee or by a pay-as-you-use pricing structure. Third, overall automation costs are also reduced, as you generally do not have to pay extra to add additional users – and adding extra users is amazingly simple. There is no need to go through a long and complicated software installation process. As the application is already on the server, simply fire-up a Web browser from anywhere, connect to the ASP server and both the application and your data are instantly available. This means that updates and maintenance are also simplified – just change the application on the central server, and every user and every location is instantly and automatically updated. Compare that to the usual scenario where someone from technical support has to visit each user's PC, disturb what he or she is doing and perform the update. Particularly for companies in multiple geographical locations, ASP greatly simplifies the management of the IT resource.

So, with all these advantages, why isn't everyone using ASP-based applications? The simple answer is that the technological infrastructure in many regions is not up to the job. The client-server nature of ASP means that high speed and reliable network communications is critical. A consistent connection of at least 1 Mbps is needed for even the most straightforward applications, while 10 Mbps is recommended for most users. Anyone who uses technology in hospitality operations on a daily basis knows that such speeds are still a dream at the moment. Many hospitality operations still use dial-up connections, with all their inherent limitations, to connect to the Internet! However, this limitation will become less of an issue as broadband connections become more common. A more serious problem is the issue of reliability. In the hospitality sector, most systems need to available 24 hours a day, 365 days a year. Were such applications to be ASP-based, a breakdown in communications could effectively cripple the operation as both the application and its data are stored at a remote location. If, for whatever reason, the hotel was unable to access its PMS on the remote server, it would effectively be deaf, dumb and blind. The simple truth is that, as they currently stand, communications channels today are simply not fast enough or reliable enough to justify using the ASP model for most hospitality applications. Having said this, the benefits of using ASP are convincing and it is likely that its use will grow in the hospitality sector, although in the initial stages its use will probably be limited to applications that are not mission critical and not so dependent on response time. Accounting, procurement and even reservations stand out as applications for which many of the hospitality software vendors are currently developing ASP-based solutions. Companies such as Microsoft® are also experimenting with ASP delivery of their general-purpose software products, so many of the current limitations will probably be solved quickly. Once the model is perfected, and more reliable broadband networking becomes more commonplace, we should see more and more hospitality software converted to the ASP model.

Marketing on the Web

For most businesses, it is not a matter of whether they should be on the Internet, but when and how! Depending on their objectives, the Internet and particularly the Web presents most businesses with a range of new and exciting opportunities. This section presents an overview of the power of the Web as a marketing and distribution channel.

One of the most important characteristics of the Web is its global market reach. Putting a company's information on the Web gives it unparalleled exposure as it is instantly available to potential customers worldwide – 24 hours a day, 365 days a year. Customers anywhere can access promotional material at a time that is convenient for them, and thus do not have to struggle to contact sales people during office hours. Such material can make use of the full capabilities of the Web by incorporating full colour photographs and graphics, sound, animation and even video, all at a fraction of the cost of producing paper-based brochures. These multimedia presentations can be updated quickly, easily and as often as necessary, which gives great potential for promoting last minute offers. For example, several hotel companies have great success with last minute weekend promotions, which allows Web surfers to book special deals at selected hotels a few days before departure. These allow the hotel company to dispose of distressed inventory and are attractive to customers because of their good value – such offers would be difficult to promote without the flexibility and two-way communications facilities provided by the Web.

The traditional way to market to a large audience is to use a 'broadcasting' approach – essentially to use a single, standardized (one size fits all) message that is designed to appeal to a broad target market. Print and television advertising are common examples of this type of promotion. The marketer controls the content (the information which is presented), the timing (when it is seen), the location (where it is seen) as well as the frequency (how often it is seen). Content is limited by factors such as the cost and capacity, and in any case, the strategy often results in a great deal of wasted exposure. Even when targeted correctly, advertising of this type is often ineffective because it fails to engage the customer. As they have no personal involvement, the advertisement doesn't entice them to purchase the product. Web marketing, however, turns many of these characteristics upside down. First, with a Web presentation, it is the customer, not the marketer, who is in control. Using hyperlinks, customers determine what they will view, when they will view it (if at all) and even the direction and order in which the information is presented. If they don't like what they find, they can be gone in a single click. However, having an electronic version of a conventional printed brochure and other paper-based promotional materials is not enough. Content and format need to be adapted to take advantage of the power and unique characteristics of the Web, and navigation tools need to be included to prevent users getting lost in the data. A web site's content should be relevant to the viewers' needs, easy to use and should include logical links to areas of further interest. Simply getting the user to visit a site once is also ineffective. Its content must change regularly, and must be absorbing enough to make users want to come back again and again.

Second, unlike traditional direct marketing techniques, it is the customer who comes to the company for information, not vice versa. The marketer is not blindly sending out mailings, hoping that they will reach someone who is interested in their subject. On the Web, it is the customer who is actively searching for information. In effect, they are 'pre-screened' because, by visiting the web site, they are showing both interest and involvement – they have a need for information (and your product, you hope) and thus are more likely to buy from who ever best satisfies this need. The fact that they have chosen to visit and are not being compelled to do so (as may be the case with television and other forms of broadcast advertisements) is significant. The Web, therefore, gives a company access to persons who are already predisposed to learning more about its products – a very desirable situation. Even when traditional advertising principles are being used on the Web – such as with banner advertising or push technology – it is precisely targeted at people who have previously demonstrated an interest in the product. For example, with search engines such as Yahoo and Altavista, a user who runs a query for sites relating to travel in Ireland could be presented with a banner advert for an Irish hotel chain along with the search results. The advertising message is not being randomly 'pushed' at the customer – they are actively seeking to pull it in.

Web promotion does not suffer from the size or capacity constraints imposed by printing costs or advertising space. As will be discussed in the next chapter, the marginal cost of building additional pages is very low, and thus, in the electric world, it is possible to include very comprehensive information for a low cost. Furthermore, unlike most other forms of marketing and promotion, expenditure on Web marketing is not used up in a single instance. With, for example, newspaper advertising, your marketing efforts are wrapping fish and chips next day. A web page, on the other hand, continues working for you until you decide to remove or change it. By hyperlinking pages together in an appropriate fashion, the Web marketer can create an ultra-comprehensive personalized multimedia brochure that is instantly available twenty-four hours a day, seven days a week, to potential customers all over the world. This allows viewers to take a customized tour and explore your products and services based on their individual needs and interests – not based on a standardized mass-market sales message. Widely different information requirements can be easily and economically accommodated. Instead of having a single message targeting many customers, many different messages can be aimed at individual customers for a very low marginal cost. Such a personalized 'sniper' approach allows customers to get the information they want quickly and easily and is acknowledged to be more effective than traditional 'shotgun' methods, but would be difficult and expensive to achieve using conventional marketing methods.

Other characteristics of the Web further facilitate this personalized approach. In addition to its potential for 'narrow-casting', the ability of the Web to facilitate two-way communication is a useful marketing tool. This two-way dialogue forms an important component of relationship marketing, and is an important factor in building customer loyalty. Customers can effortlessly communicate with companies to find product information, ask questions or negotiate prices, all with just a few keystrokes. Just as easily, companies can contact customers to clarify their needs or inform them of new products. Features such as email, Web forms, CGI and Java® Applets positively encourage marketers to interact with consumers. Interactivity of this type is high tech, and can be very subtle and persuasive. The computer can remember the individual's responses, which in turn makes it possible to customize the messages flowing back to the customer to reflect their individual likes and preferences. This high level of responsiveness makes the Web unique among marketing media. Perhaps Amazon.com, the online book store (www.amazon.com), provides the ultimate example of this phenomenon. This web site monitors the actions of users and assesses their preferences and habits based on the pages they access and the products they purchase. Amazon then maintains contact with each user by sending periodic email messages, which are automatically customized to match that individual's interests and buying habits, thus helping to reinforce the relationship and making the user return to the web site. Similarly it automatically develops personal homepages for all its users, filling each page with recommendations for products that it feels (based on its analysis of their past actions) will interest each individual customer. This level of personalization has been very effective for Amazon, and it has been facilitated entirely by the two-way communication power of the Web.

Review questions

1. Distinguish between the Internet and the World Wide Web.
2. What is an IP address?
3. How do you get assigned a domain name?
4. What is the function of a DNS?
5. Name four common domain name suffixes.
6. What is the difference between a URL and a domain name?
7. Describe the function of three common Internet services.
8. What is the function of a Web browser?
9. What are the two most common browsers in use today?
10. Explain why large files are broken down into packets to be transported over the Internet.
11. What is HTML?
12. What is the function of a hyperlink?
13. From the user's perspective, what are the three main problems with using the Internet?

14. Explain the difference between a search engine and a directory listing.

15. In relation to search engines, what is a spider?

16. What does a HTML tag do?

17. Explain the purpose of a hyperlink.

18. What is the function of a browser plug-in?

19. Give two examples of common plug-ins and what they do.

20. What is the difference between an intranet and the Internet?

21. What is a virtual private network (VPN)?

22. Explain what is meant by ASP?

23. Why does using an ASP approach allow you to use less powerful hardware?

24. Do you need any special software to access an ASP-based service?

25. Explain why the Web is a superior marketing medium.

26. How does the Web encourage interactivity between the customer and the company?

27. How does the Web facilitate personalization?

28. What type of information is typically distributed through an intranet?

Discussion questions

1. As we discussed in the chapter, customers associate speed with quality of service. On the Web, speed of response can be very variable. What factors determine the speed at which the surfer receives a web page when they try to access your site?

2. The security of credit card transactions has been identified as a major obstacle to electronic commerce. Explain why people might be concerned about entering their credit card details to complete a transaction. Are these fears justified? How could a hotel help allay these fears to encourage electronic booking?

3. Explain why Web-based marketing is thought to be more effective than other forms of advertising, promotion and distribution. Give examples of how you could use these advantages to better market your hospitality business.

4. ASP technology has the potential to greatly reduce the cost of deploying technology based system across an organization. Explain why using such an approach reduces total cost of ownership (see Chapter 11). What factors are limiting its widespread adoption in the hospitality sector?

5. Hotmail is probably the most well-known example of an ASP-based application. Explain how Hotmail conforms to the ASP concept, and highlight the advantages for its owners of using such an approach.

6. Many companies create what are in effect online versions of their paper brochures as their first web site. Explain why this is not a very effective way of taking advantage of the power of the Web for marketing, promotion and distribution purposes. What should they do instead?

6 Developing a web site

Depending on what you want to create, developing a web site can be a fairly simple or an extremely complex process. While developing an extensive, database-driven web site would difficult and should be left to professional web developers, most people are capable of developing something less ambitious if they are willing to do a little research and invest a little time. Irrespective of whether you are creating a site yourself or paying a professional to do the development, a similar series of steps needs to be followed. This section outlines that development process, and provides a variety of guidelines to help you focus on the key issues and ensure that your site works the way you want it to work first time.

The web site development process

Step one – setting objectives for your web site

While it might seem obvious, you cannot create a web site until you first of all decide what you would like your web site to do. One of the main reasons why businesses become dissatisfied with their web site is that they fail to define at the outset what the site is supposed to do and how its performance will be measured. As a result, someone is always disappointed with what is being done, thus no matter what happens the site is doomed to failure.

When setting web site objectives, at a simple level, you need to decide what you want your web site to do. Do you want to have a small number of web pages to make people aware of your product and to which you can refer them if they would like to find out in-depth information about your facilities and attractions, or do you want customers to be able to make bookings (either by email or by accessing inventory and rates for themselves online), or do you want to try to develop a relationship with them electronically by monitoring their online activities and behaviour and customizing subsequent interactions with, and messages to, them? Each of these objectives is both possible and acceptable, depending on what you actually want to do. They correspond to three basic theoretical levels – *informational*, *transactional* and *ecommerce*, which together form a continuum along which you need to position your site. Where you choose along this line will to a large extent determine many of your subsequent decisions, so choose carefully, as making the wrong decision at this stage can lead to problems and frustrations later.

Step two – register your domain name

Once you have decided what you would like your web site to do, the next step is to identify and register your domain name or web address. When trying to identify the most appropriate domain name for your web site, there are a few issues that you need to consider. First, remember than many people trying to find your site will start by simply typing your business name followed by '.com', so if that web address is available it is important to register it. The other domain suffixes (.org, .net) are not as popular and thus far less valuable, although the new .biz extension promises to be the .com of the future. Don't forget the country-specific extensions of the countries in which you are currently located, or in which

Figure 6.1   Searching for a suitable domain name

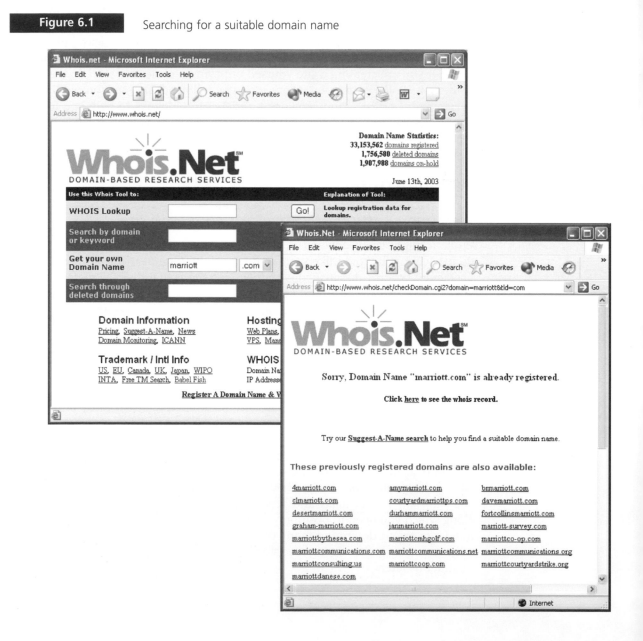

you might be located in the future. Remember that domain names are allocated on a first come, first served basis, and it can be worthwhile registering domain names that you do not need right now but which might be useful in the future. When you come back, they might be no longer available. You should also consider registering common misspellings of your name. For example, companies such as Marriott (whose name is easily spelt incorrectly) stress the value of having registered www.marriot.com, www.mariott.com and www.mariot.com as well as many others. When choosing a domain name, remember that they can be up to 67 characters in length, can contain letters, numbers and dashes ('-') but cannot contain spaces or other punctuation marks.

As was discussed in Chapter 5, Web addresses are allocated on a first come, first served basis within each domain. The simplest way to check if the one that you want is still free is to use one of the many commercial domain registration web sites such as www.whois.net which connect directly to the central repository of web addresses and can see instantly if your desired address is still available (a quick glance through the back of any computer magazine will give you the URLs of many such sites). If the one you want is already taken (as is very likely these days as much of the Web real estate has already been sold) then the service will usually show you the contact details of the person who currently owns it, and will also usually suggest a variety of other similar addresses that are still available and in which you might be interested. It's important to note that you do not actually buy a domain name – you pay a fee to use it for a particular period of time (usually two, five or ten years) after which it goes back into the pool of available names unless you choose to renew it and pay another fee. Once you have found the domain name that you want, registered it and paid the registration fee, your new domain name will become active within 24 to 48 hours – it is not immediate because it takes that amount of time to communicate the new domain name and its associated IP address to all the domain name servers (DNS) throughout the world.

Where someone else has already registered the address that you would like, you can always try to buy it from them. However, with good Web addresses often changing hands for hundreds of thousands (or even millions) of dollars, this may be a little beyond your budget. Sometimes, however, you can get the address in another way. Where you have an existing trademark or trade name that is similar to the domain name in question, and the current owners do not, then in some cases you can get possession of the address cheaply and relatively easily. In an effort to cut down on cybersquatting – where enterprising individuals registered thousands of Web addresses in the hope that someone, some day would want them and to which they could sell them at a massive profit – ICANN (the Internet Corporation for Assigned Names and Numbers – the organization responsible for allocating Web addresses on the Internet) has introduced guidelines for web address dispute resolution. Basically if the address in dispute is identical to or confusingly similar to an existing trademark, if the current owner has no legitimate claim on the name and is using the domain name in bad faith, then ICANN can reallocate the address to the trademark holder. Using this procedure costs in the region of US$2000 instead of the blank cheque usually associated with taking legal action for trademark infringing, gives a result in weeks instead of months and to date 80 per cent of disputes have been found in favour of the trademark holder. However, it is important to note that this procedure only applies to the top-level domain names and getting a country specific domain name still means either buying it from the owner or undertaking long and costly legal action to prove that it conflicts with your trademark.

Step three – build your web pages

Once you have decided on your objectives and registered your domain name, the next step is to create the web pages themselves. As we saw in Chapter 5, most web pages are written in a language called HTML (Hypertext Mark-up Language) that uses special tags to instruct the Web browser as to how to display the different elements of the page. There are several different ways to create these HTML pages:

- At the most basic level, the developer can develop the pages manually by writing the HTML code directly on a text editor (such as notepad on Windows®). Obviously this is a technical and time-consuming task, as the developer must be both fluent in HTML and will have to painstakingly manually check and test his work for errors as each page is developed. However, this approach does have the advantage of great flexibility in terms of what can be done, and certainly many developers use it to make small changes in pages, even if they do not use it to do the bulk of their development work. It does suffer from two major disadvantages – the need for a high degree of technical knowledge (trying to read complex HTML makes deciphering Egyptian hieroglyphics look simple!) – which makes it unsuitable for all but the most competent of developers, and the difficulty in trapping and identifying errors as most text editors provide very limited facilities to aid in the development process.

- An alternative approach is to use the conversion facilities available on many common software packages. For example, a developer could lay out a page on Microsoft® Word exactly as he would like it to appear in a Web browser, complete with text and graphics in the desired locations and hyperlinks to other pages, and by choosing 'Save As HTML' from the save menu, the HTML code for that page would be automatically generated. This approach is perfect for situations where the developer only wants to create a limited number of pages, but again the lack of facilities to aid in the development process make it unsuitable for use in creating larger and more complex sites.

- For that reason, most developers use specialized Web development software such as Microsoft® FrontPage® or Macromedia® Dream Weaver®. These types of packages hide the complexity of HMTL under a simpler user interface, and, in addition to helping to actually generate the HTML code for each page, usually provide a range of other facilities to aid in the development of larger sites. For example, such packages make the creation of frames – in effect mini-pages within web pages – relatively easy and include facilities to check that your pages are technically correct, are compatible with the most common Web browsers and will download at an acceptable speed. Such applications also help manage all the loose ends on your site – a point that becomes increasingly important as the site grows in size and complexity. Most include facilities for checking for broken links – either internal as a result of deleted or moved pages or graphics, or externally as a result of changes in other sites. This may sound trivial but don't forget that the web site is the first impression that many people will have of your company, and if the site is poorly designed and managed, with broken links and indifferent material, it may well be their last!

- One other approach is also worthy of mention. Where the site contains a large number of similar pages (for example on an ecommerce site with a page for each product, or on a hotel company site with a page for each hotel) a database-driven approach may be more appropriate than creating HTML pages. With this development strategy, a single template is created for the common page, with indications of where the textual, graphical and other elements should be placed. The data for each page are maintained in a separate database and merged with the template in response to requests from the users – thus generating the HTML code for each page on the fly. The advantage of this approach is that individual pages do not have to be developed and maintained for each product or hotel. Changing the layout of the template will automatically change the layout of all the pages based on it. And it is easier to maintain the base data using the facilities of the database rather than attempting to update product details on a large number of individual pages every time something changes. For example, using a database it would be easy to decrease the price of all your products by 5 per cent – you could do it with a single database command if you wished – a sharp contrast to having to edit each page individually, find the place where the price is quoted and update each one manually.

Apart from the technical aspects of creating pages, their content is obviously of prime importance. While an in-depth discussion of what you should and should not include on your pages is too major a task to be included here, there are a few broad general guidelines that will help you get started.

Page elements

A wide variety of different types of content can be built into each page. These include the following:

Text   In most cases, words will make up the majority of the content of your pages. Since we write all the time, it's easy to think that anyone can write content for the Web. However creating Web copy is not the same as writing for any other medium, and several issues need to be borne in mind. First, Internet users are an unforgiving audience with very short attention spans, so keep sentences short and punchy. They tend to jump from page to page in no particular order and at most scan the copy. Therefore 'chunking the copy' is essential when creating the web site content. Each page must stand alone, be short and punchy, and allow the reader to grasp the essence of the message literally at a glance. As a result, it is important to break up blocks of text with headings and subheadings to facilitate skimming. Also remember that not all the readers of the page will be human. As will be discussed below, the content included on the page, and the way in which it is included, is one of the key issues that determines placement in the search engines.

Graphics   Some well-chosen graphics add real value to a page, both livening up dull pages of text and giving surfers some visual information. However, they have to be used with care and there is a fine balance that must be observed. A picture speaks a thousand words but that doesn't mean that you have to try to fit an entire book into one page! Graphics should look good, reinforce the graphic design (see below) but at the same time stay out of the way. Size is obviously important! The bigger and richer the picture, the longer it takes to download. Current research indicates that web pages (both text and graphics) should be kept under 40K – a size that takes about 13 seconds to download using a 56K modem and the point at which most surfers start to get twitchy!

To achieve this, in most cases you will need to slim down your graphics, which can be accomplished in two ways – by optimizing their quality or by reducing their physical dimensions. Many graphics are far higher in resolution than they actually need to be for use on the Web. For example, most scanners capture pictures at a minimum of 400 dpi, and some digital cameras have a default setting of 1000 dpi, yet the highest resolution that can be viewed on a computer monitor is 72 dpi! Obviously such output is too heavy for use on a web page, and such images need to be run though optimization programs to slim them down to an acceptable file size. Choosing the correct file type for graphics is also important. In general, Jpg files work best with photos and other full colour material, while Gifs are better at displaying computer generated material such as logos. Reducing the physical size of your images will also decrease the amount of data that needs to be downloaded. One way of using smaller graphics is to position them as 'thumbnails' – small graphics built into the text, which add graphic appeal but cannot really be viewed properly (and more importantly, do not slow down the page download). If a user wants to see more detail on a graphic, they can click on it and it will load a larger, richer version of the same file. Even using these techniques, finding an acceptable compromise between file size and image quality can be difficult, and in many cases it is worth asking what the image adds to the page. If it doesn't add something meaningful, it is often better to omit it completely and save the bandwidth.

Animation   Animations are a step up from static graphics in terms of complexity. Two different types are common. Animated Gifs use series of static pictures displayed rapidly in succession to create the illusion of animation (in much the same way as kids draw cartoons with minute changes on the corner of a book and flick through the pages to see the pictures 'move'). Flash, on the other hand, uses a programming language to create true animation, but the recipient has to have a plug-in installed in their browser to view it. In both cases, the animation can add interest to a page, if used appropriately, but sometimes they can be more distracting than enhancing. A good analogy is that an animation is like someone jumping up and down waving a flag while you are trying to read! And of course, animations increase page size and thus decrease download speeds. As a result, animations should only be used sparingly, and only in places where it is appropriate.

Sound   While it is possible to include sound on a web page quite easily, most people agree that it should only be used in very limited circumstances. The biggest problem is that to generate audio output at an acceptable quality, quite large files have to be downloaded. However, it can be useful to create atmosphere in certain situations. For example, some nightclubs incorporate background music (sometimes they let you choose your own from a selection) while you browse through their site.

Video   Once again the main difficulty with video is one of size – for example 10 seconds of Mpeg video would be about 600K and take about 4 minutes to download over a 56K modem! This obviously limits the usefulness of video on the Web, but it has good potential for the future. Broadband use is growing, which will permit more surfers to view such files, while technologies such as streaming video allow the video to start playing before the entire file has been downloaded, thus decreasing the wait time for the user. In the meantime, it is probably a good idea to provide alternative content for those who cannot handle such large files. For example, interactive 360 degree photos, such as those facilitated by both QuickTime® and IPIX® technologies, can add that level of interactivity to a web page at an acceptable (although still quite big) file size.

Graphic design

You only have seconds to make an impression, so make sure that your homepage makes an immediate impression. At the same time, it should match your offline image, so if you are an upmarket hotel company then the page should scream luxury and quality, while if you target the younger generation the design should

Figure 6.2

Hard Rock Hotel's web site reflects its offline image

project an image of hipness and fun. Remember that in the online world you only get one opportunity to get this right – one click of the mouse and the potential customer is gone for ever. Whatever image you choose, it is important to be consistent and establish a graphic identity – some combination of page elements, fonts, colours and layout that immediately allows the surfer to recognize your site. Think about it for a second – wouldn't you recognize an Amazon.com page without looking at its logo? That just shows you what a good job they have made of establishing their graphic identity! As mentioned above, in many cases your graphic design will flow from your offline promotional material, but it is important to be consistent – in brochures, in adverts, on your web site and in email marketing.

Internal content

One of the main reasons visitors view a web site is that they derive value from the information you provide there. Thus your web site is a prime opportunity to provide a single, one-stop shop for both customers and potential customers to find out anything they might want to know about your company, all without tying up any customer service resources. As a result, you should try to include anything the potential customer wants to know, or might potentially want to know, about your company on your site. Many businesses have found that they have made substantial cost savings by developing a comprehensive web site, as customers can find answers for themselves rather than calling or otherwise contacting the company with their questions.

Obviously organization is a key issue. You should start with general information and become more specific as you move down through the hierarchy of pages. Remember that the marginal cost of adding pages is very low, and that the interactive nature of the Web allows the surfer to plot their own route through this sea of data. Since the surfer chooses what they want to look at, they will never see the hundreds (if not thousands) of detailed pages in which they have no interest. Yet those who need that specific information will find it, and thank you for providing it with their business.

External content

When designing your web site, remember that the guest is not just interested in your hotel – their prime concern is the success of their trip – and you should therefore help them to plan this trip in any way that you can. On your web site, this might include incorporating links to airlines and car hire companies servicing your destination, links to destination sites, links to local attractions and events or building in facilities for calculating currency conversion, seeing the weather forecasts, displaying interactive maps or allowing them to plan their journey with route planning facilities. It is worth pointing out that in all of these cases, you do not need to develop any technology or compile any information yourself – each one of the above can be sourced electronically through virtual partnerships with third parties, and either linked to or built invisibly into your web site.

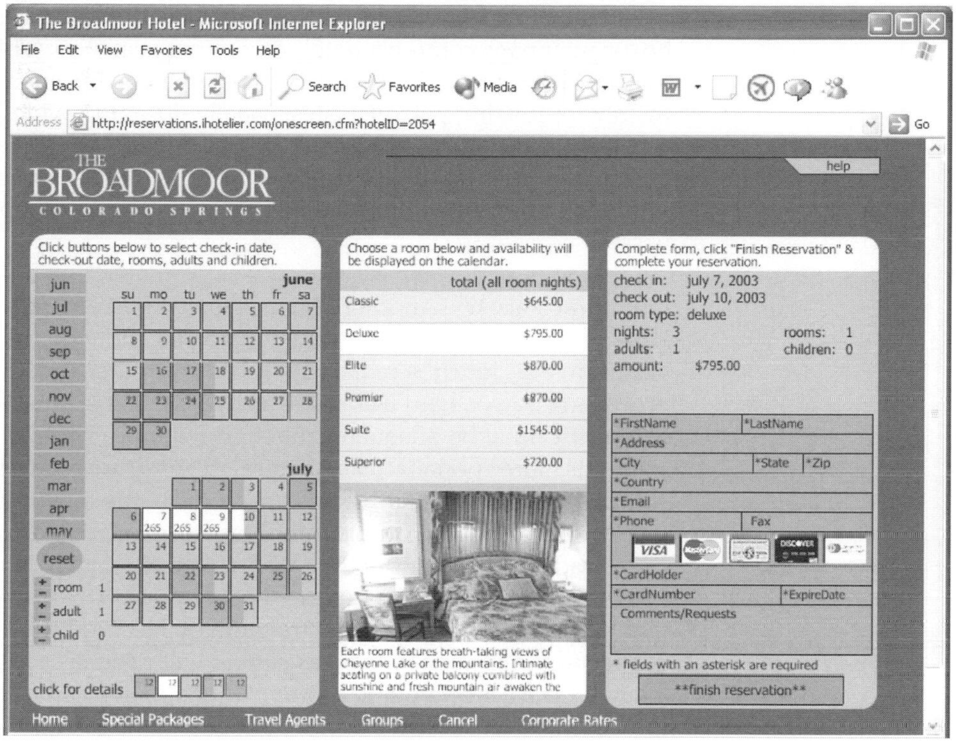

Figure 6.3

The Broadmoor's reservations screen

Reservation facilities

While content is important, when developing your web site you need to bear in mind that the most important purpose of a hotel web site is usually to encourage and facilitate reservations. Real-time booking facilities are essential. In the past, customers would tolerate email reservation request forms and long delays in receiving confirmation of their booking, but their expectations have become higher as they have become more experienced with using the web. Real time, online, reservation facilities (in the language of their choice) with instant confirmation in now the minimum level of service that they will accept, and if you are not willing to provide such facilities, your competitor, just a click away, will!

Step four – hire a host

With your web pages designed (or initially designed, as we will see later), the next step is to find some Web space on which to host them. Here there are three basic options – use free space provided by your Internet Service Provider (ISP), run your own Web server or use the facilities of a virtual host.

Free space   Practically all ISPs give you a limited amount of Web space on which to host some pages when you sign up for an account that allows you to connect to the Internet. Apart from issues of speed and reliability, the main drawback with using such facilities is the difficulty in associating it with your domain name. Although technically possible (using a Web redirect service), in most cases you will end up with an unusable Web address like www.members. hostingcompany.com/~abchotels.com – not really a usable or marketable commercial Web address. Furthermore, most free hosting spaces, as they are intended mainly for hosting personal sites, usually do not provide the database, CGI and other technical facilities that most commercial sites need to run successfully. Clearly this solution is only useful for very simple sites, and given the low costs involved in the other two solutions, is really of minor importance for most businesses.

Own Web server   Another option is to purchase, install and maintain your own Web server with its own permanent connection to the Internet. In terms of hardware, not much is required – just a computer with an adequate amount of processing power, hard disk space and memory. For simple sites, even a last generation PC may be adequate, although for more complex sites and ecommerce solutions more specialized and dedicated hardware may be required to handle the volume of traffic. Similarly software to drive the server is easy to acquire, with most of the companies that produce browser software allowing site developers to download basic versions of their Web server software for free, or to purchase more full featured versions at a very reasonable price. A permanent dedicated connection to the Internet – usually in the form of a leased line – is also needed. Dial-up connections are not adequate as surfers will need access to your server 24 hours a day, 7 days a week, not just when you happen to be connected to your dial-up ISP. All that's left now is the difficult part – configuring the server and keeping it up and running. Maintaining your own server means continually monitoring it to insure that it is online, working properly and serving up its pages at acceptable speed. You also need to update the server software as patches are introduced to fix bugs and close security loopholes, and also may need to scale up your hardware and/or bandwidth as the volume of traffic coming to your server grows. Overall, this is a big commitment, but has the advantage of allowing you full control over all aspects of how your server operates. However it is a whole lot of work!

Virtual hosting   The third option overcomes many of the limitations of the other two solutions. Using a virtual server allows you to have your own space on your own server with its own domain name but frees you from the necessity (and hassle) of running your own hardware and software. Specialist companies run vast server farms – buildings full of Web servers with super-resilient power supply, fire protection and security, permanently connected to the Internet by high-speed lines. Contracting with one of these companies to provide your hosting space frees you from both the capital and maintenance requirements of running your own equipment by providing a guaranteed level of service in return for a fixed monthly fee. Different levels of fees give you access to different levels of service (e.g. your own Web server vs. space on a shared server, more Web space for your pages, more capacity for monthly traffic, faster response times, server redundancy, load balancing and guaranteed minimum levels of downtime), while the virtual server provider can also usually provide advanced features such as database facilities, more advanced security or credit card processing if required. And, since the virtual provider focuses solely on selling hosting services, they tend to be experts at maintaining service standards, and thus you do not need to worry about updating software, monitoring traffic levels or other maintenance tasks. By outsourcing in this way, you greatly simplify the technical aspects of running a site – you just have to specify the facilities that you need, pay for them periodically and let the service provider worry about keeping everything running and connected. Using a virtual server also adds tremendous flexibility. For example, if your web site is very successful and attracts many visitors, you can quickly find that your original configuration (in terms of processing power to service the server requests and bandwidth to carry the resulting traffic) is not adequate. If you were running your own equipment, you would need to go through the expensive and time-consuming process of upgrading your hardware, transferring your site and organizing a connection to the Internet with more capacity. However, with a virtual server, you can contact the hosting company and arrange a switch over to a higher capacity system, something that, because of the specialized nature of hosting companies, could usually be done literally at the flick of a switch and completed in minutes rather than days or weeks.

Step five – publish your pages

With your Web space organized, the next step is to take the pages that you created earlier from your local PC (where only you can see them), and publish them onto the Web server so that they are available to everyone. This can be done manually using file transfer protocol (FTP), which essentially manages the transfer of files from one electronic location to another. However, most Web development packages also provide facilities to help automate the publication process, and to check that the pages published are the most up-to-date available. From the point at which they are loaded onto the Web server, your pages will be available for the whole wide world to see at the domain name that you have previously registered.

Step six – promoting your web site

In the movie *Field of Dreams* we repeatedly hear the phrase 'If you build it, they will come'. The problem with the Web is that unless you tell people about it, they cannot come, because they simple will not know it exists. Actually building your web site is only half (or even one quarter) of the battle. A more significant challenge is attracting (and re-attracting) visitors to your site so that you can sell to them. The more you manage to attract and the longer you can keep them there, the more opportunities you have to build your brand and/or sell your product.

This section explores the subject of online marketing and promotion, and is thus focused on how to drive business to your web site. Although a variety of different techniques will be discussed, it has to be remembered that one of the most effective ways of attracting business to your site – direct navigation – has already been mentioned. Put simply, the most common way that users find your site is by directly typing your domain name (or what they think is your domain name, or what your domain name should be) into their Web browser. For a large number of users, this is the first thing that they will try. So having the appropriate set of domain names (particularly the .com but also the country specific domain names) is critical. Of course this strategy only works if the potential customer is aware of your existence – if they are not aware of you, how can they type your domain name? Many of the other techniques discussed in this chapter focus on overcoming this problem by gaining visibility with the appropriate consumer. The use of links (reciprocal or paid), search engine placement, banner adverting and even email marketing all focus on reaching out to customers and making them aware of your product. But it is important not to forget the traditional media. To reinforce Web use, the site's URL should be incorporated onto everything – business cards, brochures, letterhead, adverts in newspapers and TV and everywhere else!

Links – it's not called the Web for nothing!

Apart from direct navigation (see above), links are the most common way that users find your web site. Because of the way in which the Web has developed, surfers expect to find links to related subjects or complementary products on most Web pages. There are even special sites, known as portals, which are essentially little more than collections of links on a specialized subject area. Their value lies in allowing the surfer to connect to other sites related to their area of interest rather than in the content and facilities that they themselves provide.

Links can basically be of two types – reciprocal or paid. Reciprocal links, as the name suggests, work on the principle of 'You scratch my back and I'll scratch yours'. One participant in the agreement places a link on one/several of their pages for the web site of their partner site, and in return the second participant places a similar link on their web site back to the original web site. No money changes hands, but both partners cooperate with each other to enhance the usefulness of their web sites and provide a surfing experience for their users. Such agreements usually work best with complementary products. So, for example, a hotel might place links on its web site for a car hire company, or local restaurants or attractions. In return, the companies to which it has linked would also include links on their pages to their 'recommended accommodation provider' or 'accommodation partner' or maybe just to 'places to stay'.

Paid links are an entirely different story. Creating paid links is akin to placing an advert in a newspaper, except that there are some fundamental differences in terms of how it is paid for and in how accurately its success (or otherwise) can be measured. With a paid link, you enter into a contractual arrangement with a site to include a link on one or more of their pages in return for payment. The latter can take the form of either a fixed sum (simply for just displaying the link for a specified period of time) or a cost per click (CPC), where you pay a small sum each time a visitor to their site clicks on that link and comes to your web site. The first scenario is similar to traditional advertising, where you are essentially paying to be included, and there are a large number of online directories that essentially use this approach. For example, on BusinessMeetings.com, you pay an annual fee to be included in the directory listing of hotels that cater for the business, conference and convention market. While it is possible to judge the performance of such listings by measuring the number of visitors that click-through, you have no guarantees in advance as to how useful or successful a particular fixed fee link is going to be, and you could just be wasting your money. A more attractive scenario would be to pay based on performance, as in the pay-per-click option, and also with banner adverts and associate schemes as will be discussed below.

Search engine placement

Another way of trying to drive business to your web site is to actively manage your listings on the search engines. When trying to locate a particular site that satisfies their needs, many users turn to their favourite search engine and enter various phrases (known in technical terms as 'keywords') that describe what they are looking for. The search engine then goes through its database and extracts a list of the sites that it thinks most accurately match the question and thus should satisfy the information needs of the searcher. Exactly how each search engine arrives at its answer is a trade secret, but each tries to deliver answers that are relevant so that surfers will continue to use it as their search engine of choice.

The first step in trying to maximize traffic from the search engines is to register your site with the ones on which you want to be listed. Although in certain circumstances, a search engine may accidentally discover your site all on its own, in most cases you have to make each engine aware of your existence by going to the site and filling in a form to tell it your URL (and sometimes some other information about what your site does). Obviously there are a lot of different search engines out there, and registering with each one individually could take some time. For that reason, many people make use of online services such as Submit-it!, which allows you to submit your pages to multiple search engines in one go and thus save a lot of time and frustration.

Once the engine has been alerted to your existence, it will send a special piece of software, known as a 'spider' along to examine your site, try to figure out what each page is about, explore each link on each page, and ultimately put each page into a classification for inclusion in its search database. Exactly how these spiders perform these classifications is based on a constantly changing secret algorithm, but certain factors are known to help increase your ranking. (**Warning** – as this changes frequently, it is best to consult an online source that is refreshed more often than a printed book to see the most current data on what works and what doesn't. Also you need to be aware that each spider has its own idiosyncrasies and thus what will increase your rankings in one search engine may have a detrimental effect on ranking in the others!)

Links Having links into, out of and between your pages is known to help increase your ranking in the search engines. Most spiders examine not only the

Table 6.1	Rank	Engine	Percentage share
Most popular search engines (May 2003)	1	Google	55.2
	2	Yahoo	21.7
	3	MSN Search	9.6
	4	AOL Search	3.8
	5	Terra Lycos	2.6
	6	Altavista	2.2
	7	Askjeeves	1.5

Source: http://www.onestat.com

number of links but also the quality of these links. Thus links (paid or reciprocal) to and from very popular sites will have more of an effect than links to/from a site that no one ever visits.

Page structure   To make life easy for the spider, each page on your site should concentrate on one subject. Remember that while you are trying to sell a product, the spider is trying to classify your page. So focusing on a single issue, and moving from the general to the specific in the text of your page, helps the spider to more thoroughly and accurately work out the subject matter of the page, resulting in more accurate classifications and thus higher listings. So instead of having a limited number of pages on your site, each trying to be all things to all people, you should break your content up into smaller, more compact and more specialized pages which the spider can analyse and classify more easily. And remember that you can still include all the content you want by including links between pages, which will help increase your rankings further, as discussed above.

Word frequency and word placement   Related to the above point is the issue of the text itself. Obviously spiders make use of both the page title and the content of the page (particularly the text) to perform their classification. Therefore specific words reflecting the subject matter of the page need to be included several times in both the headings and body text of the page. Most search engines now advise that you use the relevant keywords 'frequently but not obsessively'. This is because in the past, page designers used to try to fool the spiders by using strategies such as 'word stuffing' – including a word hundreds of times in the background of a page in a deliberate attempt to influence the spider. However, once a large number of sites starting doing this, it became ineffective as the search engine companies changed the spider classification algorithm; now repeating the same word or phrase too many times will decrease rather than increase a page's ranking. The actual placement of words on the page is also important. The subject of the page needs to be present both in the page title and also several times towards the top of the page. And, as your teachers always told you, when writing your pages, always move from the general to the specific, just like writing an essay or a term paper!

Meta tags   Many spiders use meta tags – invisible code from the header section of the web page – to help them perform their classification. Meta tags are not normally visible to the surfer, but they do give the visiting spider certain information about the page. While there are many different individual tags, the three most important are the 'Title', 'Description' and 'Keywords' tags. The purpose of the title tag is self-explanatory – but having an accurate and concise title is extremely important as it is one of the main clues used by the spider in classifying the page as was discussed above. It also appears in the listing of results when the search engine displays an answer to the user and thus may be critical in determining if a user clicks on your site or one of the others listed. The content of the description tag is also used for both classification purposes and is displayed in query results, as can be seen from Figure 6.4. So, once again, accurate and compelling content are vital here to influence both the spider and the surfer looking at the search results. Last, most spiders, at least to some extent, use the text listed in the keyword meta tags to help in their classification process, so each page

The content of your
meta tags determines
what appears in the
search engines

needs to have an individual set of keywords and phrases that accurately reflect its content. This last point is worth emphasizing. Each page can have – and should have – a unique set of meta tags. Since each page is different in terms of its content (and, one hopes, its objective), it makes no sense to have a standard set of keywords – each set needs to be individually customized to the content of the page in question.

Paid search engine listings

While everyone should take some steps to try to improve their rankings in the search engines, investing a great deal of time and effort may not be entirely justified. Most search engines feature sponsored or featured (i.e. paid) links at the top of their search results, so spending a lot of time trying to improve your ranking may not make that much difference at the end of the day. Either by paying for particular sets of keywords, or as a result of preferred partner contracts, large companies ensure that they always come out top of the search results. While some search engines ethically identify these links as sponsored or partner links, many do not and simply integrate such listings directly into their search results. In any case, the question must be asked as to whether the surfer distinguishes between sponsored and normal links when viewing search results, or do they just click on the links that come up first, presuming that they are the ones that most closely match their needs?

Anyone can participate in the sponsored results section if they wish (and of course, if they pay!). Companies such as Overture.com allow you to bid on keywords, or sets of keywords, on a pay-per-click basis and supply their content to many of the main search engines as sponsored matches. For every keyword, you bid a certain amount per click, and your position in the listing shown to the user by the search engine is determined by the amount of your bid relative to those of the other sponsors. Thus it's easy (if expensive) to jump to the number one position simply by bidding more per click than anyone else. While using this strategy is attractive as it is performance related – if no one enters the keywords in question, or if no one clicks on your listing in the results screen, then you pay nothing.

However, if you are both successful at picking the right keywords and encouraging people to click through to your web site, then using pay-per-click can get very expensive very quickly. Imagine bidding €1 per click for a particular set of keywords (this is not an unreasonable amount – for example, at the time of writing the keywords 'Paris Hotel' had a highest bid of about €3 on Overture.com) and having thousands of people click though to your site – this would result in a bill for thousands of euros. Would it be worth it? Of course that would depend on the success of your site at converting *lookers* (visitors) into *bookers* (purchasers) – which you can measure using the log file analysis software discussed later in this chapter. Your conversion ratio will help you determine how much you should bid for each keyword. For example, if you have a 5 per cent conversion ratio, bidding €1 per click would result (on average) in a cost per reservation of €20. However it is worth also pointing out that it should be easier to convert visitors who arrived at your web site through this route (assuming of course that you picked the correct keywords) as they are actively searching for the product that you are selling and thus may be more predisposed towards purchasing in comparison to your average visitor.

Banner advertising

Another way of driving visitors to your web site is banner advertising. Almost since the beginnings of the Web, eye-catching banner adverts have 'adorned' web pages exalting us to click on them to take advantage of their offers. Currently banner adverts are getting more and more intrusive – taking up more space on web pages, incorporating Macromedia® Flash® and other forms of animation, sending floating logos cascading across the screen or even taking over our browsers completely with multimedia messages incorporate both sound and video. However, ever since their initial use, debate has surrounded their effectiveness. Detractors claim that today few people even notice banner adverts any more, and that even fewer click on them. This has resulted in a click-through rate of less than 1 per cent if all the pages on the Web are considered as a whole. But if banner adverts are really so ineffective, why do so many companies continue to use them? Spending on Internet adverts already exceeds spending on advertising in cinemas worldwide and continues to increase at a rapid rate. The simple truth is that banner adverts can be effective if they are positioned appropriately, as will be discussed below. With Web marketing, even more so than traditional print based adverting, choosing the right location for your advert is the key issue.

Banner adverts take many different forms and can be placed in a variety of positions on a page (see Figure 6.5). To place a banner on a particular site, you can either approach the owner of the site directly or make use of the services of an Internet advertising agency such as Doubleclick.com. The latter approach means that instead of having to identify sites for your banners yourself, you give the agency broad guidelines on the types of sites and type of audience that you would like your adverts to reach, and leave the rest to them.

Irrespective of whether you go direct or you use an agency, banner adverts are paid for using either a pay-per-display or pay-per-click model. With pay-per-display, a commonly heard term is CPM (cost per 1000 impressions, M being the Roman numeral for one thousand). CPM is how most sites quote the cost of displaying a banner advert, with CPMs of €30 being typical for mid-popularity web sites. Related to CPM is CTR, which stands for click-through rate, meaning the percentage of people who view a particular page containing an advert that click on the advert. Click-through rates have fallen drastically over the past few years as people become more used to using the Web and more resistant to the charms of banner adverts as a result of over-exposure. CTRs of about 0.3 per cent are now common on many web sites. Combining these two anagrams gives you a third – CPC (cost per click) – effectively the amount it costs (on average) to drive a visitor to your web site. Figure 6.6 takes this calculation a stage further by incorporating conversion rates to show how you can calculate how the cost of displaying a banner advert ultimately ends up allowing you to calculate your cost per booking. Given these sorts of figures, using paid listings on the search engines doesn't seem so uneconomical after all!

Figure 6.5

Types and positioning of banner adverts

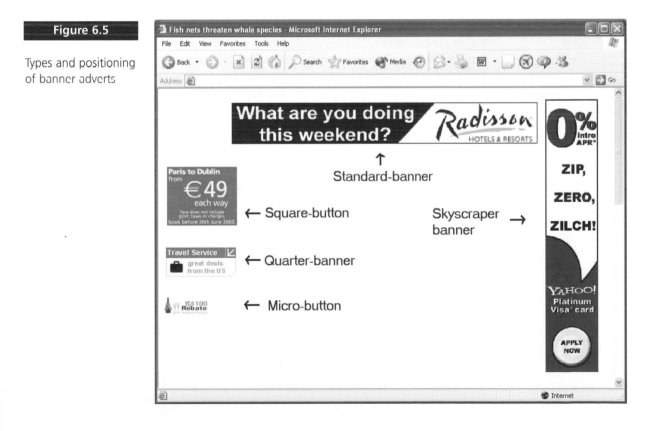

Figure 6.6

Calculating the cost
per conversion

Cost per thousand impressions (CPM) = €30.00

Click-through rate = 1 in 400 or 0.25%

Therefore

Cost per click (CPC) = €30 divided by 100 divided by 4 = 60c

Web site conversion rate (number of lookers who become bookers)
= 3% or 1 in 33

Therefore

Cost per conversion = 60c by 33 = €19.80

So how do you decrease this booking cost? Obviously you need to focus on the three elements discussed above – by increasing CTR, by increasing the conversion of visitors in buyers once they arrive at your web site or by decreasing the CPM. The latter simply may not be possible, as really the only way to do it is to place banners on less popular sites, which although they charge less, would obviously result in lower volumes. Both of the other strategies – increasing CTRs and increasing conversions – depend largely on making either the advert or the subsequent offer more attractive to the Web surfer. Doubleclick suggest the following ways to increase the CTR – using animation in the banner, posing questions (particularly cryptic questions) to generate user involvement and using action phrases such as 'Click Here!' The CTR can also be improved by ensuring that the offer is relevant to the surfer, both by carefully choosing the sites on which the advert is displayed and also by limiting the surfers to which the advert is displayed by careful use of filters. These allow you to specify various criteria that limit the occasions on which your advert will be displayed, and can be used to ensure that only the surfers that you think will be interested in your offer get included in your cost per thousand impressions. So, for example, when placing a banner advert on a particular site you might specify that you only want the advert displayed to surfers who look at pages related to travel to Dublin, or to surfers who have purchased travel from the site before and have already booked a flight to your city. Using relevant filters brings two benefits – they reduce the overall cost of a banner advertising campaign (since properly used, it should reduce the number of times that an advert is displayed) and they increase the effectiveness of the campaign as they increase the relevance by only showing it to 'qualified' surfers.

However, as discussed earlier, the biggest problem with the pay-per-display approach is that you have no guarantee as to the advert's effectiveness. It can be displayed thousands of times (thus generating a hefty bill for you) but might not generate any visitors for your web site. From the perspective of the advertiser, pay-per-click is obviously more attractive. As the name suggests, unlike pay-per-display, where the advertiser pays irrespective of whether anyone clicks on the advert or not, pay-per-click is performance based – the advertiser only pays whenever someone clicks on a particular advert and comes to their web site. While pay-per-click rates are higher, typically in the region of €1 per click, people coming to your web site as a result of such adverts may be easier to convert, as they have actively clicked on your advert and thus must be more predisposed towards your product that a typical surfer.

Associate schemes

Another performance-related method of attracting visitors to your web site is an associate scheme. However, this goes one step further – instead of rewarding other web sites for driving visitors to your web site, with an associate scheme you reward your associate partners only when their actions result in a sale. Obviously this is very attractive for the advertiser – no sale, no cost!

Perhaps the best way to explain what is meant by an associate scheme is looking at how Amazon uses this strategy to get wider distribution for its products. Any web site can start selling books by become an Amazon Associate. Having completed an agreement online, they can build their own Web pages describing the books of their choice, either using their own content or incorporating content from Amazon's site. When a customer wants to buy a product on such site, clicking on the 'purchase' button will take them (invisibly if it is a private label arrangement, but usually just directly) to that product's page on the Amazon web site. If they complete the purchase process, the Associate is rewarded with a share of the revenue generated from that customer's visit. Such a process allows smaller sites to engage in ecommerce without having to develop the infrastructure to handle ordering, payment and the logistics of delivery. At the same time, the parent company benefits from increased exposure – as associates concentrate on promoting themselves, and thus indirectly their parent site – but only pays when the associates efforts are successful. It's the perfect example of a performance-related reward system, all enabled by the Web.

Email marketing

Making your offer relevant is again a key issue when using email marketing. Many businesses now routinely send electronic marketing messages to their customers. These take many forms – from emails promising special offers to electronic newsletters highlighting new developments in the company to personalized greetings to individual customers celebrating special occasions such as birthdays or wedding anniversaries. In fact the ease with which messages can currently be created and sent has given rise to one of the greatest marketing challenges of our time – unsolicited email or SPAM. Named after the pink luncheon meat, SPAM has now reached epidemic proportions and practically everyone's email inbox is constantly under strain. Nearly 40 per cent of all Internet email is unsolicited and unwanted, and a recent survey estimated that the typical email user in the United States receives an average of 2000 unsolicited emails each year, with the number growing rapidly as each day passes. People are drowning under a wave of emails offering everything from Russian brides to domain name registration to Viagra! SPAM wastes time and saps productivity and consumers are starting to react violently to unsolicited messages. So what can you do to avoid adding to this deluge, and more importantly, make your email messages stand out?

When considering undertaking some email marketing, the two key issues are permission and relevance. While it is possible to purchase the email addresses of prospects from a variety of sources, such unsolicited email is not only ineffective in that it wastes resources, but may in fact be counterproductive in that it may annoy the recipient enough for him to actively avoid your product. To use email marketing effectively, you have to build up your own database of email contacts, each of whom has explicitly given their permission to communicate with them. Such a database can be built up in a variety of ways – from offline sources such as Frequent Guest Programs or competitions to online sources such as a registration form on your web site. In either case, the guest should be asked to opt-in – to tick a box indicating that they give you permission to send them targeted communications. The alternative (all too often used) opt-out method, where the user needs to tick a box to indicate that they do NOT want to be included in a marketing database is a trick that often works in the short term but nearly always generates resentment in the long term. In fact, to be 100 per cent sure that consumers do actually want to receive messages, many companies now use a system of double opt-in. Whenever someone initially indicates that they want to be included in the database, the company will send them an initial message confirming their request, to which they must reply if they actually want to be added to the database.

To further enhance the usefulness of the data, it can also be a good idea to allow the person registering to specify the subjects about which they would like to receive mailings and special offers. Given the amount of SPAM that most people now receive, many consumers are becoming more reluctant to surrender personal details, and having the ability to limit the marketing messages they receive to those that should be of interest in important. And finally, whichever method you use to add names to your database, and whatever answers the guest gives as to what mailings they want to receive, the most important thing you have to do is respect their wishes. If they indicate that they do not want to receive promotional messages from you, don't send any even though you have their contact details. If they only want to receive messages about weekend golf packages, then just send them offers related to this theme. Nothing is more guaranteed to upset the recipient than masses of irrelevant promotional emails. Even one or two off-topic messages will ensure that the offer that's definitely of interest to them will be send unread to the trashcan! However, correctly targeting messages generates high response rates. Two per cent is common, and response rates of 15 to 20 per cent are possible with well conceived, well targeted personalized offers.

Another important issue with email marketing is the actual content of the email message itself. Needless to say, the subject line should reflect the offer being made in the email. If you have followed the guidelines mentioned above, recipients have both indicated an interest in receiving promotional emails from you, and the message that you have sent them corresponds to their interests. Thus the text in subject line is a key way to make your message stand out from all the unsolicited messages they receive. Highlight both your company name and the nature of the offer. (In addition, the majority of the current efforts to confront the menace of SPAM focus on prosecuting senders who use false or misleading subject lines for fraud, so watch out!) Figure 6.7 shows an example of an

Figure 6.7

Anatomy of a perfect
email marketing
message

interesting promotional email. The message begins with the logo of the company to help establish credibility with the receiver, and also includes a set of simple graphical buttons that stress the main products sold by the company and can also be used to take the recipient to the relevant section of the sender's web site. Immediately following the opening material is a graphic clearly showing the benefit or 'pay-off' from this message – in this case a thermometer indicating low prices. The main body of the email displays the details of the offer – in this case specific flight combinations in which the receiver has previously indicated interest in receiving. These are followed by a 'Book it!' link – a call to action that not only prompts the receiver to make the booking but also takes the potential purchaser to a unique page on the sender's web site, thus allowing response to this particular email marketing campaign to be more easily measured. Two banner adverts for complementary products are then included, which, with some shrewd business thinking, may in themselves actually have generated enough income to pay the costs of the entire email marketing campaign, and these are followed by the 'small print' – the terms and conditions of the offer. The email finishes with a section that allows recipients to unsubscribe from future mailings, update their profile or change and refine their interest preferences, essential facilities that help to build up trust with recipients and reinforce the impression that they are giving their permission for you to send marketing messages to them.

The sample email in Figure 6.7 is quite obviously a HTML email. As with web pages, this could be written manually in HTML code or generated using a HTML editor such as FrontPage or Dreamweaver®. However, most companies choose to use more specialized packages specifically designed for email marketing when implementing anything but the simplest campaigns. In addition to helping to create the HTML for the email message itself, such tools also normally provide email list management and campaign reporting facilities to help manage the logistics of a campaign. The former helps automate the process of administrating email lists composed of thousands of subjects, automatically removing recipients who wish to unsubscribe or email addresses that consistently bounce. Campaign reporting facilities help you measure the effectiveness of each promotional message, giving you valuable information such as the number of emails sent, the number that were successfully delivered and (given appropriate facilities) the number opened. Such data can be combined with data from the company's web site logs to establish how many people subsequently clicked through to the web site and even how many made a purchase. Detailed data such as this makes it easier to experiment to find the types of offers that are best, as it is relatively easy to establish what works and what doesn't with your own particular set of customers.

Steps seven, eight and nine – maintaining your web site

Your web site is up and running, and we hope attracting customers and (if that was your aim) facilitating transactions. Now is not the time to sit back and relax! Undeniably, the most important factor for building a successful web site is maintenance – not just keeping the site up and running, but also keeping it up-to-date and constantly refining it to make it better. Unfortunately many people think that once a site has been created, it is finished. In fact, that's just the starting point!

To encourage people to visit and return, your site must be constantly updated. You need to continually monitor what's happening and act quickly to refine and improve your site to ensure that it continues to do its job as effectively as it can. In addition, rankings on the search engines must constantly be monitored and managed. Remember a web site is not just for Christmas, it's for life!

One of the simplest elements of maintenance is adding additional content to your site. As we discussed earlier, the marginal costs of adding pages to your web site is very low, so continuing to develop it by adding additional content will make it both more interesting to regular visitors and also more attractive to new ones. Consider adding sections that cater for special interest groups, for example, meeting planners, couples planning their weddings or honeymoons, travel agents or any other large customer segment that regularly does business with your property, as well as developing content in the languages of your major markets. Having more in-depth content than just the regular 'brochureware' increases the 'chewiness' of your site, makes it more attractive to the search engines (and thus may get you ranked higher), helps keep people on the site longer and thus gives you more opportunities to convert them into customers. At the same time, the interactive nature of the Web means that surfers can create their own self-guided tour through your site and can ignore the content in which they are not interested. But don't add material indiscriminately. You also need to monitor the effectiveness of the material which is already there, and make adjustments or even cut out the dead wood to make your site cleaner and more effective. Tools such as Webtrends allow you to analyse the server log files and develop a clear picture of what visitors to your web site actually do. Log files contain a wealth of information – what pages have been viewed (and not viewed), how long surfers spend on each page, the most popular paths (i.e. the sequences of pages that people usual follow through the site), where they come from (both physically and the site they visited before they came to your site), and much more. Information such as this allows you to develop an understanding of surfers behaviour on your site and thus refine both your content and features to more closely match the needs of your customers.

Summary

This chapter has outlined the eight steps typically involved in creating a web site. Even though most readers will never actually sit down at a computer and complete all of these steps for themselves, it does help them to focus on the key issues involved in the development process so that they can discuss them intelligently with their professional Web development team – whether that be technical staff within the company or a specialized outside Web development company. The process is not that complicated (otherwise how would there be millions of sites out in cyberspace created by ordinary people like you or me)? Creating a simple site is easy, and the great thing about the Web is its tremendous flexibility. If you don't like what you have created, you can change it again and again until you get it right, or get rid of it completely if you want, and no-one will ever know the difference. Stop thinking about it and just do it!

This chapter has also briefly discussed the main methods of marketing your product electronically. As has been shown, there are a wide variety of techniques available, and each requires continued effort on the part of your company for it to be successful. When using links or banner adverts, you need to spend time finding and partnering with relevant sites so that your offers reach the right customers. Managing your ranking on the search engines is also on ongoing process, while, to be effective, email marketing requires more than just a once off message. There are of course a large number of third party companies available to help you (for a fee), whether it is to find prospective partner sites for your banner adverts or to try to bump your web site up higher on the list of search engine results. Irrespective of whether you rely on internal staff or outsource, it has become clear that management of your company's representation on the Web is essential. And from the above discussion, it can be seen that the overwhelming theme throughout each of the techniques is that the message presented must be relevant to your customer. Such an approach fits well with the trend towards individual service and personalization currently being seen throughout society as a whole. In this era of electronic communications, a mass-marketing approach is becoming less and less effective and the customer truly is becoming king.

Review questions

1. What are the three most basic categorizations of web sites?
2. Why is the domain name that you choose important?
3. How many domain names should your register?
4. What happens if you fail to renew your domain name on time?
5. How long does it take a newly registered domain name to become active? Why?
6. Explain what is meant by cybersquatting.
7. What conditions need to be true for you to regain control over a disputed domain name using the ICANN dispute resolution procedure?
8. What are the main limitations when using a text editor to create your web pages?
9. What are the main limitations when using conversion facilities to create your web pages?
10. When should you consider using a database-driven approach to create your web pages?
11. What advantages does a database-driven approach bring?
12. Name three different elements that you can include on a typical web page?
13. What should be the maximum size of your web page? Why?
14. When should you use a Gif as opposed to a Jpg to display a graphic?
15. Why is it important to include links for your pages to other web sites?
16. What is meant by a virtual host?

Case Study *Four Seasons Hotels and Resorts*

for quick display but can be enlarged with a simple click on the image. Also on each page is quick access to what Hayward calls 'the pay-off', hotel package information that includes rates and reservations. 'You have to think about how people use the medium' Hayward says. 'And that is why we have links on every page to the pay-off, the packages. You have to make it easy for people to get there.'

At www.fourseasons.com, Michael Hayward, director of marketing planning, has focused on creating a site that takes full advantage of the Internet's strengths while being careful to stay away from cute gimmicks such as flashing logos or moving images that can slow page downloads. For instance, the site opens on a clean, attractive page with a borderless frames set-up that includes three small pictures, a basic menu and a simple 'welcome' greeting.

In the 'Worldwide Properties' section, each Four Seasons hotel is clearly listed on the page by name and broken out by region, so that visitors don't have to click through numerous hyperlinks to get to a desired property. And in an effort to serve two types of site visitors at once, Hayward has included both detailed hotel information for the casual browser and a quick printable factsheet for the travel planner in a hurry. In addition, each hotel tour includes 20 high-resolution photos, each of which is small in size

Hayward has packed so much efficiency into the web site that visitors can find just the information they want in the least amount of time possible. Hayward has even included a detailed meeting planners' section with request-for-proposal capabilities and a customized golf section with pages graphically tailored for golfing guests. 'We chose golf because there is an identifiable target audience and there is a viable online community dedicated to golf', Hayward says. He also sees this targeted, customized Web marketing strategy as a viable approach for attracting spa customers and wedding planners.

The site's pièce de résistance is the welcome sign on the homepage. Each time visitors return to the site after the initial visit, the 'welcome' sign turns into a 'welcome back' sign. This small personal touch is the icing on the cake of an extremely user-friendly and attractive approach to Web marketing.

17. In the context of web-site creation, for what is FTP typically used?

18. In terms of publicizing your web site, explain the importance of direct navigation.

19. Distinguish between recipical and paid links.

20. Links can be paid for using either a fixed fee or a pay-per-click model. What are the advantages and disadvantages of each method?

21. In the context of a search engine, explain the function of a spider.

22. Give three examples of factors that may influence your position on the search engines.

23. Why do some companies pay to be listed higher in search engine results?

24. What are the main limitations of banner advertising?

25. Explain how to reduce your cost per click.

26. What is the relationship between CPM and the cost of generating a single reservation on your web site?

27. Explain how associates schemes work. Why are such schemes more attractive (to the seller) than CPC payment models?

28. Explain the difference between opt-in and opt-out.

29. What is meant by 'double opt-in'? Why do companies use it?

30. Identify three ways to make your email marketing more effective.

31. What is the purpose of a server log file?

32. What is meant by 'chewiness'?

Discussion questions

1. Examine the hotel web site of your choice. Analyse it critically in terms of its page content, graphic design, internal content, external content and reservation facilities. Suggest ways in which the site in question could improve each of these elements.

2. Critically compare the three hosting solutions suggested in this chapter in terms of cost, control and facilities provided. How should a hotel company developing their own web site decide which strategy to use?

3. Try to find a hotel of your choice on the major search engines (www.google.com, www.altavista.com and www.yahoo.com). In each case, examine the first five links shown in the search results. Are these links to the web site of the hotel in question, or to the web sites of various online intermediaries (as will be discussed in Chapter 8)? Using the information contained in this chapter, try to work out why each site has come up at the top of the list.

4. Most people receive a large amount of SPAM email messages. Examine a SPAM message of your choice. Explain why such a message is unlikely to be effective. If all such SPAM messages are similar, why is the volume of SPAM increasing?

5. From customers who originally clicked on a banner advert to reach your site, your cost per reservation is €75.00. Explain the factors that influence this figure, and, by implication, how you might reduce this cost.

Hotel electronic distribution

A profession, no less than a craft, is shaped by its tools. The profession of marketing, its theories, its practices, and even the basic sciences that it draws on are determined by the tools at its disposal at any moment. When the tools change, the discipline adjusts, sometimes quite profoundly and usually quite belatedly. The introduction of television advertising 50 years ago was just such a disruptive event and marketing theory and practice are still responding, evolving their understanding of how the tool works and how its effects should be measured.

The points made by Deighton (1996) in a discussion on interactive marketing are especially relevant today in the hotel sector where one of its most powerful marketing tools – electronic distribution – is developing rapidly. Although traditionally not renowned for its prompt embrace of technology, electronic marketing and product distribution have quickly gained acceptance in hotels. Hoteliers need to be aware of current developments in this evolution if they are to benefit from its full potential. This chapter examines the ways in which information technology is being applied to marketing and distribution in the hotel industry. It looks at the global distribution systems (GDS), whose developers were pioneers in the application of information and communications technology to the field of distribution, and traces the efforts of hotel chains to make their product available electronically, as well as discussing the problems encountered by smaller independent hotels in taking advantage of the opportunities presented by electronic distribution. The distribution theme continues in the next chapter, where the effect of the World Wide Web on how the hotel product is being sold electronically is addressed.

Global distribution systems

Global distribution systems (GDS) were originally developed to help solve a variety of challenges in airline operations. Among the most pressing of these was the difficulty in finding the information needed to book an airline ticket. Although the airlines periodically published their schedules and fares in booklets, which were then distributed to travel agents, finding accurate and current information was a complex process. If a customer wanted to book a flight from, say, Paris to Berlin, the travel agent had to identify which airlines flew on the requested route, and then locate and examine each of their schedules to establish if they had a flight which met the customer's needs. Once a suitable flight had been identified, the travel agent then had to contact the airline's reservations department to see if seats were available and be quoted a fare. Both the flight details and the fare quoted were then passed onto the customer for approval, after which the travel agent had to contact the airline again, reconfirm the details and make the actual booking. Clearly this process of *searching – calling – booking* was unsatisfactory for all concerned. The travel agent had to maintain stocks of airline schedules (which were often out-of-date as soon as they were published) and also had high telecommunications costs from contacting the airlines to check availability and fares, and again to make bookings. In addition, the amount of time which it took to deal with each customer enquiry, find relevant information and make the subsequent booking, made day-to-day agency operations very expensive when labour and communications costs were taken into account. It was also not very attractive from the customer's perspective, as it usually involved a considerable delay between when a flight was requested and the booking was confirmed. Last, for airlines, selling their flights in this manner was far from ideal, as they had to maintain an expensive reservation staff to process enquiries and reservations from travel agents, while at the same time paying commission on each booking – thus in effect paying twice for the same work!

The airlines also had a further problem – storing and managing vast amounts of information. Each carrier had to maintain comprehensive details about flight schedules, fares, seat availability and passenger reservations in order to operate. The sheer volume of data and the speed at which it could change led the airlines to turn to computers in the late 1950s. The original reservation programs were developed as internal control systems – for use by the airline's own reservation staff to manage seat availability more efficiently. When dealing with an inquiry from a travel agent, the reservation agent was able to find information and make bookings quickly and easily using a computer terminal linked to the airline's central database. However, airline managers quickly realized that it would be more effective to allow travel agents to access the central system directly. Therefore, as computing and communication costs both began to tumble in the early 1970s, airlines began to place terminals in their high volume agencies to allow travel agents to search for information and make bookings for themselves. Clearly this was far more efficient that the searching – calling – booking process described earlier. Being able to access the reservation database directly reduced the time necessary for travel agents to both find information for the customer and to make bookings, and also eliminated much of the communication costs associated with the older manual system. It also gave them instant access to real-time availability and pricing information, which led to a substantial improvement in the quality of their customer service. Direct access was also beneficial from the airline's point of view, as it was less expensive to purchase and distribute appropriate equipment to allow agents to access the system electronically than to hire additional staff to deal with increasing volumes of business.

In 1978, deregulation of US airline sector gave a tremendous impetus to the growth of computerized reservation systems. In essence, deregulation triggered the arrival of new airlines and more airlines competing on the same routes. While this ultimately meant cheaper prices for consumers, it also meant more flights, more fares, more limitations and ultimately more confusion. The use of a computerized system was essential to try to untangle the complex web of information. However, deregulation also had another effect – the increase in the number of flights led to increased competition, resulting in a reduction in the price of seats. Travel agents, who receive a fixed commission on what they sell to the customer, were thus threatened by falling revenues. To counteract this, they began to place emphasis on cross-selling other travel products (such as hotel accommodation and car hire) along with airline seats. Having grown comfortable with their airline reservation systems, agents wanted to also be able to source information about and make bookings for such travel products on their computer terminals. At the same time, the GDS needed to increase their revenues, because despite the increased number of flights being sold, there were simply not enough airline bookings being processed to meet their high operating costs. These two factors prompted the GDS to start using spare capacity to offer non-air travel products on their systems. One of the first products to be included was hotel accommodation.

Hotel distribution on the GDS

The initial way in which hotels distributed their product over the GDS was by loading their room types, descriptions and price categories directly onto the airline reservation system database. As a result, this information was available to, and the hotels bookable by, thousands of travel agents worldwide. This was advantageous to each of the participants. Hotels benefited by being distributed to a wider audience, travel agents benefited by being able to book a broader portfolio of products through their computer system, and the GDS benefited through increased booking volumes which helped to offset their operating costs.

However, while listing the hotel on a GDS made it available to thousands of travel agents worldwide, problems arose because of the data architecture of the system. As they were originally designed to distribute airline seats, their database structure was specifically designed to store information about that product. An airline seat is relatively homogeneous – one seat is more or less the same as any other on the same route. The hotel product, on the other hand, is very diverse. Even a relatively standardized hotel with a very simple rate structure could have, for example, four room types (suite, double, twin and single) and three rate categories (rack, corporate, leisure), giving a total of twelve combinations (e.g. suite at rack rate, suite at corporate rate, etc.). Of these twelve different rooms/rates combinations, the structure of the GDS database meant that only some of the rates available could be loaded. This was a major limitation, as the type of rate required is one of the main decision factors used by travel agents and their clients. For example, if the client requires a corporate, government or promotional rate, and one is not listed on the system, the hotel will not be included in the initial search results and thus will be eliminated from further consideration.

The rigid database structure also limited the hotel from a marketing perspective. For example, after the initial search described above, travel agents usually 'drill down' to see a more detailed description of each hotel that catches their attention. This second screen is, in effect, like an advertisement, and is particularly important, as this is how a property differentiates itself from its competitors. However, the database structure greatly constrained such efforts as it only allowed very limited information about the product itself to be stored. As a result, the detailed descriptions necessary to effectively portray a property or to describe a package could not be incorporated onto the system. Furthermore, because of the space restrictions, simplified, abbreviated and truncated descriptions often

```
DENVER INTL ARPT CO 20FEB-21FEB 1NT 1 ADULT M1
8 HY REGENCY DENVER $6 C 1750 WELTON STREET 22SW L
USD  A1K - 170.00 A2D - 170.00 BUS - 185.00 CLB -
195.00  COR - 160.00 SEN - 128.00 GOV - 68.87 TVL -
80.00
```

had to be used, frequently to the point where product differentiation and even clarity were sacrificed.

Aside from the lack of flexibility, hotels also experienced problems in getting information into the database in the first place. Loading data was relatively technical, as each system used different protocols and syntax and thus each system had to be maintained separately. In many cases, the data to be loaded already existed in computerized form, but needed to be converted and reformatted to fit the structural requirements of the GDS database. As a result, many hotels used third party services to handle updates for them, which further increased the cost of using a GDS as a distribution channel. Updating data was also time-consuming, often resulting in a long lead time between when the hotel wanted to change a piece of data and when it appeared live on the system. This meant that hotels could not make effective use of the GDS as a channel for distributing special packages and promotions unless they were fed into the system several months in advance.

These three problems – limited number of rates displayed, inadequate descriptions and lack of special offers – meant that travel agents did not have complete confidence in the hotel information provided by the GDS. In particular, the fact that all the rates available in a particular property were not displayed led travel agents to mistrust the computer system, as they were often quoted different availability and prices when they telephoned either the hotel's central reservations office or the hotel directly. As a result, travel agents did not use their systems to book hotel rooms to the same extent as with airline seats, and much of the potential of listing hotels on the GDS was being lost. Although the GDS subsequently undertook massive renovations of their hotel sales modules to address these problems, it was too late. Having struggled for so long to fit multiple rates, unstandardized room types and descriptions of diverse services into the highly rigid database structure of the GDS, everyone agreed that the continued development of the GDS databases to accommodate hotel data would be impractical. An alternative strategy was proposed. Rather than loading hotel products onto the GDS, the hotel companies began to develop their own separate computerized systems with a database structure more appropriate to the hotel product, and subsequently linked these systems electronically to the GDS to provide access to the powerful and valuable travel agent market.

Hotel central reservations offices

The growth of travel in the 1960s, which prompted airlines to develop computerized reservation systems, put similar pressures on hotels. Individual properties were receiving growing numbers of telephone calls, letters and telexes from potential customers wanting to book accommodation. Large clerical squads were needed to sort mail, type letters, send telegrams and handle other requests. Bottlenecks were frequent, administration costs were sky-high and experienced staff were in short supply.

An opportunity for rationalization was recognized by many of the American hotel chains. They noted the inefficiencies of the existing system and determined that the best way to serve the customer, and at the same time provide a valuable service to their member hotels, was to centralize the reservations function into central reservation offices (CROs). These functioned in a similar manner to the reservations offices operated by the airlines, except of course that the product being sold was hotel rooms, not airline seats. The CRO kept track of the rates, availability, special packages, negotiated rates and descriptions of each property, and allowed customers to book any room in the chain by contacting a single central location. The booking process was further simplified by the introduction of toll-free telephone services in the United States in the mid-1960s, which allowed potential customers to make a single free telephone call to enquire about and book any of the chain's hotels anywhere in the world. The UK-based budget hotel group Travelodge provided a good example of how a CRO could operate efficiently. In all its marketing, the group published only a single toll-free number that connected the customer (whether a travel agent or independent traveller) to the central reservations office. Individual reservation numbers for each property were not published and individual lodges did not handle advanced reservations, instead referring all enquires to the CRO. In this way, reservations staff and operating costs on a group basis were kept to a minimum. Particularly interesting was its philosophy of never being full. Should the particular lodge requested not have rooms available, accommodation was automatically offered at a nearby alternative. Today's call centre technology also allows the level of customer service to be greatly enhanced. Before picking up the phone, the telesales agent can have access to detailed information about the caller's past history and spending, future reservations, demographic data and even links to promotional material that the customer has already received, all of which can be used to personalize the service provided to a very high level.

Centralizing the reservation function also brings other advantages. Bottlenecks are reduced while, at the same time, reservations agents are used more intensively than they would be at unit level as centralization helped to average out the busy and slack periods. A more professional level of customer service is possible because of the use of dedicated, well-trained staff, and service quality is also more consistent as centralization makes it easier to monitor and control. Overall the lesson is clear: a centralized booking environment is faster, more efficient and, if well designed, far more economical to operate than unit level reservation offices. Only two major costs remained; telecommunications, as the CRO had to pay for the provision of the toll-free service; and the labour cost of the reservations agents needed to answer phones and process other enquires. It didn't take companies long to work out that these too could be reduced by allowing customers direct access to their systems electronically.

Computerized reservation systems

Initially, central reservations agents processed bookings by checking on 'availability blackboards' displayed on the walls of the centre, or in massive books which were updated by hand. However, as booking volumes grew, these manual operating methods were quickly overwhelmed and hotel companies introduced computers to help manage the increasing workload. By developing their own systems, hotel companies gave themselves both the opportunity and the flexibility to make the systems more closely match the requirements of the hotel product. Free from the constraints of the GDS, the new systems were capable of incorporating extensive product details written in full, abbreviation-free English, along with an unlimited number of rates and room types. These developments made the systems far more effective as both an informative and marketing tool, as they gave the hotelier the opportunity to differentiate based on product quality and features and just not on price.

Travel agents also benefited from the development of CROs and CRSs. Traditionally, they had used published travel guides such the *ABC Guide* to find information when looking for a hotel to meet a guest's needs and budget. While these provide considerable information on facilities, etc., they rarely showed accurate room rates, as they are published infrequently and would become outdated too quickly. As a result, travel agents had to contact the hotel directly to determine rates and availability, which usually involved expensive long distance telephone calls. The advent of the CRO, which provided a toll-free number to find information about and to make bookings in any hotel in a chain, greatly helped to reduce costs and encourage the booking of hotel rooms by travel agents. However, as travel agents were already familiar with the use of computer systems for information search and booking purposes as a result of their use of airline reservation systems, it was logical that hotel rooms be made available in the same way. From the travel agent's perspective, the cost of finding information and processing a booking electronically is much lower. Using an electronic system, a travel agent with a client flying to Glasgow can check availability in hotels in the area on the required dates, see what room rates each is offering and make a booking in seconds and at minimal cost. Making the same booking manually would involve several long distance phone calls and possibly a fax to confirm the details, which together with the time expended would probably make the transaction unprofitable. In monetary terms, Thomas Cook estimate that the cost of making a hotel booking over the telephone is approximately £3, as opposed to 76p to reserve the same room electronically. As a result, many agencies now actively discourage their staff from using manual search and booking methods, and operations not available on computerized systems lose out. Furthermore demand for hotel rooms from travel agents has also increased as a result of commission caps introduced by the major airlines. Travel agents have had to look for additional sources of income, and hotel sales, particularly at the luxury end of the market, are a convenient complementary product. Thus hotels not represented on electronic channels risk losing out on these incremental sales.

Figure 7.2	`**HOC INSIDE AVAILABILITY** WELCOME TO HYATT ...COME`
	`ON IN`
A typical listing on	
the hotel CRS	`REF USD RATE HY 09962 REGENCY DENVER`

```
**HOC INSIDE AVAILABILITY** WELCOME TO HYATT ...COME
ON IN

REF USD RATE HY 09962 REGENCY DENVER
1 185.00 RACK/CORPORATE REGENCY CLUB
      DLUX RM W/ KING OR 2 DBL BEDS ON 25TH FLOOR W/
      MOUNTAIN OR CITY VIEWS WORK DESK 25 INCH TV FULL
      BRKFST MON-FRI

2 160.00 RACK/CORPORATE HYATT GUEST ROOM
      SUPERIOR RM W/ KING OR 2 DBL BEDS LOCATED ON
      FLOORS 4-20

3 175.00 RACK/CORPORATE BUSINESS PLAN
      DLUX RM COMP BKFST COFFEE MAKER IN-ROOM FAX
      MACHINE IRON W/BOARD AND BUSINESS CENTRE
```

Levels of GDS connectivity

While many of the processes and data which travel agents needed to be able to book hotels electronically were already present on the reservation systems, it obviously wasn't feasible to place terminals in each travel agency as had happened with the airline systems. The solution lay in developing a link between the new hotel reservation systems and the GDSs. In this way, travel agents could access the hotel products electronically through their existing terminals without encountering the database structure problems noted earlier, and the hotel chains didn't have to make massive investments to develop their own distribution network.

Several different levels of connectivity are possible. These are differentiated by both the speed at which they can return a confirmation code to the person making the booking and by where the data being displayed is actually stored.

* The lowest level of connectivity is known as *manual*. In this case, the hotel product descriptions and rates are hosted on the GDS database as in the scenario discussed earlier. Travel agent bookings are handled using a series of manually processed electronic requests and responses commonly known as queues. These are basically electronic messages that are sent to a GDS terminal located in the hotel chain's CRO. The reservation agent examines each booking request, checks availability, makes the booking and returns another electronic message containing a confirmation code back to the travel agent, with the speed of response depending, to a large extent, on staff efficiency at the CRO. Obviously this is a very basic level of (non-electronic) connectivity which can result in considerable delays for the travel agent, and is also inefficient from the hotel chain's point of view as it involves process-ing reservation in two places – on the GDS and on their own internal reservations system.

- *Type B* connectivity is more advanced in that the process is automated and the travel agent receives a confirmation number directly from the hotel chain's CRS without human intervention. A further enhancement is known as *Type A*, where the confirmation is received within seven seconds. This speedy response means that the travel agents know that the booking will be confirmed while their customer is still present, and thus they are far more likely to book hotels offering this at least level of connectivity. In both of the latter cases, the description data and rates are still stored on the GDS database, with the hotel CRS computer only being contacted to check availability, make the booking and generate the confirmation number. As a result, only the abbreviated descriptions and limited number of rates hosted on the GDS are available to the travel agent.

- Seamless connectivity, the highest level of connectivity currently available, solves this problem. In this mode, the GDS database is no longer used, and all the data displayed on the travel agent terminal has been instantly and automatically extracted from the hotel CRS. It allows the travel agent to see directly into the hotel chain's CRS – in effect using the GDS as a form of electronic gateway. This is a huge step forward as it eliminates the truncated description, limited number of rates and confidence issues discussed earlier. Comprehensive product descriptions can be displayed on the travel agent terminal, which allows hotels to market themselves based on their product merits, rather than on price alone. Also, as it draws information from the hotel's CRS, seamless connectivity permits a complete listing of the rates available. This helps eliminate the mistrust that travel agents have traditionally felt in relation to hotel GDS data. Now the availability and rate data shown on their screens is exactly the same as that at the CRO, and there is no point in phoning the CRO in an effort to obtain a lower rate. In addition, seamless connectivity eliminates the problem of having to update multiple databases, thus decreasing both costs and the chances of error.

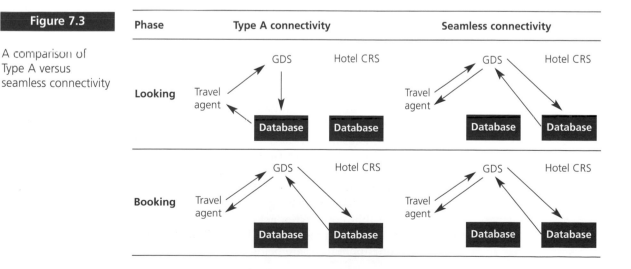

Figure 7.3

A comparison of Type A versus seamless connectivity

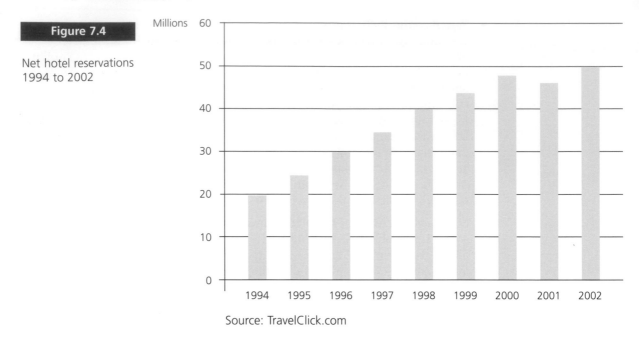

Net hotel reservations
1994 to 2002

Source: TravelClick.com

Each of the major GDS has implemented the ability to offer seamless connectivity on its system. The net result of this and the other enhancements discussed earlier is significant and sustained growth in the number of hotel reservations processed over the GDS, to the point where for many companies it has become a mainstream channel of distribution.

The allocation issue

A key issue with CRO and CRS operation is where to store the room inventory. Most hotel chains have traditionally chosen to let the actual inventory reside at the property level, with an allocation or some sort of free sale status available at the central level that permits bookings to be made. With this system, each hotel makes a certain number of rooms on each date available to the CRO. The central office therefore doesn't have to contact the unit to check availability every time there is a booking request. The potential rooms are 'blocked' at the property level and are effectively regarded as already sold. This system has always been unpopular and problematic. Unless it is closely monitored, there can be synchronization difficulties; for example, if a CRO hasn't managed to fill its allocation, then the possibility exists that rooms can be available while reservations are being denied at the unit level. Similarly, if high occupancies are expected and the unit manager reduces or eliminates the allocation, there is a risk that bookings could be denied at the central office while rooms are still available at the unit level. Problems also arise with regard to rates. Allocated rooms are essentially sold at a predetermined price, regardless of market fluctuations after the allocation is initially made. As a result, prices can vary depending on where the customer contacts, and many discovered that they could often get better rates by phoning the property directly than they could through the CRO or through their travel agent, or vice versa.

Two different approaches are being used as possible solutions to the 'allocation problem'. The first is to develop bidirectional interfaces that automate communications between the CRS and the unit level PMS to facilitate keeping the two databases in synch. When a room night is booked through the CRS, the individual property's database is automatically notified and updated. Likewise, each time a reservation is booked directly at the property, the CRO is updated. As a result, the chances of underselling or overselling a property are significantly reduced. The major obstacle to this strategy is the proliferation of different PMS packages used by most hotel groups. This diversity makes the development of such interfaces impractical. Until each chain chooses and implements a standard PMS configuration in all its units, this arrangement is unlikely to become commonplace. An alternative, and possibly more efficient, method of achieving the same goal is the use of 'single image inventory'. Instead of having separate reservations databases at the CRO and the unit property level, many CRS and PMS are being re-engineered to share the same room inventory database, usually located at the CRO level. All reservations are maintained on the CRS, and arrival details are automatically downloaded to the PMS on a nightly basis. Property level staff can either access the CRS to process inquiries and take bookings, or else can take advantage of developments in telecommunications technology to transparently re-route the caller to the CRO. The major advantage of single image inventory is that since everyone (property level reservations staff, the CRO and even travel agents through the CRS/GDS) is effectively working with the same data, systems can never become unsynchronized. Thus the last room can be sold equally well to a walk-in guest at the property, to someone on the telephone at the CRO or even to the travel agent over the GDS, and always at the correct price! Single image inventory also has the advantage that resources are not wasted in maintaining multiple databases. Changing rates and updating descriptions on a variety of different systems is time-consuming, and with each additional database, there is increased chance of error. With single image inventory, information is updated once on a single database and is immediately available to everyone.

The management of inventory at group level allows some very interesting yield management tactics to be used, particularly where the hotels are located near to one another geographically, and facilitates the collection and maintenance of important management information. The centralized database forms a vast data resource, which offers interesting opportunities for analysis and reporting. Consolidation of company-wide data allows management to easily track local, regional and global performance, trends and preferences. The latest data mining techniques can be used to compile precise marketing, sales and operational reports, such as, for example, travel agent tracking (by individual hotel, city, region and total corporate). The warehouse can also be used to support chain-wide guest history/customer loyalty schemes, not just for individuals but also for companies and intermediaries. For example, a detailed breakdown of the number of room nights sold, the percentage of cancellations and no-shows, and the average rate at which bookings are made can be found for each bulk purchaser with which the company does business – not just for an individual property but across the chain as a whole. This information on the customer's previous pattern if business gives the company fantastic bargaining power when negotiating rates or commissions. It's not just the upmarket chains that are taking advantage of this opportunity. Cendant Corporation, whose brands include Days Inns, Howard Johnson, Knights Inns, Ramada, and Super 8 spent nearly €75 million on a project to equip each of their properties with a standard PMS connected to a central system with reservations, data warehousing and reporting facilities, all with the objective of mining the subsequent data resource.

Reservation systems operation

Irrespective of whether the reservation is being made at the unit or the central level, the method of actually processing the reservation is relatively standard. The process starts with an availability enquiry. The date of arrival needed is entered, along with the type(s) of room and the number of nights required. The system will respond by displaying room availability for the requested period and, on some systems, the rate to be offered to the client. If the requested accommodation is unavailable, the system may allow overbooking up to predetermined limits.

If rooms are available, the client's name, address and telephone number are entered, along with details such as method of payment, the source of business and any special requirements. Utilities to help speed up the reservation process may be provided. For example, some systems allow the zip or postal code to be entered first: from this most of the address can be filled in automatically by the computer, and only minor details such as the street number need to be edited. Similarly, if the guest has stayed in the hotel before, or is a member of the chain's loyalty club, such details may be automatically drawn from the guest history system. When all the details have been entered, a confirmation number is generated by the reservation system, which the guest can quote if the reservation needs to be changed at a later date. An individually addressed letter, fax or email, confirming the details of the reservation, is later generated as part of the night audit.

Figure 7.5

A reservation inquiry screen

Room Availability / Rate Details for Falmouth Beach Resort Hotel

Availability for Sailing Weekend (Single/Double/Extra/Child)

Room	Saturday 13/02/99	Sunday 14/02/99
Standard–Double	110/220/110/25	110/220/110/25
Standard–Twin	110/220/110/25	110/220/110/25

Offerable Rates

Negotiated Rates

Packages: Sailing Weekend

Arrival Date: 13/02/99 # Adults (11 & Over): 2 # Children (Under 11): 0 # Nights: 2 # Rooms: 1

Rate Detail for

Date	Description	Single	Double	XP Chg	Child Chg	Quantity	Total
13/02/99	Sailing Weekend – Standard – Double	.00	220.00	.00	.00	1	220.00
14/02/99	Sailing Weekend – Standard – Double	.00	220.00	.00	.00	1	220.00

OK   Ignore   Pkg Features   Currency: British Pound   Total Charges: 440.00

Call Tracking   06/02/99   13:52

Figure 7.6

A typical reservation
entry screen

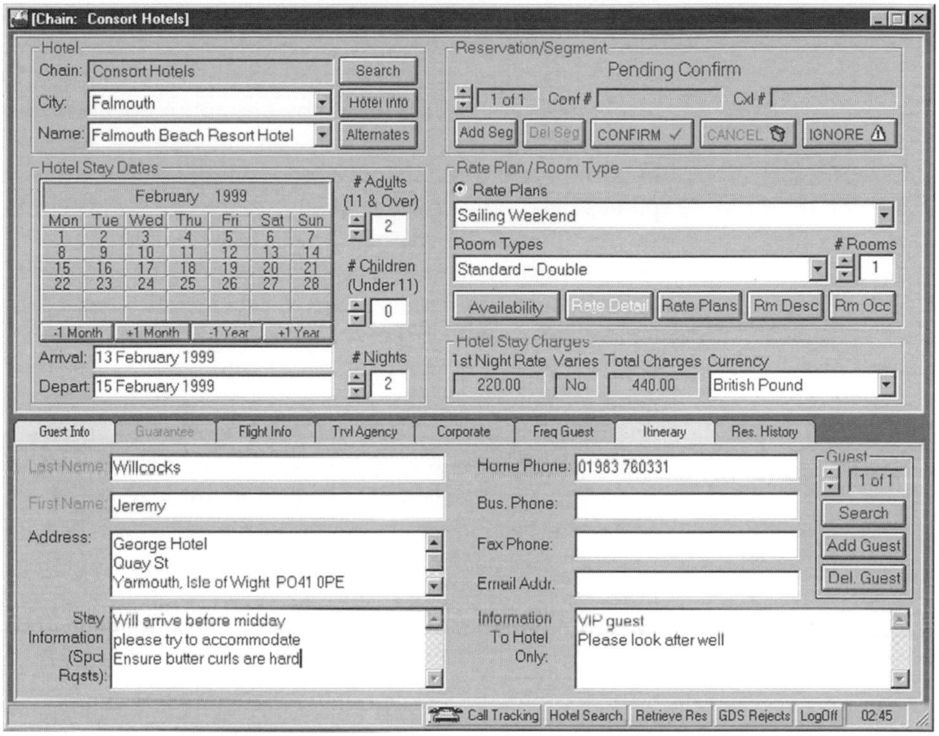

Most systems also accept group reservations, which operate in a slightly differ-ent manner. First of all, a master reservation is set up with the group details and a block of rooms is allocated to the group. A special rate for the group may be offered and programmed into the system. Special accounting instructions (such as billing a master folio for all accommodation and breakfast charges and the individual room folios for all other charges) can also be set up at this stage, thus helping to eliminate unnecessary work for the front-office staff. Individual group members can then make their own reservations, and are allocated rooms from the reserved block.

Switch companies

As we have seen, connectivity has become a competitive necessity for most hotel chains. Travel agents have rapidly come to expect that hotel products are available on their computerized systems, and are increasingly basing their buying decisions on the detailed information they find there. However, it is both expensive and technical to interface a CRS with the GDS computer systems. Recent estimates put the cost of developing just the software portion of such a link at approxi-mately € 250,000. While developing a link with just one of the major GDS might be operationally and financially feasible for larger hotel companies, links with each of the big four (Sabre, Amadeus, Galileo International and Worldspan) are needed to ensure maximum exposure in the worldwide marketplace. To do this, of course, would be prohibitively expensive as it would entail four times the cost and technical headaches.

To overcome this problem, two companies; THISCO (The Hotel Industry Switching Company) and Wizcom developed similar concepts of a universal switch – a bidirectional interface between the airline GDS and any hotel central reservation system. Transactions are automatically 'translated' by the switch so that there is compatibility between the systems. As a result, instead of having to build multiple interfaces between their CRS and the airline systems, hotel companies need only develop a single gateway – between the CRS and the universal switch – which allows them to connect to all the major systems. As well as being less technical, such a solution gives access to the GDS at a relatively low cost.

Switch companies also help to provide additional services. For example, travel agents who send guests to a hotel are supposed to be paid a commission of approximately 10 per cent of the room revenue for the referral. However, in general, many hotels are slow to pay this commission, which makes travel agents unenthusiastic about selling hotel rooms. Centralized commission payments systems help to simplify and speed up the payment process and make travel agents surer of payment. Once they are a member of the system, each travel agency receives a single monthly cheque representing all the commissions due from all member hotels, along with a detailed statement showing every reservation, every cancellation and every no-show in the hotels represented by the system. Payments are made in the agent's local currency, thus helping to reduce bank charges. Similarly, costs and administrative work for the hotel are reduced. Only a single cheque, made out to the clearing organization, is needed to pay all the commissions due and a concise report accurately details business received from each travel agency. With such a system everyone is a winner, as travel agents can book hotels with confidence and hotels get increased levels of business from travel agents!

Figure 7.7

The Switch Company Concept

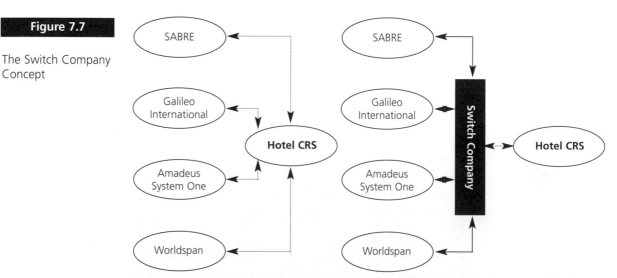

Without a switch company, the hotel CRS has to develop multiple interfaces (shown by the dotted lines above) to link with the GDS. Where a switching company is used, only a single interface needs to be developed.

Hotel representative companies

One of the factors limiting the growth of hotel electronic bookings is that only a particular type of hotel is well represented on the GDS. By and large, all the GDS provide access to the same 30,000 or so hotel properties, which tend to be members of the large international hotel groups. Travel agents, however, need their systems to provide information about all types of hotels – domestic and international, chain and independent, large and small. As Richard Brooks (senior director of rooms management for Stouffer Hotels) points out:

> Information is the most important commodity a hotel has to give travel agents. By not having an effective state-of-the-art CRS, you severely limit the information you can provide them and consequently their ability to sell your hotel.

Thus there is increasing pressure on all hotels, but particularly on smaller groups and independents, to find a way of making themselves available electronically, despite the considerable difficulties involved. The dominance of the large groups on the GDS can, in part, be explained by the prerequisite of having a computerized reservations system. HSSS Ltd, a leading firm of UK-based hospitality technology consultants, point out that the start up cost of even the simplest centralized system is at least £100,000. Enhancements such as developing interfaces with the GDS increase costs substantially. Even though the benefits of CRS use and accepting electronic bookings are equally compelling for smaller hotel groups as for the larger ones, such levels of investment are difficult for smaller groups to justify. The large chains are able to afford such systems as they have high booking volumes which reduces the transaction cost; they usually target the business traveller, where high prices mean high margins; and also can spread the capital costs across a large number of units. Two alternative strategies being used by smaller companies to overcome this problem and gain economies of scale are to band together into a marketing consortium or to outsource their reservations function to a third party provider.

Well-known examples of marketing consortia include Utell, Best Western, SRS Steigenberger and Leading Hotels of the World. While most such 'alliances' provide a wide range of services, including advice on marketing and promotion, advertising efforts and sometimes even 24-hour international toll-free central reservation facilities, it is their cost-effective access to electronic distribution which is their key selling point. Outsourcing of the central reservations function in this way has become increasingly popular. A 'generic' level of service is relatively basic, where calls to the CRO are answered with a simple 'Hello, Reservations'. More costly is the 'private label' option, where reservations agents respond to calls with the hotel's name – for example with 'Good Morning, ABC Hotels reservations'- which helps retain corporate identity. In both cases (and perhaps more importantly), hotels are listed on the CRS, and thus are available to travel agents through the GDS. They therefore get the benefits of electronic distribution with a minimum of capital costs. Operational costs are also more predictable as they are generally transaction based. Because having access to the latest features and technology is a key selling point when attracting new members, third party service providers also tend to place a lot of emphasis on developing their reservation systems to incorporate the latest technologies. Thus a hotel company can gain access to continued state of the art facilities at a relatively low cost by using such a strategy.

An alternative to using a third party reservations service is to outsource only the data processing component of the reservation process. In such cases, the hotel operates their own voice reservation centres, but uses computer services owned and operated by an outside company. The owners of the system generate extra revenue by 'subletting' spare capacity on their system, while the renter gets access to electronic distribution facilities without the capital expenditure and technicality of purchasing and maintaining a computer system. Once again, costs are highly predictable, with expenses based on transaction volumes plus a fixed monthly fee. Limitations associated with using generic display screens and booking functions are balanced by the immediate availability and proven performance of the system, combined with no responsibility for its maintenance and freedom from substantial capital commitment.

Destination management systems

An often quoted statistic is that in the USA, well over half of hotel reservations come in through a central reservations system, but that in Europe, the norm is less than 10 per cent. Why is this so? One of the major reasons is the way in which the hotel industry outside the USA is structured. Branding (whether owned or managed) is much less common in Europe. For example, less than 30 per cent of hotels in the UK are members of a chain, group or consortium. As we have seen, computerized systems have traditionally been used to distribute a homogeneous product. With chain hotels, you can be relatively certain of the physical characteristics of the product you have booked. A room in any of the major hotel brands will have standardized facilities and amenities (for example, two double beds, an en-suite bathroom, a telephone and a television). However, where the hotel is unbranded, there tends to be more diversity. Contrast the room described above with one in an independently owned Irish country house. There may only be one bed (but it could be a four poster), there might not be any telephone or television and the bathroom might be down the hall. And the room right next to it would be completely different. The possibilities for variation are infinite. Indeed, most of these types of properties market themselves not on their similarities, but on their differences. In order to incorporate them onto a computerized reservation system, very comprehensive descriptions are needed to not only explain the physical characteristics of the product, but also to try to give a sense of their intangible qualities to the prospective buyer. Also the issue of cost cannot be ignored. Hotels outside the US tend to be smaller and thus less likely to be able to afford to use electronic channels in the first place. Even when the hardware and other systems costs are ignored, many CRS and representative companies charge joining fees, periodic subscriptions or require minimum monthly sales volumes, which tend to be cost-prohibitive for smaller operations. In addition, many smaller operations sell a relatively low price/low margin product, and thus fixed transaction fees represent a higher proportion of revenue than is the case with their higher priced, more business-focused cousins.

Even though the majority of hotels tend to be small, collectively they are very important to the economies of many regions. For example, tourism is Ireland's third largest export, a significant generator of foreign currency and one of the country's largest employers. Smaller operations tend to retain more of the flavour of the locality than their 'branded' competitors, and in many cases are the building blocks of the attractiveness of a city, region or country that attracts tourists in the first place. However, they tend to be particularly weak in terms of marketing knowledge and ability. Not only are they unaware of the techniques and tools available, but their efforts tend to be uncoordinated, inconsistent and ill-targeted, which results in low effectiveness. As a result, many governments feel it necessary to help tourism operations to actively promote both themselves and their region. This is usually achieved through regional tourism organizations (RTOs), which have as their mandate the promotion of all the tourism operations in a distinct geographical region. Marketing is this way is more effective than the efforts of individual suppliers as people are not attracted to a region by the facilities on which, it turns out, they spend the most money — accommodation and catering. They come to enjoy other attractions, but they have to eat and sleep somewhere!

RTOs help to promote a region in several ways. Prior to the trip, they act as a central source of information, mailing brochures and responding to mail and phone enquires. They actively promote the region at tourism exhibitions/travel shows and often maintain marketing offices in their major foreign markets to distribute information to potential visitors. During the trip, RTOs help provide information through a network of tourism information centres (TICs) where visitors can make enquires and pick up brochures over the counter. Some of these offices also make reservations with hotels or other suppliers, sometimes for free or (more than likely) for a fee or commission. This reservation-processing function is important as it is generally accepted that the consumer wants more than just information when planning a trip. Inevitably, his ultimate aim is to make a booking, and the easier it is to find information, check availability and complete the booking, the more likely visitors are to both initially choose the destination and subsequently be satisfied with their experience.

However, providing such information and reservation services is problematic. Tourism is probably the ultimate dispersed industry. Tourists, whether business or leisure, come from everywhere and go everywhere – which means that everyone's information requirements are unique. Even for the same room on two different days, there may be quite different information requirements. With tens of thousands of small suppliers and millions of individualistic purchasers, the permutations of information expand to a fearsome level. As we have already seem, GDS and CRS, with their primarily business client/travel agent focus and restricted database structure, are not capable of servicing this very complex and demanding mix of needs. A different type of distribution system, more adapted to the needs of smaller, leisure-focused suppliers, was needed. This led to the development of a new kind of distribution system focused specifically on the needs of both the RTOs and the smaller tourism supplier. These systems are known by a variety of different names, including, amongst many others, destination information systems (DIS), destination marketing systems and destination management systems (DMS). Although their precise content varies, they all share a common philosophy – they have been designed to distribute information about (and increasingly process reservations for) a diverse and comprehensive range of tourism-related products, usually from a distinct geographical region. As a result,

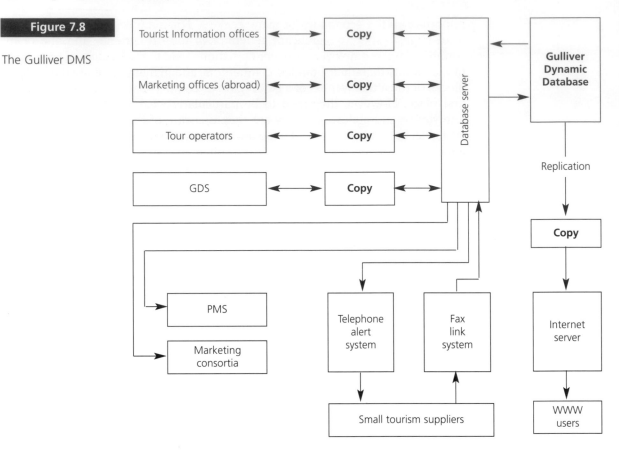

Figure 7.8

The Gulliver DMS

they are more inclined to include smaller suppliers instead of just the major hotel chains. In most cases, their development has been driven by the RTOs, and thus their focus tends to be on leisure rather than on business travel.

Being relatively new, DMS are still in a state of evolution. Some systems are information focused – in effect acting a resource that can be used to help satisfy the tourist's need for information. Systems of this type are often used by TIC counter staff to assist in responding quickly and efficiently to customer queries. For example, if a visitor is searching for a luxury hotel room by the beach, with TV and babysitting facilities at a cost of €100 per night, a query can be entered into the system and the set of properties that match the criteria printed for the customer. DMS help to improve this type of travel counselling by ensuring that all options are presented to the customer and also by assisting the counsellor in structuring the traveller's request. It thereby reduces the time spent on servicing each inquiry, and at the same time increases the quality of service provided. The system is even more effective if the database is made directly available to the public using technologies such as CD-ROM's, teletext, multimedia touch screen kiosks or the World Wide Web. Such a strategy allows visitors to find information for themselves, thus dramatically reducing costs.

Simply providing access to tourist information on its own is not very effective as a distribution strategy. Customers searching for information want to make a reservation with as little trouble as possible. As a result, many DMS include booking facilities so that potential customers can find the tourism product that meets their needs, check availability and rates and then make a booking in one seamless process. This brings several advantages to the RTO. Apart from the immediate revenue from fees or commissions, being able to book electronically gives TICs many of the benefits which travel agents experienced when they first started using electronic systems, including reduced costs, faster response times, improved customer service, increased control and reduced administrative work. While initially these reservation facilities may be limited to use in the TICs or by a telesales centre, increasingly RTOs are trying to provide such facilities directly to customers over the World Wide Web, and we will look at this in the next chapter.

Review questions

1. Explain why making bookings manually is ineffective for (a) the travel agent and (b) the travel supplier.

2. Why were the global distribution systems (GDS) originally developed?

3. Why did the GDS begin selling products other than airline seats?

4. What are the advantages of using a GDS:
   (a) For the travel agent?
   (b) For the tourism supplier?
   (c) For the customer?

5. Why, in the past, were travel agents distrustful of the hotel information on their GDS systems?

6. Describe the main functions of a central reservation office (CRO).

7. Explain why operating a CRO is more cost-effective than having unit level reservations departments in each of the hotels in a chain.

8. Why do travel agents want to be able to book hotels reservations through their computer systems rather than over the telephone?

9. What is the main disadvantage of having manual connectivity between the CRS and the GDS?

10. Distinguish between Type B and Type A connectivity.

11. Why does the travel agent prefer to make bookings with hotel companies that offer Type A connectivity?

12. Describe what is meant by seamless integration.

13. Why don't more hotel groups use bidirectional interfaces between their CRS and their properties?

14. What is the main advantage of single image inventory?

15. What is the main function of a universal switch?

16. What effect does the use of a universal switch have on
    (a) Capital costs
    (b) Transaction costs?

17. Why do travel agents prefer hotels that participate in a centralized commission payment scheme?

18. Why do many smaller hotels prefer to use third party reservation services rather than develop their own CRS?

19. Distinguish between private label and generic levels of reservation services.

20. What are the advantages and disadvantages of outsourcing the reservations function?

21. Why are leisure-orientated hotels generally not included on the GDS?

22. Why do regional tourism organizations try to promote independent travel suppliers?

23. What are the main functions of a destination management system (DMS)?

Discussion questions

1. What channels of distribution would be most suitable for use by:
   • An airport hotel?
   • A resort property in a remote location?
   • A city centre B&B?
   What factors should you take into consideration when making your decision?

2. Compare and contrast the cost to a hotel of a reservation that is made:
   • By a travel agents through the GDS
   • By a customer by telephoning the CRO
   • Direct to the property over the Internet.
   In each case, think about the various fees, charges and commissions that have to be paid. Would the value of the booking have an effect on the total cost?

3. Call the toll-free number of the hotel company of your choice and try to make a booking for the property of your choice. Immediately afterwards, call that property directly and request a similar product on a similar date. Were the rates that you were quoted the same? Explain why. What factors might influence your answer?

Hotel distribution on the Web

While Chapter 7 discussed the traditional electronic distribution systems used in the hotel sector, the development of the World Wide Web as a commercial medium in the early 1990s has prompted great change in the way that the hotel product is being sold. Each of the participants in the traditional distribution chain (travel agents, GDS, CRS, third party reservation system providers and even DMS) has begun to sell its product directly over the Web. In addition, a variety of new pure-play travel web sites have appeared, with the result that there are now a large number of alternative (sometimes competing, sometimes complementary) electronic routes over which a customer can potentially book a hotel room. This chapter tries to demystify how the Web is affecting hotel distribution. It also describes the main players in the hotel electronic distribution arena today in order to act as a guide for anyone trying to manage distribution over this growing range of Internet-based channels.

The arrival of the Web

Until the early 1990s, hotel electronic channels of distribution were as described in Chapter 7 – a cosy status quo between the CRS and the GDS. Each system cooperated, rather than competed, with each other, participants operated a closer user group and relationships were effectively linear, with each participant playing a mutually beneficial role. Use of such electronic distribution was beneficial in terms of the numbers of bookings generated, but was also expensive and lacking in flexibility. As we saw, the majority of channels were routed through the GDS, which has implications in terms of cost (as the GDS providers demand a fee for each transaction processed), audience (as GDSs are mostly used by travel agents and other business travel oriented clients) and format of information content (as GDSs are limited by their textually-based interface). Gradually commissions and other reservation costs began to grow and hotel companies began seeking alternative ways to distribute their product.

From 1994 onwards, the development of electronic commerce on the World Wide Web provided just such an opportunity. Most companies began experimenting with online distribution, and it has had a profound effect on the way in which the hotel product is marketed, distributed and sold. Perhaps the most significant effect is the shake up in the relationship between distribution channels participants that it has caused. In addition to cooperating, most companies now compete with each other through their own consumer-orientated web sites. Hotel chain CRSs, the GDSs, third party reservations system providers, destination management organizations and even the Switch companies have all introduced consumer-orientated web sites, all with the objective of transacting business directly with the customer, thereby bypassing intermediaries lower down in the distribution chain. Companies from outside the travel sector have also noted the potential of online travel distribution and entered the arena. These new 'pure-play' intermediaries took advantage of the Internet boom of the 1990s to get established, and are rapidly starting to dominate the sale of online travel. Lacking the constraints imposed by pre-existing relationships with traditional players, such companies have been free to introduce innovative business models that could possibly change the way travel is distributed. In effect, the Web has acted as a catalyst, prompting growth, change, complexity and increased competition in hotel distribution. The number of potential routes between suppliers and customers has expanded rapidly, and most of these channels are becoming interconnected, with each offering multiple points of sale to the customer. As a result, an understanding of the major types of systems available and of likely future developments is necessary in order to be able to manage hotel distribution successfully.

The online travel market

For several years travel has been the most popular product sold online. The Internet is the perfect medium for selling travel products as it brings together a vast network of suppliers and a widely dispersed customer pool into a centralized market place. Unlike physical products, fulfilment is not a problem with travel as, in most cases, communicating a confirmation number to the customer is sufficient to complete the travel transaction.

Actual dollar estimates of the current size of the online travel market (and forecasts for the future) vary greatly, as can be seen from Table 8.1. However, most analysts consistently agree that spending on travel is about one-third of the total online business-to-consumer (B2C) transactions, and that spending on travel will increase by at least a factor of two over the next three years. Looking at sales figures alone is not enough to recognize the importance of the Web to the travel sector as it ignores bookings influenced by, but not completed, online. For

Table 8.1	Analyst	Estimate 2001	Estimate 2002	Forecast 2005	Forecast 2006	Forecast 2007
Online leisure and unmanaged business travel (US$ billion)	**Forrester Research**	14.2	22.7		38.7	50.0
	PhoCusWright	13.3	40.1			
	CNet		31.0			
	HVS	23.0		63.0		
	Jupiter Media Metrix	24.0				64.0

Note that the above figures represent leisure travel and unmanaged business travel only, and do not include the rapidly growing managed corporate travel segments.

Source: Compiled from multiple sources as part of ongoing research

Table 8.2	Characteristics	Bookers	Lookers	Sideliners
The online travel consumer	Mean age	35	36	37
	Mean income	€71,000	€53,200	€39,400
	Male (%)	59	56	66
	Married (%)	60	58	50
	College degree or higher (%)	52	34	25
	Months online	34	27	22
	Travelled for leisure in the past year (%)	97	82	55
	Have used a live travel agent (%)	43	30	10
	Mean leisure trips per year	3.1	2.6	2.1
	Mean amount spent per year on leisure trips	€2,152	€1,458	€907

Source: The state of online travel (2000) Gomez.com

example, research by the Travel Industry Association of America estimates that around 64 million Americans now plan their journeys using the Internet, but that only about two-thirds of them actually booked their trips online. As a result, their revenues are not included in figures quoted above. While the reasons behind this may be complex (security concerns, complexity of the trip, need for human contact, etc.), the proportion is significant and clearly actual sales are not a true reflection of the importance of the Web in influencing the choice of the travel product.

The growth figures predicted above are not surprising, considering that hotels can be distributed in many different ways on the Web. The advantages are clear; by addressing the consumer directly, the hotel is able to bypass the GDS, resulting in substantially lower costs and making it possible to distribute lower margin products. The absence of requirements in terms of database structure gives it the flexibility to distribute heterogeneous products, while the ease of entry, low set-up costs and the fact that no special equipment is needed make it attractive as a distribution medium for smaller tourism operations. Lastly, its multimedia capabilities and its global reach make it very effective as a marketing medium. Because of these advantages, many analysts agree that nearly 20 per cent of all hotel bookings will be made over the Web by 2005.

Hotel distribution on the Web

To take advantage of these opportunities, hotels can basically use three different strategies to distribution over the Web – through a chain or consortium site, by setting up their own site or by listing themselves on one of the travel mega sites.

Hotel company web site

Practically all of the major hotel chains maintain a web site for promotional and booking purposes. These typically contain information on the company in general, and on company-wide schemes such as loyalty clubs, special promotions, corporate partnerships, etc. Most include a search engine, which makes it easy for potential customers to find the product that meets their needs. For example, users can enter the location and any other desired criteria (such as having a swimming pool or babysitting facilities) into a Web form, click submit, and the site responds with a list of the properties which meet their needs. Profiles of each property can then be displayed, which typically include textual descriptions supplemented by photos, and, of course, reservation facilities. These can range in complexity from reservation requests, where the user fills in an on-screen form to request avail-ability – the form is then sent electronically to the hotel and they wait for a reply; to real-time booking facilities where the user accesses an interactive database that is capable of processing the entire booking electronically, instantly and without any human intervention. As we discussed in Chapter 6, the latter is now the minimum level that the customer is willing to accept, and for a hotel company to offer less could have severe commercial consequences.

Independent hotel sites

Sites for independent hotels tend to be more varied and harder to find. Most contain only a few static web pages, but sometimes the flexibility of not having to conform to corporate guidelines means that smaller operations can have innova-tive, effective and comprehensive sites. The Vicarage Hotel in London (http://londonvicarage.com) is a good example of such an approach.

> The site is separated into various sections. The first is the *Introduction* with gives information on The Vicarage itself. Room rates and breakfast menu are presented in the *Details* section. *Highlights* include information on Notting Hill Carnival and New Year's Eve in Trafalgar Square. *Directions* are given from the airport and the Tube. *Frequently Asked Questions* presents a list, with questions ranging from check-in times to the parking situation. A guide for *What's On In London* with information on the Tube and London Museums is included, as well as pictures of Vicarage employees, the view from the B&B and The Vicarage's taxi man.

Perhaps the number of bookings it generates best measures the success of this web site. After two months of operation, Web bookings outstripped the previous number one source of business at The Vicarage. Some of the reasons for its success may be that the site includes information not only on the B&B itself, but also general tourist information on the surrounding area. It also does this in a very user-friendly manner, which encourages use by people new to the Web.

Intermediary sites

The third way of exploiting the potential of the Web is through the travel mega sites – virtual travel malls combining travel products from different sources and offering the user a standard mechanism to search through information and make reservations. The majority offer a full travel service, and allow users to search and receive instant confirmation for flights, car rental and hotels using the same data-bases available to travel agents over their terminals. One of the key selling points of the mega-agencies is that they offer products from competing suppliers. On a hotel company web site, browsers are limited to viewing and purchasing just the products of the brand in question. Unfortunately most consumers do not purchase travel in this way, and while some are loyal to particular brands, most at least want to see the alternatives that are out there and might satisfy their needs.

In addition to their 'commercial' information and booking facilities, most mega-agencies also provide a range of other useful resources for the traveller. These often include general travel advice, destination guides containing information on area attractions, travel news, local weather reports, currency converters, dynamic location maps and even point to point driving instructions. Such facilities make them more attractive to the consumer because in most cases, someone booking an airline ticket also needs a hotel, or needs to find out something about the destination, and would like to know about visas and health requirements. As a result, consumers are increasingly turning to the online travel agencies who provide a one-stop travel shop for all the travel needs of today's harassed consumer and also provide choice, convenience, comparison shopping and even cost advantages. The major mega-agencies currently servicing the hotel sector are discussed in the next section.

The online mega-agencies

The suitability of travel for online distribution and few barriers to entry have resulted in a very large number of companies facilitating the sale of travel online. However a small number of companies (dubbed the mega-agencies) have quickly emerged to dominate the sector. Brief profiles of each of these companies are shown below.

- **Expedia**: Founded in 1996 and headquartered in Bellevue, Washington, Expedia really lives up to its motto of being 'Everything in Travel'. It offers the widest product selection of all the mega-agencies, as well as localized versions serving specific markets in the US, UK, France, Germany, Canada, Australia and Italy. Its origins lie in the Microsoft® Corporation, which has provided it with one of its key differentiators – superior technology. For example, Expedia is able to integrate published and unpublished rates on the same web page, a functionality that increases its conversion rate and ability to cross-sell products. Furthermore Expedia has been one of the pioneers in changing the business model used to sell travel online, placing emphasis on both the merchant model and dynamic packaging, as will be discussed below. All of these factors have resulted in Expedia controlling about 40 per cent of all online travel sales, making it currently the largest online travel retailer. It uses WorldSpan as its primary bookings engine for its non-merchant model inventory (see below). In 2002, Expedia was purchased by USA Networks, and thus can be considered a sister company of Hotels.com (discussed below).

Figure 8.1

Expedia.com

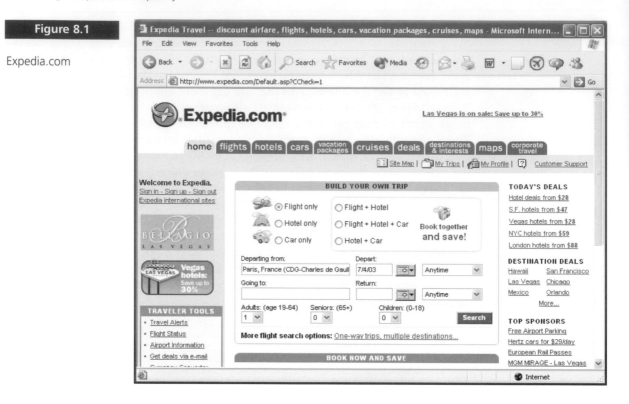

Figure 8.2

Travelocity.com

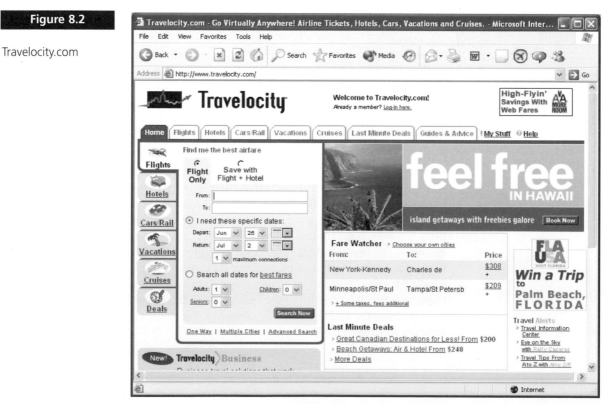

- **Travelocity**: Launched in 1996, and headquartered in Fort Worth, Texas, Travelocity is effectively intertwined with Sabre – one of the major GDS. The company itself is a child of the Sabre Corporation and uses the Sabre GDS as its reservations engine. The March 2000 purchase of Preview Travel – at that time the third largest online agency behind Expedia and Travelocity – catapulted it into the number one position, although it has since been once again overtaken by Expedia. Travelocity is a full service travel agency, offering a broad range of products to both leisure and corporate clients.

- **Priceline**: Founded in 1997 and headquartered in Norwalk, Connecticut, Priceline is famous for the use of its name-your-own-price business model. Unlike traditional retailing, where the seller sets the price to be paid, Priceline allows customers to nominate how much they are willing to pay for a particular product and then invites suppliers to take up their offer. In return for being able to choose their own price, customers have to be willing to give up something, which in the case of travel is the ability to specify a brand. This was a revolutionary idea that empowered customers, who immediately embraced it, resulting in Priceline becoming profitable long before its larger competitors. The success of the Priceline model depends on two factors – price-sensitive but brand-neutral customers and permanent excess capacity – both of which are clearly visible in today's marketplace. The fact that brand is not disclosed to customers prior to purchase makes Priceline particularly attractive as a distressed inventory distribution channel to the many suppliers worried about the effect of discounting on their brand image.

- **Hotels.com** (aka Hotel Reservations Network, HRN, HotelDiscounts.com): Unlike the other leading companies, Hotels.com is unique in that it does not attempt to provide a full travel service but instead specializes in discount

Figure 8.3

Priceline.com

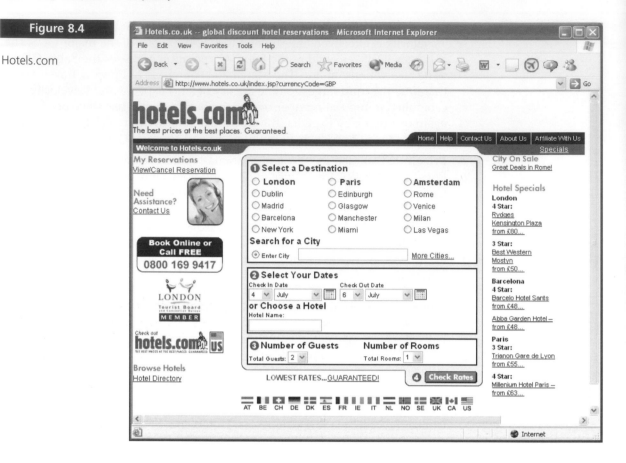

Figure 8.4

Hotels.com

hotel rooms – typically at savings of up to 65 per cent off regular hotel rates, according to the company's publicity. A subsidiary of USA Interactive of Dallas, Texas (who also own Expedia), it started as a hotel consolidator in 1991 and moved onto the Internet in 1995. Hotels.com's business model remains that of a consolidator, but it uses the power of the Internet for distribution. It negotiates room blocks with individual hotels at discount prices, and then sells them to consumers at prices below what they would normally find on other channels, their margin being the difference between what they pay the supplier and charge the customer. Nearly one-third of all hotel rooms, or 500m room nights a year, go unsold, and Hotels.com fills this gap using a model in which it takes no inventory risk and enjoys a 30 per cent gross profit. Hotels.com is also unique in its extensive use of associates (over 30,000 in 2002) – independent web sites that use Hotels.com booking engine to process bookings in return for a shared commission.

- **Ebookers**: Having their origins in the 'bricks and mortar' UK-based travel agency Flightbookers, Ebookers launched on the Internet in 1999 and is regarded as one of the most successful of the European online agencies. It has a presence in 11 European countries (Italy continues to elude it), operates in ten languages and specializes in discount fares. Ebookers has negotiated special deals with over 120 airlines, which give it fares 15 per cent to 75 per cent below published rates, and also sells normal scheduled air

Figure 8.5

Ebookers.com

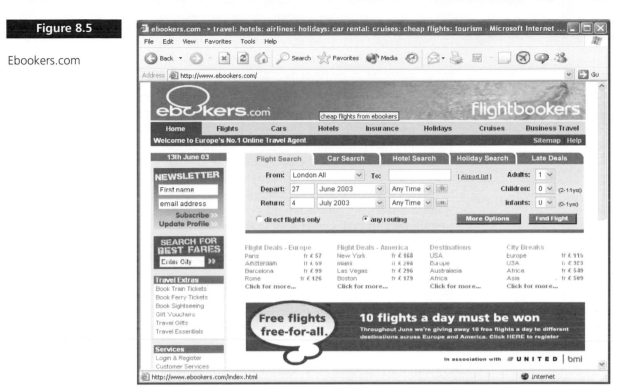

Figure 8.6

Lastminute.com

travel. In addition, it offers discount rates on hotels, car hire, packages, special interest travel and even insurance. However, primarily because of the current size of the online travel market in Europe, it is dwarfed by the other mega-agencies in terms of overall revenues.

- **Lastminute.com**: Based on the idea of matching supply and demand, last-minute.com offers consumers the opportunity to purchase a broad range of travel-related products at discount prices but with a very short lead time – hence the name 'last minute'. Currently the product range offered includes airline tickets, hotel rooms, packages, entertainment tickets, restaurant reservations and gifts. Lastminute operates in a range of countries, including the UK, France, Germany, Italy, Sweden, Spain, the Netherlands, Belgium, Australia, South Africa and Japan, has over 6.8 million subscribers to its weekly newsletter and has proved a hit with consumers – it is consistently the only site to appear in the top 10 most popular travel sites in Britain, France, Germany, Sweden, Italy and Spain. Lastminute is popular with suppliers as well, allowing them to dispose of distressed inventory that might otherwise go unsold. One of Lastminute's biggest threats comes from a concern among suppliers as to the effect including their product on such discount sites has on their customer's perception of their brand.

HSMAI claims that hotel chain sites currently are highly effective, with the majority of Internet bookings flowing through them rather than through the Web intermediaries. However, most agree that this will soon change. Unlike the situation with the airlines, who have managed to build a dedicated online community of loyal customers, increasing numbers of hotel bookings are being routed through online intermediaries instead of through supplier's sites. The reasons for this trend seem clear – consumers are increasingly demanding a one-stop shop when making and booking their travel plans. Why visit a single hotel company's web site when by visiting one of the online mega travel agency sites, consumers can comparison-shop between different brands, make their reservation and also book their flight and car hire all in one location. While travel suppliers could theoretically compete by increasing their range of product offering (in fact some are trying, as witnessed by SNCF's – France's national rail operator – introduction of hotel reservations and car rentals; hyatt.com's incorporation of air and car booking facilities; and dollar.com's incorporation of air and hotel booking facilities), they are still faced with the problem of lack of choice in their core product – unless of course they start selling their competitors' products on their corporate site – and also perhaps from a perceived lack of impartiality in the minds of consumers. As a result, it has become clear that there is a trend towards online mega-agencies as the primary source of online bookings in the future.

The big get bigger

While the current political and economic climate is having a disastrous effect on the majority of tourism industry companies, the majority of mega-agencies discussed above continued to increase both revenues and profits, despite reduced (or even eliminated) commissions from the airlines. Most are profitable and exhibiting high rates of growth (see Figure 8.7). This section examines how these

| Figure 8.7 | Online agency gross bookings 1999 to 2002 |

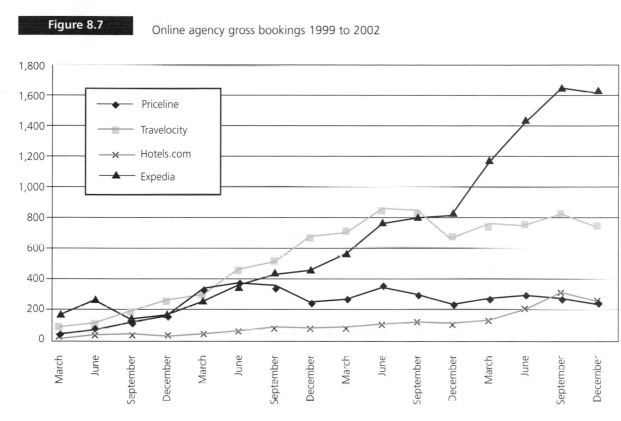

mega-agencies are bucking overall economic trends and consolidating their position in controlling the distribution of online travel.

- **Market size:** As was discussed above, both the size of the overall travel market and the proportion sold online continues to grow. Figures from the Travel Industry Association of America indicate that about 10 per cent of all travel in the US is currently sold online, and that this will rise to 14 per cent by 2005. As both the size of the market is growing and the online agencies are capturing a bigger portion of the pie, they are continually strengthening their position and increasing their power.

- **Geographical spread:** To date, most attention has focused on the US travel market but this is changing. Europe is predicted to overtake the US in terms of the value of bookings made online in the very near future. The potential of Europe is clear; a population of 380 million (40 per cent more than the US), 155 million Internet users compared with 133 million in the US and an average of 33 days' annual vacation compared to 13 in the US. Although it is more complex to do business in Europe as a result of multiple languages, taxation and legal systems, it is also more profitable as negotiated fares and rates are more common, allowing intermediaries to build in margins of up to 40 per cent on their sales. And in Europe, intermediaries get 30 days to pay suppliers instead of the 7 in the US, giving valuable cash-flow advantages. As a result, mega-agencies operating primarily in Europe do not need to make huge sales to be profitable. Similarly the growing Internet population in Asia-Pacific offers yet untapped potential – a fact that is sure to be exploited by both Hotels.com and Expedia, who have both recently opened offices in the region.

- **Product mix:** Currently airline tickets are the most commonly purchased online travel item, representing over three-quarters of all transactions. Online agencies are highly dependent on such sales, which is problematic as most of the major airlines have severely restricted commission on regular airfares sold online. Many have capped commissions to €10 per segment irrespective of the value of the booking, and several are eliminating commissions altogether. In addition, the online agencies are suffering from increased competition for airline ticket sales as the airlines try to encourage customers to book directly on their own branded web sites (we will discuss this later). While some mega-agencies have reacted by adding a service fee, most are trying to diversify the range of products they offer to customers over their sites, and, as a result, the percentage of hotels, car rentals and vacations sold online is expect to grow significantly. While in most cases the complementary products being sold offer higher commission levels than those associated with airline seats, the appeal of lodging is higher transaction volumes. According to Rich Barton, CEO of Expedia, air travel accounts for €270 billion of the world travel and tourism market, but lodging is far bigger at €350 billion and is to a large extent unexploited. However, selling hotel rooms using the traditional agency model is relatively unrewarding, paying only eight to ten per cent of a relatively low selling price. To increase their return, the online agencies are currently focusing on two strategies – the merchant model and dynamic packaging.

The merchant model

In contrast to the agency model used by both offline and online travel agents, where the retailer distributes a product in return for a predefined and fixed percentage commission, under the merchant model the supplier contracts in advance for bulk purchase of inventory at discount prices and then resells these products at a margin that it determines for itself in response to market demand. While in some cases the agency actually takes control of the inventory, usually it only contracts the right to book a product, committing to a cut-off date at which point it will inform the hotel if it has not sold the room in question. If it fails to sell the room in question, it does not suffer any loss as long as it informs the hotel on or before the cut-off date. Expedia has been very successful with its 'Expedia Special Rate' programme – a version of the merchant model. Hotel.com's entire business model is based around this concept.

Packaging

If the merchant model described above sounds strangely like the way in which tour operators work, then you will not be surprised by the attempts by the mega-agencies to create and sell their own packages. Most online agencies already sell vacation packages supplied by traditional tour operators using the agency model. However most are also trying to create their own packages based on the inventory of flights, hotel and car hire products made available to them from their use of the merchant model. By combining several components together, they can add a more substantial margin, with a corresponding positive effect on profitability. Once again Expedia appears to be leading the field. Each time a user makes a reservation enquiry, along with the answer Expedia will also propose various packages of air, hotel, car hire, etc., in an attempt to both increase average spend as a result of the cross selling and generating higher profit margins. Several mega-agencies are also currently developing the technology to package dynamically – to allow the consumer to swap around components of the package interactively by selecting from a menu of flight, hotel and other components. In this way, customers would be able to create their own customized packages – one that is right for them rather than a mass-market product.

Both of these strategies have been very successful for those who have implemented them successfully. For example, Expedia now claims that four out of five of its hotel rooms are sold using the merchant model rather than the supplementary agency inventory it pulls out of WorldSpan. Merchant revenues (comprising Expedia Special Rates and revenues from packaging), have tripled to €97 million or over 60 per cent of sales, reflecting the company's changing sales mix – which has ultimately resulted in higher levels of profitability.

Corporate travel

The mega-agencies have also noted the potential of the corporate travel market and have introduced intranet and extranet-based facilities to service the needs of corporate travel buyers. According to American Express, travel is the third largest controllable expense in most companies. Such spending has traditionally been unmanaged, resulting in wasted expenditure. Although most companies have corporate travel policies, in practice they are difficult to implement and control.

Intranet technology can help by linking the company directly to preferred suppliers, through which all travel bookings must be made. When an employee clicks on travel on the company intranet, they are taken directly to a specific page on the mega-agency's web site, into which they enter details of the services they require. This request is then sent electronically for authorization by the appropriate people, and then automatically booked, thus helping to further streamline the process and reduce costs. Formal corporate travel policies (such as, for example, that employees must spend less than £100 per night on accommodation) and negotiated rates can be incorporated into the system and enforced automatically. Most systems can also send the traveller's bill to their company's accounting department after the trip, and provide a variety of management information to help the travel manager control the company's travel spending more effectively.

The power and the glory

The online mega travel agencies are blooming at a time when many tourism suppliers are struggling for survival. Already there is danger of an oligopoly situation, as the top five online travel services control nearly 60 per cent of the entire online travel market. One of the effects of this dominance is that it has changed the nature of the power relationship within travel distribution. Traditionally the suppliers, particularly the airlines, have been firmly in charge, as demonstrated by commission caps and cuts over the past ten years. However, scale has allowed the online agencies to become far more powerful. For example, Expedia reacted to a United Airways decision that it would cease paying any commissions to online agencies by changing the way it displayed fares for United flights on its sites. While still listed, Expedia customers had to go to another page to get United's prices, even if they were the cheapest or most convenient on selected routes. Few consumers took the extra effort, and United sales plunged until the airline reversed its decision and Expedia resumed displaying fares in less than 24 hours. Clearly the volume of business that Expedia was bringing to United put it in the driver's seat. Similarly the online agencies now generate sufficient volume for many suppliers who have to concede to agency 'requests' for payment for placing their fare listings higher on a Web page or make them the first ones seen by customers, even though they may not be the lowest priced. If suppliers refuse to pay fees, they risk being displayed in unfavourable positions or even being shut out of sites altogether.

Suppliers have reacted to this shift of power in two ways: by giving their customers increased motivation to book directly on their own branded web sites and by forming alliances with their competitors to create mega-agency-killer web sites.

- **Direct sales:** Currently, both traditional bricks and mortar travel agents and the online agencies such as Expedia and Travelocity communicate with travel suppliers by passing information and reservations through the global distribution systems (GDS); suppliers pay a transaction fee for every booking processed. Although levels vary, current estimates put the charge at about €14 per trip for an airline booking, and about €3.50 for each hotel booking routed through the system. In addition, suppliers also pay commission to the travel agent. Given the growing volume of bookings originating from electronic sources, suppliers have an increasing incentive to bypass both the GDS and the online agencies and transact business directly with the consumer.

  As a result, increasingly suppliers are rewarding customers for booking directly by giving them extra frequent flyer miles, tiered benefits and special prices. Hoteliers in particular have become much more aggressive in their pricing strategies, and want everyone to know that the best deals are available on their own web sites. For example, 6C now gives a lowest rate guarantee on its own web site. Its offer is simple – if the consumer can find the same product at a cheaper price on another online channel within 24 hours of making a booking, the company will match the lower price and give the customer an additional 10 per cent discount. Such steps go a long way towards reassuring customers that they are getting a fair deal. However,

driving bookings to a supplier web site is a difficult battle to win. Despite considerable effort, the majority of suppliers have failed to significantly change their distribution mix. Their own branded web sites are in general quite successful at selling to frequent travellers and loyalty club members – in effect to their existing customers – but not so good at attracting incremental business. The online agencies, with their broader choice and product categories, offer the chance to attract new business and also make a valuable contribution in terms of keeping planes and hotels full. The merchant model based on net prices discussed above may help to preserve this relationship. With this strategy, both parties win – the supplier gets to set the minimum acceptable rate that they are willing to accept as the net rate offered, and the online agency can achieve an acceptable level of
profitability by adding their own margin before sale to the customer.

- **Industry cooperation:** As discussed above, one of the reasons that travel suppliers have not been successful at divert significant amounts of business to their own web sites remains that in most cases consumers want a one-stop shop offering both brand choice and the ability to satisfy all their travel booking requirements in one go – something that is clearly not available on a single company's branded web site. For this reason, many leading travel suppliers have formed industry alliances with a single aim – to divert business away from the mega-agencies. Unlike individual supplier web sites, online-agency-killers can offer the broad range of both brands and products demanded by today's online consumer, while their ownership by consortia of suppliers rescues them from claims of bias or unfavourable practices. For suppliers, the benefits of such cooperation are clear – no agency commission and in most cases reduced transaction fees as many of these new sites bypass the traditional GDS databases and connect directly with supplier databases. By bonding together travel suppliers are able to get the best of both worlds – scale to be able to effectively compete with the mega-agencies, but at a lower cost. To date, four major companies have emerged – Orbitz, Hotwire, Opodo and TravelWeb.

Orbitz

The original giant-killer, established by five major US airlines in a direct attempt to reduce the power of the online travel agencies. Orbitz began selling tickets in June 2001, and by the following February it had topped € 1 billion in revenue and become the third largest online travel web site. Such quick success alarmed rivals, who attribute much of Orbitz's gains to its 'most-favoured nation' status, a designation that guarantees that it gets its 30 founding airlines' lowest fares, making it particularly attractive to price-sensitive customers. Obviously its rivals claim that this arrangement gives Orbitz an unfair advantage. However, federal regulators have probed these relationships for antitrust violations and so far have allowed it to operate unfettered. Currently, for most of its 455 airlines, Orbitz must still contact a GDS to confirm pricing and availability and book the tickets. However, it recently introduced its 'Supplier Link' technology, which allows its search engine to bypass the GDS databases and connect directly to the airlines' reservations systems, resulting in savings in transaction costs for the airlines concerned.

While not as cheap as booking directly, many suppliers consider this a reasonable amount to pay for the market reach given by such a widely promoted system.

Hotwire

Launched in 2000 today Hotwire is partnered with 33 international airlines, more than 4000 hotels and several major car rental companies. Hotwire's concept basically follows the Priceline name-your-own-price business model. Customers are asked to be flexible on certain details, and in return are given significant discounts off published prices. Hotwire hotels are guaranteed to be the lowest available, backed by Hotwire's 'Double the Difference' low price guarantee.

Opodo

Originating from 'Opportunity to do', Opodo is essentially a European version of Orbitz with some key differences. Established by nine leading European airlines, in contrast to the disintermediation strategy adopted by Orbitz, Opodo will continue to use Amadeus (one of the major GDS) as its technology partner, yet still promises to deliver reduced distribution costs to its travel suppliers and improved choice, value and service to its customers. Currently up and running in three European countries (Germany, France and the UK), the company has publicly stated its ambition to be profitable and the market leader in Europe by 2004.

TravelWeb (aka Hotel Distribution Systems and HDS)

Following the example of developments in the airline sector, five major international hotel companies partnered with Pegasus Solutions (the technology provider behind THISCO) to form a new company with the aim of making hotel rooms available to multiple travel web sites via direct connections to hotel central reservation systems. Once again, the prime motivation is to reduce transaction cost by disintermediation, and to present a viable alternative to the mega-agencies to consumers. However, unlike the airline sector, where the partners in Orbitz and Opodo control the majority of available seating, the effect of such systems is likely to be less in the hotel sector. Lodging is highly fragmented, and Travelweb controls only a fraction of the hotel rooms in North America, and even less outside the US. To challenge Expedia and Hotels.com – who each boast partnerships with more than 4000 hotels worldwide – TravelWeb needs to greatly expand its number of members.

Conclusion – a battle of the Titans

Trouble is brewing in online travel. While suppliers would ideally like consumers to book directly, they face severe competition from the one-stop shop mega-agencies. Even though the latter already control more than half of all online travel, forecasts predict that they will grow further in importance and further dominate the sale of travel online. Many people point towards the giant-killers such as Orbitz, Opodo, Hotwire and TravelWeb as the solution. Although they are not as efficient as distributing directly, these new services do offer a lower cost of distribution and are more attractive to the consumer than single brand sites because of the choice that they offer. The rapid rise of Orbitz – from nothing at launch to the third largest US online travel agency in only nine months – is seen as a sign of hope by many. Clearly the mega-agencies feel threatened – the launch of each giant-killer has been met with claims of uncompetitive monopolistic practices, and almost every one has had to undergo investigation by either the US Department of Justice or the European Commission. However, in addition to complaining, the mega-agencies have been smart – switching to selling discount inventory under the profitable merchant model and promoting higher margin products like vacations and cruises as never before, which has resulted in them becoming stronger than ever. The giant-killers will have to fight long and hard to kill off such established online players. And they are unlikely to go without a fight. Both Travelocity and Expedia are among the top 10 agencies in the world, have made large investments in both technology and branding, have multiple years' experience not just in selling travel online and establishing their brands, but also in competing with each other, and thus are unlikely to be easily threatened. What is likely to happen could best be termed warlike coexistence – as in the offline world, suppliers, online agencies and agency-killers will exist side by side to serve the leisure and unmanaged business traveller.

Case Study *Fairmont Hotels and Resorts*

Like most hotel chains, Fairmont Hotels and Resorts know that the future of cost-effective distribution is to generate the bookings on your own site. As the traveller became more comfortable with making online reservations, it became a priority to develop one of the best, if not the best, online hotel sites.

Known as an old world luxury hotel chain, featuring such storied hotels as The Fairmont San Francisco, The Fairmont Banff Springs, Fairmont Le Château Frontenac and The Plaza New York, Fairmont Hotels and Resorts had to do more than develop a good site. It needed to create a cost-effective way to communicate the many Fairmont experiences from city to resort hotels, to warm and cold weather destinations, all combining old world charm with new world technology. After much planning and consideration, Fairmont launched an ambitious e-business initiative designed to deliver the industry's most customized and personal travel experiences,

reduced costs and streamlined processing, and increased sales and stronger guest and employee relationships. Their new site offered enhanced services that reinforced the brand promise of providing 'places in the heart'.

According to Jens Thraenhart, Director of Internet Strategy, 'Our progress is dependent on the properties embracing Fairmont's online initiatives and extending the Internet strategy into their local destinations.' As a result, the company made great efforts to involve each of the properties. A decentralized content management system and a centralized guest data warehouse enabled the hotels to update content, promotions and special events, as well as access guest information to create a personalized experience at the property level.

Specifically the goals of the Fairmont.com site were as follows:

Case Study *continued*

- Online experience and content management: to create an online experience that is consistent with the offline brand message that differentiates Fairmont from other luxury hotel companies and creates value to its customer segments.
- Optimizing resources and reducing costs: to provide efficient, online methods for fulfilment of collateral and reservations as well as delivering an exceptional customer experience online.
- Customer relationship management: to create meaningful and personalized offers to site visitors thus strengthening relationships with existing customers and creating new relationships with first-time users.
- Web pricing, distribution and online marketing: to offer support to hotels to enable them to offer competitive pricing on Fairmont.com and integrity through all Fairmont's channels.

By combining high-class with high tech, Fairmont Hotels and Resorts got the word out via direct marketing about the site's new features. Customers received emails driving them to customized landing pages, which list special offers and promotions. Some of the features visitors found included:

- Expanded booking features where guests not only can book rooms but also book select activities such as dining, tennis, golf and spa treatments.
- Destination maps where a click will transport

Case Study *continued*

you anywhere in the Fairmont world with drop-down menus for accessing cities and individual hotels.

- The Fairmont Planner, a clever, interactive planning tool that allows customers who are looking for a destination but don't know where to find Fairmont properties that match their individual experience needs.
- A virtual concierge that offers complete destination information in each destination. Rating is offered by an unbiased firm, 10Dest. Ranging from a full listing of area restaurants to parks and museums to location attractions, there's detailed information available at a stroke of the keyboard. There's even a Concierge Recommends list, sponsored by the hotel concierge, listing their very favourite recommendations and special events.

Results

In terms of web site activity, monthly visits increased steadily from 250,000 visits per month at launch to 586,000 visits twelve months later. Of those that can be tracked, 29 per cent are return visitors. Over the first 12 months of operations, bookings increased 270 per cent with an approximate 8–15 per cent increase per month. In relation to overall bookings at Fairmont Hotels, online numbers steadily increased from 0.93 per cent at launch to 2.17 per cent. Revenue generated on Fairmont.com more than doubled in the 12 months after the launch. In addition, on average one out of every four guests completing a room reservation booked an additional activity, with dining reservations being the most common. Such progress has been recognized by the media with *Internet Travel News'* Site of the Week, July 28, 2002, reporting that '. . . Fairmont.com easily outdoes the competition on their originality and features, without affecting the quality of the content'.

Courtesy of Jens Thraenhart, Director Internet Strategy, Fairmont Hotels and Resorts

Practical questions

1. Web reservations exercise

Think like the customer!

Use each of the specified channels to attempt to make a reservation for a standard double room for the Novotel in New York and the East-side Marriott in New York, for one night commencing 12 August. Obviously you do not need to complete the transaction – just go as far as where you are quoted a rate for the date specified. (Note that all properties may not be available on all channels, so if you cannot find it, don't worry.)

Record the number of rates listed and the monetary amount of the lowest publicly available rate displayed for the product specified. (Ignore any special rates such as AAA rates, senior citizen rates or anything else that the general public cannot normally purchase). Record rates in US dollars (www.xe.net/ucc can be used to make currency conversions).

(a) Use Expedia.com (www.expedia.com) to see if you can book each of the hotels.

(b) Use the chain site (e.g. www.hilton.com), if there is one, to make the same bookings.

(c) Use TravelWeb.com (www.travelweb.com) to see if you can book the same hotels.

(d) Use Hotels.com (www.hotels.com) to see if you can book the same hotels.

(e) Use Orbitz.com (if you are in the USA) or Opodo.com (if you are in Europe) to book the same hotels.

(f) Search for each of the hotels on Google. In each case, select the site that comes out top of the list and try to make a booking.

(g) Call the toll-free number of the chain to try to get a better rate (you should be able to find this number from the Web, shouldn't you?).

(h) With any other channel with which you are familiar, identify the lowest rate that you can find for your hotel on those dates.

Are the pricing strategies logical? Is there a connection between the cost of distributing over the channel and the rate(s) being offered there? What is each company doing to encourage customers to book directly?

Review questions

1. What effect did the development of the Web as a commercial medium have on the traditional intermediaries involved in travel distribution?

2. Why are figures showing online sales not a true representation of the importance of the online travel market?

3. From the hotel's perspective, explain the benefits of selling a room directly to the customer over the Web.

4. What are the three basic ways that a hotel can make itself available for sale online?

5. Why do consumers tend to use mega-agency sites rather than supplier sites when shopping for travel products online?

6. Expedia and Travelocity use which type of traditional intermediary as their information and bookings engine?

7. Explain how the name-your-own-price model works from the consumer's perspective.

8. What are the main advantages for of the name-your-own-price model for the hotel being sold?

9. What are the main advantages of sites such as Lastminute.com for the hotel being sold?

10. Explain the difference between the agency model and the merchant model (a) from the hotel's perspective and (b) from the intermediary's perspective.

11. Why are the mega-agencies placing increasing emphasis on packaging as a future strategy?

12. Explain the benefits of an intranet-based managed corporate travel system (a) for the travel manager of the company using it, and (b) for the hotel.

13. Give two examples of efforts by travel suppliers to re-divert sales away from the mega-agencies and back to their own direct sites.

14. Why are initiatives such as TravelWeb less likely to succeed than ones such as Orbitz and Opodo?

Discussion questions

1. Putting yourself in the position of a customer booking a business trip, compare your experience on the following sites; www.expedia.co.uk, www.lastminute.co.uk and www.6C.com. Which site is more likely to help you to organize your trip most efficiently? Why? Would your answer be the same if you were trying to organize a leisure trip?

2. Examine the web sites of both easyJet (www.easyjet.com) and RyanAir (www.ryanair.com). Both are highly successful and generate nearly 90 per cent of all bookings for their respective companies. What implications does this success have for the cost structure and profitability of these companies? From your examination of the sites, what strategies do these two companies seem to be using to generate bookings through this channel? Could hotel companies follow the same strategy? Why/why not?

3. You are the yield manager of a hotel property in which a significant amount of your business originates through one of the online mega-agencies. The company in question comes to you and says that it is shortly going to change from using the agency model to the merchant model. What implications does this have for your hotel? What would happen if you refused to participate in such a new pricing strategy?

4. Try to book at table at the restaurant of your choice using any online channel available to you. Can you actually make the booking? Why is booking a restaurant table so much more difficult that booking a hotel room or an airline seat? (Hint: Could the value of the transaction have something to do with it?)

9 Hotel computer applications

The use of dedicated computer systems for day-to-day support in hotels has become commonplace. This chapter reviews the major types of computer application used to support property level hotel operations and management. These include property management systems (PMS), which automate the front office of the hotel and act as the cornerstone of hotel technology, as well as a growing range of auxiliary or supporting systems including electronic door locks, energy management systems and call accounting systems. As we saw in Chapter 3, each of these systems can be and often is used separately. However, they operate much more efficiently when linked together to form an integrated hotel system. Although each system is discussed separately below, the importance of their integration should always be borne in mind. Figure 9.1, repeated from Chapter 3 (Figure 3.38), emphasizes this.

Property level reservation systems

Although the topics of electronic distribution and reservations systems were discussed in depth in Chapters 7 and 8, one facet is worth repeating in relation to hotel operations. Most hotels continue to maintain a reservation system at the property level, despite the benefits of single image inventory. This manages the room inventory for the individual hotel, tracking availability, helping to sell individual and group reservations and generate reports such as arrivals lists, reservation forecasts, travel agent commission due and pre-registration cards. Although its importance will decrease as usage of electronic distribution grows, direct reservations are still the most important source of business for most hotels and thus it makes sense to have a reservation system at the property. Where the hotel is part of a chain or consortium, this unit level system should be interfaced or integrated with the central reservation system to help increase coordination and reduce confusion. Irrespective of whether part of a chain or an independent property, the reservation system should in any case be integrated with the PMS, so that guest details can be automatically transferred to maximize efficiency and minimize retyping.

Property management systems

The front office is often described as the centre of all hotel activities. It not only acts as the main contact point between the hotel and the guest, but also provides information to and receives information from practically every other department

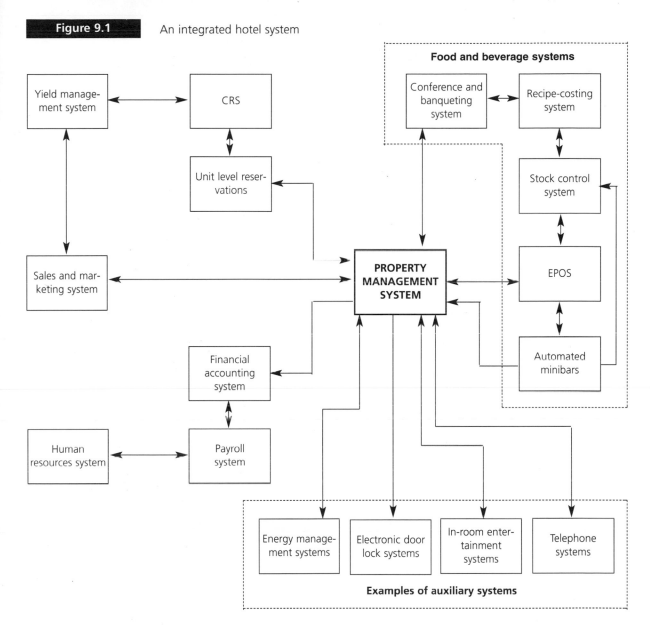

Figure 9.1   An integrated hotel system

in the hotel. A property management system (PMS) helps manage these interactions, and at the same time acts as an information hub for the other computer systems. The functions of a PMS may be broken down into the following different categories, each of which is discussed in more detail below:

- **Registration** – allocating vacant rooms to incoming guests and marking those rooms as being occupied;
- **Housekeeping** – tracking which rooms are occupied, waiting to be cleaned, waiting to be inspected, or ready to be passed back to the front desk for allocation to incoming guests;

- **Guest accounting** – tracking all guest charges and payments and producing the final guest bill;
- **Night audit** – automatically performing end-of-day routines such as posting room charges to each guest folio.

Registration

Upon arrival, a guest must check in or register in the hotel. Where the reservation system and the PMS are integrated, their personal details should already have been electronically transferred to help speed up the registration process and eliminate unnecessary re-keying of data. Usually a pre-registration card (Figure 9.2) will have been printed as part of the previous night audit, which the guest can simply sign to confirm the details and complete the check-in process. Guests without reservations can fill in a paper registration form and this information can then be entered quickly into the computer system.

Most systems allow reservations to be retrieved using either the guest's name or the reservation confirmation number. Once the reservation is displayed on the screen, a room can be allocated from the list of vacant rooms displayed by the system. This is then marked as being occupied to prevent it being allocated in error to another incoming guest. Similarly, group registration is greatly simplified using a computerized system. Rooms can be pre-allocated on the basis of a rooming list sent in advance by the organizers. On arrival, the entire group – for example, a bus tour – can be registered in a single step – literally at the touch of a button! Although traditionally check-in has happened at the reception desk, the growth in the use of technology-based systems has resulted in new and innovative ways of registering the guest. For example, many hotels now use laptop or hand-held computers to facilitate the check-in process, either at an office-style desk at which the guest can sit in comfort in upmarket hotels, or by taking the computer to the guest to allow registration in queues at high volume hotels such as at major airports or in Las Vegas, or even in transfer busses en route to the hotel. These devices allow hotel staff to wirelessly connect to the hotel PMS, retrieve the guest's reservation, capture a signature digitally on screen, swipe the guest's credit card and even generate an electronic key, all at a location remote from the front desk. Companies such as EuroDisney, who need to process

Figure 9.2

A pre-registration card

The Abbey Tavern

O'CONNOR, P. Mr	Arrival date	26 Apr 99
	Nights:	3
12 Eglinton Rd	Room type:	Double
Donnybrook		
Dublin 4		

Signature: _____

Your attention is drawn to 'The Hotel Proprietors Act' which is displayed at Reception thousands of check-ins each day, use such technology on the Eurostar train from London, to make life easy for the guest by avoiding queuing on arrival at the property and to take some of the pressure off the front desk.

Technology can also facilitate self check-in using kiosks in the lobby of the hotel. Again these can be used to avoid queues, or even to eliminate the front desk entirely, as is the case with budget brand such as Accor's Formula 1, thus saving on labour costs for the hotel while at the same time allowing guests to check-in 24 hours a day. However, while providing such facilities as an option can be a good idea, forcing guests to use them by providing no alternative may be counterproductive as in most cases guests still prefer the (however flawed) human touch. Self-check-in kiosks are normally more powerful than hand-held devices and normally allow both guest with a reservation and walk-ins to register, perhaps allowing them to choose a room from an interactive map of the property, swipe their credit cards and generate their room key, as well as acting as an information point (or virtual concierge) to allow guests to find out more about the hotel and surrounding area. Some hotel companies have even begun to question why the guest needs to register on arrival in the first place, and have started to provide facilities whereby guests (usually their frequent guests) can register on the day of arrival from anywhere using the Internet or the cell phone, and receive their room number by email or by text message. On arrival they can go straight to their allocated room and use their frequency card to open the electronic door lock – now that's service!

Irrespective of how the registration occurs, where the PMS is integrated with the other systems, the process of room allocation makes all the auxiliary systems aware that a new guest has registered. As a result, each system will provide its services to the newly occupied room. For example, the telephone system will allow calls to be made from the room's telephone, the energy-management system will blast the room with warm or cool air to get it to an acceptable temperature, and the electronic door-locking system will issue a new magnetic key specifically for the new guest. A billing folio is also opened automatically for the guest so that charges in the hotel's bars and restaurants can be posted to the room number by the EPOS systems. All of this happens automatically and invisibly, greatly helping to enhance guest service.

Housekeeping

The housekeeping or accommodation management department is responsible for cleaning and maintaining both the guest rooms and the public areas of the hotel, and its work needs to be closely coordinated with that of the front office. Good communication between these departments is therefore essential because the front office needs accurate and up-to-date information on the status (vacant, occupied or dirty) of every room in order to operate effectively. Some systems facilitate this using the telephone system. When the room attendant has finished servicing a room, he or she types a code into the telephone, which alerts the PMS that the room is ready for inspection. It can then be checked by the floor supervisor, who enters another code to inform the PMS that it is clean and ready for allocation to incoming guests. As a result, the front desk is aware immediately when rooms are ready for new guests, and does not have to keep guests waiting unnecessarily. The PMS also assists the accommodation manager by automatically providing lists of which guests are departing or staying over. Some systems will even help to equally distribute the cleaning load between room attendants, and produce assignment sheets automatically.

Guest accounting

A folio is automatically opened at registration to allow charges to be posted to the guest's account. This folio must always be kept accurate, up-to-date and capable of being produced for the guest on demand. Most systems allow each room to have more than one folio, which can be useful where guests are sharing rooms, or where a guest needs one folio for business expenses and another for personal extras, such as drinks or in-room movies.

Charges may be divided into two categories:

1. Some, such as the room rate, are posted automatically. This is important as, today, because of the use of yield management systems, most hotels normally have many different room rates. This makes it easy to post an incorrect rate accidentally, which either loses revenue for the hotel or infuriates the guest! A PMS, however, should always correctly identify the rate originally quoted to the guest at the time of reservation, and post it accurately to the guest's folio. Other automatic charges, such as taxes or service charge, can also be calculated automatically and accurately, helping to reinforce the professional image of the hotel.

2. Other charges are posted as the guest uses various hotel services such as bars, restaurants and leisure facilities. Sometimes these are posted manually from a paper docket system, but more recently the trend has been to use integrated EPOS systems to post charges directly and instantly onto the guest's account. So, for example, as soon as the guest orders in the restaurant, the charge appears on their folio. Similarly, when the guest types their room number into the remote control of the television to confirm that they wish to watch a pay movie, the charge for this movie is automatically posted on their folio. Such automation helps to reduce clerical errors and also prevents guests checking out without paying for services.

When posting charges (or payments) manually, several security features may be encountered. The clerk posting the transaction normally has to enter an identification code, which can be used to identify the person who made the posting in the event of a dispute at a later date. The room number and the amount to be posted to the account are then entered. A security code (such as the first four letters of the guest's surname from his or her signature) may then have to be entered to complete the posting. This helps prevent items being charged to the incorrect room number or by someone who is not staying in the hotel. Any payments received from guests are summarized on the cashier's shift report (Figure 9.4), which helps to improve cash control. All transactions are also recorded on an audit trail, which is automatically printed onto paper several times a day. This lists the details of every transaction, and can be invaluable to reconstruct guest bills if the computer system breaks down.

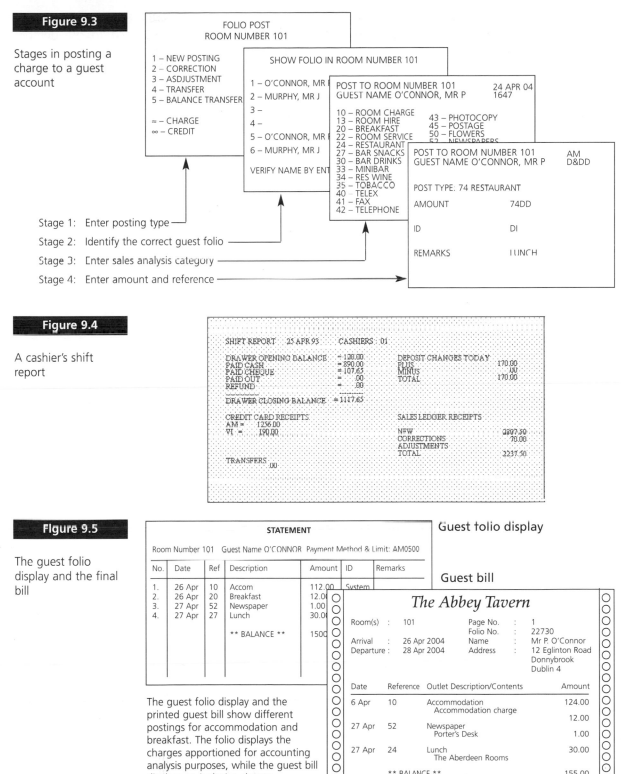

Figure 9.3

Stages in posting a charge to a guest account

FOLIO POST
ROOM NUMBER 101

1 – NEW POSTING
2 – CORRECTION
3 – ASDJUSTMENT
4 – TRANSFER
5 – BALANCE TRANSFER

≈ – CHARGE
∞ – CREDIT

SHOW FOLIO IN ROOM NUMBER 101

1 – O'CONNOR, MR P
2 – MURPHY, MR J
3 –
4 –
5 – O'CONNOR, MR P
6 – MURPHY, MR J

VERIFY NAME BY ENT

POST TO ROOM NUMBER 101   24 APR 04
GUEST NAME O'CONNOR, MR P   1647

10 – ROOM CHARGE   43 – PHOTOCOPY
13 – ROOM HIRE   45 – POSTAGE
20 – BREAKFAST   50 – FLOWERS
22 – ROOM SERVICE   52 – NEWSPAPERS
24 – RESTAURANT
27 – BAR SNACKS
30 – BAR DRINKS
33 – MINIBAR
34 – RES WINE
35 – TOBACCO
40 – TELEX
41 – FAX
42 – TELEPHONE

POST TO ROOM NUMBER 101   AM
GUEST NAME O'CONNOR, MR P   D&DD

POST TYPE: 74 RESTAURANT

AMOUNT   74DD

ID   DI

REMARKS   LUNCH

Stage 1:   Enter posting type
Stage 2:   Identify the correct guest folio
Stage 3:   Enter sales analysis category
Stage 4:   Enter amount and reference

Figure 9.4

A cashier's shift report

SHIFT REPORT   25 APR 93   CASHIERS 01

DRAWER OPENING BALANCE   = 120.00   DEPOSIT CHANGES TODAY
PAID CASH   = 890.00   PLUS   170.00
PAID CHEQUE   = 107.65   MINUS   .00
PAID OUT   =   .00   TOTAL   170.00
REFUND   =   .00

DRAWER CLOSING BALANCE   = 1117.65

CREDIT CARD RECEIPTS   SALES LEDGER RECEIPTS
AM =   1256.00
VI =   190.00   NEW   2297.50
                                      CORRECTIONS   70.00
                                      ADJUSTMENTS
                                      TOTAL   2237.50
TRANSFERS   .00

Figure 9.5

The guest folio display and the final bill

STATEMENT

Room Number 101   Guest Name O'CONNOR   Payment Method & Limit: AM0500

No.	Date	Ref	Description	Amount	ID	Remarks
1.	26 Apr	10	Accom	112.00	System	
2.	26 Apr	20	Breakfast	12.00		
3.	27 Apr	52	Newspaper	1.00		
4.	27 Apr	27	Lunch	30.00		
			** BALANCE **	1500		

Guest folio display

Guest bill

The Abbey Tavern

Room(s) :   101   Page No.   :   1
                           Folio No.   :   22730
Arrival   : 26 Apr 2004   Name   :   Mr P. O'Connor
Departure : 28 Apr 2004   Address   :   12 Eglinton Road
                                            Donnybrook
                                            Dublin 4

Date	Reference	Outlet Description/Contents	Amount
6 Apr	10	Accommodation	124.00
		Accommodation charge	
			12.00
27 Apr	52	Newspaper	
		Porter's Desk	1.00
27 Apr	24	Lunch	30.00
		The Aberdeen Rooms	
		** BALANCE **	155.00

The guest folio display and the printed guest bill show different postings for accommodation and breakfast. The folio displays the charges apportioned for accounting analysis purposes, while the guest bill displays an inclusive charge

To check-out, the guest must either pay the total due on their account, or (usually by pre-arrangement) have their balance transferred to the debtor's system (see Chapter 11). Upon check-out, the PMS alerts housekeeping that the room is ready to be cleaned, and also informs each of the auxiliary systems that the room is no longer occupied. As a result, the telephone system will no longer allow calls to be made from the bedroom's telephone, the EPOS will not accept charges for that room number, and the electronic locking system will not allow the former guest back into the bedroom.

Night audit

Each night various tasks, such as automatically posting the room charge to each guest's account, must be performed. In addition, all the accounts must be cross-checked to ensure that everything balances. These tasks were traditionally carried out manually by a team of night auditors. However, these tasks are routine and repetitive, which ultimately makes them boring. For example, imagine posting the room charges manually in a 100-bedroom hotel. Each guest folio would have to be examined in turn, the quoted room rate found, the charge posted and the new balance due calculated. Exactly the same procedure would have to be repeated for each of the other 99 rooms! However, this 'routineness' makes these tasks very suitable for computerization. The night-audit module automates these procedures and uses the power of the computer to ensure accuracy and reliability. And, because the computerized system works at electronic speeds, the audit is completed in minutes rather than in hours.

Some common procedures carried out automatically as part of the night audit include:

- **Posting room and tax**. As discussed above, the correct room rate must be posted to each guest's folio each night. Using a manual system, this alone could take several hours, and can be troublesome. The amount of time saved, and the increase in accuracy achieved, by automating this one procedure can often be sufficient reason to install a PMS in the first place.

- **Changing the system date**. The night audit is usually the last transaction in the hotel's day. Once everything is balanced, the system date is changed and all daily summary totals are reset to zero.

- **Performing system back-ups**. Where a computer is used in the front office, a vast amount of valuable data (such as reservation information and details of guest charges) is collected and stored electronically. If the system failed and all this data was lost, the hotel would be in a very difficult situation. For that reason, a system back-up (making a copy of all the hotel's data files) must be performed on a regular basis. In the event of a system failure, data can be restored from the back-up and only the transactions entered since the last back-up are lost. Such back-ups are normally carried out nightly, as part of the night-audit procedure.

- **Printing historical reports**. Various reports summarizing the previous day's and period-to-date's business (such as a nationality analysis, a department-alized sales analysis report, or a report summarizing revenue by source of business) are generated by the system to keep management informed about the hotel operations.

- **Printing operational materials for the next day**. These include status reports such as expected arrivals and departure lists, and other operational items such as pre-registration cards and confirmation letters. Folios for guests who are expected to depart in the morning may also be printed to help speed up the check-out process. In some cases, these are slipped under the bedroom doors of departing guests in the middle of the night so that they can use self-check-out facilities in their room (see below) to avoid queuing at the reception desk in the morning.

Ancillary systems

This section gives an overview of various systems which, although not part of the PMS itself, interface with it and increase efficiency and control. Many of these systems generate valuable incremental revenue for the property, while in other cases the provision of the system becomes a differentiator in the mind of the guest, helping to make the property stand out in a sea of similar-looking hotels all providing the same facilities and amenities. As a result, the number and complexity of ancillary systems is growing rapidly, and, while the list below mentions those most commonly found in the hotel industry, it is by no means exhaustive. Each system is then discussed in detail in the following sections:

- Electronic door-locking systems;
- Energy-management systems;
- Call accounting and telephone systems;
- Internet access;
- TV-based services;
- In-room safes.

Many catering-related systems that operate in the hotel environment, such as EPOS systems and minibars, also interface with the PMS. These are discussed in detail in Chapter 10.

Electronic door-locking systems

Given the public nature of hotels, security is obviously important. The locks on hotel doors are usually of good quality, which has the side effect that their keys are expensive to cut. Unfortunately, guests have a habit of accidentally taking the room key with them when they depart. When this happens, the door lock has to be replaced because someone could return with the 'stolen' key at a later date and get back into the room, and of course hotels make it easy for the thief by listing their address and the room number on the plastic tag attached to the key. A further disadvantage with conventional keys is that some members of staff (such as housekeepers or duty managers) have special keys, known as sub-masters or masters, which are capable of opening most of the locks in the hotel. If one of these is lost, every lock affected has to be changed!

Figure 9.6

Alternative types of
electronic keycards

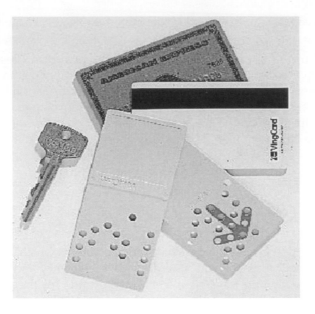

An electronic door-locking system uses small plastic cards instead of metal keys. The combination that opens the door can be recorded on these cards in a variety of ways: either by punching holes in the card, by storing it on a magnetic strip on the rear of the card or by storing it on the embedded chip of a smart card. Because of the way the system works, it does not matter if the guest forgets to return the key at check-out as the combination in the door lock is changed and a new, unique key issued for each new guest.

Electronic door-locking systems are generally set up in one of two ways. Some systems use a stand-alone 'in-the-door' microprocessor, while others use an online system that is connected by wiring to a computer at the front desk. The stand-alone systems operate by storing a predetermined sequence of combinations in each lock and on the computer that issues the keys. The door lock 'knows' that a new guest has checked in when it reads the key with the next combination in the sequence. However, problems arise when the door locks and the front-office computer become unsynchronized. For example, if a door key is issued but never used, the computer at the front office will move on to the next combination but the door lock will not. As a result, when the next guest checks in and is issued a new key, it will not open the door because the lock is one step behind in the sequence and is expecting a different combination, and the newly arrived guest is left standing in the corridor with his luggage! With an online system, the computer communicates directly with the lock and cancels the previous access code as soon as the guest checks out. When a new guest arrives and a new key is issued, the lock is immediately informed of the new combination. Online systems also offer higher levels of security as they can be programmed to sound an alarm if a door is left ajar or opened forcibly. However, online systems tend to be much more expensive, particularly because of the cost of installing wiring between each door lock and the front-office computer.

With an electronic door-locking system, staff keys are also more secure. If a master key is lost or stolen, combinations in the door locks can be scrambled quickly and easily to prevent anyone gaining access to guest rooms. (With an online system, this can happen literally instantly, as all the locks in the hotel can be reprogrammed to ignore the combination on the missing key with the touch of a button from the central computer. With a stand-alone system, someone would have to go to each individual lock with a hand-held computer and update its individual database; a process that while easier than actually having to physically change the locks in each door is still time-consuming and frustrating.) Keys can also be time-limited (thus preventing their use when the employee is off duty) or limited to particular areas (for example, a floor housekeeper's key might open all doors on one floor, but not on any other floors). Most systems can also maintain an audit trail to track which keys have been used to enter each room, and this computerized record can now be submitted as evidence in legal proceedings. However, while this facility can allow management to track who has entered a particular room within a certain time period, gathering data from a block of rooms can be time-consuming. Each door lock would have to be addressed individually and its data downloaded because it is the door, not the key, which stores the information. If a smart-card-based system is being used, and you are worried about where a particular employee has been, you don't have to read 500 locks, you can just read the information stored on the smart card's chip. In any case, knowing that the system can track their whereabouts so easily is a major deterrent to wrongdoing for most employees.

Energy-management systems

Now that most guest's room have a TV, a hairdryer, a refreshment centre, business equipment and many other in-room facilities, more electricity is being used throughout the hotel and managing energy costs has become a priority. Unfortunately conserving power is usually not a priority for most guests, and many frequently leave their rooms with all the lights turned on, the television blaring and the air-conditioning running at full steam. Very basic mechanical systems, such as turning off the air-conditioning when the balcony door is open, can result in major power savings. However, by using technology-based systems, hoteliers can now take control of room lighting, temperature and electricity and minimize energy use while at the same time maintaining guest comfort and control. For example, energy-management systems can automatically reduce heating or air-conditioning in unoccupied rooms or areas of the hotel. If a guest is allocated a room in that area, the system blasts it with warm or cold air to return it quickly to an acceptable temperature. Electronically controlled systems allow more accurate control to be maintained over temperatures, which can lead to further energy savings. For example, temperatures can be kept accurate to within ± 0.2°C, as opposed to ± 3°C with mechanical thermostats, which means that average temperatures can be reduced. Thus, to achieve a minimum temperature of 18°C with a thermostat cycle of ± 3°C, an average temperature of 21°C is required. Using a computerized energy-management system with a cycle of ± 0.2°C, this can be reduced to 18.2°C, which can lead to energy savings of up to 10 per cent.

While some systems work by using the guest's key card as a physical trigger, for example by requiring the guest to place their key card in a special holder by the bedroom door to activate the room's power services, more advanced systems use sensors in the room, and some basic logic built into the energy control unit to provide a more invisible level of service. When the door opens and the sensor detects the presence of a guest, room services are activated and control over temperature is given to the guest, bounded only by the outer limits set by the hotel (to prevent pipes freezing in winter and the air-conditioning running flat out in summer). If the guest goes to sleep and there is no detectable movement (although most modern sensors are sensitive enough to detect the guest's breathing even while asleep), the systems still know the room is occupied, as the door hasn't opened. If the door opens and movement is still detected afterwards, the room is obviously still occupied. Perhaps someone came in, or the guest dropped a room service tray in the corridor for pick-up. Only when no movement is sensed after the door has opened will the system set itself to 'no-occupant' mode and turn off the power and adjust the temperature. When used throughout the hotel, energy-management systems of this type can generate savings of between 30 and 60 per cent. (A useful little service that is related to this system allows house-keeping to avoid disturbing the guest unnecessarily. By building an invisible

---

Figure 9.7

Energy-management system savings

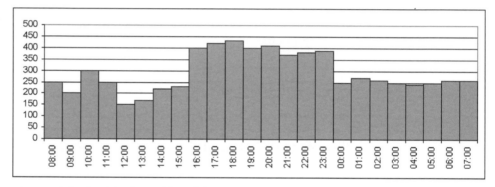

Average daily electricity demand (watts) for one room at the Travelodge without any energy management system installed.

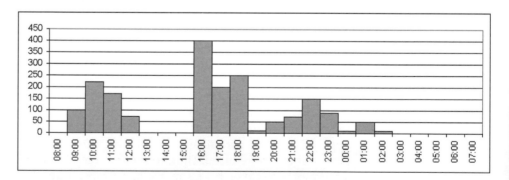

Average daily electricity demand (watts) for one room at the Travelodge with energy management system installed.

Annual electricity bill of the Travelodge *before* installation of energy management system: UK£30,000
Annual electricity bill of the Travelodge *after* installation of energy management system: UK£12,000

Source: Lowe Group publicity brochure

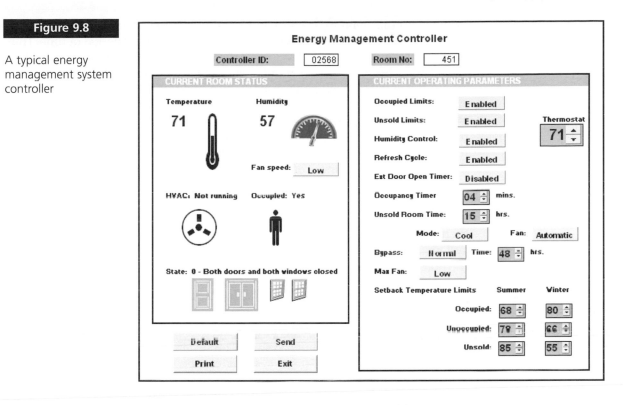

Figure 9.8

A typical energy management system controller

indicator into the door to show whether the room is occupied or not, hotel staff can use a small hand-held device to see if the guest is in the room, even if he is sleeping and has forgotten to put out the 'do-not-disturb' sign, and thus make sure he is not interrupted unnecessarily.)

Call accounting and telephone systems

Telephone systems are one of the most common uses of technology in hotels. Direct-dial facilities from the guest bedrooms are provided by a piece of equipment known as the private automated branch exchange (PABX). This is basically a computer system that connects the hotel's internal telephone system to the outside world and manages the allocation of lines to incoming and outgoing calls. A typical hotel could have, for example, one hundred telephone extensions in guest rooms and administrative offices. Obviously not all of these are used simultaneously, and thus a smaller number of incoming lines are required to provide dial tone access. So, for example, the hotel may have eight incoming lines, which are then allocated on an as-needed basis to the individual extensions. The downside is, of course, that there will be times when all of the outside lines will be busy and thus no more incoming or outgoing calls can be serviced. An important question, therefore, is how many outside lines are needed in a typical hotel? While in the past most hotels had one line for every twelve bedrooms, now many hotel chains require a ratio of one line to every six rooms. The reason for this is the growth in the number of guests carrying laptop computers and using the telephone in their bedroom to connect to their company network or the Internet.

While voice calls tend to be short in duration, data calls tend to be much longer – thus tying up one of the valuable outside lines for a longer period of time. Thus, in order to provide adequate levels of service and allow other guests to get a telephone line when they want it, more outside lines are needed. However, justifying the investment in installing these addition lines is difficult, as many of these calls are to toll-free or local numbers and thus adding more lines often results in little increased telephone revenue – catch 22! For this reason, many hotels are concentrating on providing business travellers with other ways of accessing the Internet, for example by providing high speed Internet access from the guest room rather than increasing the number of telephone lines coming into the hotel.

Another systems works alongside the PABX to provide direct dial facilities. The *call accounting system* records the number dialled from each extension, its duration and calculates the charge for each call. This data can be printed onto paper and then manually posted onto the guest's account or, in the case of an integrated system, automatically posted directly onto the guest's bill. The main advantage for the hotel is increased control. Because the time of the call and the number dialled is recorded, it is more difficult for the guest to dispute having made the call and, because the charge is posted automatically on completion of the call, guests cannot check out without paying for all their telephone calls. Most systems will also not allow calls to be made from unoccupied rooms, which helps prevents fraudulent use of the telephone system. The system also monitors administrative telephone extensions, and good systems can be set up to highlight the most expensive calls, the longest calls and most frequently dialled numbers to help discourage employee telephone fraud. Other facilities provided by telephone systems include automatic wake-up calls (often in multiple languages), caller identification and voicemail. Caller identification displays the name of the guest (taken from the PMS) on a screen and allows staff to provide guest name recognition, thereby increasing the perception of customer service. Voicemail allows spoken messages to be left for guests who are not in their rooms, which is much more efficient than having a telephone operator scribble a message on a piece of paper. All messages are automatically stamped with the time and date they were recorded, and can be replayed on any phone by dialling into the voicemail system and entering an appropriate room number and security code. More advanced

---

Figure 9.9

A call accounting system profit report

Telephone Profit Report Room 101

Report for calls 3/4/03 to 4/4/03

Type		Number dialled	Dur	Time	Date	Cost	Profit	Charge
DODD	LCL	7453353	17	21:35	04/03/2003	0.14	0.61	0,75
DODD	INT	001-852-5256272	2	22:03	04/03/2003	4.97	9.23	14.20
DODD	INC		11	22:45	04/03/2003	0.00	0.00	0.00
DODD	INT	00-44-785525566	37	22:56	04/03/2003	22.59	39.83	62.42
DODD	L2N	1-800-7921516	2	09:04	04/04/2003	0.84	0.60	1.44
DODD	INT	00-44-4133440822	2	09:30	04/04/2003	2.64	5.92	8.56
DODD	LCL	6784566	3	09:35	04/04/2003	0.14	0.61	0.75

Total Telephone Costs ------ 31.32
Total Telephone Profits ------ 56.80
Total Telephone Charges ------ 88.12

systems feature a link to the PMS and the reservations system, so that guests checking in at the front desk can be made aware of messages left for them before arrival, and these voicemails can be automatically transferred to their room's voicemail box. Many business-focused hotels are now trying to increase the level of service that they provide to their guests by providing voicemail facilities for a limited time after the guest has checked out of the hotel.

One of the major limitations of traditional hotel telephone systems was that the wire connecting them to the wall limited their mobility. Many hotels now provide the guest (and often their employees) with cordless phones. Not only is this more convenient for the guest within the room, but many digital cordless phones allow calls to be made and received anywhere in the hotel, thus eliminating the problem of trying to track down the guest for an important call when he is not in his room, and also making it easier and more convenient for the guest to make calls, thus helping to increase telephone revenue. Some hotels are even going a step further and providing valued guests with cellphones that can be used anywhere in the destination for the duration of their stay, with all calls automatically being charged to their billing folio on the PMS.

Internet access

The Internet's mass appeal as a business and entertainment tool has forced hoteliers to think about the ways in which they can provide Internet access to their guests. A 2003 survey of business travellers carried out by *Hotel and Motel* magazine found that 54 per cent of business travellers now require access to the Internet during their stay. Several different options are available to provide this, including through network points in the guest room, from the hotel's business centre, from Internet kiosks located in the hotel lobby or even wirelessly through the public areas of the hotel. The demand for Internet access in the room is having an effect on the number of telephone lines needed in most hotels, but justifying the investment is difficult because of the low incremental revenues. The solutions detailed below may be cheaper and may also be able to generate additional revenues – resulting in increased profits – from the guest.

One strategy for providing Internet access involves partnering with the TV/movie/cable provider to provide Internet access through the television system. Using infrared keyboards and mice, guests can browse the Web and manage their email page (which may be all that they want to do) without tying up any of the hotel's phone lines. Such systems suffer from the disadvantage that they do not have the capability to upload or download files, and may suffer from some security fears as guests worry about what residual data remains on such systems once they have logged off. Business travellers (the primary market for Internet access) usually need access to applications and data on their own laptops, so Internet access through the television is not attractive to anyone but the casual browser. To cater for more demanding users, another strategy is to provide high-speed Internet access in selected hotel rooms, and to promote these heavily among guests demanding Internet access. For example, the I-Port system allows customers with laptops equipped with a network card to access the hotel's network at speeds up to 50 times faster than is possible over a telephone. This involves extending the hotel's ethernet network to the rooms in question and providing network points into which guests can plug their laptops; which is a costly solution, as wiring has to be run to each guest room. Two other solutions have emerged. Newer systems use the existing telephone wire (but at a different frequency so that guests can still make calls while using the network) to deliver high-speed connectivity to the guest room. And many hotels are now introducing wireless networking by placing wireless access points strategically throughout the public areas of the hotel (and sometimes in guest rooms as well) to allow guests to connect their WiFi-enabled laptops. Naturally, since in each case the level of service is better than what can be achieved over a conventional telephone line,

| Table 9.1 | Summary of options to allow guest laptops access to the Internet |

System	How the guest uses it	Cost to hotel	Pros	Cons
Standard telephone line	Plugging their laptop modem into the RJ-11 port on the side of the telephone	Monthly line rental plus the cost of the call, which is offset by the amount charged to the guest	System is already installed and working in most properties	Slow speed (max 56 Kbps). Ties up the hotel's phone lines
ISDN	Via dedicated digital phone line(s) and a special ISDN modem	Expensive monthly rental plus the cost of the call, which is offset by the amount charged to the guest	Faster and more reliable than a standard telephone line. May be used in pairs to given even higher speeds	Requires dedicated lines and special modems. Low usage levels
Ethernet	Using the network card built into the guest's laptop	Wiring to guest bedroom. Increased bandwidth on hotel's network to cope with increased traffic	Very fast! Easy to set up – literally plug in and play. No incremental costs	Wiring is expensive. Security issues with allowing guests access to hotel network
Wireless	Using a WiFi card built into their laptop, or any other wireless-enabled device	Wireless access points strategically located throughout building	Access anywhere. Revenue generation opportunities from guest and non-guests	Technical to operate
DSL	Via DSL modems in the guest room, connected to their laptop via USB ports or network cards	DSL modem in each guest room	Uses existing wiring. Very fast download speeds	Expense of purchasing and installing modems

the hotel can charge a premium for its use. Rates of about €20 per day are common, providing a very useful and lucrative additional revenue stream for the hotel. However many hotels, particularly those that deal primarily with business guests, are now starting to provide such facilities for free or at least building them into the room rate as part of their normal range of amenities for guests, and most people agree that such facilities will become a standard service for guests, just like the television and the telephone, in the near future.

TV-based services

A television, offering access to local, cable, satellite and pay channels, has become a necessity in practically every guest room. According to technology consultant Ted Horner, nearly 93 per cent of guests use the television during their stay, and it is rare these days to find a hotel room without a large television set cluttering up the corner. Providing such facilities is obviously expensive from both a capital and an operational point of view but the cost can be offset somewhat by using the television to provide a range of additional services. For example, the television is increasingly being used as a device to give information to the guest. Often it is used to display a welcoming message, in the language of the guest, immediately after check-in. Telephone messages and other information such as special promotions available in the hotel or even room-service menus can also be displayed on screen. Some security systems automatically switch on televisions to broadcast evacuation information orally and visually in the event of an emergency. Many systems allow the guest to view their PMS billing folio on screen, and some facilitate check-out from the room, thus allowing the guest to avoid queues at the front desk in the morning. Guests typically review their bills on the screen and, provided everything is in order, press a one-digit approval button on either the telephone handset or the television remote control. However, having to get a copy of the paper printout greatly reduces the usage of in-room check-out by business clients, as they need a printed copy of the bill in order to reclaim their expenses. As the availability of an instant receipt would greatly increase usage, some hotels are overcoming this problem by using the printer or fax machine in the guest room to instantly produce a copy of the bill that the client can take away with them.

Revenue generating facilities that can be provided include pay-movie channels, Nintendo-style games and even interactive shopping. Pay-movies usually use dedicated channels playing a selection of movies in rotation 24 hours a day, and include a timing device so that after a brief preview, the system asks the guest to type their room number into the remote control to confirm that they wish to keep watching and are willing to accept the charge. More advanced systems feature DVOD (digital video on demand) – basically a video jukebox that allows the guest to watch a large selection of movies at a time that is convenient for them (rather than on a preset schedule), and also allows the guest to pause and rewind if they so wish. As we saw earlier, the TV is also being used as an Internet connectivity device through the use of cordless keyboards and mice, and many hotels with a leisure clientele provide interactive video games on the television to keep young (and not so young) guests occupied. Each of these systems increases the number of services provided to guests, while at the same time generating incremental revenue for the hotel.

In-room safes

An in-room safe is not new technology, but it is something that most business travellers expect because they are travelling with thousands of dollars worth of technology. In addition to cash, business travellers typically carry a laptop computer, a cell phone and perhaps a PDA that need to be stored safely while the guest is not using them. (Some modern systems offer a power outlet actually inside the safe so that guests can charge their laptop while it is in storage). As with door locks, the least sophisticated come with a keyed lock. Others use the same magnetic card from the door lock as their key, but most hotel room safes now make use of a four- or six-digit combination that can be set personally by the guest to control access. Newer safes are starting to use biometrics, allowing guest to open the safe with their thumbprint.

What facilities do hotel guests actually want?

Figure 9.10 gives an idea of the types of facilities that are currently being provided in hotel guest rooms.

However, the question must be asked – what in-room facilities do guests actually want? Research has shown that that the business guest has very specific but simple needs. These include a large work desk, an ergonomic chair, a room safe big enough to store their laptop computer and appropriate lighting to allow them to get some work done. Desk level power is useful to facilitate their use of a laptop computer, while a clearly labelled telephone jack allows them to connect to the Internet to check email or connect to their company network. The latter is particularly important as many hotels still hard wire their telephones into the wall, which prevents the laptop being connected in the first place, while others use digital phone systems that can damage laptop modems if connected by mistake. Many business clients also require printing facilities, although opinions are divided as to whether an in-room printer/fax/copier or a hotel business centre is the best way to satisfy this need. Another alternative is to have a partnership

Figure 9.10

In-room systems available to guests

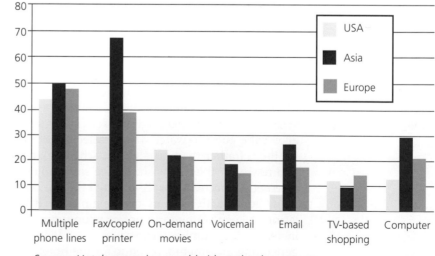

Source: *Hotels* magazine, worldwide technology survey

with a company that provides online printing solutions, whereby the guest uploads the files to be printed to a web site, and these are electronically rerouted to a printer located near the front desk or concierge desk. Sometimes the simplest things, such as a power or telephone jack converter, can make all the difference.

While leisure guests are less demanding in terms of business facilities, they increasingly want the types of amenities they take for granted in their homes, such as good quality television sets, hi-fi and computer games. As the technology and entertainment facilities available in the home continue to develop, hotels must keep pace if they are to maintain an adequate level of service and comfort. Resorts need to provide similar levels of technology to business hotels, because while people often want to get away from it all, they often need to bring their office toys along with them to keep in contact with the rest of the world. While presented in a more unobtrusive way, resorts need to provide similar levels of connectivity, security and service to attract the demanding business client who wants to get away from it all while still staying in touch. Those who are not interested in it can ignore it, but those who need it will be extremely grateful that you provided it.

Case Study

Journalist Bill Howard is very clear about what he wants in the guest room

I'm sorry, but to me 'business traveler's room' should mean more than two packets of Starbucks coffee next to the in-room coffee maker and a copy of *USA Today* dropped outside the door at 4.00 A.M. If I'm paying a surcharge for a 'business' room, there should be something tangible, such as a computer desk, and an ergonomic chair so that I don't have to pull over an armchair and try to raise the seating height with two pillows from the bed. Secondly, a combination printer/fax machine. One that is functional. With paper! With ink still in the cartridges! With a printer cable! With spares available at the front desk at 11:00 P.M. These are the only three things that justify an extra fee.

It goes without saying that the phone should have an RJ-11 jack built in, or there should be a wall jack expressly labeled 'modem' or 'data'. From time to time, you find unlabeled RJ-11s in the room, and you're never sure whether it's a data line, a second jack for the room's single phone line, an abandoned line or a digital line that could fry your modem. Labeling is important because the hotel staff aren't likely to know anything about what type of line it is, particularly when I need to use it at midnight! There ought to be power outlets near the desk, and if any of these are switched, there needs to be a big warning label. There is nothing more frustrating than arriving into a hotel after a long flight with a dead laptop battery, plugging it into charge and then finding next morning that it's still dead because when you turned off the switch by the door to put out the lights, you also turned off all the power outlets in the room. And since, because of energy management systems, many hotels now only provide power when you are in the room, they should provide one or two clearly labeled outlets that stay live all the time so that you can charge your laptop while you're away from your room. One last thing – every room should have a room safe big enough to hold a laptop computer. And every desk should have an attaching point for a Kensington lock security cable.

Adapted from: Howard, Bill, 'Practical sense for road warrior', *PC Magazine*, October 1997.

Perhaps the easiest way to decide if a facility is necessary is to look at the hotel's guest and ask: Will the facility markedly increase guest satisfaction? Will it give the hotel a marketing advantage over its competitors? Will it help provide more efficient service? Will it help to substantially reduce operating costs? If the answer to all of these points is 'No', then there is little point is installing that facility in your rooms. One further point is also important. We also need to consider the abilities and comfort levels of the guest with technology. Too often the guest is intimidated or confused by in-room technology: transparency in terms of ease of use is critical. For that reason, some companies have introduced technology concierges – specialized staff to help troubleshoot the in-room systems and help guests with general computer-related problems. However all your staff should know how to both operate and troubleshoot the systems. When a guest is having trouble with their pay-per-view movie system at midnight, the technical staff are unlikely to be around as they all went home at 6 o'clock! Of course a much better solution would to be make all of the in-room systems so simple that even your mother (or perhaps my mother) could use them intuitively!

Case Study *Using computerized systems in small hotels*

Nick Jackman, manager of the Gatwick Skylodge Hotel, describes the effect of installing a computer system in a fifty-bedroom airport hotel.

With most guests only staying one night and an average of 90 per cent occupancy, we have an extremely heavy load of paperwork. Before the computer was introduced, all the confirmations and invoices were typed and room bookings were kept in the traditional way. Now the computer is used for everything from the initial telephone inquiry to the final billing. The staff like it because it gives them more time to spend on more interesting work, and it gives the hotel a more professional image, but above all it relieves us of all the tedious administrative and paperwork chores. At the end of every day the computer totals the transactions performed in the previous 24 hours, breaking down payments into payment types (Access, American Express, Visa, cash or cheques). At the moment the daily information is printed out and then sent to the Skylodge accounts department in London, although it is hoped that soon the daily totals will be sent to the accounts department automatically over an electronic link.

The system installed in the hotel is basically a property management system (PMS). This is interfaced with the group's central reservation system, and reservations are automatically downloaded three times a day. Most of the Skylodge's customers have reservations, although the hotel also picks up a lot of walk-in business from the airlines when flights are delayed or cancelled. The telephone, minibar and video-on-demand systems are all interfaced with the PMS to allow charges to be posted automatically, as is the EPOS system in the bar and restaurant. Although these interfaces were expensive to develop, Jackman feels that they were worth it.

In the past, we had a lot of problems with late charges, as guests often managed to check out without settling all of their bills. With the new system, everything is posted automatically and immediately, thus helping to greatly increase control.

Case Study *continued*

As well as performing the end-of-day routines before morning, rather than the middle of the next afternoon as before, Jackman is able to access and analyse the performance of the hotel with great ease. The revenue is broken down into accommodation, no-shows, room hire, VAT, restaurant, bar, telephone, newspapers and other extras, so that management is able to see how areas of the business are performing. 'I feel that all the analysis is a lot more reliable now. Before, there was a lot of room for error.' Before the system was installed, Jackman and his staff had to keep the same records, generate the same acknowledgment letters, draw up the bills and analyse the business to the same degree as does the computer system. The difference is that everything is now done automatically.

Previously we had several members of staff permanently tied up doing the work which the computer does now. No one has lost their job, but our staff are now able to spend a lot more of their time at the front desk looking after the guests, which is obviously more pleasant.

Practical questions

These exercises are designed to familiarize you with many of the transactions that you would encounter working in both the reservations section and the front office of a typical hotel. To complete the exercises successfully, you must process each transaction in the order shown (tick them off as you finish them). If you skip any, some of the later transactions or reports will not work!

Day one: reservations department – morning

You have just started work in the reservations section of the Heather Hotel. Enter each of the following transactions into your reservations system.

- ☎ Mr Fergus Brown wishes to make a reservation for a single room for two nights starting tomorrow. He is a businessman who stays regularly, and pays the commercial rate of £50.00 per night. A deposit is not requested. His address is 12 George's St, Amsterdam.

- ☎ Miss Edel Clancy wishes to make a booking for both a double and a single room for a single night starting tomorrow. She has been offered a rate of £40.00 per person per night (p.p.p.n.) for the double room and £55.00 for the single. Her address is 'The Oaks', Manchester, UK. A deposit of £40.00 is requested.

- 🖥 Mr Fred White arrives at the front desk and wants a double room for tonight. He is charged the rack rate of £70.00 p.p.p.n. His address is Widget Enterprises, Lisdoonvarna, Co. Clare. Enter his details and allocate him a room from the list of vacant rooms displayed.

❑ ☎ Mr Brown rings and cancels his reservation.

❑ 🖃 Miss Clancy sends a deposit of £50.00.

❑ ☎ Dr George Harris wishes to make a reservation for a double room for one week, commencing tomorrow. He is offered a rate of £40.00 p.p.p.n. His address is 13 Grange Rd, Rathfarnham, Co. Dublin. Because this reservation is for such a long period, it must be guaranteed. Dr Harris uses his credit card as a guarantee method – Visa 5432 2345 2567.

❑ ☎ Mr Brown rings and cancels his cancellation. Re-enter his booking.

Day one: front desk – afternoon

Congratulations! You have done so well this morning in reservations that the front-office manager has decided that you should work at reception. Enter each of the following transactions into your PMS:

❑ ☎ Make a reservation for John North for a double room for one night, arrival tomorrow.

❑ 💻 Enter a chance arrival, for a suite for three nights at a rate of £100.00 p.p.p.n., for Mr Richard West. Assign an appropriate room to Mr West.

❑ 📄 Examine and print the guest list. If you have done everything correctly so far, there should be two people currently registered in the hotel (Mr White from earlier today and Mr West from the last transaction).

❑ 📄 Examine and print the arrivals list for tomorrow. (There should be four people listed.)

❑ 📄 Examine and print the expected departures list for tomorrow. (There should only be one person listed.)

❑ 💻 Examine Mr West's and Mr North's folios. There are no charges listed on their accounts yet. Why not?

❑ 💻 It is the end of the day. Run the night audit, post room and tax, and change the system date.

Day two: front office – early shift

❑ 💻 Examine Mr West's folio again. There should be a charge for accommodation on his account. Where did this originate?

❑ 📄 Examine the arrival list. Is Mr North's name on the list? Is Mr West's? Explain why one is on the list and the other is not!

❑ 💻 Mr North has arrived. Register him and assign a suitable room to him. He will settle his bill in cash.

❑ 📄 Post the following charges to the relevant guest accounts;

Mr White	Breakfast	£14.00
Mr West	Newspapers	£2.30
Mr North	Breakfast	£21.00
Mr North	Leisure Club	£5.00

❑ 💻 Mr White wants to check out. He pays his bill in full in cash. Accept this payment and check him out.

❑ 💻 Mr Brown and Dr Harris arrive. Register each of them in turn and allocate appropriate rooms to them.

❑ 📄 Examine the arrivals list. Who has yet to arrive?

❑ 📄 Examine tomorrow's arrivals list. Why is it blank?

❑ 💻 Mr Brown comes to the front desk and tells you that he needs two bills, one with just the accommodation charge and the other with his incidentals. Arrange this on the system

❑ $ Dr Harris makes a prepayment of £200.00 using his Visa card. Credit this to his account.

❑ 📄 Print your cashier's report. Explain where both the cash and the credit-card totals originated. (Hint: do not forget the deposits taken when you were working in reservations.)

❑ 💻 Mr North's toilet is leaking! Check which rooms are vacant and change him to a new room.

Review questions

1. What does each of the following abbreviations mean:
   (a) PMS;
   (b) CRS;
   (d) EPOS;
   (c) PABX?

2. Name the major constituent modules of a PMS.

3. What are the five functions of a reservation system?

4. Name the most common ancillary systems which interface with the PMS.

5. Describe the effect that registering a new guest has on the:
   (a) Guest accounting module;
   (b) EPOS system;
   (c) Telephone system;
   (d) Energy-management system.

6. Why might a guest require two separate account folios?

7. What five tasks are typically carried out by a night-audit procedure?

8. Explain how energy-management systems can help to reduce power consumption.

9. What factors should you take into account when evaluating a new in-room facility for your hotel?

Discussion questions

1. What benefits are gained by using an integrated hotel system as opposed to many independent systems?

2. The PMS has been described as the core of all the computer systems in the hotel, around which all the other systems revolve and all information flows. Explain why this is so important.

3. Automatic self-check-out, either in the hotel room or at ATM-style machines in the lobby, is becoming common. What are the advantages of such a system for both the guest and the hotel? Why then are such systems not used in every hotel?

4. A vast amount of data about customers is collected each day by hotel computer systems. Explain how this data could be useful for other purposes.

5. Compare stand-alone and online electronic door-locking systems in terms of both the level of security provided and their cost.

10 Catering computing systems

Technology is playing an increasingly important role in food and beverage operations and management. Equipment such as combination microwave/convection ovens, blast chillers, induction hobs and a wide variety of other technology-based systems are now commonplace in many kitchens. The use of information technology-based (IT-based) systems is also gaining ground. IT-based systems that focus primarily on food and beverages form an essential part of the integrated hotel system introduced in Chapter 3. As was discussed, recipe-costing systems, stock-control systems, electronic point-of-sale (EPOS) systems, conference and banqueting systems and specialist systems such as minibars all interact with the PMS to help ensure the smooth running of the hotel. Of course, not all catering operations are part of a hotel. Restaurants, fast food outlets, industrial catering and institutional catering (in areas such as hospitals, prisons and schools) all have their own individual management and control needs, which are very different to those of a hotel. As a result, several other systems which do not form part of the integrated hotel system are also discussed in this chapter. These include automatic vending systems, cashless payment systems, nutritional analysis systems and beverage-control systems. Figure 10.1 shows how these additional systems interact with the more common catering-oriented ones. As with hotel-oriented applications, each catering system often functions independently. However, the systems are much more efficient and effective if integrated to share common data. Indeed, integration brings such increases in productivity that an integrated system is often known as a *catering information system*.

Recipe-costing systems

A recipe-costing system uses up-to-date prices to calculate an accurate cost for food and beverage products. Based on these costs, selling prices that guarantee a particular level of profit can be established.

Irrespective of whether a manual or a computerized system is being used, *standard recipes* are often used to calculate the cost of each dish. Each food and beverage item has to be examined and standardized in terms of its portion size, ingredients and method of preparation. Traditionally, this process generated a series of paper recipe cards, each of which listed the ingredients needed to produce the dish in question, and an accurate costing based on the quantity of each ingredient used. However, the costing was only accurate while prices remained static. If the price of butter, for example, changed, then each recipe card that contained butter had to be found and its cost recalculated. Obviously this was too time-consuming to be done every time each ingredient price changed (which could be every day when dealing with fresh produce), so many operations simply increase their 'estimated' recipe costs in line with inflation. As a result, their calculations quickly became inaccurate, often resulting in eroded profit margins.

Computerized recipe-costing systems reduce the amount of time and effort needed to keep recipe costs up to date by automatically recalculating costs whenever ingredient prices change. Every recipe that contains an ingredient whose price has changed is accessed and is cost updated in seconds. As a result, recipe costs are always accurate, meaning that profit margins are guaranteed.

Recipe-costing systems operation

Recipe-costing systems use a database of ingredients to build up an accurate cost for each recipe (Figure 10.2). The actual data stored vary from system to system, but data such as the ingredient name, the unit by which it is purchased, and its price are normally included. A wastage factor, which can be used to allow for bone or trimming, is often also included to help calculate a more realistic cost for the recipe. Ingredient prices can be entered manually, or, in the case of an integrated system, can be drawn automatically from the stock-control system. In such cases, ingredient prices and, as a result, recipe costs are always accurate and up to date.

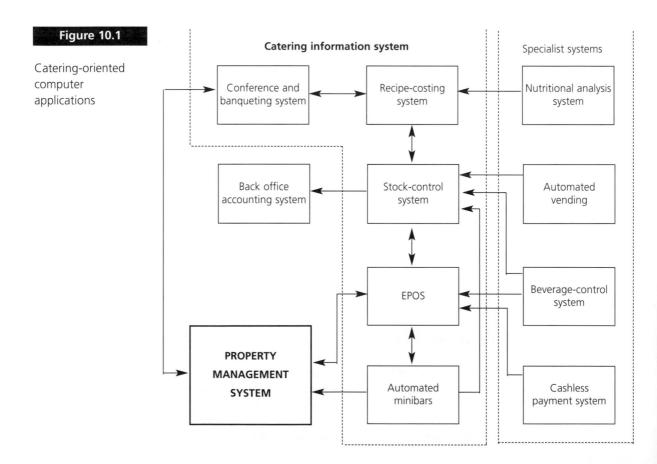

Figure 10.1

Catering-oriented computer applications

A recipe-costing
ingredient screen

Section 7 – Ingredients

Code	Description	Unit	Date	Factor	Cost
BCN	Bacon trimmings	LB	25Jan99	1	0.30
BPEP	Black pepper	Jar	25Jan99	1	0.90
BRSUG	Brown sugar	LB	25Jan99	1	1.20
BSTOCK	Brown stock	Litre	01Jan99	1	0.08
BUT	Butter	LB	25Jan99	1	1.30
CCHS	Cream cheese	LB	25Jan99	1	0.99
CHS	Cheddar cheese	LB	25Jan99	1	1.45
CRM	Cream	Pint	30Jan99	1	2.20
CURPOW	Curry powder	Oz	25Jan99	1	1.10
EGG	Eggs	Doz	02Feb99	1	0.90
FBD	French bread	Each	25Jan99	1	0.58
FLR	Flour	LB	26Jan99	1	1.10
FSTK	Fillet steak	LB	25Jan99	0.9	2.30
GAR	Garlic	FLR	25Jan99	1	0.15
HERBS	Fresh herbs	PCKT	25Jan99	1	0.30

To create a new recipe, a recipe identification code and a description are entered. This creates a new computerized 'recipe card' to which ingredients can be added (Figure 10.3). When an ingredient's code is entered, the unit by which it is purchased and its purchase price are automatically displayed. The quantity required for the recipe is then entered, and its cost is calculated and added to the other ingredient costs to give the overall cost of the dish.

The cost of items that are produced in bulk in the kitchen (such as pastry, stock or sauces) can be calculated using *sub-recipes*. These can then be incorporated into

Adding an ingredient
to a recipe.

Sirloin steak
SSTK   £2.40 (each)

Cream
CRM   £2.20 (pint)

Black peppers
BPEP   £0.90 (jar)

Red house wine
REDHS   £7.00 (bot.)

Mushrooms
MUS   £3.70 (Chip)

Onions
ONI   £0.80 (lb)

Peppered steak
Main1   £40.20

Peppered steak (Main1)   £40.20
10 Por   1+50%   £60.30

Note: Each ingredient sits on a branch of the tree. Its cost price and the quantity used are combined to give a total cost price, which in this case is £40.20. Note also how a predefined mark-up of 50 per cent brings the selling price for ten portions to £60.30.

other recipes using a process known as *nesting*, which eliminates having to duplicate the same combination of ingredients in several different recipes. For example, if several dishes contained puff pastry, the ingredients, such as flour, eggs and butter, could be entered into each one of the individual recipes. Alternatively, a sub-recipe could be created for puff pastry (and the ingredient details entered just once), and the sub-recipe incorporated as an ingredient in each recipe (Figure 10.4). In this way, the cost of the puff pastry is included in each of the other recipes, but much less data has to be entered. Within recipes, sub-recipes work in exactly the same way as normal ingredients. If the price of a sub-recipe ingredient changes, then the cost of every recipe in which it has been incorporated is automatically updated.

Most systems can provide a report showing the ingredients and quantities needed to produce any recipe in the system (Figure 10.5). This can then be used as an order list or, in the case of an integrated system, sent electronically to the stock-control system as a store's requisition. If more than the standard number of portions are needed, the program will calculate the quantities required automatically. This feature can save a lot of time and help prevent mistakes. For example, say a standard recipe produced 20 portions of a dish. If 170 portions were required, using a manual system the chef would have to multiply the quantity of each ingredient in the standard recipe by (in this case) 8.5 to find the quantity needed to produce 170 portions. This would obviously be time-consuming, and it would be easy to make mistakes in the calculations. A computerized system carries out these calculations automatically and accurately in seconds.

Recipe-costing systems can also cost entire menus by combining a series of recipes. Other charges, such as room hire, administration charges, labour costs, and charges for wines and spirits can be built into the menu cost by including them as 'ingredients'. An accurate cost per head can be calculated and a listing of the ingredients and quantities needed to create the menu can be printed in exactly the same way as with a 'normal' recipe. Ingredients present in more than

Figure 10.4

A recipe card incorporating a sub-recipe

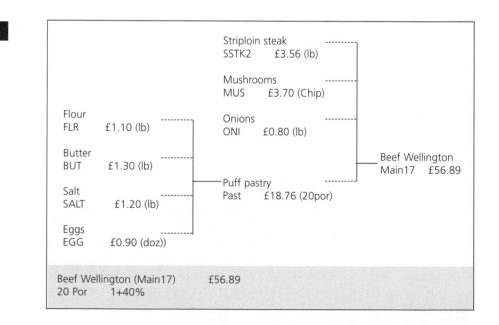

Figure 10.5

A printed ingredient list for a recipe

		Quantity		Rate	Cost
Ingredients					
BUT	Butter	4	Lb	£1.30	£5.20
EGG	Eggs	1/2	Doz	£0.90	£0.45
FLR	Flour	4	Lb	£1.10	£4.40
ONI	Onions	1	Lb	£0.80	£0.80
MUS	Mushrooms	1/5	Chip	£3.70	£0.74
SALT	Salt	1/32	Lb	£1.20	£0.04
SSTK2	Striploin steak	10	Lb	£3.56	£35.60
					£47.19
Sub-recipes					
PAST	Puff pastry	20	Por	£18.76	£18.76
					£18.76
Final recipes					
Main17	Beef Wellington	20	Por	£56.89	£56.89
					£56.89

one recipe are added together to give a total figure for each stock item. Once again, this list can then be used as a guide for ordering or, in the case of an integrated system, automatically sent to the stock-control system as a requisition.

Stock-control systems

A stock-control system helps manage and control the flow of stock through an organization by recording the value of each stock item in different locations (such as the central stores, the dry stores and the kitchen) and tracking stock movements into, out of and between each of these locations.

The concept of stock control is based on the accounting principle that an item's opening stock, plus its purchases, must be equal to its closing stock plus the amount consumed. If these are not equal, then what is known as a *variance* exists, which means that some of the stock is missing. However, carrying out stock control manually is very labour-intensive and time-consuming. For example, to check a single product, the amount of that product delivered and issued over the period has to be calculated by totalling the delivery dockets and requisitions respectively. The previous period's closing stock figure would then have to be found, and the theoretical closing stock figure calculated. Then the quantity of the item actually in stock would have to be established by performing a stocktake and physically counting the amount of the product in each storage location. Last, the theoretical and the actual figures would have to be compared to see if a variance existed. All that effort for just a single stock item! In any reasonably sized catering operation, the same process would have to be performed for hundreds, if not thousands, of products on a regular basis.

Using a computerized system, all the boring, repetitive and error-prone calculations are carried out automatically. Most of the data needed (apart from the actual stock figures) is already available on the system (for example, opening stock is available from the previous period, purchases from the records of deliveries and returns, and issues from the record of requisitions from the sales units) and the calculations can be carried out in seconds by the computer. As a result, the likelihood of errors is reduced and the stock-control process can be carried out more frequently (or even in real time) with little extra effort.

Stock-control systems' operation

Separate modules of the stock-control system deal with deliveries, issues and stocktaking. However, before the system can be used, each item of stock must be set up on the system (Figure 10.6). Each product is allocated a unique identification code, and its description and pack size are entered. The item's purchase unit (for example, a 12 kg sack), issue unit (1 kg) and reorder level are also entered, as well as details of the nominated suppliers if appropriate. Given the vast number of stock items used by a typical catering operation, these details can take a considerable amount of time to set up, but are essential for the smooth operation of the stock-control system.

Deliveries

The goods inwards clerk enters details of deliveries into the system as the stock items arrive at the central stores. When entering a delivery docket's details, the

| **Figure 10.6** | An ingredient set-up screen |

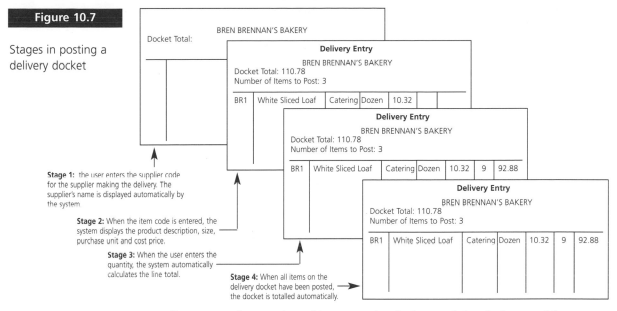

Stages in posting a
delivery docket

Stage 1: the user enters the supplier code
for the supplier making the delivery. The
supplier's name is displayed automatically by
the system

Stage 2: When the item code is entered, the
system displays the product description, size,
purchase unit and cost price.

Stage 3: When the user enters the
quantity, the system automatically
calculates the line total.

Stage 4: When all items on the
delivery docket have been posted,
the docket is totalled automatically.

user first enters the number of items on the docket and the docket total for use as
a cross-check (Figure 10.7). As each stock-item code is entered, the system
displays its description, purchase unit and size to help prevent posting errors. The
quantity delivered and the price on the delivery docket are then entered. When
everything on the docket has been input, the system calculates the total value of
the delivery and compares it to the docket total entered by the user at the beginning. This helps identify mistakes (in either the delivery docket or the data
posted) before the items are added to current stock. If both figures tally, the
quantity of each stock item is added to inventory in the central stores and the
delivery docket total is sent electronically to the creditor's module of the accounting system to be paid.

Issues

Stock is issued from the central stores when a requisition is received from one of
the sales or production areas. Traditionally the head chef, who estimated the
amount of each ingredient needed to produce the menu for the day in question,
drew up these requisitions manually. To ensure that enough of each ingredient
was available, these requisitions tended to overestimate the amount required,
which resulted in wastage and therefore higher costs. As has already been discussed, a recipe-costing system can be used to calculate the exact quantities
needed for any multiple of a recipe, which eliminates the estimates and thus helps
to reduce wastage. If the recipe-costing system and the stock-control system are
interfaced, then the requisition can be sent electronically, thus reducing paperwork. Once an item is requisitioned, the store inventory figure is reduced by the
amount issued. Over-issues because of pack sizes (for example, where 340g of an
item are needed and only 1 kg packs are available) are noted and taken into
account when the same production kitchen requisitions the same item again.
Even if it is not tracked, the excess issued is, in any case, less than one unit, which
means that control is much tighter than with a manual system.

Figure 10.8

A stocktake sheet

Stocktake Sheet – Dry Stores

Shelf number	Description	Size	Number
567	Heinz Baked Beans	450g	_____
568	Heinz Baked Beans	900g	_____
569	Heinz Baked Beans	2000g	_____
570	Batchelors' Peas	450g	_____
571	Batchelors' Peas	900g	_____
572	Knorr Stock Cubes – Beef	100g	_____
573	Knorr Stock Cubes – Chicken	100g	_____
574	Knorr Stock Cubes – Veg.	100g	_____
575	El Pasco Taco Sauce	10oz jar	_____
576	Plain flour	1kg	_____
577	Self-raising flour	3kg	_____
578	Whole grain flour	1kg	_____
579	Sugar (white)	1kg	_____
580	Sugar (brown)	1kg	_____
581	Sugar (cubes)	1kg	_____
582	Salt	500g	_____

Stocktaking

At the end of any period, a closing stock figure is calculated from the information held in the system. This is a theoretical figure – it represents the amount of each stock item that should be left in the stores. A stocktake must then be performed to check the actual levels of each item in stock. The stock-control system helps by printing blank stock sheets, which are organized in a way that should help to speed up the counting process (Figure 10.8). For example, they could be printed in an order that matches the locations of shelves in the stores. The quantities counted are then entered into the system, using data input screens laid out in the same order as the stock sheets. Some systems use small, hand-held computers to record stock levels directly and transfer them electronically into the stock-control system. Because the data does not have to be manually transcribed, the process is speeded up and another potential source of error is eliminated.

Once the data from the stocktake has been entered, the theoretical and the actual stock figures can be compared and any differences highlighted. This is usually done on a variance report, such as the one shown in Figure 10.9.

Other features

In addition to tracking stock movements, stock-control systems also provide other facilities to help manage stock within the business. Two of the most useful of these are *usage rates* and *automatic reordering*. The amount of each stock item issued during each period is recorded and used to calculate a usage rate. This

Figure 10.9

A stock variance
report

Item	Unit	Cost	O/S	Pur	Ret	Iss	C/S Stock take	VAR
Bacon trimmings	LB	0.30	10	82	0	47	45	43	−4
Black pepper	Jar	0.90	2	4	0	1	5	5	0
Brown sugar	LB	1.20	5	12	0	13	4	4	0
Brown stock	Litre	0.08	3	8	0	10	1	1	0
Butter	LB	1.30	12	56	0	47	21	11	−10
Cream cheese	LB	0.99	2	4	4	1	1	1	0
Cheddar cheese	LB	1.45	12	37	0	39	10	19	0
Cream	Pint	2.20	7	28	0	31	4	4	0
Curry powder	Oz	1.10	80	0	0	26	54	54	0
Eggs	Doz	0.90	4	24	0	20	8	8	0
French bread	Each	0.58	7	100	0	93	14	14	0
Flour	LB	1.10	18	20	0	27	11	11	0
Fillet steak	LB	2.30	26	35	0	41	10	2	−8
Garlic	FLR	0.15	84	0	0	79	5	5	9
Fresh herbs	PCKT	0.30	17	0	0	15	2	1	−1

clearly identifies which items are being used most, and which are barely used at all. In the former case, the items can be purchased in bulk, or quantity discounts can be negotiated, while stock levels of items in the latter category can be reduced, thus freeing valuable working capital.

If a minimum stock level is entered when each stock item is being set up on the system, then the stock-control system can automatically identify which items need to be reordered. This helps ensure that items are never out of stock. The reorder list details the individual stock items, sizes and quantities that need to be ordered, along with the name and telephone number of each supplier. Some systems can automatically generate purchase orders, have them authorized electronically by the appropriate managers, and fax or email them directly to the nominated suppliers. At its most advanced level, such systems are known as e-procurement systems.

E-procurement systems

Purchasing is not regarded as a very glamorous task in most organizations. Purchasing everything from bread and milk to napkins and paperclips involves finding suppliers, negotiating prices, filling in requisitions, approving and sending orders, processing deliveries, reconciling invoices and authorizing payments (along, of course, with lots of administrative work at every step of the way). But purchasing is an essential function and the business cannot operate without it.

Little wonder then that there is so much excitement about the growth in business to business (B2B) marketplaces and the resulting potential for e-procurement. E-marketplaces, at a simple level, bring buyers and sellers together on an electronic portal, and provide a range of facilities to simplify the purchasing process. They reduce the search costs of purchasers and the marketing costs of suppliers, and are particularly useful where both buyers and sellers are fragmented (i.e. the marketplace is not dominated by any big players), as is the case in the hospitality sector. In the past, using anything but the simplest e-procurement system involved large-scale investment in proprietary hardware and software. However, the growth in the use of the Internet as a commercial medium has simplified the introduction of company-wide e-procurement systems into hospitality organizations. In particular, the development of Internet-enabled ASP-based systems (see Chapter 5) has made it easy for companies to use e-procurement with little or no investment, making the facility available to both large and small firms quickly and easily.

E-procurement can be defined as using information and communications technologies to automate the entire purchasing process – from identification and selection of suitable suppliers through to eventual payment for the product. Most systems provide buyers with electronic access to a broad range of suppliers. This allows them far more choice than they would typically have with a manual system, because the hassle and cost of finding and dealing with multiple suppliers means that most companies concentrate on a select few. This list of suppliers can either be comprehensive to give purchasers more choice or limited to corporate-approved vendors in order to ensure consistency in terms of the products being used across a chain. In either case, vendors listed on the system typically display an electronic catalogue of their products (complete with colour photos, comprehensive descriptions and detailed technical specifications). Where there is an existing relationship between the supplier and the purchaser, the system may display pre-negotiated prices for each product, or alternatively it may facilitate the RFP process when setting up a new dialog. Most systems also provide facilities that make it easy to compare products across multiple suppliers, thus easing price comparisons. Orders (from multiple suppliers if necessary) are created by selecting the desired products from each supplier's catalogue to create an electronic purchase order. The latter can then be routed to the relevant person within the organization for authorization, although in some cases the e-procurement system itself will act as a first filter, ensuring that only the right people can buy the products that they are authorized to buy from the suppliers that they are authorized to buy from. Once electronically rubber-stamped, the authorized orders are channelled automatically to the relevant supplier. Most systems also give the purchaser the ability to track the status of each order and will record it as waiting for authorization, ordered, en route or delivered. Deliveries can automatically be reconciled against outstanding orders for the supplier in question, which can trigger a process whereby deliveries are automatically matched to invoices and cleared for payment. The e-procurement marketplace often facilitates this too in an effort to reduce the amount of administrative work associated with the purchasing process. Most systems also provide comprehensive reporting facilities to show purchase costs and usage patterns, and also to identify and control off-contract purchasing.

E-procurement systems deliver value by streamlining the entire purchasing process, introducing efficiencies at every step in process. Such systems promise to deliver major cost savings in a variety of ways. First, by facilitating access to a broader range of suppliers and products than would typically be possible using a manual system, it gives purchasers more choice and the potential to find cheaper prices. Savings of 15–20 per cent are typically found when a company changes from a manual to an e-procurement system. Some systems promise bigger savings by consolidating orders from multiple purchasers together and negotiating bulk discounts from suppliers. The costs associated with processing an order are also generally reduced when dealing with an electronic rather than a manual system. Ordering materials manually is generally regarded as being expensive, with figures of €100 to €150 not uncommon if the labour costs of processing, authorizing and controlling purchases are taken into account. With an electronic system, such costs are greatly reduced as all of the administrative tasks are taken care of automatically.

E-procurement also helps to reduce costs in a third way – by reducing or even eliminating maverick purchasing. Most companies use nominated suppliers with whom they have negotiated special discount prices for the products that they normally buy. However, particularly in a dynamic industry like hospitality, purchases are often made outside of such contract as a result of bad planning or unforeseen circumstances. The National Association of Purchasing Managers estimates that in many firms nearly one-third of items are purchased off-contract at price premiums of between 15 and 30 percent. In addition to having higher cost prices, such maverick buying further increases costs as such orders do not go through the normal purchasing and control process (often they are bought out of petty cash) and then generate extra administrative work. E-procurement systems, with their access to a broad range of suppliers and strong analysis tools, can help to minimize such purchases thus reducing costs. The last benefit of using e-procurement is that the use of an automated system can help to speed up the entire purchasing and fulfilment cycle (in some cases reducing the cycle from weeks to minutes), making planning easier for the manager and perhaps leading to a reduction is stock levels as less material has to be kept as a safety margin since stocks can be replenished faster. Taken together, all of these benefits can result in substantial cost savings, which is why so many hospitality companies are currently experimenting with the use of e-procurement systems.

Electronic point-of-sale systems

Ever since the first owner of an inn stored his takings in a shoe box and tried to keep a mental account of daily sales, restaurateurs have struggled with the problem of balancing money taken in with food and beverages served. Unfortunately in the days of shoe box control, the money left at the end of the day rarely tallied with the amount of goods sold. Bartenders miscounted how many pints of ale the large party by the fireside had actually drank, servers forgot to charge the traveller from out of town for his dessert and the innkeeper saw his profits slipping through his fingers (and in some cases into the pockets of his employees).

More effective control procedures developed over the next few hundred years. One of the most commonly used techniques here is the three-fly order docket. With this system, the waiter retains one copy for reference; another is sent to the cashier's desk to compile the guest bill (and subsequently reconciled with the kitchen copy for control purposes) while a third is sent to the kitchen to actually order the food itself. However, handwritten restaurant orders cause a variety of problems. The kitchen often cannot read badly written orders, resulting in delays, errors and confusion. Cashiers can easily misplace supplemental dockets for items such as drinks or desserts, thus losing revenue for the operation. Balances are often incorrectly calculated, and items such as sales tax or service charge take time, mental arithmetic ability and patience to calculate. For example, recent research has shown that as many as 16 per cent of all handwritten guest checks are incorrectly totalled, usually in favour of the guest. At the end of the day's work, the manager is left with a large number of paper dockets to be matched with each other and tabulated before the control process can even begin. All this takes time, and each delay makes the information it produces less and less useful. Using an electronic point-of-sale (EPOS) system can help to solve many of these problems, and can also bring a variety of other benefits to the operation.

In looking at the use of technology-based systems in this area, its important to differentiate between EPOS and the electronic cash registers (ECR) that proceeded them (but which are still widely used). ECRs are primarily stand-alone units that add up prices for customer bills and hold daily/periodic sales totals. EPOS systems, on the other hand, have a more comprehensive range of capabilities including keeping track of current food and beverage orders, transmitting orders electronically to the production area, helping to ensure the accuracy of guest bills and, in the case of interfaced systems, automatically posting charges into the PMS account folios of guests registered in the hotel. The two biggest controllable expenses in restaurant operations are labour cost and food cost, and the

Figure 10.10   A typical EPOS layout

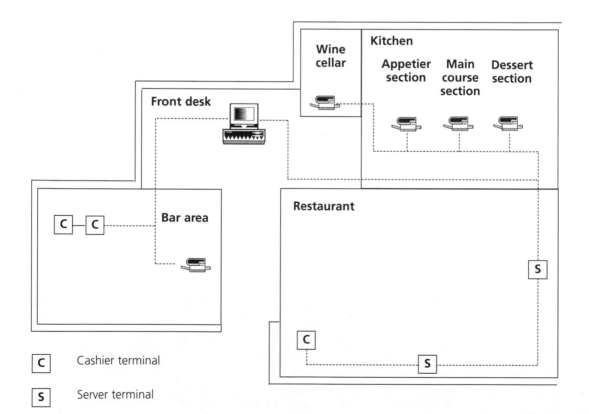

right EPOS system can help operators to lower costs in both areas while at the same time enhancing customer service.

The main function of an EPOS system is to record the guest's order. This is entered into a terminal by the waiter, and is then relayed through the system to remote printers in each of the production areas. Orders are automatically routed to the correct printer so that appetizers appear at the appetizer preparation area, drinks at the bar and so on (Figure 10.10). These printed orders are clear and legible (something that cannot be said about most waiters' handwritten dockets!), which helps reduce mistakes. They are also automatically time-stamped and numbered consecutively, which makes it easier for the chefs to know which item is next to be prepared. On some systems, the production area can even alert the waiter through the system when an order is ready to be picked up.

The result of using an EPOS system is that time previously wasted walking from the dining room to the kitchen or bar (to drop off orders, call items away or check whether an order is ready) is saved. The waiter therefore has more time available, which can be spent interacting with the guest, leading to increased guest satisfaction, and also means that more guests can be served by the same number of waiters. Control is also greatly increased, as unless an item is entered through the EPOS, the kitchen will not produce it. As a result, all items served – desserts, drinks, and coffees – end up on the guest bill and the potential for lost revenue is reduced. The need to manually reconcile both copies of the orders is also eliminated, as the EPOS system automatically tracks open cheques, voids, comps, and discounts, thus helping to increase control and reduce fraud. Some systems even include links to the video surveillance systems, and can be programmed to record what's happening when certain transactions, such as for example the employee ringing up a void or a no-sale, occur. EPOS systems also automate a lot of the paperwork that managers have traditionally been expect to complete. By reducing the amount of time that managers need to spend sitting at their desk crunching numbers, an EPOS can free managers up to focus on the most important aspect of their job – managing people.

Types of EPOS

There are several types of EPOS system available, and these vary greatly in terms of both their complexity and their price. For example, EPOS may be counter-based or hand-held, may use a cash register-style keyboard, a membrane keyboard or a touch screen, and may be stand-alone or part of a mini-network (or cluster) of terminals (Figure 10.11). The use of a touch screen brings many benefits and is becoming very popular. The display area of a touch-screen terminal is less cluttered than other types of EPOS because hierarchical menus can be used. For example, when the waiter begins taking an order, the unit might display 'buttons' for Appetizers, Main dishes, Desserts and Drinks. When one of these options is chosen (for example, Appetizers), the screen clears and a new menu with the appetizers available is displayed. Because only relevant options are displayed, there is less chance that the user will become confused, which makes training easier and helps to prevent mistakes. Additional prompts can be included to encourage up-selling. Hand-held terminals are also becoming popular as they allow orders to be transmitted from the table side to the production area using

A counter-based
touchscreen EPOS
terminal (left) and a
hand-held EPOS
terminal (right)

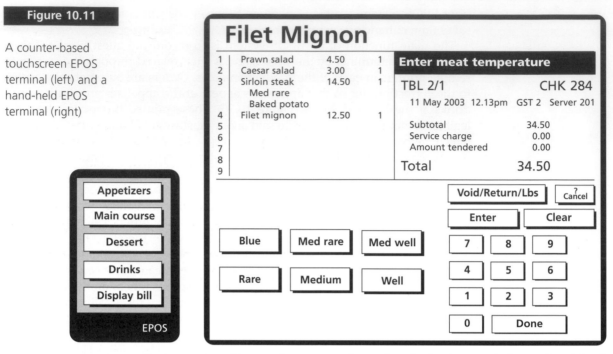

wireless networking and, as a result, saving both time and the waiters' feet! In addition they have been found to greatly increase speed of service, resulting in higher average checks and increased turnover of tables.

EPOS operation

While taking an order, the waiter is prompted by the system to help reduce mistakes or omissions. For example, when an order for a steak is taken, the system will ask how the customer would like the steak to be cooked, and will not accept any other input until the customer's choice has been entered. Similarly, if the steak is served with a choice of baked potato or salad, the server will again be prompted to enter the customer's preference (Figure 10.12). Facilities such as these help to increase guest satisfaction, as the order is taken quickly and efficiently, with no omissions. From the kitchen's point of view, each order is complete, so time is not wasted clarifying exactly what has to be cooked for the guest.

Most systems also have a facility that displays the selling price of each item ordered. The most frequently ordered dishes are usually allocated dedicated keys on the keyboard, and less commonly sold items are accessed using price look-up codes (PLUs). The EPOS also performs all the calculations (in terms of both totalling the bill and calculating service charge or VAT) automatically. As a result, guest bills are always accurate and up to date. The printed bill is clear, concise and itemized, which can help to prevent disputes with the guest over charges (Figure 10.13). EPOS systems usually allow several prices to be stored for each item, which can be useful when different prices are required at different times. For example, a bar might have one set of prices for a 'happy hour' and another set of 'normal' prices. Without an EPOS, staff would have to remember both sets of

Figure 10.12

Hierarchical menus on a hand-held EPOS system

Choose

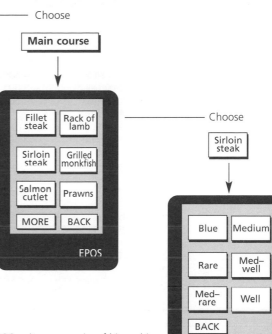

The touch screen on the hand-held EPOS unit uses a series of hierarchical menus. When the 'button' for main courses is pressed at stage one, a sub-menu, showing the available choices for that day, is displayed. Similarly, at stage two, when 'sirloin steak' is chosen, the user is automatically prompted to enter cooking details. As a result, the server cannot forget to ask how the guest would like the steak cooked.

prices, which gives rise to opportunities for errors or even fraud. On an EPOS, the prices can be switched from one set to another instantly using a management code, thus ensuring that the correct price is always charged. Naturally, the cashier terminal also acts as a normal cash register and tracks the amount of money received by each waiter. Links with credit-card systems can check the credit worthiness of cards and obtain authorization codes automatically when the guest's credit card is swiped through the magnetic card reader. In the case of a hotel, if the EPOS is integrated with the PMS, the bill total can also be posted onto the guest folio automatically, thus reducing the danger of the guest checking out without paying.

Management reports

Apart from improving the working lives of waiters, EPOS can also help to make managers' lives easier. With a manual system, managers spend a lot of time auditing guest checks, trying to work out sales mix, closing out registers and generally trying to keep control over operations. With an EPOS, most of this is done automatically, and a wide variety of management information is produced automatically to help them do their jobs better. For example, reports outlining the pattern of business throughout the period can be obtained automatically. This allows busy and slack periods to be identified. Staff performance can also be

Figure 10.13

An itemized guest bill

```
                    GUEST BILL

Table 12          Covers:  2
Waiter: Paul

Prawn salad        4.50      1      4.50
Caesar salad       3.00      1      3.00
Sirloin steak     14.50      1     14.50
   Med. rare
   Baked potato
Filet Mignon      12.50      1     12.50
Bot house red     11.50      1     11.50
Choc eclairs       2.50      1      2.50
Sel ice cream      2.00      1      2.00
Coffee             0.90      2      1.80

Sub-total                          49.80
Service @ 12.5%                     6.23

TOTAL                              56.03

       THANK YOU – PLEASE CALL AGAIN
```

Menu prices are automatically entered by the system, helping to prevent the incorrect price being charged.

Calculations, such as the one shown here for service charge, are carried out automatically, thus further reducing errors.

Figure 10.14

Examples of management reports provided by EPOS systems

SALES REPORT

Date: 18.04.03
Period: Lunch

Item	Number	Sales
Appetizers	34	86.50
Main dishes	79	571.00
Pasta	14	72.80
Salads	5	34.60
Desserts	41	96.20
Beverages	103	135.40
Wine	31	177.90
Bar	107	246.86
Cash	87	1064.50
Credit cards	11	856.76
Void		
Refund		
Complementary		

SALES ANALYSIS

Date: 18.04.03

Item	Number sold		Ranking
	Today	YTB	
Sirloin steak	12	1361	1
Prawns	8	1296	2
Black sole	7	803	3
Tagiratelle carbonara	10	765	4
Chicken kiev	5	751	5
Chicken cordon bleu	8	699	6
Stuffed mushrooms	1	675	7
Potato skins	18	610	8
Choc eclairs	11	597	9
Fresh fruit salad	0	20	77
Gr salmon cutlet	1	1	78
Seafood lasagne	0	0	79

assessed from the system. For example, reports showing each employee's total sales (in terms of either revenue or number of items sold), or showing the distribution of their sales over the shift, are available and make it easy to identify the workers who are performing best for evaluation and motivational purposes. While most of this information could be obtained using a manual system, the amount of time and effort which would be required to find it would make it uneconomical. Where an EPOS is used, this information is available at literally the touch of a button, which makes it easier for management to get the information needed to help run their operation.

Case Study *Chart House Restaurants*

Chart House Restaurants prides itself on upholding its 45-year old mission: the creation of a memorable dining experience through the seamless mix of high quality food, service, atmosphere and location. Operating approximately 70 upmarket steakhouses throughout the United States, the company had no point-of-sales system at most of its locations, and the few that were installed were dissimilar. The management of the chain believed that the lack of an effective EPOS system was having a negative effect on sales, creating training difficulties and threatening the quality of its customer service.

The situation began to manifest itself in a number of ways. Errors on guest checks were cutting into profits. Training new employees took as long as three weeks and the waiting staff was spending time managing paper orders that could have been spent more productively interacting with customers. For that reason, Chart House decided to install an EPOS from HIS on a network of Windows® NT-based computers throughout all of its restaurants. In choosing this system, its objectives were clear. 'We wanted a Windows®-based POS that would decrease training time, reduce errors and allow the restaurant staff to spend more time with the guest', according to Vice-President of Information Systems John Townsend. At the same time, the company needed a good return on investment. 'Our goal was to improve customer service while paying for the system within 18 months as a result of the tangible savings derived from the benefits we envisioned.'

They certainly achieved this goal. By capturing in the system all the desserts and beverages served by waiting staff without collecting for them, as well as correctly charging the guests rather than handwriting a price for each item and mentally calculating the total, Chart House estimates that its sales have increased by an average of 1.5 per cent per restaurant. 'The sales increase attributable to this EPOS translates into nearly $23,000 per restaurant per year – nearly $1.5 million company-wide', says Townsend. The new system has also reduced training time – an important issue given the industry's high turnover rate. The simplicity of the new system has allowed Chart House to reduce the amount of time needed to train a waiter to accurately enter a guest order, making it possible for them to cut the time its takes for a new waiter to be qualified to wait on guests from three weeks to one. That's a saving of $9000 per restaurant per year, about $750,000 when extended throughout the company. And lastly the system has helped the restaurant improve its service, something that is extremely important to Chart House. 'By allowing orders to be entered quickly and accurately, the system frees up waiters to spend significantly more time with the guest', explains Townsend. 'This allows the staff to provide a higher level of service and more comprehensive explanations of the items on the menu.' While the benefits of this are more difficult to quantify, Townsend believes that the added service typically results in increased sales due to a higher guest return rate and higher per sales per guest.

Table management systems

Handling reservations and seating people in a large, high volume restaurant is a complex job. Often the restaurant loses business because the host or hostess does not know what tables are available at a particular point in time. Valuable time is wasted walking the room checking table status, particularly if it is not possible to see the entire layout from the hostess desk. Potential sales are lost when parties of two are seated at tables for four because the hostess wasn't aware that a two-top was vacant on the other side of the restaurant. And while all of this is going on, guests are waiting and getting more and more frustrated.

Table management systems, which are closely related to (and often integrated with) the EPOS system, are particularly useful in such situations. Instead of trying to manage reservations and walk-ins on a paper chart, restaurants can make use of dedicated systems that assist in managing bookings and seating. A comprehensive table management system should be able to track pre-booked and walk-in reservation requests, help the host or hostess to allocate these bookings to tables in an effective manner, automatically notify waiting guests when a table is ready and provide management with useful information on party size, reservation lead times and server productivity. One of the most basic features of a table management system is the ability to record and process advanced reservations – something traditionally done in a paper diary. However, using a computerized system brings a range of benefits, including the ability to automatically recognize repeat customers at the time of booking and prompt the person taking the reservation to give them the recognition they deserve. With walk-in guests who cannot be seated immediately, the system helps manage the waiting list and match waiting parties up with tables as they become available. In some cases the system can be used to automatically alert waiting customers that their table is ready, either through an electronic sign or using pagers issued to the guest when they request the table. Paging systems allow staff to locate customers quickly and easily, no matter how busy the restaurant, bar or venue, and even allow guests to wander off to nearby shops or attractions if they so wish, secure in the knowledge that they will be notified when a table becomes available. In loud venues, pagers that vibrate rather than beep can be used, allowing such a system to be used in locations where aural pages ('Smith, party of four, your table is ready') would not work. Such a system saves staff a lot of time trying to locate a particular customer, and presents a more professional and organized image. Many operations that have implement it find that there are far fewer walkouts by customers who give up on waiting, and that wait times are reduced by 20 and 30 per cent as a result of better communications between waiters, hostesses and customers.

Another key function is to manage current table status information (vacant, occupied or reserved), which is particularly important in large operations where the hostess cannot see the entire restaurant from the desk. Without such a feature, tables can often be lying idle while guests queue impatiently at the door, simply because no-one has informed the hostess that the table is again ready to receive customers. Integration with EPOS allows a guest bill to be opened automatically as soon as the table is assigned, thus helping to increase control, and some systems will also alert the waiter responsible for that table that a new party has been seated and is waiting to be served. Many systems also indicate elapsed time of service on each table, so that the user can estimate when a particular table is likely to become free, and can even be set up to alert a manager if the amount of time a table has been waiting seems too long. When the guest pays the bill at the end of the meal, the EPOS system can be set up to return the table to a vacant status automatically, after a reasonable delay to allow the waiting staff to clear and reset it. As a result, you never have the situation where someone can forget to let the hostess station know that the table is ready for the next batch of customers.

Conference and banqueting systems

At first glance, taking a reservation for a conference room may appear to be no more complicated than taking a normal reservation for a bedroom. However, booking a conference room is far more complex for several reasons:

- Conference rooms can usually be subdivided into different sub units, each of which can either be sold on its own, or joined with other parts. This makes accepting a booking complicated, because if a subsection has already been reserved, then the entire room cannot be sold to another client at the same time.

- A function room can be sold several times each day. For example, a heavily booked room might have a breakfast meeting, another meeting later in the morning, a lunch service, a meeting in the afternoon and a function in the evening. To allow this to happen, the conference and banqueting system uses hours (or sometimes even quarter-hours) instead of days as a booking time frame.

- Each booking has different set-up and clean-down times depending on the size of the room, the type of meeting and the style of seating required. For example, it would obviously take much longer to set up a room for a meal service than for a classroom-style conference. When taking reservations for conference rooms, time has to be allowed between bookings for these activities.

- A variety of other 'reservations' are dependent on the conference reservation. For example, a conference reservation may include orders for various food and beverage items (such as coffee breaks or lunches), requests for audio-visual equipment, and even normal hotel room reservations for conference participants. Organizing these requirements means coordinating with almost every other department in the hotel.

As the name suggests, *conference and banqueting systems* assist in managing and controlling reservations and billing in the hotel's banqueting department. Such systems are important as each event handled by the conference sales office is potentially worth thousands of pounds in revenue (not only in terms of room hire, but also in terms of associated food, beverage and accommodation sales). As a result, it is essential that each event is handled professionally, that each potential client's queries are followed up quickly and efficiently, that the activities of all departments are well coordinated, and that everything operates smoothly on the day(s) of the event.

Prospect management

Computerized conference and banqueting systems help to achieve this in a number of ways. The better systems start by assisting the sales office to manage prospective clients. Because each booking has such a high potential revenue, as many inquiries as possible must be converted into actual bookings. The sales office must appear to be efficient and well organized, as it is often the first point of contact with the client. Unfortunately, in many cases, sales people spend much of their time completing paperwork and preparing reports for management. With a good computerized system, many of these administrative functions are auto-mated, and salespeople can instead concentrate on what they do best: identifying and following up leads and thus increasing sales. Good systems help them do this by incorporating a contact management module at their core, which helps record inquiries and leads, and at the same time, track correspondence with potential clients. Many systems automatically prompt sales people to follow up inquiries. For example, some systems present the user with a 'to-do' screen on login, which highlights priorities and special notes for that day, thus helping to insure that salespeople do not forget to call back or send material to a client when they promised to do so. As a result, the client gets the information they were promised when they were promised it. Most systems also provide facilities to keep a log of what was discussed in phone calls, and track what letters, proposals or contracts have been sent to which clients. As a result, everyone in the sales office can find out the status of each client or each inquiry, simply by consulting the system.

Managing reservations

The key to a successful conference and banqueting reservation system is the *bookings diary*. The traditional paper diary had a page for each day with the names of the function rooms listed down the left-hand side and the time in half-hour units listed across the top. When a reservation was taken for a particular room, the relevant squares were filled in or 'blocked' to indicate a booking. As a result, sales staff could see at a glance which rooms were vacant, this helping to prevent double bookings. However, the diary quickly became confusing as tentative bookings were added and removed, events were switched from one room to another, and details of bookings changed. When handling reservations, most computerized conference and banqueting systems follow this same grid principle, creating a replica of the function diary pages on the screen (Figure 10.15). This gives the system has a familiar look and feel, and as a result, staff have less trouble adjusting to using the computerized system. Function rooms can be blocked by dragging a mouse over the relevant squares on the computer screen, with differ-ent colours used to indicate different types of booking (such as tentative or confirmed). This, however, is where the similarity with the manual system ends. Double bookings become a thing of the past, as good systems will simply not allow two events to be confirmed for the same room at the same time. The system can be set up to automatically add appropriate set-up and clean-up times to ensure that there is enough time between bookings. The 'block' on the computer screen becomes the central source of information about that reservation. Each block on the diary screen has an attached event record (Figure 10.16), which stores data about the client and requirements for the event in one place and is instantly available to all of the sales team at the click of a button. This increase in coordination ultimately results in both increased productivity for the sales staff and increased customer satisfaction. Even at the simplest level, it overcomes one of the major limitations of the ledger – more than one person can have access to the data at the same time over the computer network and no-one has to wait for the physical diary to become available. In fact many systems allow sales people to access the database remotely to check inventory or make bookings by dialling in over a modem or by connecting over the Internet. By using such facilities, a sales person can sit in the client's office, answer all of the their questions instantly, check availability, quote up-to-date rates, prepare personalized contracts and close the sale there and then if necessary! All of this is obviously far more effective than having to do multiple sales calls and follow up with faxes and letters.

Coordination

The ability to track requests for equipment is very important. In any conference area, there is a limited amount of equipment such as chairs, overhead projectors and video units. If equipment needs are not recorded, there may be a shortage of particular items when several events are in progress at the same time. If this shortage is foreseen, extra equipment can be rented or borrowed from outside sources. The computerized system helps to identify when shortages will occur by attaching a list of the equipment required to each booking. As each piece is reserved, it is removed from the list of equipment available, which means that

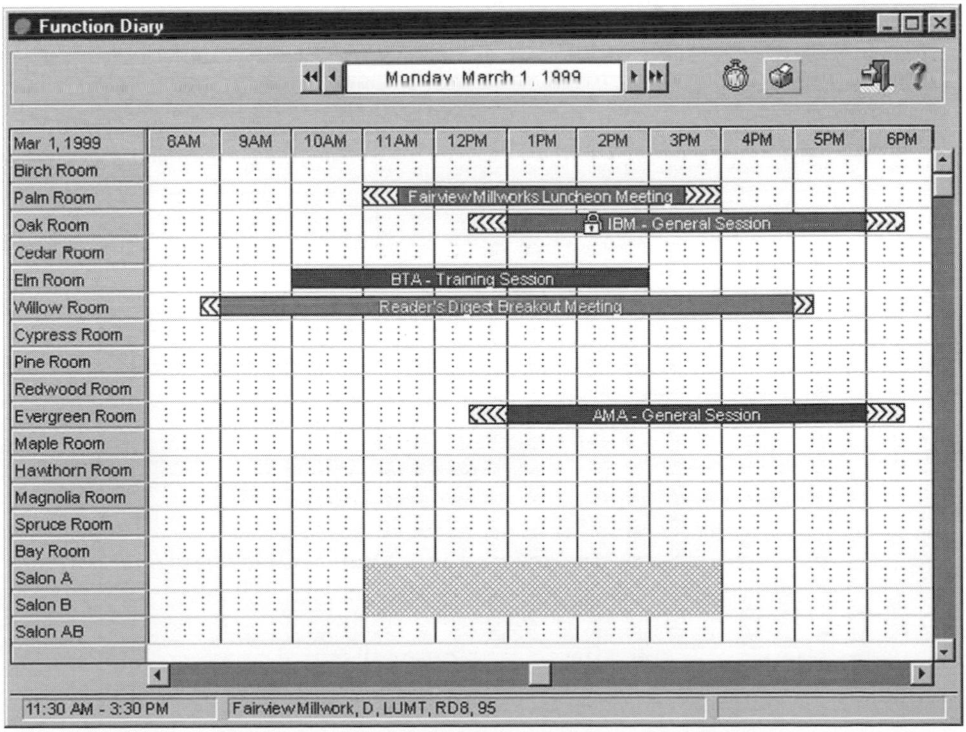

Figure 10.15

The diary screen of a computerized conference and banqueting system someone else cannot book it. As a result, it is clear from an early stage when extra items are needed, and these can be organized well in advance.

Some systems also assist in the generation of graphic room layouts, and facilitate the production of seating plans and nametags. Room set-up diagrams are useful in that they ensure that both the client and the hotel are agreed on how the room will be laid out for an event. Some packages allow the client to access a certified model showing the size and shape of each meeting room on the Internet, add objects such as tables and chairs and in effect design the room set-up for themselves, safe in the knowledge that whatever they design on screen can work on the ground. Programs are designed to prevent tables being placed close together and line-of-sight guides can help tell them where to position (or perhaps not position) the projector screen or the speaker's lectern. Once the diagram is complete, it can be sent electronically to the sales department of the venue where in addition to being attached to the event's record, it can be used to automatically generate equipment requirements and printed to guide the staff setting up the room on the day of the event. Some systems also assist in drawing up the table plan – managing the seating list for each table and automatically producing tent cards and place cards as well as the alphabetical list to place by the door.

In addition to preventing double bookings and helping to manage equipment rentals, conference and banqueting systems also help to prevent other mistakes. For example, the system prevents operational mix-ups, such as trying to put a conference for 500 people in a room that can only accommodate 300. As all the client's requirements are attached to the booking, none of them can be forgotten or misplaced. Even when a booking needs to be moved to another location or time slot (which can be a nightmare in a ledger-based diary), all of the attached

Figure 10.16   Online facilities allow the customer to design the room layout

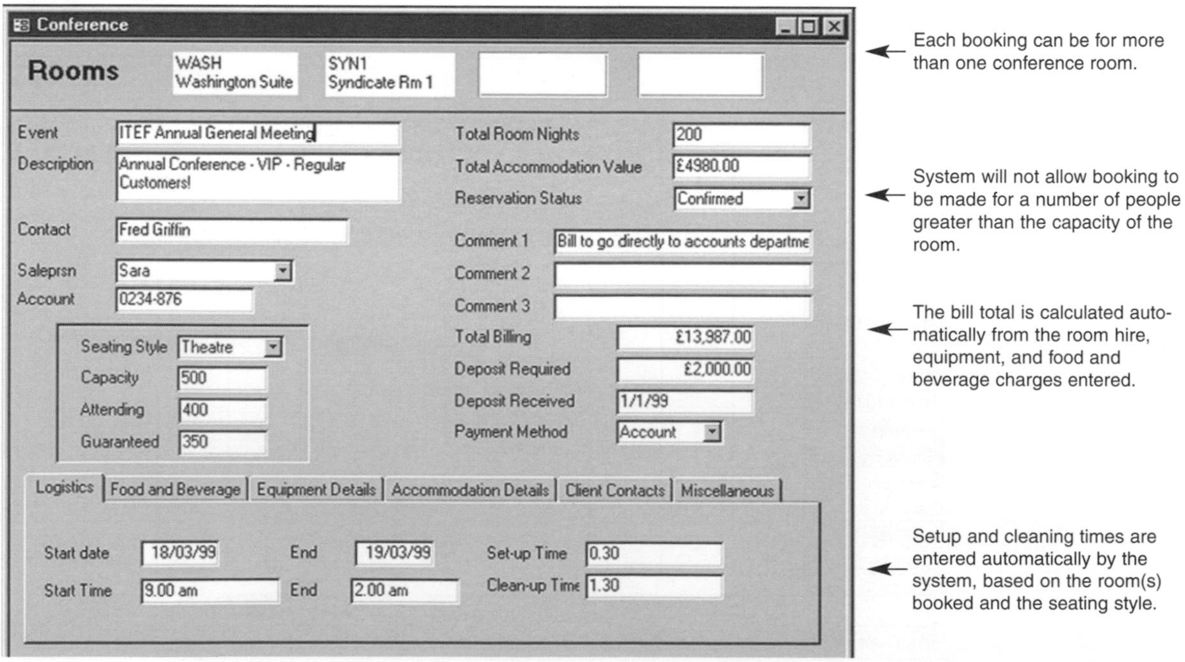

Each booking can be for more than one conference room.

System will not allow booking to be made for a number of people greater than the capacity of the room.

The bill total is calculated automatically from the room hire, equipment, and food and beverage charges entered.

Setup and cleaning times are entered automatically by the system, based on the room(s) booked and the seating style.

details are automatically adjusted when the block is 'dragged and dropped' to its new location on the grid.

Similarly, much of the inordinate amount of paperwork associated with the sales department is done automatically. For example, once the details of the booking have been agreed with the client, most systems can produce a professional, desk-top-published contract in seconds. Most of the reports required for both day-to-day operations and for management are automatically produced. Summary lists of equipment needed, and detailed lists of the equipment to be placed in each room for each event, can be printed to guide the staff setting each room. Similarly, food and beverage reports showing the service time and the dishes required can be accessed on the system, which makes it easier for the catering department to plan production and service. Some systems are particularly strong in this area. For example, Newmarket's Delphi system's Power BEO (Banquet Event Order) report is particularly powerful, tracking everything from room layout to the colour of the napkins, and presenting it in a way that is particularly suited to use by the staff setting up and running the event. Links with the PMS allow the person taking the function booking to check on room availability and, if necessary, make a block booking for the conference participants. The system can also assist with client billing. With a manual system, charges for room hire, equipment rental, and food and beverage service have to be gathered from various departments, which means that charges can often accidentally be omitted. Again, the computerized system helps simplify the process. In most

Figure 10.17

A conference reservation record

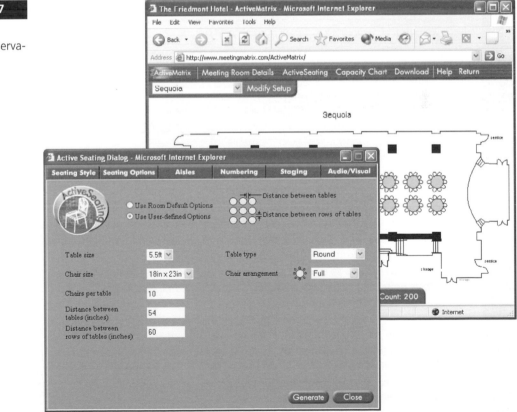

cases, charges are added to the client's bill automatically. For example, room hire and equipment rental charges are added to the bill at the time of booking. Charges for food and beverage service can be posted automatically through an interface with the EPOS system. As a result, a clear and accurate itemized bill, detailing the total amount owed, is immediately available for the client. All of these administrative features help to manage the details of each event and reduce the potential for errors. As a result, staff have to spend less time 'fire-fighting' and events run much more smoothly for the customer.

In summary, the use of a computerized conference and banqueting system makes the complex task of event management easier. Accidental overbooking is eliminated (although deliberate overbooking can be accommodated). Reports detailing exact equipment and food and beverage requirements can be accessed for each day, so every department knows where and when their services are required. All charges are automatically posted to the clients' bills. As all aspects of the booking (the rooms booked, the equipment used, the food and beverages required and the accommodation blocked) are linked together, it is easy for management to assess the value of each booking because all information is immediately available in a single place on the system. Some systems can even forecast the anticipated profit from the event (provided the expected scenario pans out) and show the impact on the period's budget. This helps the manager judge immediately if the event in question is a good piece of business to take or not, and what the impact is likely to be on the hotel's total conference and banqueting performance for the period.

Case Study *Jury's Hotel Dublin and the NFS conference system*

Jury's Hotel Group is now one of the largest hotel operators in Ireland. Their central Dublin hotel, based in Ballsbridge, is the largest conference venue in the city, with about 20 conference rooms and a very large banqueting suite, capable of hosting events for over 500 people. Until recently all conference operations had been run manually, generating a large volume of paperwork, with all the challenges that this entails. It was decided to install a computerized conference and banqueting system and, following an assessment of the systems on the marketplace, the CABS system from NFS software was selected.

CABS is now used to handle all aspects of conference operations, from the booking of rooms to the creation of function sheets and other client communication such as confirmation letters and contracts. In addition, all internal reporting for operational purposes (such as the generation of departmental reports for all the functional areas – catering, housekeeping, room planning, equip-ment and accommodation) is done using the system. 'The most significant improvements we have seen are in the operational area', comments Keith White.

> In the past we were spending several days each month preparing and amending function sheets, as well as doing a host of operational and revenue reports. This is all now all done automatically by the computerized system, saving an immense amount of time.

Suzanne, head of the conference office at the hotel, comments

> Initially we were nervous about not having a diary, something physical that we could refer to easily if something went wrong. Now after using the computerized system for a few months, we wonder how we coped without it!

Specialist catering computer systems

The catering industry is very wide and diverse, and different types of outlet have different information technology needs. Some of the more common specialist systems, namely minibars, automatic vending systems, cash-less payments systems, nutritional analysis systems, beverage-control systems and club management systems are discussed briefly below.

Minibars

For a long time, in-room dining meant a chocolate mint on the pillow when you returned to your room last thing at night. Now many hotels are providing guests with the means to serve themselves a much wider range of products in the room. Many hotels (and some upmarket hospitals and convalescent homes) now provide minibar systems in their bedrooms to help enhance guest service. Instead of telephoning room service for drinks, guests can serve themselves from the minibar. Bottles and cans of beverages (and increasingly a variety of other products such as snacks, suntan lotion and disposable cameras) are displayed in special holders linked to sensors. When a guest removes an item, the transaction is recorded and automatically posted on the guest's bill. (Where children are occupying the room – or when the hotel has a guest who should not be served any more alcohol! – the unit can be locked electronically from the front desk, through this same interface with the PMS.) In only a decade, minibars have gone from an expensive and unproductive facility that many hotels had to provide to a major profit centre. Some long-stay properties even feature all-in-one units that include a fridge, a freezer and a microwave in one device to allow guests to prepare a hot meal for themselves in their room. Today a well-run minibar system can rank third in a hotel's profit picture, immediate after rooms and F&B. Sales can be quite substantial, with nearly one-third of guests using the minibar during their stay and average sales of about €3 per guest per night not uncommon.

One of the often-quoted problems with minibars is incorrect or disputed charges. For example, problems often occur when a guest takes an item out of the unit and then decides that he or she does not want it. Once the item is removed from the drawer, the charge for it is automatically posted onto the guest bill and putting it back will not change that! In some cases, this leads to a dispute at check-out. However, such disputes are a relatively minor problem, and were more of an issue when minibars were new and the subject of curiosity. To minimize the problem, some systems give the guest up to 30 seconds to change his mind and replace the item before posting the charge to the guest folio. Replaced items are marked as 'handled' and a minibar attendant can be sent next day to check that such items have not been tampered with or refilled with water!

In addition to ensuring that the guest is charged for every item consumed, using a minibar system makes restocking easier. Without a computerized system, each unit must be checked each day and the missing items replaced. The minibar system, on the other hand, provides a summary list of the items needed to restock all the units (Figure 10.18). It also provides another report, organized by room number, which shows which items are missing from each unit. As a result, time is not wasted checking units that are full, which means that the entire process of

Figure 10.18

Minibar operational
reports

Stock requisition – Robobar system

Stock number	Description	Size	Number
101	Power Irish whiskey	Mini	37
102	Jameson Irish whiskey	Mini	5
107	Smirnoff vodka	Mini	69
109	Gordon's gin	Mini	57
110	CDD gin	Mini	12
200	Coca-cola	16oz can	91
201	7-Up	16oz can	34
251	Club white lemonade	16oz can	87
252	Club tonic water	16oz can	51
253	Club bitter lemon	16oz can	3
410	Champagne	Snip	2
411	House wine (white)	Half bottle	1
412	House wine (white)	Mini	17
413	House wine (red)	Half bottle	0
414	House wine (red)	Mini	3
1070	Peanuts (salted)	30g	44

```
m 109
don's Gin              1
b Tonic Water          1
nuts (salted)          1

m 110
----- OK----------

m 111
eson Irish Whiskey     4
noff Vodka             2
b White Lemonade       2
a Cola                 2

m 112
don's Gin              3
p                      1
nuts (salted)          1

m 113
se Wine (Red)          1
nuts (salted)          2

m 114
ers Irish Whiskey      1
b White Lemonade       1
```

```
Room 108
7-Up                   1
Peanuts (salted)       1

Room 115
------- OK----------
```

restocking can be completed in a much shorter time. Having replaced a traditional 'honour' bar with a computerized minibar system, many hotels have found that a single full-time employee can service as many as 400 bedrooms a day. Guest security is also increased, as hotel employees do not have to enter each room to see whether the minibar needs to be restocked. Last, control over stock is increased, as only the exact amount of stock needed to refill all of the units needs to be issued from the stores.

Automatic vending machines are closely related to minibar and are used to provide food and beverage service in remote locations or at unsociable hours. Most systems work on the same principles as minibars. Summary reports showing the exact quantities of each menu item needed to refill the unit can be obtained from the system, greatly simplifying the restocking process. Units that do not need to be restocked do not have to be visited, which helps to eliminate wasted journeys.

Nutritional analysis systems

Nutritional analysis packages are typically used to analyse the calorific and nutritional content of meals and help identify deficiencies in diet. In general, they are only used in very specialist areas, such as by nutritionists, by dietitians and in hospitals.

The system works by maintaining a database of the nutritional values of a large range of foodstuffs. The food consumption of the patient (in terms of both the

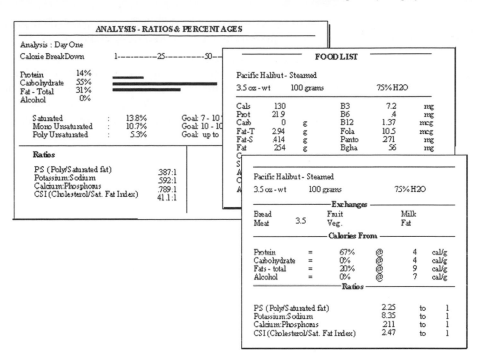

Reports from a
nutritional analysis
package

items and the quantities) is recorded over a period of time. This is then entered
into the system and, using the database, analysed. This analysis is compared with
the recommended intake, which is once again calculated by the system on the
basis of the age, weight, height, gender and activity level of the patient. Reports
showing deficiencies or excesses in the diet can then be obtained (Figure 10.19).

The use of a computerized system allows the diet to be analysed in more depth
than could be achieved using manual methods. Most systems check the levels of
over a hundred vitamins, minerals and other food components such as amino and
fatty acids, and allow factors such as the cooking methods used to be taken into
account. The system also completes the analysis quickly, which frees the nutri-
tionist to spend more time interpreting, as opposed to calculating, the results.

Cashless payment systems

Many catering outlets are introducing cashless payment systems, which allow
customers to use cards instead of cash to pay for their purchases. Cards are loaded
with credit, either through a vending machine or in a central cash office, and are
debited each time the customer makes a purchase. This technology is also
becoming common within resorts (with companies such as Club Med) or on
cruise liners. The single card can be used to pay for meals, drinks, shop items,
beauty treatments and even telephone calls.

The elimination of cash transactions brings a variety of advantages. Security is
less of a problem, as opportunities for theft are reduced. There is less need for
floats, as change is usually not given, and thus both banking charges and the
amount of administration associated with counting, banking and reconciliation is
also considerably reduced. Since customers (in effect) pay for their purchases in

advance by loading their card with credit, cash flow is also improved. The system brings advantages to the customer as well. For example, a card-operated cashless payment system is used in a variety of secondary schools in the UK. Once loaded, the card can be used to buy meals in the cafeteria, and after each transaction the child is given a receipt showing how much credit is left on their card. The elimination of cash helps to reduce bullying and also helps to ensure that children are spending their dinner money on food and not on something else. The system can also be programmed to recognize if a child is eligible for a subsidized meal and to charge the appropriate price. Thus subsidized children can buy food alongside those paying full price without any risk of anyone noticing. Some systems can even produce end of term reports outlining the eating habits of each child, to be sent to parents.

Beverage-control systems

Another specialist system is the beverage-control system, which uses electronic and computerized components to increase control over the sale of alcoholic drinks such as beer and spirits. In general, stock control is easier when dealing

Figure 10.20

A beverage-control system using flow meters

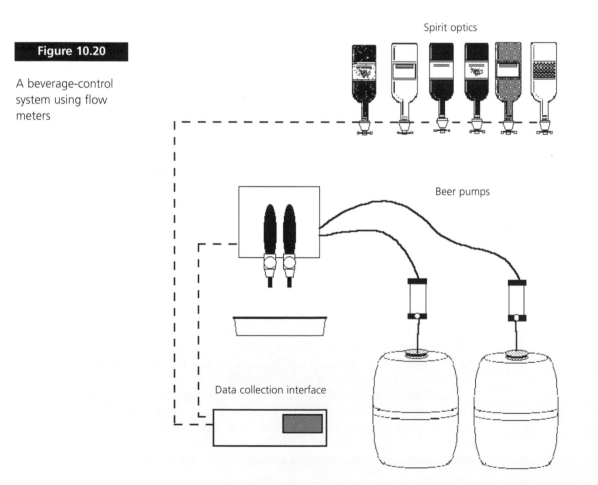

with beverages than with food items because the sales units are pre-portioned into bottles. The exceptions are, of course, draught beer and spirits, which are where most abuse occurs. Short measures are served, thus cheating the customer, or else drinks are given away free, thus cheating the bar. A comparison with petrol stations shows how bad control is in this area. Spirits and beers are far more expensive than petrol. However, every petrol station manager knows exactly how much fuel is sold each day, and has revenue to account for every single drop. How many bar managers can say the same?

Electronic flow meters help increase control by measuring the amount of liquid passing through a beer pipe or spirit optic (Figure 10.20). In general, the system interfaces with the EPOS system or the electronic cash register in the bar, so that once an item is dispensed, it must be paid for, by either the customer or the bar staff. However, even without this feature, control is greatly increased. A list of exactly what has been dispensed, and its potential value, can be generated at the end of each sales period. Any discrepancies between what has been entered into the cash register and what has passed through the beverage monitor can be highlighted, thus helping to spot abuse.

Case Study *Bass Tavern's beverage control system*

The relaxing ambience of the local pub may seen like an unlikely setting for new technology, but Bass Taverns, one of the biggest breweries in the UK, also runs one of the country's most impressive computer networks. Inside each pub, Bass has installed a miniature local area network that connects devices called 'scatter-pads' located in multiple locations behind the bar. These record every over the counter sale and connect to touch screen tills, a back office PC and onwards to a server located at head office. Each pint pulled is recorded by flow meters on the beer lines, which measure, to the nearest quarter pint, how much beer has been dispensed, and the till, tipped off by the flow meter, expects a payment. If one is not made, the system sends a warning to the pub manager and to the network control centre.

Each manager has a networked PC in his office, into which he feeds stock details, work rates and cash takings. Each night, Bass's central computers contact each pub connected to this machine and download the stocks consumed, which means that at the central level, Bass has an exact up-to-date picture of what is happening in each outlet. A regional manager, who can now supervise over 100 pubs, can monitor every bottle of whisky and pint of beer in real time as it is sold over the counter. Bass has also introduced an automatic ordering system, using the stock control data polled each night to set up automatic deliveries to the pubs. This is linked directly to the brewing arm of Bass, so that the brewers can estimate demand more accurately and cut down on wastage. The system has also changed the way managers organize their staff. Because the system can tell which staff sold what drinks at different periods throughout the night, the manager can set staff schedules so that they are working at the times when they sell most. They can also tell the staff that sold the most drinks, made the most money and made the most mistakes.

Adapted from 'But can it mix a gin and tonic?' *The Sunday Times*, 27 June 1993, p. 14.

Club management systems

Private clubs, whether sporting clubs such as golf and tennis clubs, or something more quintessentially English like gentlemen's clubs, are in many ways similar to traditional food and beverage outlets. Irrespective of their type, most provide extensive dining and entertainment facilities (and sometimes even banqueting and accommodation facilities) to their members. Many of the systems discussed earlier (including restaurant reservations systems, recipe costing systems, stock control systems, EPOS and conference and banqueting systems) are also often used in clubs.

However, most clubs have some unique features which necessitate dedicated software systems. For example, the prime purpose of a club is usually to serve its members; thus both recognizing and managing these members is very important. Club management systems aid in this process by tracking membership details, demographic information and preference data in an effort to provide a more personalized level of service. For example, most systems store the spouse's/children's names so that family members can be addressed by name when they visit with the member. Other systems store more personal details such as birthdays/anniversaries and meal preferences to try to provide a sense that the club knows the member better than a normal restaurant or bar. Many systems also now store photographs of members, both to aid recognition and also as a security feature to prevent imposters charging items to the member's account or using the clubs facilities.

While member recognition is important, the main function of most club management systems is to help manage the club's finances. Most aid in the collection of membership dues, as well as helping to automatically produce monthly bills for members for drinks, meals and the use of the club's sporting or other facilities. The latter can be particularly complex, as clubs have multiple points of sale, including bars, restaurants, sports facilities, pro-shop, fitness centre etc., each of which may be charged to the member's account on a per use basis or may be included in their monthly dues depending on their category of membership. Good coordination and control are thus essential to ensure that bills are correctly calculated and that revenue is not being lost due to missed charges.

In addition to helping to manage member accounts, most club management systems also have a range of other functions depending on the type of club. For example, in a sports club, the system would typically help manage reservations for sports facilities such as tennis or squash courts, lessons and appointments with fitness instructors and gold tee times. Some can help organize competitions and league tables or even help fitness instructors to devise and monitor personal fitness programmes for individual members. All of these facilities help to enhance the level of service provided by the club, making life easier for the staff and giving a better experience to members.

Practical questions

The practical questions in this chapter are divided into three sections, dealing in turn with recipe-costing, stock-control, and conference and banqueting systems. Each set of exercises can be completed independently, but it would be more beneficial to complete them in sequence, as the concept of integration between the systems is developed.

Recipe-costing systems

1. An intermediate recipe

Table 10.1 shows the list of ingredients and quantities that have been agreed upon as a standard recipe for twenty portions of puff pastry.

Table 10.1

Puff pastry

Ingredient	Quantity	Ingredient code?
Flour	1.8 kg	
Butter	1.2 kg	
Salt	0.25g	
Water	285 ml	

(a) Go to the ingredient section of your recipe-costing package and find the code for each ingredient. If the ingredient is not listed, assign it a code and insert its description, wastage factor and price.
(b) Once you have noted all the ingredient codes, cost the recipe using your system.

2. Final recipes

Tables 10.2, 10.3 and 10.4 show the ingredients and quantities for the standard recipes for ten portions of Beef Wellington and twenty portions of apple pie. Create an intermediate recipe for short crust pastry and create final recipes for each dish.

Table 10.2

Beef Wellington

Ingredient	Quantity	Ingredient code?
Fillet steak	2.7 kg	
Butter	225g	
Mushrooms	1.4 kg	
Onions	0.9 kg	
Salt	25g	
Puff pastry	10 portions	

This will be served with:

New potatoes	1.8 kg	
Parsley	75g	
Carrots	2.3 kg	

Table 10.3

Shortcrust pastry

Ingredient	Quantity	Ingredient code?
Butter	0.9 kg	
Sugar	0.3 kg	
Salt	1 tbls	
Eggs	3	
Flour	1.4 kg	

Table 10.4

Apple pie

Ingredient	Quantity	Ingredient code?
Shortcrust pastry	20 por	
Apples	2.7 kg	
Butter	85 g	
Cinnamon	7g	

3. Price changes

(a) The price of butter doubles! Change the price in the ingredient section and note the effect on the costings. (Note: you may have to choose an option on the applications menu to get the recipes to recalculate.) Why does each recipe cost increase?

(b) The price of onions goes up by 60 pence per kilo. Change the cost price, recalculate the file and note the effect on the selling prices. Why has only a single recipe cost increased?

(c) Create another recipe for an appetizer, called seafood cocktail, and decide on the constituents yourself. Remember to note the ingredient codes before beginning to construct the recipe.

4. Costing an entire menu

Your conference and banqueting manager would like an accurate costing for the menu shown in Figure 10.21.

The proposed banquet is for seventy people and the total price quoted should include (in addition to food cost) the following charges:

(a) a room-hire charge of £100.00;
(b) five waiters at £20 per shift;
(c) seven bottles of house red wine at £120 per case;
(d) six bottles of house red wine at £130 per case.

Figure 10.21

Menu for Question 4

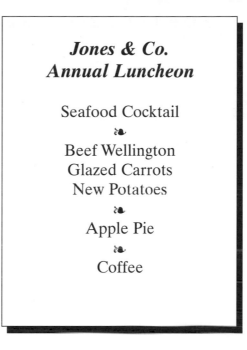

Jones & Co.
Annual Luncheon

Seafood Cocktail

🍃

Beef Wellington
Glazed Carrots
New Potatoes

🍃

Apple Pie

🍃

Coffee

Using your recipe-costing package, cost the above menu. Quote a price per head that will result in an overall 40 per cent mark-up on the event.

Stock-control systems

You have been appointed food and beverages manager of a new hotel that is planning to computerize its stock control. A new system is on trial in the hotel and you must assess its usefulness.

Before it can be used, details of all suppliers and their products must be entered into the system. Initially, to familiarize yourself with the system, you have decided to set up three suppliers and five products. You will then use the system to control these products for a day and examine the management reports available.

1. Data set-up

Table 10.5 shows details of the suppliers that you will initially use. Details of the products to be initially set up on the system are shown in Table 10.9. Set up each supplier and product on your system.

Table 10.5

Details of suppliers for Question 1

Supplier number	Supplier name	Address		Telephone
10	Brennan's Bakery	Kilmore Industrial Est	Dublin 12	345678
11	Grant's of Ireland	Eniskerry Rd	Co. Dublin	123456
12	Musgrave Brothers	Sandyford Ind. Est.	Co. Dublin	987654

2. Entering the opening stocks

A stock take has been performed to establish the current stock levels of each item. Enter the results shown in Table 10.6 as the opening stock on the system.

Product name	Current stock
Sliced white bread	8
Croissants	0
Heinz baked beans	27
Jameson's Irish whiskey	19
Gordon's gin	10

3. Day-to-day operations

Your system is now ready for use. Listed below are some of the typical transactions which would be encountered in the stores area. Use the stock-control system to process each one.

(a) Three dozen sliced white bread loaves and two dozen croissants are delivered from Brennan's Bakery.

(b) The requisition shown in Figure 10.22 is received from the main bar. If the items are currently in stock, issue the entire requisition. If you do not have enough of an item, issue as much as possible and note the shortfall on the requisition.

Figure 10.22

Requisition from main bar

> ## Stores Requisition
>
> Date: No. 1281
>
> Please supply to: *Main Bar*
>
> | | |
> |---|---|
> | *Jameson's* | *3* |
> | *Gordon's* | *1* |
> | *Sliced bread* | *7* |

(c) Two cases of Jameson's whiskey are delivered.

(d) The requisition shown in Figure 10.23 is received from the kitchen. If the items are currently in stock, issue the entire requisition. If you do not have enough of an item, issue as much as possible and note the shortfall on the requisition.

Figure 10.23

Requisition from
production kitchen

Stores Requisition

Date: No. 1282

Please supply to: *Production Kitchen*

Jameson's	*1*
Sliced bread	*8*
Heinz beans	*21*
Croissants	*8*

(e) Two cases of Heinz baked beans are delivered.

(f) Another delivery of two dozen sliced white bread loaves arrives from Brennan's.

(g) The kitchen needs another fourteen sliced loaves!

4. Reconciling theoretical and actual stock

It is the end of the day. You now want to see if the system has worked properly, but first of all you must do a stock take to establish the actual closing stock.

(a) Print a stock sheet to make doing your stock take easier.

(b) Shown in Figure 10.24 is the completed stock sheet. Enter each item's closing stock into the system.

Figure 10.24

Stock sheet

Stock Sheet – Main Stores

P. No.	Product	Quantity
100	Sliced white bread	8
110	Croissants	0
200	Heinz baked beans	27
700	Jameson's Irish whiskey	19
720	Gordon's gin	10

(c) Run the variance report. Do variances exist on any of the products? What might have caused these variances?

(d) Run the reorder list option to find out whether any products need to be reordered.

Conference and banqueting systems

The following exercises demonstrate the power of a conference and banqueting system. They are divided into two stages: setting up the system and actually using the system to take bookings.

1. Setting up the system

Your hotel is pleased with its experiments with computerization in the stock-control area. It has now decided to purchase a computerized conference and banqueting system. Once again, you have been asked to set up the system. Details of the conference rooms, the menus available and the equipment available must be entered before the system can be used.

The hotel has three function rooms: the Tara, the Kinsale and the Rosslare. Exact details of each room are listed in Table 10.7. In addition, the hotel has two syndicate rooms, each of which can accommodate twelve people in a boardroom style. Their shape makes them unsuitable for any other style of seating. The charge for use of these rooms is £10 per hour.

Table 10.7		*Tara*	*Kinsale*	*Rosslare*
Details of function rooms	Dimensions	20 by 25 metres	10 by 25 metres	10 by 10 metres
	Set-up time	30 minutes	30 minutes	15 minutes
	Clean-down time	45 minutes	45 minutes	30 minutes
	Capacity			
	Reception	1000	600	200
	Classroom	450	300	120
	Theatre	700	370	160
	Banquet – round tables	£400	£180	£100
	Banquet – rectangular tables	£500	£260	£110
	Charge rate			
	Per hour	£40	£30	£20
	Per half-day	£150	£100	£60
	Per day	£280	£180	£100

Using an integrated system, the costs of food and beverage items would be drawn directly from the menu-costing system. Unfortunately, because computerization is relatively new in your hotel, the systems are not yet integrated, and the details have to be manually re-entered into the new system. Shown in Table 10.8 are the prices of the items that you will offer initially. Enter each onto the system. Shown in Table 10.9 is a list of the audio-visual equipment available for use in the conference area.

Table 10.8	Section	Recipe	Selling price
Prices	Appetizers	Seafood cocktail	£3.00
		Prawn bisque	£3.75
		Chilled melon	£2.00
	Main courses	Beef Wellington	£10.80
		Roast turkey	£8.50
		Chicken cordon bleu	£8.00
	Desserts	Apple pie	£2.00
		Baked Alaska	£2.20
		Chocolate mousse	£2.00
	Beverages	House red wine	£8.00
		House white wine	£8.00
		Irish spring water	£1.00
		Orange juice	£1.00

Table 10.9	Equipment	Number available
List of equipment	Conference chairs	400
	VHS video player	1
	90-cm colour television	1
	Flipchart	2
	Amplifier/microphone	2
	Podium	2

2. Using a conference and banqueting system

Details of the hotel's conference facilities and equipment have been set up on the system and it is now ready for use. Process each of the following inquiries and bookings.

(a) On 2 January 1995, Jones & Co. wish to hold a banquet for its best customers. They wish to book the Tara Room provisionally from 7.00 p.m. onwards. They expect 200 people to attend. They will have the menu shown in Figure 10.21 above. In addition, they will need a podium and an amplifier/microphone for a sales presentation.

(b) On the same night, XYZ Electronics wish to have a meeting for some of their sales reps. Approximately forty people will attend. Book the Rosslare Room from 7.00 p.m. onwards. No food or beverages are required, but they will need a podium, a TV and a video for the presentation. They have been offered a room-hire charge of £200.

(c) Murphy Group Sales wish to have a conference in your hotel on 2 January. Two hundred and fifty people will attend and they wish to book the Tara Room from 2 p.m. until 8 p.m. They will require thirty bottles of red and thirty bottles of white house wine. A room-hire charge of £380 has been agreed.

A podium, an amplifier/microphone and a flipchart are required for a presentation.

(d) As the Tara Room is already reserved, make the above booking for the Kinsale Room. Murphy Group pay a deposit of £200 immediately.

(e) Examine the bookings chart for 2 January. Notice how the times when each room is booked are shaded on the screen, and how different types of shading are used to indicate confirmed and tentative bookings.

(f) Jones & Co. confirm their booking and pay a deposit of £200.

(g) Print an equipment requirement list for 2 January.

(h) Print a food and beverage requirement list for 2 January.

Review questions

1. Explain what is meant by a standard recipe.

2. Give two reasons why using a computerized recipe-costing package is more efficient than using manual methods.

3. Why do some recipe-costing packages incorporate a wastage factor?

4. What is meant by the term sub-recipe?

5. What is the basic accounting principle which underlies all stock-control packages?

6. What is the main advantage in using a computerized stock-control package compared to manual methods?

7. Explain why there might be a difference between the theoretical stock figure calculated by the stock-control system and the figure found at the stocktake.

8. What is meant by a usage rate?

9. Name three functions of an EPOS system.

10. Explain how an EPOS system can increase the productivity of your waiting staff.

11. What factors make a conference reservation more complex than a normal room reservation?

12. Why might a hotel install minibars in their guest bedrooms?

13. Explain how the use of a computerized system simplifies the restocking process of both minibars and vending systems.

14. What are the two main functions of a nutritional analysis package?

15. Explain how a computerized system can help improve control over draught beers and spirits.

Discussion questions

1. A catering information system (CIS) is composed of several independent computer systems, each of which is capable of operating on its own. However, the CIS is much more effective and efficient if the systems are integrated. Discuss, using appropriate examples, how these systems are integrated and why this integration increases the productivity of the overall system.

2. Within a large hotel, the computer systems in both the hotel and the catering area interact constantly. Why do these interactions occur? Explain, giving appropriate examples, how they increase management's control over operations.

11 Back-office systems

The phrase back-office system is used to describe the administrative-focused computer systems commonly found in a hotel and catering computer operation. These systems generally work behind the scenes and are designed to automate key business functions rather than serve the customer directly. Examples of some of these systems have already been discussed in previous chapters for the sake of clarity. For instance, stock-control systems, which are clearly internally focused, were discussed in Chapter 10 because of their importance as a component of the catering information system. Other examples of back office systems, discussed below, include:

- **Payroll systems**, which automate the calculation and payment of wages and salaries;

- **Personnel systems**, which store and analyse information about employees, as well as helping to delivery of training;

- **Labour scheduling software**, which aids in drawing up employee rosters, while at the same time helping to minimize labour cost;

- **Accounting systems** which automate the process of drawing up periodic financial reports;

- **Marketing systems** which help analyse the market position of the hotel; and

- **Maintenance management systems**, which help coordinate the maintenance department of a hospitality organization.

Payroll systems

In any business with more than a few employees, calculating payroll can be a very time-consuming process. Income tax and national insurance charges must be calculated for every employee. Pension and health insurance deductions have to be made, and cumulative period-to-date figures have to be stored and periodically reported to the tax authorities.

Even calculating an employee's wage before tax can be complicated and time-consuming. The number of hours worked by each employee must be established and multiplied by the appropriate rate per hour. Where extra hours have been worked, the number of hours of overtime must be calculated and the appropriate rate applied. Other payments, such as shift allowances or bonuses, may also have to be added to the basic wage. The hospitality industry has several peculiar characteristics that make payroll calculation particularly complicated. For example, because employees are often multi-skilled, they can work in several departments, each with different hourly wage rates, during any one particular pay period, which makes calculation of the amount owed to them both complicated and confusing. Similarly, where service charge is collected, this has to be distributed (and taxed), which further increases the complexity of the calculations.

Computerized packages assist by automating the calculation of payroll figures. The main benefit gained is that the time needed to complete the task is greatly reduced. In many cases, the entire process can be shortened from days to hours. As a result, where wages are paid frequently, major savings of time (and, as a result, cost) are possible. The number of hours worked can be entered into the system from a time sheet (Figure 11.1), or transferred automatically from an electronic device such as a time clock located near the employee entrance. In some cases, hotel and catering computer systems can act as time clocks. For example, if workers use an EPOS system or a PMS, it can be set up to record the logon and logoff time of each employee, and automatically report the number of hours worked to the payroll system. Such an approach also helps ensure that employees are only paid for the hours for which they are scheduled. For example, without the logon check, an employee who is supposed to start work at noon, but who arrives and clocks in on the time clock at the door at 11:30 may inadvertently be paid for their 30-minute pre-work coffee break. However, where payroll is based on the time that they logon on the restaurant EPOS, it becomes more difficult for them to sign on before their official starting time.

Once the gross wage is known, the amount of tax due can be calculated using data from the employee's master file (Figure 11.2). This lists demographic information (such as whether the employee is married or single), along with data that is relevant in calculating taxation, such as the employee's tax-free allowance, tax rate and period-to-date totals. By combining these two sources of information, the package is able to calculate the amount of tax due for the period. Itemized pay slips, listing all deductions, and personalized paycheques can then be produced automatically by the system (Figure 11.3). Where payment is made in cash, a facility known as a 'coin counter' can calculate exactly how many of each note and coin are needed to make up the wage packets.

Figure 11.1

An employee time sheet

RESTAURANT

Time Sheet
Week ending: 21 August 1999

Name	Monday	Tuesday	Wednesday	Thursday	Friday	Saturday	Sunday	Total
Anderson, James	8		8	8	8	9	8	49
Baker, Clive	8	8	4	8	8	4		40
Dunne, Joe	9	8			8	8	8	41
Fagan, Tom	8	8	8	8			4	36
Hogan, Richard	4	8	8			8	8	36
Twoomey, Fred			8	10	8	6	8	40
Total hours	37	32	36	34	32	35	36	232

Figure 11.2

An employee master file

EMPLOYEE MASTER FILE
Private and Confidential

Employee no:	67845		Address:	127 Anglesea Rd
Surname	Smith			Donnybrook
First name	Fred			Dublin 4
			Marital status	Married
Social insurance no.	1236789A		Payment period	Monthly
Tax table	C			
Annual tax-free allowance	4230		Social Insurance category	A1
Salary to date	8000		Number of contributions	32
TFA to date	2810			
Cumulative tax paid	2018			

Figure 11.3

Personalized payslips and cheques produced automatically by the payroll system

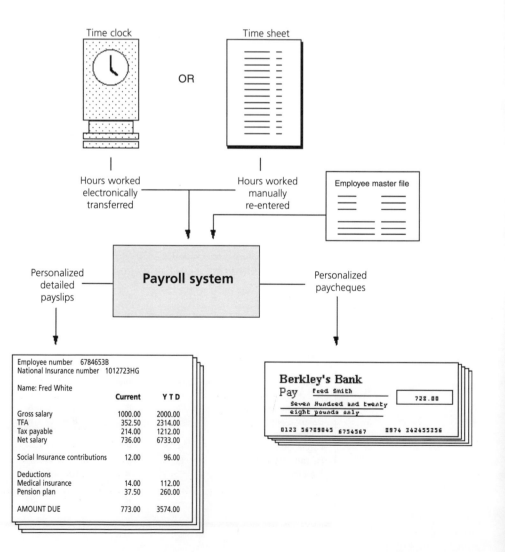

Using cash or cheques for payroll is costly in terms of bank charges and administrative time. To help reduce these costs, many systems allow payments to be made by bank transfer. The system draws up a list of names, bank account numbers and amounts due to each person. This is sent electronically to the bank, the funds required for payment are automatically removed from the firm's bank account, and the relevant amount due to each employee is paid directly into their bank account. Costs for the business are reduced, as only a single transaction is necessary for the entire payroll, thus saving on bank costs, and employees get paid more quickly, as they do not have to wait for their paycheques to clear.

Payroll systems automatically maintain cumulative period-to-date totals of gross income, tax paid and net income for each employee. As a result, completing income tax reports at the end of the year is greatly simplified. Forms such as the P60 summary of pay and tax for each employee, and the P35 annual tax return for the Inland Revenue, can be printed straight off the system. Similarly, a P45 for a departing employee can be produced literally on demand as all the necessary information is available and up to date on the system.

Personnel management systems

Because of the links between the payroll and the personnel departments, their computer systems tend to work closely with each other. In some cases, personnel management systems incorporate payroll as part of their functions. However, it is more common to have separate systems because each department has separate functions, and since the computer systems supports the department, different approaches are needed. As was discussed above, a payroll system's main purposes are to produce pay slips and track cumulative payroll figures. Its data is mainly quantitative, and it produces fixed-format reports periodically. Personnel systems, on the other hand, store more qualitative information about employees, and are designed to answer *ad hoc* questions about this data on an as-needed basis. At the same time, it can be beneficial to interface the two systems. For example, data such as the employee's name, marital status and annual salary are included on both. Integration means that this common data can be managed in one place, and that the data is consistent in both departments.

Personnel management systems typically store a variety of information about each employee, as can be seen from Table 11.1. This data can be analysed in various ways to produce useful information for the personnel manager. However, such systems are still relatively uncommon in the hotel and catering industry. This could be because they give most benefit in businesses that employ a large number of people. Individual hotels or restaurants tend to employ a relatively small number of staff, and thus using a complex computer system to help manage personnel might therefore be unproductive. However, as European Union Human Resources policies and guidelines become more comprehensive, it will be increasingly difficult to store all the required information, draw up the necessary reports and schedule staff, while, at the same time, conforming to all the regulations without using a computerized system. Personnel management systems are of great help in these tasks, and their use is likely to continue to grow within the sector.

Table 11.1	Data typically stored on a personnel system		
Personal data	*Position data*	*Tax data*	*Disciplinary data*
Surname	Job title	Social Insurance number	Number of times late arrival
First name	Department	Annual tax-free allowance	Number of certified
Title	Status (permanent, temporary, casual)	Tax category	absences Y-T-D
Address	Commencement date	Gross earnings Y-T-D	Number of uncertified
Telephone no.	Annual salary	Tax paid Y-T-D	absences Y-T-D
Date of birth	Hours per week	Social Insurance Class	Details of verbal warnings
Gender	Days annual holidays	Number of contributions	Details of first written warning
Marital status	Salary review date	Y-T-D	
Next of kin			Details of second written warning
			Dismissal date

Labour scheduling systems

A new facility on many personnel systems is labour scheduling, which assists in drawing up staff rosters and managing labour costs. This is a particularly difficult task as the staffing requirements of each shift have to be balanced against the times at which individual employees are available for work. Juggling these variables to arrange a roster can be very complex and time-consuming, yet it is often entrusted to relatively junior and untrained staff such as department heads or assistant managers. Many rosters are organized based on convenience rather than efficiency, leading to higher labour costs than might be necessary. Given that labour makes up such a high proportion of costs in the hospitality sector, it comes as no surprise that the area is ripe for the application of information technology to try to make the process more efficient.

On a computerized labour-scheduling system, staffing requirements – in terms of both staff numbers and skills required – are fed into the system, which then uses mathematical optimization techniques to draw up rosters that, in addition to minimizing costs, optimize staff usage and put the right people, in the right numbers, in the right places at the right time. The system can be set up to minimize labour costs by making as much use as possible of permanent staff and by avoiding overtime. Confusion is reduced, as each employee receives a detailed, individually printed report showing where and when he or she is scheduled to work (Figure 11.4). The system also automates the production of schedules, cutting down on the amount of time that managers have to spend on administrative tasks. The softer benefits (no less real but harder to quantify) include better customer service as a result of always having enough staff available to cater for the level of business being experienced, and happier staff as they are less likely to be rushed off their feet or bored senseless, which again translates into better customer service. And when everyone is happy, this is usually reflected on the bottom line.

Figure 11.4

A computer-generated roster and employee time sheet

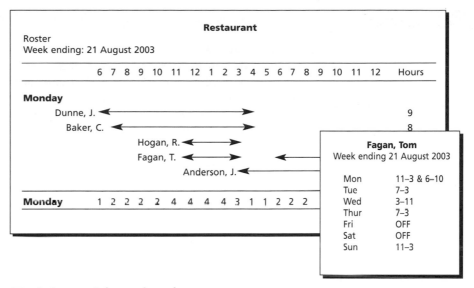

Training with technology

Imagine training all of your receptionists on new check-in procedures, from the comfort of their own home. Having explained and demonstrated what to do, each trainee could be quizzed for recollection and understanding, and given a certificate confirming that they had achieved the learning objectives of the course. Or think about holding an annual company retreat for all the food and beverage managers in your hotel chain, without them ever having to leave their units. These scenarios are not wishful thinking, but possibilities made practical by the application of technology to the problem of training in hospitality organizations. Videotapes, CD-ROMs, cable TV and the Web are revolutionizing the way in which we can deliver training.

Training has not always been a priority for many hospitality organizations. While some training (such as on-the-job training on operational issues) is common, more abstract training on, for example, safety, security or good hygiene practices, are usually not delivered as often as they should be. However, increased legislative pressure, and the litigious nature of both customers and employees makes such courses essential. Not only can technology be used to deliver these and other courses, at a time and place that is convenient for the employee, it can also be used to make sure that the employee does not skip over portions of the course and to test their understanding on completion. In the event of a dispute or court case at a later date, there is no way that an employee could plead ignorance or that they did not understand the course, as records from the system could be produced as evidence that they both took the course and passed the exam. Using computer-assisted training is also far more cost-effective than running face-to-face training. In many cases, pre-developed courses are available covering many training topics, and these can be bought literally off the shelf. Even where customized training needs to be developed, costs can still be considerably lower than organizing and delivering live courses across a geographically dispersed hotel or restaurant chain. While technology is not a panacea, it can be used to assist in the training process and make life easier for both managers and workers. As a result, while there will always be a place for both one-to-one and classroom training, more technology is likely to be used in the delivery of training programmes.

Pre-recorded videotapes are probably the oldest form of computer-assisted learning. However they suffer from a major disadvantage in that they are relatively static – they have a fixed content that is difficult to update or customize. Similarly (particularly in the US) cable or satellite TV can be used to deliver training courses, but like videotape, these are limited in that they permit very limited interaction between the trainer and the trainee. The latter just sits and watches the broadcast. Although using video-conference could overcome this problem, such facilities are expensive and require specialized equipment. CD-ROM-based training courses, on the other hand, only require a standard computer and can offer more interactive elements by allowing users to have more control over the content, speed and format of the course. For example, on a CD-ROM, the user could choose to view a more detailed explanation of a particular item if they were not familiar with the issue, or a less detailed explanation if they were already aware of it. Such increased control makes the course more interesting and engaging for participants, thus helping them to retain more of the content.

CD-ROMs can also be set up so that once a particular portion of the training material has been completed, the programme will test the trainee and not allow them to move onto another session until they have answered enough questions in the test correctly. Where their knowledge is insufficient, it can go back over particular segments of the material and make the trainee take the test again until they get it right. Some CD-based training programmes will automatically print a personalized certificate of completion so that supervisors will know that the training has been finished satisfactorily. Many training packages that were originally distributed on CD-ROM are currently being converted to DVD, where the higher storage capacity allows both more training material and richer media to be incorporated onto a single disk. The Web is also being used extensively for training purposes. Apart from its obvious function as an outstanding source of information for employees of all levels, there are an increasing number of training and educational courses being delivered online. The advantages are similar to those of CD-ROM-based courses, with the added benefit that they can be viewed by anyone anywhere, without having to go to the trouble of distributing a physical CD-ROM or DVD.

Accounting systems

Several of the systems already discussed could be described as accounting related. Both stock-control systems (discussed in Chapter 10) and payroll systems (discussed above) play an important part in the accounting process. This section, however, focuses on those systems which deal with the core accounting functions of drawing up financial reports and statements.

The traditional, paper-based method of accounting involves recording transactions in three ledgers: a sales ledger, a purchases ledger and a nominal ledger (sometimes also known as a general ledger). Because a 'double-entry' system is used to help ensure accuracy, entries have to be made in multiple ledgers to record each transaction. Computerized packages simplify the process by completing transactions in a single step. All necessary ledger entries are made automatically by the software. In addition, electronic links to other computer systems allow many of the postings to be made automatically. For example, the majority of entries in both the debtor's ledger and the creditor's ledger originate as postings in the PMS and the stock-control system respectively (Figure 11.5).

Accounting systems are usually purchased in modules, each of which deals with different aspects of the accounting process. Each module can work as a stand-alone package, or can be integrated with other modules to give a complete computerized accounting system. Modularization allows businesses to use only those modules that are useful to them. For example, the restaurant sector has a very high percentage of cash transactions and rarely extends credit to its customers. As a result, a debtors' ledger module is generally not needed in most restaurants. Using an accounting system that is modularized would mean that they could purchase and use the creditors' ledger and nominal ledger modules and not bother with the debtors' ledger, thus reducing system complexity as well as the purchase cost. Modularization also allows businesses to computerize in stages. Functions can be automated one at a time, with new modules not being introduced until the existing ones are working properly and successfully integrated into the work environment.

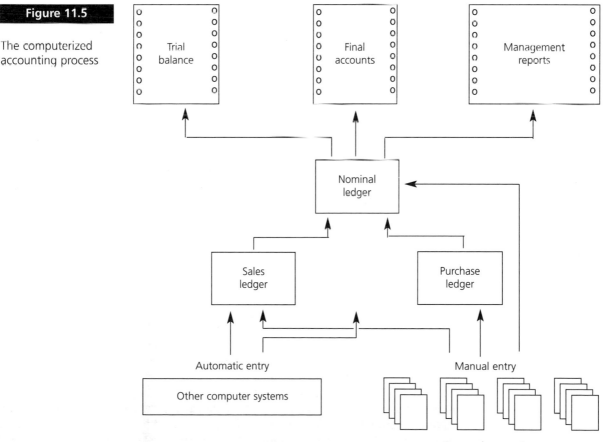

Figure 11.5

The computerized accounting process

The three most commonly used modules in an accounting system are the debtors' ledger module, the creditors' ledger module, and the nominal ledger module.

Debtors' ledger module

The debtors' ledger records the details of all credit sales made by the business. Using a computerized system ensures that customer accounts are always accurate and up to date, and means that end of month statements can be produced promptly (Figure 11.6). As most customers wait until they receive their statement before paying, producing these quickly helps to reduce the collection period.

The module also provides important management information which makes it easier to manage debtors efficiently. For example, the *credit limit report* alerts management when clients are nearing their credit limit, thus helping to minimize bad debts. Similarly, the *aged debtors' report* helps speed up debt collection by highlighting how long each debt has been outstanding (Figure 11.7). The system also automatically prints reminders to be sent to clients whose payments are overdue. All these facilities allow managers to better manage debtors, reduce the collection period and improve cash flow.

Creditors' ledger module

The creditors' ledger records all purchases made by the business. Like the debtors' ledger module, it also provides valuable reports and management information. For example, one of the reports produced by the module is the *payments schedule*, which lists the amounts due to creditors in a calendar-like format (Figure 11.8). This helps in two ways. First, it ensures that payment is made on time, thus making use of discounts, and second, it prevents payment being made too soon, thus making maximum use of the 'free' credit given by suppliers.

Nominal ledger module

The main function of the nominal ledger is to produce the final accounts: the *trading account*, the *profit and loss statement* and the *balance sheet*. These are the main financial reports which assess the performance and profitability of the business.

The nominal ledger itself is composed of a large number of accounts arranged using a hierarchical coding system known as the *chart of accounts*. This coding system must be organized effectively, as it determines both the quality and the quantity of the analysis that can be performed on the data in the system. For example, all sales could be posted to a single account, but this would make a comprehensive analysis of sales very difficult. Alternatively, sales could be broken down in several sub-categories (such as accommodation, food, beverages, etc.) as shown in Figure 11.9. Using a structure such as this would provide much more information about the composition of sales, and, because of the hierarchical structure of the codes, a single sales figure could still be produced by consolidating all accounts beginning with the digits '40'. The balance from each account is used to draw up the *trial balance*, from which the final accounts are produced. The trading account, the profit and loss statement, and the balance sheet are produced automatically by the system (Figure 11.10). Furthermore, different analyses, such

Figure 11.6

A monthly debtor's statement

Heather Hotel
CUSTOMER STATEMENT
1/10/2003

Credit terms: 30 days – please pay by 1/11/03

Account number: 10030   ABC Tours
316 Elm Park Road
Dalkey
Birmingham
BR1 2BG

Date	Invoice No.	Charge	Payment	Balance
01/10/03	Bal. forward	1956.00		1956.00
04/10/03	Payment		750.00	1206.00
07/10/03	107918	102.00		1308.00
15/10/03	107956	250.00		1558.00
1//10/03	107978	89.00		1647.00
25/10/03	107999	107.50		1754.50
26/10/03	Payment		560.00	1196.50
				1196.50

Current	One month	Two months	Over three months
448.50	334	316	18

Figure 11.7   Debtors' ledger management reports

Heather Hotel
AGED DEBTORS REPORT   23 August 2003

Customer number	Customer name	Contact name	Total one	Credit limit	Current month	One month	Two months	Three months	Over three months
10002	ABC Tours	Fred Brown	1194.50	1200.00	543.50	334.00	316.00	13.00	0.00
10005	Loged Antiques	Jade Logan	170.00						
10010	XYZ Electronics	Ann Howard	6790.00						
20000	Studio Travel	Joe Smith	79.00						
20010	Emerald Tours	Adam Black	4571.00						
20050	Arthur Fox & Co.	Lisa Murphy	17.50						
20100	Blakes Bus Tours	John Murphy	399.00						

Heather Hotel
CREDIT LIMIT REPORT   **10/09/03**

Customer number	Name	Telephone	Date of last payment	Credit limit	Current balance	Available credit
10002	ABC Tours	437-0123	01/09/03	1200.00	1194.50	5.50
10003	Franklin Tours	544-3765		400.00	443.58	0.00
10000	Armstrong & Sons	310-9876	13/07/03	200.00	234.98	0.00
10650	Western Holidays	343.6750	05/03/03	400.00	390.75	9.25
21900	Mitchell Solicitors	987-3643	05/09/03	200.00	341.50	0.00

Figure 11.8   The payments schedule

Heather Hotel
Creditors' ledger payment schedule
1/10/99

Supplier name	Credit terms	Discount	Amount due in							
			7 days	14 days	21 days	28 days	2 months	3 months	>3 months	Total
ABC Catering Suppliers	30 days	5%	57	112	98	89	3			359
Browns Wine Merchants	30 days	7%	678	1894	561	1044				4280
Catering Equipment Ltd	60 days	5%	120	618	91	276	709	174	174	2162
Fitzgeralds	30 days	3%	623	2195	183	1000				4001
Guinness Group Sales	60 days	5%	1278	789	3497	1855	3812	102		11333
Hogans Meats	30 days	2%	94	261	232	196	293			1076
Jeff's Bakery	14 days	1%	184	230	224					638
Kilkenny Poultry	45 days	3%	834	267	943	681	956	10		3691
Limerick Butchers	30 days	3%		107	34	71	23			235
Monaghan's Confectionery	30 days	3%	28	41	67	45				181
Naughtan's Travel	45 days	3%	312	120	268	233	388	57		1378
Porter Taxi Service	30 days	5%	12	63	45	40	8			168
Queen's Catering Suppliers	30 days	3%	276	854	456	529				2115
Roach's Seafood Suppliers	30 days	3%	92	94	105	97				388
Wicklow Meats	30 days	3%	65	184	87	112				448
Total			4653	7829	6891	6268	6295	343	174	32453
Cumulative total			4653	12482	19373	25641	31936	32279		

Figure 11.9

A trial balance showing the chart of accounts

Heather Hotel
Nominal Ledger Report – Trial Balance
1/10/99 – Page 1

Ref.	Account name	Debit	Credit
0010	Freehold property	249900.00	
0020	Kitchen equipment	10520.00	
0021	K/E depreciation		1360.00
0040	Furniture & fittings	56230.00	
0041	F&F depreciation		10563.00
0050	Motor vehicles	12500.00	
0051	M/V depreciation		1250.00
1001	Stock	3641.00	
1100	Debtors control account	14672.00	
1200	Bank a/c		563.00
1210	Cash in hand	15500.00	
1230	Petty cash	312.00	
2100	Creditors control account		7836.00
2200	Tax control account	7563.00	
2210	PAYE		3850.00
2211	National Insurance		1563.00
2300	Leases		1063.00
2310	Hire purchases		230.00
3000	Ordinary shares		300000.00
3100	Reserves		42560.00
4000	Accom. sales		90530.00
4010	Food sales		45600.00
4020	Beverage sales		23700.00
4030	Conference sales		65950.00
4040	Sundry sales		542.00
5010	Rent received		6000.00
6201	Advertising	2057.00	
7100	Postage and stationery	635.00	
7401	Printing	400.00	
7500	Wages – full-time	36750.00	
7510	Wages – part-time	6382.00	
7800	Insurance	1500.00	

The hierarchical system of numbering used in the 'Chart of Accounts' can be seen in the first column of the trial balance report shown here. For example, all sales figures begin with the digits '40'. Similarly, all expenses begin with the digit '7'. As a result, single figures for particular categories can easily be calculated by simply consolidating all accounts beginning with certain figures.

Notice also how gaps have been left in the numbering scheme to allow extra accounts to be added at a later stage

as profitability, liquidity and financial ratios, can also be calculated automatically, thus freeing the manager to spend time interpreting (instead of calculating) these statistics.

Apart from the obvious increase in accuracy, the main benefit that comes from the use of computerization in this area is that accounts can be produced far more regularly than would be possible using manual methods. Most companies find that using a computerized system they can produce final accounts on a monthly, weekly or, if so desired, daily basis with less effort and expense than it took to produce accounts once every quarter using a manual system. Because accounts can be produced more often, management are able to react much faster to changes in performance, and control over the company's finances is much tighter. Financial results are also more timely in that they are available closer to the period to which they relate. Using a manual system, it might take one or two weeks to complete all the postings for a period, balance each account, draw up the trial balance and compile the final accounts. On a computer system, the entire process can be completed in just a few minutes! In fact, the main cause of delays is usually waiting for invoices or other dockets to arrive from outside companies that still use manual systems.

Figure 11.10 The Trading Account, Profit and Loss Statement, and Balance Sheet

Heather Hotel
1/10/99 – Page 1

Nominal-ledger report – profit and loss statement

	Current month	Year to date
Sales		
Accommodation	7875.00	90530.00
Food	6300.00	45600.00
Beverage	1970.00	23700.00
Conference	7863.00	65950.00
Sundry	32.00	542.00
	24040.00	226322.00
Purchases		
Food	2004.00	17890.00
Beverage	970.00	10965.00
Sundry	15.00	156.00
	2989.00	29011.00
Gross profit	21051.00	197311.00
Profit and loss statement		
Overheads		
Advertising	420.00	2057.00
Postage & stationery	76.00	635.00
Printing	0.00	400.00
Wages	5760.00	43132.00
Insurance	150.00	1500.00
General expenses	50.00	563.00
Electricity	712.00	6357.00
Telephone	97.00	1830.00
Depreciation	1010.00	13173.00
	8275.00	69647.00
Net profit	12776.00	127664.00

Heather Hotel
1/10/99 – Page 1

Nominal-ledger report – balance sheet

	Current month	Year to date
Fixed assets		
Freehold property	249900.00	249900.00
Kitchen equipment	10520.00	10520.00
Kitchen equipment depreciation	(1360.00)	(1360.00)
Furniture and fittings	56230.00	56230.00
Furniture and fittings depreciation	(10563.00)	(10563.00)
Motor vehicles	12500.00	12500.00
Motor vehicles depreciation	(1250.00)	(1250.00)
	315977.00	315977.00
Current assets		
Stock	3231.00	3641.00
Debtors	14882.00	14672.00
Deposits and cash	14312.00	15812.00
Tax pre-paid	6163.00	7563.00
	38588.00	41688.00
Current liabilities		
Creditors	8932.00	7836.00
PAYE	3850.00	3850.00
National insurance	1563.00	1563.00
Hire purchase	190.00	230.00
Bank account	2063.00	563.00
	16598.00	14042.00
	21990.00	27646.00
	337967.00	343623.00
Financed by		
Ordinary shares	300000.00	300000.00
Reserves	42560.00	42560.00
Leases	5156.00	1063.00
	337967.00	343623.00

Marketing systems

Marketing is a very broad subject area that focuses on identifying and satisfying customer needs. A variety of different computer applications can be used to help achieve these very broad objectives. Examples of these applications that are used in hotels include guest-history systems, database marketing systems and sales-analysis systems, all of which are discussed below.

Guest-history systems

Anybody involved in selling knows that it is much less costly and troublesome to hold on to your current customers than to spend time, effort and money trying to find new ones. For this reason, hotels have traditionally stored a lot of data about their regular customers. Guest-history departments tracked the personal details and preferences of customers who had stayed in the past, in an effort to develop a welcoming atmosphere where the guest was 'remembered' and treated like 'an old friend'.

Although some hotel groups, such as the Savoy, were legendary for the comprehensiveness and effectiveness of the paper-based systems that they used to record guest details, it is both expensive and difficult to maintain guest history manually. Computerized systems help by allowing much more information to be stored and processed with vastly less clerical effort, and also by allowing the data to be accessed more quickly and easily (Figure 11.11). In many cases, data is trans-

Figure 11.11

A data-entry screen from a typical guest-history system

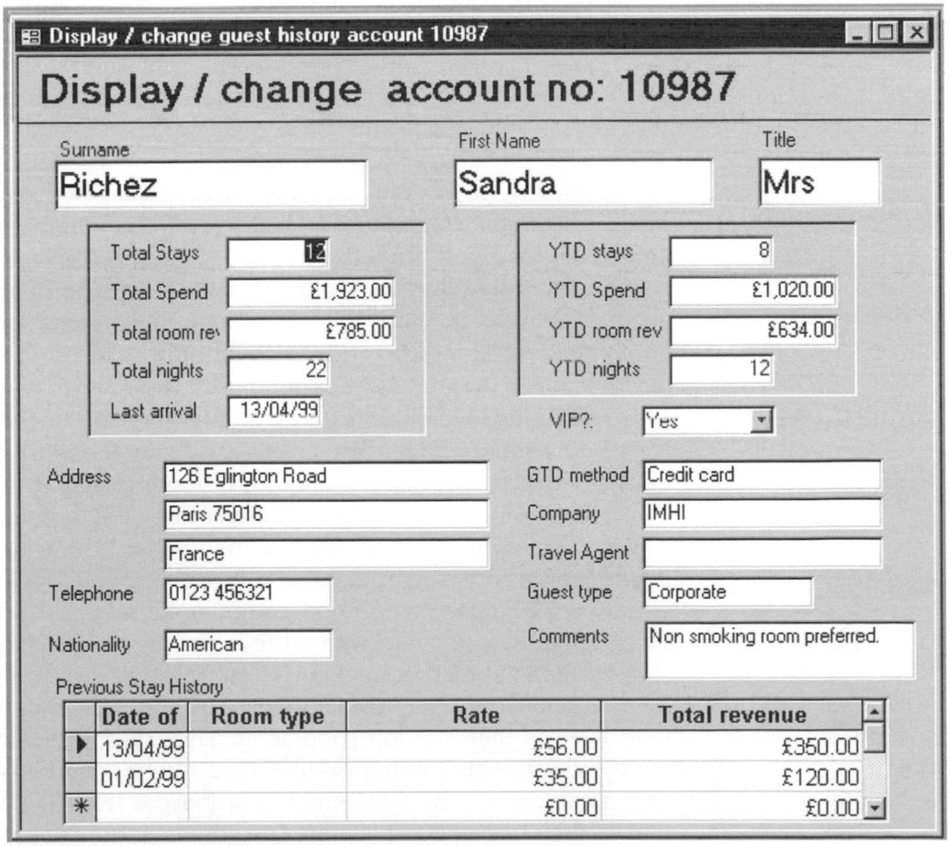

Display / change guest history account 10987

Display / change account no: 10987

Surname	First Name	Title
Richez	Sandra	Mrs

Total Stays	12	YTD stays	8
Total Spend	£1,923.00	YTD Spend	£1,020.00
Total room rev	£785.00	YTD room rev	£634.00
Total nights	22	YTD nights	12
Last arrival	13/04/99	VIP?	Yes

Address	126 Eglington Road	GTD method	Credit card
	Paris 75016	Company	IMHI
	France	Travel Agent	
Telephone	0123 456321	Guest type	Corporate
Nationality	American	Comments	Non smoking room preferred.

Previous Stay History

	Date of	Room type	Rate	Total revenue
▶	13/04/99		£56.00	£350.00
	01/02/99		£35.00	£120.00
*			£0.00	£0.00

ferred automatically from other computer systems, such as the PMS, which helps to keep the data in the database accurate and up to date. The pool of data stored in the guest-history records is very valuable from a marketing point of view. For example, it can be broken down geographically and demographically, to give an accurate profile of 'typical' guests and their spending. Using a computerized system allows such analyses to be performed in seconds, meaning that they can be carried out far more frequently than would be possible using manual methods. This better quality data can also be used in direct mail shots and to target promotional campaigns – and better targeting means improved results and less waste of advertising costs.

The use of guest history is not limited solely to hotels. Many restaurants, through the use of a frequent customer scheme and their computerized EPOS, are tracking the spending habits of their customers for marketing purposes. For example, Howard Narin, general manager of Giovanni's Restaurant and Sports Bar in San Diego, describes how using a computerized system to track take-away sales helps to target marketing efforts more precisely:

> The system saves information on every telephone order, whether delivery or pickup, and tabulates customer's average order, their most recent order, the date of the first order, etc. These records allow target mailings to be created. I can pull up all the customers on a given set of streets, or within a ZIP code, or everyone with a minimum of 50 deliveries, or the first 30 customers between a starting and ending date. With a keystroke, I can generate a target list of potential customers, all of whom meet any criteria that I specify.

Data warehouses (large storage receptacles for data), *database marketing* (programs that take customer data and use it to get or keep customers) and *data mining* (the process by which target customer groups can be distilled out of data warehouses) are all new terms being added to the language of hospitality management. Hospitality organizations have been following database-marketing principles since their inception through their use of guest history systems. However, developments in technology have presented them with an opportunity to do so much more effectively. In particular, reductions in data storage and collection costs, combined with the growth in the amount of processing power available on the desktop, mean that hotels can now collect, store and analyse the entire guest folio rather than just department totals, as was the case in the past. This means that they know more about their guests, and can therefore target their marketing efforts with greater precision in order to more closely match their needs.

An increasing trend is the combination of internally generated data with information from external sources. Increasingly these may be purchased from third party providers, who specialize in gathering demographic and lifestyle data about people in general. A good example of how to use such sources is provided by Carefree Resorts, who wanted to encourage 1000 Harley-Davidson riders to sign up for an upmarket road rally. Carefree purchased a third party list of Harley owners, and cross-referenced it with their own data to identify the Harley owners who lived in their top zip code areas. They then checked the demographics of those zip codes on another external database to identify those that had a significant share of household income levels above €125,000 – a statistic that matched that of their typical guest profile. They then choose the top zips that added up to the most qualified Harley riders, resulting in a rally that was described as a 'resounding success'.

However, if they are to use database marketing effectively, the hotel must be prepared to make a genuine commitment. Good data collection and maintenance must become a way of life for your business. Databases need constant attention to make sure that data is both accurate and current. Often it is not the technology but the procedures that undermines database-marketing efforts. For example, a major hotel chain was placing a lot of emphasis on their database as a marketing resource. At head office level, they put a lot of effort into maintaining the data, updating guest addresses, and combining multiple stays under one guest name – typical data cleaning processes. However when a guest checked into one of the units, they were typically asked to fill in or check their address. When asked if the home or business address was wanted, the desk clerks would routinely indicate that 'it doesn't matter . . . Whichever you prefer to give'. This lapse in procedures undermined the thousands of dollars spent in maintaining what management though was a clean database. Home addresses are the only link that hotel has to getting outside census demographics, psychographics and other lifestyle information to help profile its customers, and failing to consistently collect home as opposed to business addresses made their database far less valuable.

Unfortunately, despite all this potential, there is considerable evidence to suggest that hotels do not make adequate use of the data that they collect, store and process. For example, Philippe Lacour-Gayet of Schlumberger – a global technology company – points out that the hotel sector is far behind even its counterparts in the travel sector when it comes to using technology to provide better service.

> When you rent a car at Hertz as a member of their Gold Number One Club, you are treated like a king. When you arrive at the Hertz facility, your name appears on a large board with the place number where you will find your car next to it. The car is ready to go and the contract is prepared. Your driving license gets checked at the gate and you simply drive away. It's the same great treatment when you return: someone is in the parking lot with a machine connected wirelessly to the computer and your invoice is computed and prepared in less than a minute. I dream that this would happen in the hotels that I visit regularly . . . sadly, no. I have to queue to check in, say my name, fill in the form, give them my credit card, tell them what newspaper I want, what time I would like a wake up call, what breakfast I want (always the same) and then it's the same treatment when I check out. They just don't know me even though I am a frequent guest.

Sales-analysis systems

Sales-analysis systems do exactly what their name suggests – provide management with information on the breakdown of sales. Sales have traditionally been analysed using departmentalization. Totals were broken down into analysis categories such as accommodation, food and beverages. If sales are being analysed manually, departmentalization greatly increases the workload. Instead of posting just a single figure for a room rate, it must be apportioned to different departments, and several figures posted, which obviously takes more time. The number

Figure 11.12

A sales-analysis report from an EPOS system

SALES ANALYSIS REPORT						
Item	No. sold	Sell	Cost	% margin	Sales ranking	Profit ranking
Sirloin steak	1361	9.50	3.71	61	1	7
Prawns	1296	11.00	5.89	46	2	17
Black sole	803	12.50	5.60	55	3	14
Tagliatelle carbonara	765	7.00	2.56	63	4	6
Chicken kiev	751	8.50	4.39	48	5	15
Chicken cordon-bleu	699	9.00	4.67	48	6	16
Stuffed mushrooms	675	2.75	1.17	57	7	12
Potato skins	610	2.00	0.70	65	8	5
Choc eclairs	597	2.50	0.97	61	9	8
Apple pie	491	2.50	0.84	66	10	4
Lamb cutlets	367	12.00	4.90	60	11	9
Florida cocktail	109	3.00	1.80	40	12	18
Spaghetti bolognaise	97	7.00	1.34	81	13	1
Cajun chicken salad	82	9.50	3.95	58	14	11
Ice cream	56	1.75	0.78	55	15	13
Fresh fruit salad	20	2.00	0.60	70	16	3
Gr salmon cutlet	1	9.50	3.92	59	17	10
Seafood lasagne	0	12.00	3.08	74	18	2

of calculations needed to complete the analysis also increases exponentially with the number of departments used.

When electronic (as opposed to computerized) billing devices were introduced, it became easier to departmentalize sales, as the billing machine automatically allocated packages and performed all the calculations. As a result, as many 'departments' as needed could be used. If necessary, each product or service could be allocated its own department, which meant that much more detailed information was available about sales levels and sales patterns. This is in effect what happens on an electronic cash register, where each separate key is in effect a department, which makes it possible to track sales on a product-by-product basis.

Unfortunately, the analyses available from these systems are limited, not in terms of quantity but of quality. They are usually limited to the calculation of total figures for a period. Similarly, as has already been discussed, some hospitality applications (such as PMS and EPOS) provide basic sales-analysis facilities. However, these tend to relate only to the current period, because such systems are generally cleared of data at the period end (Figure 11.12). Dedicated sales-analysis packages allow more comprehensive analysis to be performed. For example, departments can be statistically compared to each other to spot trends and relationships that might otherwise be invisible. Most systems, whether manual or electronic, can calculate the average amount spent in each department. Many could also give a breakdown of the number of customers in each market segment. However, a lot of work would be required using a manual or electronic system to combine these analyses to give a *sales analysis by market segment report*, such as the one shown in Figure 11.13. The use of a computerized system not only allows an analysis such as this to be completed in seconds but also eliminates the repetitive, boring calculations normally associated with such analysis. As a result, management can perform such analysis more often, which allows a more

Figure 11.13

Reports from a
sales-analysis system

Heather Hotel
SALES ANALYSIS BY NATIONALITY
Period ending: September 2003

Percentage analysis – current period

	Domestic	USA	UK	France	Italy	Total
Sales category						
Accommodation	52	12	16	11	9	100
						100
						100
						100
						100
						100
						100
						100

						Total
						100
						100
						100
						100
						100
						100
						100
						100

Heather Hotel
SALES ANALYSIS BY MARKET SEGMENT
Period ending: September 2003

Percentage analysis – current period

	Rack	Business	Tour	Package	Conf	Total
Sales category						
Accommodation	21	32	18	13	16	100
Restaurant	12	24	14	39	11	100
Coffee shop	37	15	3	22	23	100
Room service	41	2	1	23	23	100
Bar sales	3	17	9	31	40	100
Banqueting	2	4	0	0	94	100
Meeting room sales	2	14	0	0	84	100
Leisure centre	27	3	24	12	34	100

Percentage analysis – year to date

	Rack	Business	Tour	Package	Conf	Total
Sales category						
Accommodation	19	30	22	12	17	100
Restaurant	10	21	19	33	17	100
Coffee shop	31	14	10	18	27	100
Room service	37	0	7	25	21	100
Bar sales	3	19	7	38	33	100
Banqueting	1	3	1	0	95	100
Meeting room sales	0	17	0	0	83	100
Leisure centre	22	7	23	14	34	100

accurate profile of the spending patterns of each market segment to be built up. The analysis can also be repeated frequently, which allows management to spot and respond quickly to changes in customer spending patterns.

A further development in the field of sales analysis is known as menu engineering. This process helps to identify the items on a food and beverage outlet's menu that generate the highest amount of profit in monetary terms by analysing both contribution margin and popularity. The cost price, selling price and the number of covers sold are entered into the system or imported through an interface with other computerized systems. These are evaluated, and the menu items placed into categories (traditionally stars, dogs, plough-horses and puzzles). Each category has different strategies associated with it that should help to improve overall menu performance. More advanced systems also attempt to include labour costs and thus provide more comprehensive analysis.

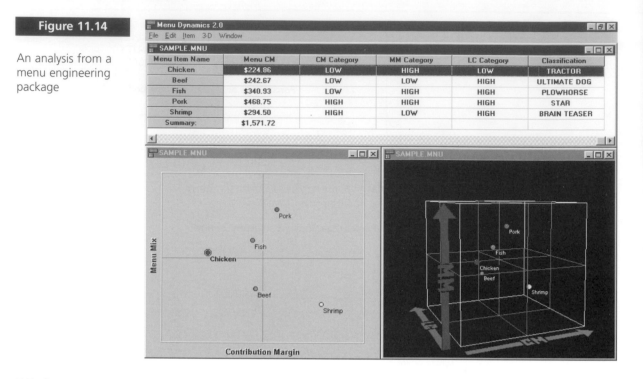

Figure 11.14

An analysis from a menu engineering package

Maintenance management systems

In general maintenance staff live a fairly thankless life. They are only ever called when something goes wrong, is broken or there is a guest complaint, while if they do their job well and everything works properly, no-one notices! Yet managing maintenance in hospitality organizations is a very complex task. On a minute-by-minute basis, a balance must be made between responding to problems and complaints and carrying out preventative work to try to ensure that complaints and breakdowns do not happen in the first place. A good computerized maintenance system can help balance these two sets of conflicting demands.

To aid in firefighting day-to-day problems, most systems automate the creation, assignment and tracking of work orders. By using its database of skills and hours of duty, the system can be set up to dispatch problems to appropriately qualified employees as they arise. In most cases, it will alert the employee to the location and nature of the problem using a paging system, and will then help track the problem until it is resolved. Other calls reporting the same problem should be recognized as duplicates and ignored, thus preventing unnecessary work checking every call. Most systems will also monitor how long each work order has been open, and automatically escalate the priority of the problem if it is not fixed within a predetermined timeframe. For example, the system could be set up to alert the maintenance supervisor if a problem is not marked as being resolved a certain amount of time after it is reported, helping to ensure that no problem is forgotten about or ignored.

Most maintenance management systems also proactively manage preventative maintenance. For example, much of the equipment in a hospitality operation needs to be serviced regularly to keep it in peak running order. With a manual system, such routine maintenance is often overlooked or deferred in an effort to deal with the large number of 'urgent', day-to-day problems – a short-term strategy that ultimately leads to even higher volumes of work in the future. With a computerized system, work orders are automatically generated and added to the daily workload to ensure that preventative maintenance is carried out periodically or after a piece of equipment has been in operation for a certain number of hours, but before a problem actually occurs. Good systems will also check that the required spare parts, etc. are in stock at the same time, or will automatically generate a purchase order so that the parts are there in sufficient time for the job to be done.

All in all, by helping to solve day-to-day problems faster, and balancing these issues against the need to carry out routine repairs, maintenance management systems help bring a sense of order and control into a difficult and complex area, leading to better customer service and ultimately higher profits.

Review questions

1. What is the main difference between back-office systems and other hospitality-related computer systems?
2. Name three benefits of using a computerized system to prepare payroll.
3. Why is it expensive to use cash or cheques to pay employees?
4. How can new technology help to reduce these costs?
5. Why should the personnel and payroll systems be integrated?
6. Explain the function of a labour-scheduling system.
7. Why are labour-scheduling systems not more widely used in the hospitality sector?
8. Explain how technology can be used to aid in training?
9. What is the main disadvantage in using videotape to deliver training courses?
10. How does CD-ROM- and DVD-based training help overcome the above problem?
11. How does the use of a computerized system help to speed up and simplify the accounting process?
12. What is the function of:
    (a) the debtors' ledger module;
    (b) the creditors' ledger module?

    In both cases, describe how the reports produced by the system help improve the cash flow of the business.
13. What is meant by the chart of accounts?
14. Why is it difficult to maintain guest history manually?
15. How does using a computerized system help maintain guest history?
16. What are the benefits of using a dedicated sales-analysis package?
17. What is the function of a maintenance management system?

Discussion questions

1. Accounting systems are sold in modules. What are the advantages of purchasing a system in this way? Would it be beneficial to be able to purchase other types of package, such as PMS, one module at a time?

2. Back-office systems are internally focused and generally do not serve the customer directly. Apart from those systems mentioned in this chapter, what other back-office systems can you identify in use in hospitality organizations?

3. Computer-based training is becoming more and more common. With regard to the hospitality industry, highlight the advantages and disadvantages of using such an approach to train operational level staff.

Selecting and installing a computer system

As we have seen in previous chapters, computerized systems are integrated into the day-to-day operations of most hospitality organizations. Implementing a new one, whether to replace an existing system or to automate for the first time, is a major task and should not be approached lightly. It requires careful planning and coordination to ensure that the system chosen matches the needs of the organization.

Selecting a new system

There is a wide variety of advice available on how select a new system so that it matches the needs of your organization and helps increase productivity. Using a standardized process helps insure that all the important points are considered and that nothing is forgotten. This section summarizes some of the key issues that need to be taken into consideration.

Perhaps the most critical question to ask when considering a new system is 'Why?'. Why expend a large amount of money, organizational energy and valuable management time in selecting and implementing a new system? Information technology-based systems are not cheap, and they take much time and employee involvement to design, select, develop and implement. In addition, most people are resistant to change (particularly change that affects their lives as fundamentally as technology) and thus question the benefits of any progress. Only after thoughtful consideration of these questions and the construction of a valid business case that clearly demonstrates the benefits of using an IT-based system should the selection process proper begin.

The selection procedure can be broken down into fifteen steps, as can be seen from Figure 12.1. Each of these is discussed separately below. However, the importance of getting impartial professional advice when choosing a system must be stressed. While a well-chosen computer system can greatly increase guest service and control, an inappropriate system will have the opposite effect, with disastrous consequences. Paying a little for appropriate advice at an early stage can help prevent a very expensive mistake.

Appoint the selection team

A cross-functional, multi-departmental team of employees should be formed to help select the new computer system. It is important that the people who will eventually use the system help to choose it and each department and level of

Figure 12.1

The purchasing
process

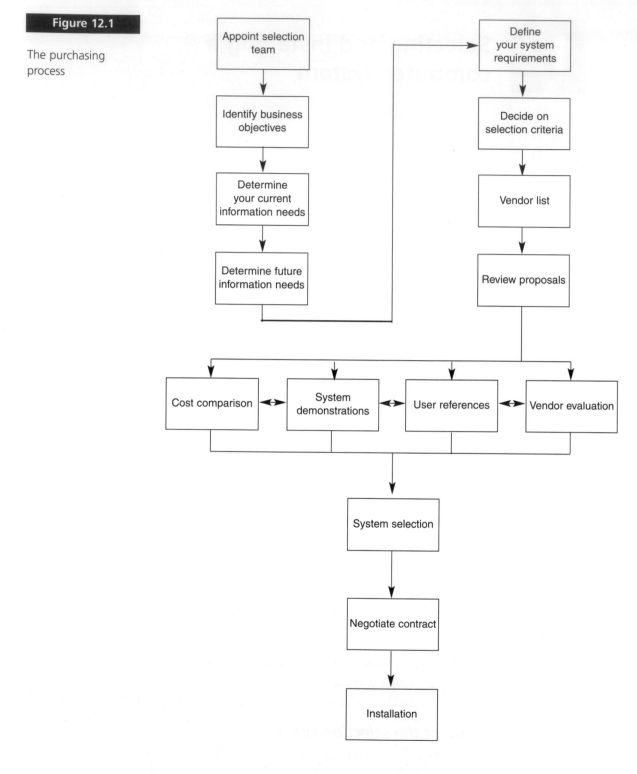

employee should be represented on this team. Involving the eventual users of the system serves two purposes. First, the broad range of experience in such a group makes the process of selecting a system and assessing how it would fit into your organization much easier. Second, involving employees from all levels helps ensure that the new system is both accepted and used. User involvement leads to the selection of a system that more closely matches the organization's needs, as well as leading to higher levels of user satisfaction. The system becomes the one that employees helped to select, not one that is being imposed on them – thus they have an interest in seeing 'their' system succeed.

A single person from the selection team should be given ultimate responsibility for making the purchase decision. This person should be responsible for determining the schedule for the process, coordinating with both users and vendors, monitoring progress and (ultimately) making the purchase decision. However, finding a suitable person to act as project leader can be difficult. The 'ideal' person should have a good knowledge of computing and technology issues, and must also be familiar with the way the hospitality business works from both an operational and a managerial perspective. Most importantly, however, the person must have a detailed knowledge of how your organization works. For this reason, it is not a good idea to use an outside consultant as the project leader, because, even though consultants (we hope!) have a thorough knowledge of both computerization and the hospitality industry in general, they are not familiar with the ins and outs of your operation. If technical help is needed to aid in selecting the system, then appropriate advice should be sought from a consultant. However, the actual decision as to which system to buy should be taken by someone inside the organization.

Identify business objectives

Before starting to choose a system, the project team must have a clear idea of the strategic objectives of the business. As we saw in Chapter 1, the use of computerization must be integrated into the overall planning process of the organization. Computer systems are just tools, and you cannot choose an appropriate tool unless you know what you are trying to achieve. Unfortunately in many cases, decisions about technology adoption are taken without any clue as to how it might be contributing to or conflicting with the company's objectives, resulting in systems being installed that operate in isolation, have little impact and quickly become obsolete or superfluous to requirements.

Determine current information needs

The precise information needed by all the people in your organization to do their jobs effectively must be identified and quantified. This is not the same thing as seeing what information is provided by your existing system – be it manual or computerized. This is merely what is currently being provided – not what employees actually want. To choose the right system, you need to establish what information is actually needed. This is usually done in two steps:

1. A review of the reports provided by your current system should be carried out. Each report should be examined in terms of the people that receive it, what use they make of each piece of data contained on it, its format (is it laid out in an appropriate way?), its completeness (is sufficient data provided or would additional or different information improve its usefulness?) and its timeliness (is it provided often enough – or too often – and fast enough?).

2. The above step helps establish the information that your current system provides. To establish your information *needs*, staff at all levels must be consulted to see how each report could be improved. Having a project team drawn from each department and from different levels of management and operations is particularly useful at this stage, as members of this team should be aware of both missing and superfluous information. Their experience can be supplemented by consulting the remainder of the staff, using questionnaires, interviews or focus groups.

Identifying information needs is difficult. In most cases, people do not know what information they want, and even if they do, they can have difficulty in communicating their needs effectively. If a specialist systems analyst is being used to help identify the information requirements, further problems often occur. Such analysts often lack experience in the user's area of specialization, making communication even more problematic, and also tend to speak a technical language, which can alienate the user further. Misunderstandings can easily occur. For this reason, once the information requirements have been quantified, they should be circulated for review to as many members of staff as possible. This allows people to double-check that what was interpreted was actually what they meant, and also helps ensure that nothing has been accidentally overlooked. Remember that it is a lot easier and cheaper to change something at this stage rather than later when the new system has been bought and implemented. However, care should also to be taken not to include too much information. Users often ask for more that they typically need to perform their job effectively. They feel it is more desirable to have too much information rather than to be caught with not enough, and do not realize the implications each extra requirement has for the overall complexity of the system. Disentangling what users really need from what they think they need requires considerable skill.

Determine future information needs

Purchasing a major computer system takes time, effort and resources, and is not a task that an organization will want to repeat often. For that reason, allowance should be made for planned expansions or developments so that, as well as satisfying the immediate needs of the organization, a new system is likely to be useful and productive for several years to come.

Decide on selection criteria

At this stage, it is a good idea to decide which features are essential and must be provided by the new system, and which would be useful but are not critical.

Detailed selection criteria should be set *now*, before sales brochures are examined and system demonstrations are viewed. Later, the variety of 'bells and whistles' viewed on different systems could cloud your judgement of what is really needed, which can often result in the purchase of an inappropriate system. If the essential features are identified and specified in advance, then irrespective of whatever system is eventually chosen, it is guaranteed at least to satisfy these minimum requirements.

However, you also need to be ready to change, at least slightly, the way in which you do your business. As discussed in Chapter 3, software vendors cater for a mass market, drawing ideas from a large pool of customers when developing applications. As a result, unless you are having the software custom written, you are unlikely to find a system that exactly matches all of your needs. Slight changes may be necessary in the way you operate your business. This in fact can be an opportunity to look at the way in which you do things and question their efficiency. Such re-engineering can bring as many benefits as the installation of the computerized system itself. So by all means make a list of the 'must have', 'desirable' and 'would be nice' features you would like the new system to have, but be aware that no system is likely to match this list 100 per cent. Your goal is to find the system that makes the fewest trade-offs at an acceptable price, and the process below should help you to achieve this goal.

Define your system requirements

Once the information needs of the organization have been identified, they should be compiled into a document known as the *request for proposal* (RFP). This sets out the specific requirements for your system and invites vendors to suggest systems that might be able to satisfy these needs.

A good RFP is composed of several parts. First of all, it should contain a *property profile*, which includes details about the operation such as its size, the typical number of transactions processed per day, and the number of different facilities such as bedrooms and restaurants. This gives the vendor a picture of the scale of the operation and allows it to be compared with other installations. This should be followed by a list of the features needed – not just the hardware and software for the system but also other expectations such as training, support levels, development of interfaces and provision of future upgrades, as well as the timescale for both response and implementation. The main component of the RFP should be a detailed description of the information that must be provided by the system. This should be laid out in a tabular format to make comparison of completed proposals easier. If a standard format is not used, then pages and pages of sales literature will have to be read to see if each system actually provides the required features.

Draw up a vendor list

The next stage is to identify possible suppliers for the system. Good sources include trade magazines, industry associations, and contacts in other hospitality organizations, as well on Internet sites such HospitalityNet.org. At this stage, it will be useful to cast the net as widely as possible in an effort to find any potential supplier for the future system. Later stages in the process will refine this list into a smaller selection that can be investigated in more detail.

Distribute the RFP

The Request for Proposal drawn up above should be sent to each of the selected vendors, along with a definite date for receipt of completed proposals. Some vendors will schedule a visit to examine the site and clarify any queries that they have about the proposal. You should try to prevent these preliminary visits from turning into sales presentations by limiting vendors to asking questions of key staff rather than actually demonstrating their system. At a later stage, once the vendor proposals have been returned and reviewed, you can invite selected vendors with suitable systems to return and present their products. Viewing demonstrations at such an early stage means wasting a lot of time assessing unsuitable systems.

Review proposals

After the closing date, each proposal should be reviewed to see whether it satisfies your information needs. If a structured RFP has been used, the initial review process is greatly simplified, as proposals can be compared directly with each other in terms of features offered. This eliminates those that are obviously unsuitable, and, as a result, allows a more detailed analysis to be performed on the remaining contenders. Many people recommend using a *weighted rating system* to evaluate proposals (see Figure 12.2). The vendor's response to each requirement is evaluated and assigned a score. Because some requirements are more important than others, simply totalling these scores will not identify the most suitable system. Instead weights are assigned to each requirement in line with their perceived importance. The weights are then applied to each score and a weighted total is calculated. In many cases, the system identified as being the most suitable will be different from that with the highest simple total, as can be seen from Figure 12.2.

The steps so far help to identify the system which best satisfies the business's information needs in theory. In reality, however, several other factors must also be taken into account. These are the performance of the system, the opinions of existing users, the vendor's track record and, of course, the cost of the system. These are assessed by the next four steps of the process.

Arrange system demonstrations

At this stage, a few contenders should appear to be the most promising. Their vendors should be invited to come and demonstrate their product to the selection team. As many of the eventual users of the system as possible should see the demonstrations, as this subjects each system to very close scrutiny from both an operational and managerial perspective.

Members of staff from each department should 'test drive' each of the prospective systems. After all, these people perform many of the tasks that are going to

Figure 12.2							

Review of bids for supply of electronic point of sales equipment
Assessment of features

Using a weighted rating system to evaluate proposals

	Unweighted scores				Weighted scores		
	A	**B**	**C**	Importance weighting of	**A**	**B**	**C**
Order Entry							
Use wireless POS terminals	3	1	3	10	30	10	30
Be capable of supporting an unlimited number of open accounts	4	1	1	3	12	3	3
Associate each open account with a waiter	4	5	7	10	40	50	70
Automatically price each dish from an internal database	2	3	5	10	20	30	50
Automatically prompt for cooking method	3	2	1	5	15	10	5
Automatically prompt for extras	5	5	1	2	10	10	2
Be capable of storing multiple prices for each product	5	1	4	5	25	5	20
Allow any terminal to print guest bills from a remote printer	4	3	1	2	8	6	2
Total score	30	21	23		160	124	182

be automated on a daily basis. As a result, they are expert on what you want the system to do and are more likely to spot limitations than managers who rarely 'get their hands dirty'. In a *Cornell Quarterly* article, Kasavana and Smith-David suggest the idea of having scripted demonstrations, by asking vendors to complete a series of pre-set transactions representative of the way your business operates. Using a script helps ensure that the same data is processed by each of the systems being assessed, thus helping to highlight differences in capabilities and methods of operations, which could have major implications in terms of the suitability of each system for your particular operation.

Check user references

Vendors usually provide a list of existing users of their system as potential references. Naturally, these should be checked, but if possible you should also try to find users who are not on the reference list in order to get a less biased impression of system performance. In both cases, ask about their level of satisfaction with the system, about the installation procedure, and about the appropriateness of the training. Find out whether there have been any problems in using the system, and about the level of support offered by the vendor when things do go wrong. It can also be beneficial to visit an operation where the prospective system is up and running, as this gives you the opportunity both to talk to the day-to-day users and to see the system in operation in a real situation, as opposed to a contrived demonstration given by professional salespeople.

Evaluate the vendor

Particularly when dealing with the automation of a critical business function, it is essential to evaluate the system vendor in terms of its size, track record and financial stability. Computer systems need constant back-up in terms of both technical support and periodic updates as the business's needs develop. Therefore you should try to ensure that the vendor is not likely to close down or go into liquidation after the installation. As we will see, ongoing support and maintenance are essential for the success of a system, and thus you should try to ensure as much as possible that the vendor you choose is likely to stay in business, at least for the foreseeable future.

Compare costs

Although it should not be the determining factor, the cost of each system must also be taken into account in the purchase decision. When comparing systems, the real cost of both installing and operating each system should be considered. This has two components:

1. **Start-up costs** are paid once, when the system is purchased, and include things such as the purchase costs of hardware, software and peripherals, training costs and data-conversion costs.
2. **Ongoing costs** are paid periodically and include things such as the cost of maintenance contracts, insurance, charges for software updates as business requirements change, the cost of training new staff and the cost of consumables such as printer stationery and ribbons.

Even this, however, does not reflect the true cost of running the system. One concept that is receiving a lot of attention at the moment is that of the total cost of ownership (TCO) of a system. The idea is that the cost of acquiring and running a computer-based system is much larger than the cost of just the hardware and software, and in fact the latter often make up just a tiny percentage of the total figure. The Gartner Group, a leading firm of technology consultants, estimate that over the lifetime of a system, some of the costs that need to be considered include (naturally) the purchase price of the hardware and software, upgrades, network infrastructure, technical and administrative support, the cost of users' time training on and learning how to use the system effectively, as well as the cost of maintenance, support and troubleshooting. All of these costs need to be compared, as some vendors sell their 'once-off' main product at a relatively low price, but then charge substantially more for other services, particularly those such as maintenance that are paid for periodically. As a result, a fairer comparison might be made by working out the cost of both purchasing the system and operating it for a fixed period.

Select the system

Having completed the last four stages – seen the system demonstrations, checked the user references, performed vendor evaluations and compared the costs – the

A percentage break-
down of total cost of
ownership

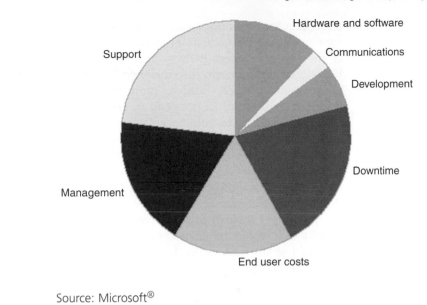

Source: Microsoft®

selection team should now be in a position to choose the system which most closely matches the needs of your business. If the selection criteria were decided in advance, as was advised above, then this step is simplified, as those systems that do not provide the 'essential' list of features can simply be eliminated. After that, the advantages and disadvantages of the remaining systems have to be balanced against their relative cost to pick the most suitable system. As much as possible, you should try to leave price out of the equation until you have narrowed your search to the two or three packages that come closest to matching your pre-determined list of essential features. If two systems satisfy your needs equally, then let price be the determining factor. Otherwise choose the system that more closely matches your needs – choosing the cheaper one, even though it does not do what you want exactly, is a false economy in the long term.

Negotiate the contract

Once the most appropriate system has been chosen, you must set about purchasing it. In some cases, you may be able to agree a better price with the supplier. In general, the price of the hardware and software itself is relatively fixed, but more favourable terms can often be negotiated for things such as training and maintenance. After prices have been agreed, a contract must be drawn up outlining the terms of the sale, such as the payment schedule, installation and training, and maintenance and support issues. As such contracts tend to be weighted heavily in favour of the vendor, you should have it checked carefully by your legal adviser and have unacceptable terms removed.

Standard systems contracts can be divided into three areas, general provisions, hardware provisions and software provisions. General provisions include details such as terms of delivery, terms of payment, saleable product warranty and provisions for breach of contract. In most cases the vendor will try to specify that the entire purchase price and the maintenance fees for the first year be paid in advance. Obviously this is not very attractive to the purchaser. In fact it is normal for payment to be made in three stages – one at the time of contract signing, one at the time of system delivery and the final payment after system acceptance testing. While the norm is to make equal payments of 33 per cent at each stage, good negotiation can lead to more favourable terms for the purchasers, for example payment of 20 per cent, 30 per cent and 50 per cent respectively. Purchasers should try to hold back as much of the final payment as possible for as long as possible, since doing so adds leverage during installation, training and system testing. Hardware provisions detail the specifications of the hardware being supplied, as well as issues such as delivery, installation, support and maintenance. Software provisions are typically more complicated. For example, as was discussed in Chapter 3, ownership of the software is generally not transferred to the purchaser. Instead they receive a non-exclusive right to use the software – usually indefinitely but sometimes for a particular period of time. When ownership of the software is not transferred, you should also try to ensure that the source code is placed in escrow. This involves placing a copy the original source code for the system in a raw form (i.e. before it has been compiled) with a trusted independent third party, so that in the event of the vendor going out of business or breaching the terms of the contract, the purchaser has access to the original program so that errors can be corrected and enhancements added.

Installation

Phew! The system has been chosen, and the selection process is finished. Unfortunately the work is only just beginning. Factors to take into consideration when installing a new system are discussed in the next section.

Installation: the end of the road?

Once the long process of choosing a computer system has been completed, it may seem that all you have to do is sit back and let the vendor install the system. Unfortunately, your work is not yet finished, as a great variety of issues must be coordinated to ensure that the installation goes smoothly. Some of the most important include:

- The timing of the installation;
- The type of changeover;
- Site preparation;
- Data entry;
- Training;
- Interfaces with other systems;
- Maintenance.

These are discussed below.

The timing of the installation

The changeover to a new computer system can be a major project in itself, requiring a great deal of coordination. Even when everything goes right, it can be very disruptive to normal, day-to-day operations. For that reason, it is important to pick an appropriate time to implement a new system. Everyone agrees that the most appropriate time is while an operation is still being built. Infrastructure requirements for the system can be incorporated into the plans at the design stage at little or no extra cost. Training can be carried out more easily and the entire installation can be coordinated so that the system is operational as soon as the hotel or catering unit starts trading. Unfortunately, most systems have to be installed in sites that are already operational. In such situations, the installation should be scheduled for a time when business is forecast to be slowest, to try to minimize disruption to customer service. It is also important not to underestimate how long an installation will take. Even the simplest multi-user system can take several days to install and test, while large, hotel-wide systems can take several weeks to get up and running, and an equal or even longer amount of time to train people to use successfully. While the system is being installed, the level of service offered to customers may decrease, depending on the changeover approach used.

The type of changeover

In addition to deciding on the timing of the installation, you must also decide how to change from using the old system to the new. Three approaches are commonly used.

- In a *parallel changeover*, both the old and the new system are used simultaneously for a period of time. This allows the accuracy of the new system to be checked, which helps build confidence that it is working properly. Disruption to guest service is minimal as the old system remains in operation until the new system has proven itself. Unfortunately it is also relatively expensive, as each transaction must be processed twice, first on the old system and then on the new. As a result, double the work has to be done, meaning more time and more staff are needed.

- An alternative approach is known as a *direct changeover*. Using this method, the old system is abandoned and the new system put into operation on a particular date. This is obviously less expensive, as two systems do not have to be used at the same time, but it is also more dangerous, as there is no 'safety net' to fall back on if the new system does not work as expected.

- A *phased changeover* approach can also be used. This is particularly useful when installing a large system composed of several modules. Individual modules can be implemented one by one, and thoroughly tested before the installation of the next module commences. However, because of the implement–test–accept cycle, completing the installation obviously takes substantially longer than using either of the other two approaches.

Site preparation

Particularly in the case of a major project, a variety of different physical preparations may have to be made to accommodate the new system. For example, network wiring or a dedicated power supply often has to be installed for use by the computer system. In some cases, alterations to the physical structure of the site may be necessary. For instance, the reception desk or the waiter stations in the restaurant may have to be changed to incorporate new equipment. Once again, detailed planning, far enough in advance, helps to minimize disruption to guest service while these alterations take place. In many cases, it is a good idea to over-configure the site, as you will almost certainly be adding more equipment as time goes by.

Data entry

The majority of computer systems have to be customized to some extent before they can be used in a particular operation. For example, a reservation system must be customized so that it displays information specific to the hotel in which it is being installed, such as the number of each type of room available, and the rate for each room. This initial set-up, known as building the databases, is usually done as part of the installation process by the system vendor.

However, even after being customized in this way, a new system is still not ready for use. Typically, a lot of data still has to be entered to make the system operational. For example, on a reservations system, details of reservation for the period immediately following the installation must be entered on the system to make the system usable. These might be stored manually on reservation forms or on an older computer system, but in either case, they have to be converted for use on the new system. With certain types of application, such as stock-control systems, this can be a very substantial task. As discussed in Chapter 10, a great deal of data must be entered about each stock item before the system is ready for use. All of this data has to be collected in a format suitable for entry onto the new system – a major task in itself. The actual data entry can be done by internal staff, or by the system vendor (for a fee, of course!). Either way, this hidden cost can add substantial expense to the overall cost of using the system.

Training

Training employees in using the new system and in how it will help them in their jobs is very important to the success of an installation. People have a natural resistance to change, and the introduction of a new and complicated computer system, along with its associated changes in procedures, can be very daunting. However, effective training, both at the time of installation and on an ongoing basis, helps to reduce fear and apprehension. If employees can see that the system is relatively easy to use and makes their jobs simpler and more fulfilling, then they are more likely to both accept and to use it.

Training is normally provided by the system vendor for an additional charge, usually as a fixed fee per day. It is normally expensive, and in most cases the cost of training will exceed the cost of the software. For that reason, there is a tendency to cut back on training in an attempt to reduce the installation costs. As a result, many employees have to learn how to use the system on the job. From a long-term perspective, however, this is a false economy, as staff are then not able to use the system to its full potential. Employees are taught how to operate systems by people who were themselves taught second-hand by people who did not have any great understanding in the first place. As information and instructions are being passed from one person to another in an unstructured manner, knowledge about the system is diluted over time to the point where no one is fully aware of all its functions and capabilities. This is known as washing-machine syndrome – 24 cycles available and only two or three ever put to use because nobody feels confident enough to try using the others.

Interfaces with other systems

The importance of linking systems together to share data has already been mentioned several times throughout this text (see, in particular, Chapter 4). Unfortunately, as we have also seen, getting systems to interface is troublesome. Despite the vendor's promises, making systems communicate with each other can be difficult, time-consuming and frustrating. If systems supplied by different vendors are to be interfaced, then both vendors should be informed as early as possible, so that the necessary interfaces can be created and any problems sorted out before the system goes online. Remember that additional hardware or software may also have to be purchased to allow the two systems to communicate, which can further add to the costs of installation.

Post-installation issues

Your new system is in, and up and running. There are just a few more issues that need to be thought about in terms of managing the system. These are support and maintenance, and security. Both are critical to the making the system work in the long term, but both are often neglected until it is too late.

Maintenance

Every computer system, no matter how reliable, will eventually break down for some reason. In hospitality operations, particularly those which are open 24 hours a day, getting the system working again as quickly as possible is essential. Support from the vendor to help fix problems is known as maintenance. Hardware maintenance contracts typically cover the cost of parts and labour to repair a piece of computer equipment which has broken down. Better contracts ensure that the repair is carried out on-site, which means that the technician comes to you and repairs it on your premises, within a specified timeframe. If the piece cannot be repaired, then it is usually replaced immediately. Alternatively the piece of equipment may have to be returned to the manufacturers, which obviously causes disruption while it is missing and can take considerable amounts of time. Software maintenance, on the other hand, is mostly carried out remotely. A technician either dials into the computer system using a modem, or gives step-by-step instructions over the telephone to a member of your staff who actually pushes the buttons. Some software vendors also provide technical support – a kind of helpdesk staffed by people who are expert in using the system and can answer questions about how to use particular features. The employees providing this service should be knowledgeable, and should be willing, be able and have sufficient time to answer questions, solve problems and provide advice. When users have someone to turn to when they reach a seemingly insurmountable problem, they are more likely to use their computer systems, and thereby develop their own level of confidence and experience, which ultimately leads to increased productivity.

The cost of maintenance is usually not included in the purchase price of the system. Instead it may be provided on a pay-per-use basis, but it is more common to pay an annual fee that is determined (in part) by the hours of cover and speed of response required. A useful industry rule of thumb is that a comprehensive maintenance contract, covering both hardware and software, should cost no more than 1 per cent of the system's initial purchase price per month. So, for example, a €50,000 system should be accompanied by a comprehensive maintenance contract costing no more than €6000 a year. (It's worth pointing out that many people manage to negotiate contracts for far less than this 1 per cent guideline.) When negotiating the contract, it is important to specify what is and what is not included. Off-site maintenance (as discussed above) is standard. If an on-site visit is necessary to fix something, is this covered? Who pays transportation costs and the travel time of the technician? Are replacement parts included? Are software upgrades included, or must they be purchased separately? Are there guaranteed response times? Guaranteed resolution times? What penalties are there if the vendor fails to meet these guarantees?

As mentioned above, the cost of maintenance will depend to a large extent on the level of support that is needed, when it is needed (five days a week or seven days a week, 12 hours a day or 24 hours a day) and service level expectations (immediate, within 30 minutes of notification, or within 2 hours of notification are standards). Because hospitality organizations have long opening hours, and require cover 24 hours a day, and because their systems are normally critical to operations, coverage times are long and response times to calls for help must be quick. These heavy demands are reflected in expensive maintenance charges. However sometimes economies can be made. Most hospitality organizations opt for a plan that closely matches their hours of operation. While in hotels this means 24/7, it does allow some savings to be made in restaurants and other types of businesses with less extensive operating hours.

Security

Computer equipment is both expensive and has a high resale value, and thus is particularly vulnerable to theft. Personal computers, monitors, printers and other peripherals all have a tendency to go missing, and thus steps must be taken to physically secure them as much as possible. There are a variety of different locking devices available for this purpose and most computers these days come with special points to which such locks can be attached. Locking points can also be attached to other peripherals and everything can be fixed to the furniture to discourage opportunistic theft. More important devices such as the file server should be located in a secure area that has restricted access, as its disappearance could be disastrous. Key equipment such as this should also be on *surge protectors* to prevent hardware damage from electrical spikes, or even on battery-powered uninterruptible power supplies (UPS) to give you time to shut equipment down properly in the event of a power failure.

Software also needs to be be protected. Original copies need to be carefully catalogued along with their serial numbers, and it goes without saying that they should never be given to employees to make personal copies. And given their value, it is usually best to either store them in a fireproof safe or off site so that they are safe in the event of a disaster. As was discussed in Chapter 3, state of the art virus protection is also essential to protect both your programs and your data. Use a virus scanner, and buy a service that automatically updates its virus dictionaries online at least once a day. Last, it can be a good idea to lockdown your configurations. This essentially prevents the user from making ill-advised changes to the machine that will cause problems that the IT department will subsequently have to find and fix. Most modern operating systems differentiate between the user of a machine and the administrator of a machine, and only the latter has the right to install new programs (or delete existing ones), change the network settings, and so on.

However, in the context of computing, security means not only physical security but also data security. The most basic aspect of data security is making back-up copies of important data. As computer systems become increasingly important to day-to-day operations and management, the data on which they are based becomes more and more valuable. When errors or crashes do happen, data can easily become corrupt and be lost completely. Imagine losing all of your future reservations, or all the billing transactions of the guests currently staying in the hotel, because of a computer crash. To enable an organization to recover from problems such as this, periodic snapshots of the system's data should be made. Then if a fault occurs, the latest copy can be reloaded back onto the system, restoring it to the position it was in before the copy was made. Obviously any transactions made in the meantime will have been lost, and will need to be repeated before normal work can resume. Human nature being what it is, where breakdowns are infrequent, we tend to neglect to make back-ups as often as we should – that is until disaster strikes and it's too late. Today's systems have the ability to make back-ups automatically – all that is necessary is to tell the system how often to run the procedure. In the past, most hotels used to make a back up nightly as part of the night audit procedure, but now that many companies are more dependent on computerized systems, back-ups are normally made several times a day. In exceptional cases, companies run mirror systems – two identical sets of hardware and software that automatically update each other. If the principle machine fails, the duplicate automatically takes over, meaning that no data is lost. Although such a solution was regarded as expensive in the past, the reductions in hardware and software costs seen in recent years now make it more feasible.

Another aspect of data security is controlling access to data. Given consumers' concerns about who can access their personal data, procedures must be put in place that limit who can view and modify guest data. Most systems allow managers to set limits on the data that an individual employee can access, as well as control what parts of the program they can use. In most cases these restrictions are controlled by passwords. So, for example, with one password an employee using a PMS might be able to check-in guests, view various reports and post charges to the guest's billing folio, but would need a different password allowing a different set of rights to accept payment and check the guest out. Passwords need to be managed carefully. Staff often share passwords, usually with the best of intentions, but often this causes problems. Systems can be set up so that passwords must be changed at regular intervals and that only passwords composed of a mixture of numbers and letters are accepted. Such steps can greatly increase security and prevent unauthorized access to the system. Steps should also be taken to prevent sensitive data from being copied. Where possible, floppy drives should be removed or disabled (special locks are available for this purpose). However, protecting data has become more and more difficult since the advent of networks, as a determined thief can simply email or otherwise electronically transfer the data he wishes to steal. Even with a good firewall, such theft is difficult to prevent. Perhaps one way of dealing with it is to have a comprehensive computer usage policy, outlining in detail what employees may or may not do with the computer systems at their disposal. This should address issues such as installing personal programs, use of the Internet and email for personal purposes, as well as copying data and should clearly outline what is acceptable and what is not. By making the organization's policy on computer use clear to employees in advance, many misunderstandings and problems can be avoided.

Conclusion

This chapter has outlined a twelve-step process to follow when selecting and installing a computerized system. Given the importance of technology for both operations and management today, making the correct choice is essential. The use of the standardized procedure outlined here should help anyone facing the dilemma to ask themselves the right questions and thus make a higher quality decision.

Practical questions

1. Using a weighted rating system to evaluate proposals

Figure 12.4 contains an extract from a request for proposal in relation to a catering system for use in the Heather Hotel. Each vendor's response to each question has been evaluated and graded on a scale of 1 to 5. Based on this assessment, system A seems to be the most suitable. However, weights have also been assigned to each question to indicate the relative importance of each requirement. Work out the weighted assessment score and check whether system A is still the most suitable. Hint: a spreadsheet could be very useful!

Figure 12.4

Extract from a request for a proposal

Electronic point-of-sales equipment

	Importance	A	B	C
Order entry				
Use wireless POS terminals	10	5	1	1
Be capable of supporting an unlimited number of open accounts	3	4	1	2
Associate each open account with a waiter	10	4	5	7
Automatically price each dish from an internal database	10	1	3	5
Automatically prompt for cooking method	5	3	2	1
Automatically prompt for extras	2	5	5	1
Be capable of storing multiple prices for each product	5	2	1	4
Allow any terminal to print guest bills from a remote printer	2	4	3	1
Order processing				
Automatically despatch order to remote printers in service locations	10	3	5	5
Alert waiter if order is not properly dispatched	5	2	2	5
Automatically time and date stamp each order	2	5	3	1
Automatically number each order consecutively	2	5	5	1
Maintain a running total of the cumulative number or items on order	1	5	1	1
Total score		**48**	**37**	**35**

Review questions

1. What are the main problems caused by a lack of control over the use of personal computers in an organization?

2. Why must you define the goals and objectives of the business before starting to choose a computer system?

3. Why should top levels of management be involved in the selection process?

4. Why should employees from each department and each level of the organization help choose the new system?

5. What is meant by the term technical support?

6. Why is it difficult to find someone suitable to act as project leader in the selection of a computer system for a hospitality organization?

7. Why should selection criteria be decided before examining the systems available?

8. What are the three main components of a request for proposal (RFP)?

9. Why should the RFP have a structured format?

10. Apart from vendors' responses to the RFP, what other factors should be taken into consideration when choosing an appropriate system?

11. What questions should you ask when checking a vendor's user references?

12. Why is it important to assess the vendor before purchasing a computer system?

13. Using examples, differentiate between start-up costs and ongoing costs.

14. What is the best time to install a new computer system?

15. Compare the advantages and disadvantages of a parallel changeover and a direct changeover.

16. What is meant by data conversion?

Discussion questions

1. Comparing the real costs of proposed systems

You are in the process of choosing a new PMS for your hotel. After carefully examining your requirements, you have decided that you need a network-based system, comprising seven workstations. Four of these will be located at the front desk, two in a separate reservations office, and one in the front-office manager's office. A search for a suitable system identified three prospective suppliers, who were invited to submit quotes for the supply of the systems. Details of their quotes have been extracted and are shown below:

- Front Desk Systems Ltd uses industry standard IBM compatible computers running over a Novell® network. It recommends using Pentium® IIIs as the client workstations, which it will supply at a cost of £1100 per unit. It will also supply the network hardware and software at a cost of £3000 for the server and £2000 for the network-operating system. Its software requires the use of a bus network topology. It will also supply its recommended printers at a cost of £300 each. The company will provide hardware maintenance for an annual fee of 7 per cent of the hardware purchase price. The cost of the PMS software itself is £4000, and ten days' training at a cost of £200 per day are recommended. Software maintenance is provided for a fee of 5 per cent of the software purchase price per annum. An interface is also required to link the new system to your existing EPOS system. The company will supply the necessary software module for £500, and an additional PC will be needed to manage and control the link.
- Hotel Control Systems recommends Pentium® 4-based computers to operate its PMS. These can be supplied at a cost of £1350 per machine. Because each workstation is more powerful, a less powerful server can be used, which costs £2000. Network software will be supplied for £2000. The company recommends a star topology and will supply printers at a cost of £350 each. Hardware maintenance is provided by a separate maintenance company which charges a flat fee of £100 per PC and £50 per printer per annum. The fee for its software is £1500, and the company recommends eight days' training at a cost of £150 per day. In addition the hotel must provide meals and accommodation for the trainers, which you estimate will cost £60 per day. The company provides software maintenance itself for an annual fee of 8 per cent of the software purchase price. Once again, an interface is needed

to allow the new and existing systems to communicate. The software for this will run on the server, and will be supplied for £500.

- Software Supplies Ltd originally supplied your existing EPOS system and will supply the software for a compatible PMS at a cost of £3000. They recommend ten days' training at a cost of £250 per day. Once again, meal and accommodation expenses for the trainers must be paid by the hotel. This company will not supply its own hardware, but recommends a local supplier who will supply the required PCs at £1200 each, the server at £3000, the network software at £1900 and the printers at £325. The hardware supplier will also provide maintenance for 10 per cent of the hardware purchase price. Software maintenance will be provided by extending your existing software maintenance contract with the company by a fixed annual fee of £250.

None of the vendors will install network wiring or the system. Instead, a specialist network wiring contractor has agreed to wire the front office and surrounding areas for £1500 in a bus topology, and £2000 in a star topology.

(a) On the basis of financial considerations alone, which system would you choose?
(b) What other factors should be taken into account? Would they change your choice of system?

References

Deighton, J. (1996) The future of interactive marketing, *Harvard Business Review* November–December: 151–162.

Haywood, M. (1990) A strategic approach to managing technology, *Cornell Hotel and Restaurant Administration Quarterly*, 31 (1): 39–45.

Kasavana, M. and Smith-David, J. (1992) Scripted computer demonstrations, *Cornell Hotel and Restaurant Administration Quarterly*, 33 (3): 74–83.

Marko, J. and Moore, R. (1980) How to select a computer system Part 1, *Cornell Hotel and Restaurant Administration Quarterly*, 21 (1): 60–71.

Index